23,68

D1085384

MARXISM-LENINISM IN
THE GERMAN DEMOCRATIC REPUBLIC

STUDIES IN RUSSIAN AND EAST EUROPEAN HISTORY

Phyllis Auty and Richard Clogg (*editors*)
British Policy Towards Wartime Resistance in Yugoslavia and Greece

Elisabeth Barker
British Policy in South-East Europe in the Second World War

Richard Clogg (*editor*)
The Movement for Greek Independence, 1770–1821: A Collection of Documents

Olga Crisp
Studies in the Russian Economy before 1914

D.G. Kirby (*editor*)
Finland and Russia, 1808–1920: Documents

Martin McCauley
The Russian Revolution and the Soviet State, 1917–1921: Documents (editor)
Khrushchev and the Development of Soviet Agriculture
Communist Power in Europe 1944–1949 (editor)
Marxism-Leninism in the German Democratic Republic: The Socialist Unity Party (SED)

Evan Mawdsley
The Russian Revolution and the Baltic Fleet

Marxism-Leninism in The German Democratic Republic

The Socialist Unity Party (SED)

Martin McCauley

BOOKS
10 East 53d St., New York 10022
(a division of Harper & Row Publishers, Inc.)

in association with the
School of Slavonic and East European Studies
University of London

First published 1979 by
THE MACMILLAN PRESS LTD
London and Basingstoke

Published in the U.S.A. 1979 by
HARPER & ROW PUBLISHERS, INC.
BARNES & NOBLE IMPORT DIVISION

Printed in Great Britain

Library of Congress Cataloging in Publication Data

McCauley, Martin.
   Marxism-Leninism in the German Democratic Republic

   (Studies in Russian and East European history)
   Bibliography: p.
   Includes index.
   1. Sozialistische Einheitspartei Deutschlands.
2. Communism — Germany, East. I. Title.
JN3971.5.A98S65 1979   329.9'43   79-11356
ISBN 0-06-494681-9

FOR
VICTOR AND GWEN

Contents

Preface   ix

Introduction   xi

Glossary and List of Abbreviations   xv

Tables and Figures   xviii

Maps   xxi

1 The German Road to Socialism   1
The International Context – The Domestic Scene – Party Membership in the SBZ – The SED Programme – The SED: Internal Developments – Cultivating the Electorate – The Oder-Neisse or Not? – The SED and the KPD One Germany or Two?

2 A Party of a New Type   47
The Allies Go Their Separate Ways – The Remodelling of the SED – The SED Becomes a Cadre Party Inside a Mass Party – The SED and the State – The *Chistka* – The Economic Base – the Uprising of 17 June 1953

3 The Factious Fifties   82
The Kremlin and Its German Policy – The New Course – The Party and the Plan – The XXth Congress of the CPSU and Its Impact on the SED – The Economic Debate – Ulbricht the Master – 'A Scar Across the Face of Berlin'

4 Socialism with a German Face   118
The New Economic System of Planning and Management of the Economy – The Political Thaw – The ESS – The Scientific-Technical Revolution – The GDR and the STR – The Evolution of the Party – Relations with the Federal Republic – A New View of Socialism – Dropping the First Secretary

Contents

5 The Honecker Era   180
   Changes in Personnel – Social and Economic Developments –
   Youth – Foreign Policy – The IXth Congress – Changes in
   Personnel – The Social Structure of SED Membership – The
   New Programme – The New Statute – The SED and the Berlin
   Conference – Relations with the Yugoslavs and the Euro-
   communists

Appendix: Short Biographies   229

Select Bibliography   249

Index   259

Preface.

The German Democratic Republic (GDR) has the highest living standards in the socialist world. She is also ahead of many non-socialist countries, as she is one of the top ten industrial nations in the world. She has achieved her pre-eminent position in the socialist bloc by dint of her own unsparing efforts. Born of chaos, destruction and great suffering in 1945, she has demanded much of her population, many of whom have not been willing to pay the price. Defeat in war cost her dear – occupation, reparations, sequestration and the knowledge that her political culture and institutions were to be influenced by Soviet practices. It was not the first time that Berlin had been occupied by Russian forces. Whereas in 1760 the local burghers had been able to buy out the occupiers, the prospect in 1945 was quite different. This time the foreign army had political ambitions as well. There was another key factor to be considered. Contrary to 1760 when there were practically no locals who wanted a Russian-style political system adopted, there were many in 1945 who wished for a socialist Germany. Although there may have been as few as 50,000 members of the Communist Party of Germany (KPD) in the Soviet zone, support for fundamental reforms which would remove the power base of the Junkers and factory owners was very significant. The question in the Soviet zone was not whether socialism would prove victorious but what face socialism would show to the world – German or Soviet? This study argues that if the working class in the Soviet zone had carried the day, German socialism would have been born. What are the distinguishing marks of this version of socialism? Traditional social-democratic views but more radical than in pre-1933 days and incorporating some KPD policies as well. Precisely since the Soviet authorities, aided by a majority of the KPD leadership, wished to prevent this, the Socialist Unity Party (SED) was brought into existence in April 1946 by fusing the KPD and the SPD, to guide the Soviet zone in the direction of Soviet socialism. Hence the SED has also had within its ranks those who would have preferred a different interpretation of socialism. The SED has often borne this in mind; for instance, until 1948 the German road to socialism was official policy and

ix

in the late 1960s Walter Ulbricht launched socialism with a German face.

This study concentrates on the evolution of the SED but is always mindful of the international context. Without the Soviet connection the SED would not have become the *Staatspartei* – the state party – in the GDR, and the GDR would not have received international recognition and entry to the UN. This has made the SED, of necessity, mindful of Soviet wishes and developments. Since the GDR has evolved her own economic system and recorded many successes, considerable attention has been paid to the economic policy of the party. Nowadays the party fails or succeeds according to the fate of its economic policy. Culture, education and religious affairs, unfortunately, have not been accorded the space they merit. They are mentioned in passing but the dictates of space have not permitted party thinking to be examined in depth.

The aims of this book are modest. It does not claim to be definitive or all-embracing. Since the author has never been permitted to sit under the table at Politburo meetings, many of the judgements must remain speculative. Regrettably *Geschichte der Sozialistischen Einheitspartei Deutschlands* (Frankfurt-am-Main, 1978) was published too late to be considered in detail. However it does not appear to contain anything which would lead the writer to change radically any of his opinions.

I am indebted to Hartmut Zimmermann for all his help and counsel during the writing of this study. Of course, he is in no way responsible for its shortcomings. I also want to thank Francis Carsten for his helpful comments on a previous draft of the Introduction.

MARTIN MCCAULEY

June 1978

Introduction

The Social Democratic Party of Germany (SPD) was the leading Marxist party in the world before 1914. At the onset of war the vast majority of SPD members heeded the Kaiser's call to battle but the few who vehemently opposed the war formed the *Gruppe Internationale* (later called the Spartacus League) in 1914. These radicals joined the Independent Social Democratic Party of Germany (USPD) in 1917. After the end of hostilities the Spartacus League dissociated itself from the USPD and together with some radicals in Bremen formed the core of the Communist Party of Germany (KPD), which came into being on 30 December 1918. Karl Liebknecht and Rosa Luxemburg were the acknowledged leaders of the KPD during the early days.

The November revolution placed power in the hands of the SPD. However it was almost totally unprepared to govern. It feared the KPD and waged a protracted struggle with the radical left.

At its first congress the KPD adopted a programme which called for contacts with fraternal parties so as to put the socialist revolution on an international basis and to secure a lasting peace. First and foremost was the Russian Communist Party (Bolsheviks) (RKP), but the tactics and habits of the Bolsheviks did not please everyone, especially Rosa Luxemburg. Fate took a hand and removed her, Leo Jogiches and Karl Liebknecht from the scene. The KPD was the first party to join the Communist International, the Comintern. Revolutionary hopes were high in Germany, and had not Lenin said that the natural home for the Comintern executive was Berlin?

Dissent was endemic in the KPD and it had little success. However the fusion of the KPD and the left wing of the USPD in December 1920 transformed the KPD into a mass party. The leadership consequently dropped its cautious approach in March 1921 after police were sent to disarm workers in central Germany. Communists were called upon to resist with all the force at their disposal. Nevertheless the contest was one-sided and much blood was spilt.

French and Belgian troops marched into the Ruhr in January 1923 and set in motion a train of events which, arguably, produced the most propitious circumstances for revolution in Germany since 1918. In August 1923 the Politburo of the RKP decided that the moment for revolution in Germany had arrived. The Soviets sent civil war veterans and military specialists. All that was needed now was a pretext for an uprising. This the Reich government provided in October 1923 when it removed the government of Saxony from office and ordered troops into central Germany. The CC plumped for armed resistance but decided to await the outcome of a conference of works' councils in Chemnitz. The conference poured cold water on the appeal for a general strike and revolutionary action; so the CC of the KPD backed down. Only in Hamburg did the uprising take place and it was suppressed without much trouble. This débâcle ended the period of hope and promise when the KPD could realistically argue that revolution was a possibility. Not until 1930 would the party be in such a position again, but by then it had been thoroughly bolshevised and was to be misled from Moscow during the critical period before the National Socialist seizure of power in January 1933.

By 1929 the KPD leadership had been purged of independent elements and was firmly in the hands of those who believed that comrade Stalin could walk on water. Typical of this trend was Ernst Thälmann, the party leader. Well-meaning, earnest, genuinely believing that a true democracy was being built in the Soviet Union, he was dull and safe and just the man to suit Stalin.

The KPD, whose membership never exceeded 400,000, became the third strongest party in the Reichstag in November 1932, when it captured 6 million votes (16·9 per cent). Its rise had been meteoric between May 1928, when it polled 3·3 million votes, and the end of the Weimar republic. It was only exceeded by one party, the NSDAP. But it was a chimera. The KPD regarded the SPD and the Weimar republic as the principal enemies. It claimed that there was really no substantial difference between the fascism of the NSDAP and that of the SPD, but the main barrage had to be concentrated on the SPD. In association with Moscow the KPD evolved a slogan that one could only fight fascism if one sought to wipe out social-democracy. The KPD did not succeed in doing this but the NSDAP finished the job the communists had begun and revealed the true strength of the KPD by demolishing it as well with breathtaking ease.

The KPD and the republic were born together and they died together. In the long, agonising night of Nazi rule, communists had ample time and opportunity to reflect on the errors of the past. No longer could democratic forces tear one another apart to the ultimate benefit of their enemies; the proponents of a new and better society had to unite in order to build secure foundations. The overwhelming majority of communists and social-democrats in Germany welcomed such sentiments.

Although most of the KPD leadership fled the country in the course of 1933 and peregrinated thereafter between Prague, Paris and Moscow, in the main the lower level functionaries stayed put. However, such was the effectiveness of the Gestapo that the vast majority of *Bezirk* secretaries, for example, were under arrest by the end of 1933. True to its analysis, the KPD had been extremely sanguine about the prospects of revolution in Germany after 1933 but by 1935 the cold water of reality had dampened its spirits. Henceforth until the defeat of Nazi Germany the KPD was only capable of offering token resistance to the oncoming fascist tide.

At the Berne conference (it actually met just outside Paris) in January/February 1939, the leadership painted a gloomy picture of events in Germany and outside. The resolutions passed did contain one which was to prove of great significance after 1945:

The new democratic republic will not repeat the weaknesses of the Weimar republic *vis-à-vis* reaction; it will carry out a thorough democratisation of the state apparatus and will adopt such measures in the defence of the newly won liberties as are necessary to render the return of a fascist tyranny once and for all impossible.

These prescient words were to find expression in the first KPD programme after the war and in the Potsdam Agreement.

The German attack on the Soviet Union on 22 June 1941 was a bitter and humiliating blow for the KPD leadership in Moscow. If their position was weak before, it now became almost untenable. Henceforth German communists would have to be the handmaidens of the Soviets and would have to become Soviet patriots rejoicing in every setback the Wehrmacht suffered. They would have to put to the back of their minds the knowledge that KPD members were fighting in some of the Wehrmacht formations.

The KPD saw to it that it was well prepared for the tasks ahead. As early as January and February 1943 consultations took place on future policy in Germany and work groups, each specialising on a specific aspect of policy, were established. A commission, composed of the leading figures in KPD circles in Moscow, was set up in February 1944. Walter Ulbricht was made responsible for political leadership in postwar Germany. Anton Ackermann was to look after economic affairs and Erich Weinert was to elaborate ways of ideologically re-educating the German population. Other leading functionaries concentrated on other aspects of policy. In October 1944, the 'action programme of the bloc of fighting democracy', drawn up by Wilhelm Pieck, Walter Ulbricht and Anton Ackermann, was put before the party leadership. A special commission, chaired by Ulbricht, to look into the problems of the work of anti-fascists in areas occupied by the Soviet Army, was called into being in February 1945. About 150 key communist émigrés were brought together in Moscow in the spring of 1945 and briefed on the political situation and their future tasks in Germany. They were informed that the German people were to be held responsible for the crimes committed by Nazi Germany; anti-fascists were to support the armies of occupation which would be stationed in Germany for a long time; as long as armies of occupation remained in Germany, there could be no question of establishing socialism; Germany was to go through a bourgeois-democratic phase, which would complete the revolution of 1848; left sectarian views that socialism should be constructed immediately after the war were to be energetically opposed. The demands of the peoples, oppressed by Hitler, for guarantees that such attacks would not re-occur were just. Reparations and new frontiers, including the Oder-Neisse line, had to be accepted. When political organisations were again permitted in Germany a 'bloc of fighting democracy' should act as an anti-fascist democratic mass organisation. It appears that the refounding of political parties was not envisaged since no agreement was reached before the Potsdam Agreement. The concept of collective guilt was aimed not merely at eradicating national socialism and the system it created, but at carrying out thorough-going social and political reform as well. A land reform was held to be necessary, the educational system had to be purged of fascist teachers and new teaching aides produced. Material from the Weimar era, according to Ulbricht, was not to be used. There could be no return to a Weimar-type republic because it had not been capable of halting the progress of fascism. The message was clear that the 'power of the war criminals, war profiteers and other reactionaries has to be smashed once and for all'. The administration had to be purged and landowners, factory owners and bankers, the promoters of militarism and fascism, had to be rendered impotent. The guidelines, for the short-as well as the long-term, were all prepared before the first Soviet soldier put his foot on German soil.

Glossary and List of Abbreviations

ABI	Workers' and Peasants' Inspectorate
ACC	Allied Control Commission
AGL	Trade Union Executive of a Section in a Large Enterprise
APO	Party Organisation of a Section in a Large Enterprise
Bezirk	County
Bezirkstag	County Parliament
BGL	Trade Union Executive in a Factory
BPCC	*Bezirk* Party Control Commission
BPO	Enterprise Party Organisation
CC	Central Committee (of the Party)
CCSC	Central Commission for State Control
CDU	Christian Democratic Union
CEMA	Council for Mutual Economic Aid (also Comecon)
Comecon	Council for Mutual Economic Aid (also CMEA)
CP	Communist Party
CPCC	Central Party Control Commission
CPSU	Communist Party of the Soviet Union
CSU	Christian Social Union
DBD	Democratic Peasants' Party of Germany
DDR	German Democratic Republic (also GDR)
DFD	Democratic Women's Association of Germany
DKP	German Communist Party
DSU	German Writers' Union
DWK	German Economic Commission
DZV	Central German Administrations
EDC	European Defence Community
ESS	Economic System of Socialism
FDGB	Free German Trades Union Association
FDJ	Free German Youth Movement
FRG	Federal Republic of Germany (also West Germany)

GDR	German Democratic Republic (also DDR)
GO	Primary Party Organisation
IG	Trade Union Representing All Workers in One Industry
JP	Young Pioneers
KAP	Co-operative Section – Crops (a large collective farm devoted entirely to field husbandry)
KB	Cultural Association
KdT	Chamber of Technology
KJV	Communist Youth Association
KPD	Communist Party of Germany
Kreis	District
Kreistag	District Parliament
KVP	People's Police in Barracks (later NVA)
Landtag	*Land* (Province) Parliament
LDPD	Liberal Democratic Party of Germany
LPG	Agricultural Co-operative (also *kolkhoz*)
MTS	Machine Tractor Station
ND	*Neues Deutschland*
NDPD	National Democratic Party of Germany
NF	National Front
NES	New Economic System
NKFD	National Committee for a Free Germany
NKVD	People's Commissariat for Internal Affairs (USSR)
NSDAP	German National Socialist Workers' Party (also Nazi Party)
NVA	National People's Army (see KVP)
PCE	Communist Party of Spain
PCF	French Communist Party
PCI	Italian Communist Party
RKP(B)	Russian Communist Party (Bolsheviks) (now the CPSU)
SAG	*Sowjetische Aktiengesellschaft* = Soviet Limited Company
SAP	Socialist Workers' Party
SBZ	Soviet Zone of Occupation
SED	Socialist Unity Party of Germany
SEW	Socialist Unity Party of West Berlin
SMAD	Soviet Military Administration in Germany
SPD	Social Democratic Party of Germany
SPK	State Planning Commission

USPD	Independent Social Democratic Party of Germany
USSR	Union of Soviet Socialist Republics (also Soviet Union)
VEB	Nationalised Enterprise
VEG	State Farm (also *sovkhoz*)
Volkskammer	People's Chamber (GDR Parliament)
VVB	Administration of Nationalised Enterprises 1952–58
VVB	Association of Nationalised Enterprises 1948–52, 1958–
WPO	Residence Party Organisation

Tables and Figures

Table 1.1   Party membership in the SBZ.   17
Figure 1.1   Organisational framework of the SED according
              to the 1st Statute (22 April 1946) and the
              guidelines for the organisational structure of the
              SED laid down by the Central Secretariat on 24
              December 1946.   27
Figure 2.1   Organisational framework of the SED in 1950
              according to the IInd SED Statute adopted at the
              IIIrd Congress, July 1950.   62
Table 2.1   Percentage distribution of the uses of the East
              German real GNP.   70
Table 2.2   Real GNP growth.   71
Table 4.1   System of Social Management.   123
Figure 4.1   Organisational framework of the SED in 1958
              according to the IIIrd SED Statute adopted
              at the IVth Congress, as amended by the Vth
              Congress.   125
Figure 4.2   Organisational framework of the SED in 1963
              according to the IVth SED Statute adopted at the
              VIth Congress.   126
Figure 4.3   The organisation of GDR industry after 1965
              (simplified).   130
Table 4.2   The Social composition of the party.   140
Table 4.3   The age structure of the party, 1966.   142
Table 4.4   Members and candidates of the CC in 1963
              according to the function they were performing
              when elected; and the proportion of graduates.   145
Table 4.5   Members and candidates of the CC in 1967
              according to the function they were performing
              when elected; and the proportion of graduates.   145
Table 4.6   Members and candidates of the CC in 1971
              according to the function they were performing
              when elected; and the proportion of graduates.   146

Figure 4.4   Organisational framework of the SED in 1971.   148
Table 4.7   Members and candidates of the Politburo and the
              CC Secretariat (elected at the VIIIth Congress,
              June 1971).   152
Table 5.1   Members and candidates of the CC in 1976
              according to the function they were performing
              when elected; and the proportion of graduates. 213

Maps

1 Germany   xxii
2 The *Länder* of the SBZ/GDR (May 1945–July 1952) with their
  capital cities   39
3 The *Bezirks* of the GDR with their capital cities (formed 23 July
  1952)   77

Germany

1 The German Road to Socialism

'He did not appear at all affected or pleased – at least that was the impression he gave. He talked to us as if it were the most natural thing in the world, after so many years, to be returning to Germany.'[1] The man was Walter Ulbricht, the place was Moscow and the date was late April 1945. The reporter was Wolfgang Leonhard, a member of the Ulbricht Group, which was to be flown to Germany even before hostilities had ceased. At last the moment for departure arrived. It was early morning on 30 April 1945. The group was to make for Berlin and to attempt the formidable task of refashioning a civil administration in the wake of the Soviet Army. The Ulbricht Group, consisting of ten functionaries, was entrusted with the key task, since it was despatched to Berlin, the capital of the Reich.[2] Berlin, even under four-power control, was expected to remain the capital of postwar Germany. Another group, headed by Anton Ackermann, was detailed to make for the Saxony-Halle-Merseburg area.[3] A third group led by Gustav Sobottka was to operate in Mecklenburg-Vorpommern.[4] Ulbricht's group was to provide civilian back-up on the territory captured by Marshal Zhukov, Ackermann in that captured by Marshal Konev and Sobottka in that overrun by Colonel-General Fedyuninsky. The military battle for Germany was almost over but the political battle was just beginning.

THE INTERNATIONAL CONTEXT

The decision of Churchill and Roosevelt, reached at the Casablanca Conference in January 1943 and taken up by Stalin in May 1943, to impose on Germany the onerous obligation of unconditional surrender implied that after defeat Germany would possess no recognised government to represent the views of the nation. The possibility of dividing up Germany was discussed originally at the first meeting of the Big Three at Tehran (November–December 1943) but nothing tangible

1

was agreed. A European Advisory Commission was set up in London in 1944 to consider the occupation of postwar Germany. At one of its meetings the British representative proposed that Germany should be divided into four occupation zones, 40 per cent of the Reich territory to be occupied by the USSR and the remainder to be apportioned among France, Great Britain and the United States. The Soviets made it clear that they did not favour mixed military contingents, each zone should be administered exclusively by one power. No unified approach on how the Reich was to be treated and ruled after defeat was agreed during the winter of 1944/45, as the Americans and Soviets could not reach agreement. At least it was agreed that denazification and demilitarisation should be common objectives. Just how these goals were to be achieved proved to be another stumbling block. The Soviet point of view was that changing economic circumstances would bring about the desired results. The subtlety of this explanation was lost on the Americans, at least at the time.

The temporary division of Germany into zones of occupation and the taking-over of supreme power by the Allied governments was agreed at Yalta in February 1945. Stalin banished all thoughts of splitting up Germany on 9 May 1945, the day after the capitulation of the Wehrmacht. The Soviet Union's goal was to preserve German unity. The territories east of the Oder-Neisse line were no longer considered by Stalin as a part of the Reich. War aims were spelled out at Yalta but, as before, there was no agreement on how Germany was to be administered after defeat. Jodl acknowledged the defeat of German forces at Reims on 7 May 1945 but the official document contained nothing on the future control system to be set up by the Allies. The Russians had agreed to a document which Jodl was to sign but late changes were made in it. This angered the Soviets, who saw it as American deceit, an ill omen for postwar co-operation. The Allied declaration of 5 June 1945 that 'there was no longer a central German government . . . capable of meeting the demands of the victorious powers' led to the Allied Control Commission (ACC) being set up to deal with all common matters affecting the whole of Germany. The Commission, since it had no executive, had to rely on the individual commanders in the four zones to carry out its decisions. The Soviet Military Administration in Germany (SMAD) was established on 9 June to administer the Soviet Occupied Zone (SBZ).[5] A Soviet Military Administration was set up in each province and *Land* on 9 July.[6] An inter-Allied military Kommandatura responsible for Berlin took office on 11 July.[7]

At Potsdam the Allies agreed that no central German government should be formed but that 'a few important administrative departments i.e. for finance, transport, industry and labour should be established'. The Allies in this context meant Great Britain, the USA and the USSR. There was a fourth Ally, France, who had been expressly excluded from the Potsdam negotiations but who was accorded full status in the ACC, with the concomitant right of veto. The other three powers, in granting this privilege to the French, forgot to make it conditional on French acceptance of the Potsdam Agreement. Bidault, representing General de Gaulle, did not feel constrained to abide by the Agreement. After all, France also had not participated in the wartime conferences of the Big Three. And she was aware of her own economic weaknesses and feared a resurgent Germany. France pressed for control of the Saar and participation in administering the Ruhr. She argued that Germany's frontiers should first be agreed before an all-German administration should be set up. Immediately after the Potsdam Conference France applied her first veto and again on 1 October. The Soviets, by Order No. 17 dated 25 July 1945, during the Potsdam negotiations established 'Central German Administrations' (DZV) in their zone. The Soviets obviously expected an all-German administration to be established after the conference. They must have found the behaviour of the French perplexing. General Sokolovsky, the head of the Soviet delegation to the ACC, apparently believed that the Americans were behind the intransigence of the French. Otherwise the United States, by applying economic pressure, could have broken French resistance. The upshot was that the Soviets raced ahead with fundamental reforms in their zone while the ACC was locked in argument over the DZV. True, the French veto was only one of the factors which influenced SMAD and KPD policy in the SBZ but none the less it was of great significance.

THE DOMESTIC SCENE

The KPD and SPD as Separate Parties (May 1945 – April 1946)
The Berlin which Ulbricht and his subordinates reached on the morning of 2 May shocked them to the core. The former capital of the Reich existed no more. Heaps of rubble, burning buildings, shells of gutted houses which resembled rotting black teeth projecting into the blue sky, carcasses of animals and humans alike, famished civilians in rags seeking shelter and food, stunned, exhausted German soldiers, carousing, inebriated Soviet Army men celebrating victory, a total breakdown of all public services – these were some of the images which met the

returning KPD émigrés. The indescribable chaos and misery had to be overcome and only the KPD functionaries and their Soviet advisers had the right to initiate action. Ulbricht had guidelines. The KPD had set up nine commissions, in Moscow on 6 February 1944, to elaborate proposals for the future of Germany. Ulbricht had been the chairman of the commission on the future political leadership of the new Germany.[8]

His first task was to establish administrations and appoint mayors in all twenty Berlin *Bezirks*. Where were the officials to come from? Well, there were the members of the various anti-fascist committees which had sprung up in the last months of the war. They were composed of members of all shades of political opinion as well as non-party people. There were the former concentration camp inmates: presumably they were not fascists, otherwise they would not have been in the camps. There were KPD members but no list of names existed, but, even if it had, most of them would have been dead or elsewhere. Ulbricht's phenomenal memory for names and places played an important role in suggesting whom to seek out. Not everyone who claimed to be a democrat, of course, turned out to be one. Egregious mistakes were made. How could it be otherwise with almost no records and about 2 million ex-members of the National Socialist Party in the SBZ?[9]

Only two posts in the *Bezirk* administration had to be occupied by communists, according to Ulbricht.[10] One was that of the deputy mayor and the other was the head of personnel. Besides this a reliable communist had to be found in each *Bezirk* who could be made responsible for building up the police. Mayors in working-class areas were to be social-democrats, those in middle-class areas, ex-members of bourgeois parties in the Weimar republic. The best qualifications for a bourgeois mayor were: 'Dr' in front of his name, a good anti-fascist record, and a capacity for working well with communists. Such an appealing package was not easy to find in Berlin in May 1945. Considerable skill was needed to put together the correct combination of officials but Ulbricht's guiding principle was crystal clear: 'it must look democratic but we must be the masters'. The greatest urgency was reserved for those *Bezirks* which were to be occupied by American, British and French forces.[11] Mayors and administrations were found for all Berlin *Bezirks* by 9 May. The Berlin administration was seen by the KPD as an example of anti-fascist co-operation. The communists hoped it would serve as a model for the rest of Germany. The Berlin administration was confirmed in office on 10 May by Colonel-General N.E. Berzarin, Soviet city commandant.

The Ackermann Group was also very active. By the middle of May almost all its members occupied important administrative posts, especially that of personnel. Fischer, Matern and Greif played a leading role in getting Dresden on its feet and influenced developments in the whole of *Land* Saxony.

A further group of key functionaries arrived in Berlin from Moscow in early June 1945. They included Wilhelm Pieck, Fred Oelssner, Paul Wandel, Johannes R. Becher and Edwin Hörnle. They were soon joined by Anton Ackermann, Hermann Matern and Kurt Fischer from Dresden. These officials then went into conference with the Berlin leadership. The decisions reached surprised some and amazed others. There were to be political parties again following the Weimar pattern. The KPD and the SPD were to be refounded. This meant that no united party of the left was envisaged. Bourgeois parties, patterned on the Deutsche Demokratische Partei and the Zentrumspartei were to be promoted. A land reform was to be set in motion in the summer of 1945. This signalled a major change in Soviet policy. Hitherto it had been accepted that individual parties would not reappear but that political activity would be circumscribed and restricted to mass organisations, embracing all shades of anti-fascist opinion. Communists in these organisations would, it was hoped, play the leading role. What had brought about the change of heart? The visit of Anastas Mikoyan, Stalin's right-hand man on German affairs, to Berlin in May appears to have been decisive in this respect.[12] The Soviets' main fear in postwar Germany was a resurgence of national socialism, which had fed for more than a decade on anti-Soviet and anti-communist sentiments. Once the German hope of a rapid victory in the USSR had receded, arrogance *vis-à-vis* the Soviet Union changed to deep-set fear of the Soviet Army. The intensity of Nazi propaganda which laid stress on the supposedly primitive, semi-civilised, half-educated or illiterate Soviet Army man had an unexpected counter-effect. When the Soviet Army began to roll remorselessly forward in 1943 and especially in 1944, the feeling that nothing could stop the 'barbarians in the east' gained ground in the Wehrmacht and in Germany. Soldiers were posted to the Eastern Front as a punishment: this speaks volumes for the image of the east. Apathy was not widespread in Germany in 1944 and 1945 but the clarion call 'the Russians are coming' was enough to strike terror into the stoutest breast. Nevertheless resistance continued right up to the day of occupation. When the Soviet Army did arrive the population accepted its fate with deep resignation and pessimism.[13] Those who believed they had most to fear from the Soviets fled westwards. Hence the Soviets were surprised to find how few people appeared to be unrepentant Nazis.

National socialism seemed to be a window which, once smashed, provided direct access to the mind of the people. This impression was the result of many factors, among them the demoralisation of defeat, the flood of refugees, the almost total conscription of the young men and the sheer physical struggle to survive. The deep roots which national socialism had formed in German society were no longer visible but were there none the less. If the population was politically apathetic in the summer of 1945, the fight to survive made them so.

Tangible evidence of the change in Soviet policy was the publication by SMAD of Order No. 2 on 10 June 1945.[14] This permitted, under Soviet control, the setting up of anti-fascist parties which declared the strengthening of democracy and the defence of civil liberties to be their goal. Trade unions and social organisations were also encouraged. The first party to reappear was the KPD on 11 June. It was followed by the SPD on 15 June, the Christian Democratic Union of Germany (CDU) on 26 June and the Liberal Democratic Party of Germany (LDPD) on 5 July. The four parties met in Berlin on 14 July and agreed to establish a bloc of anti-fascist democratic parties. A committee, composed of five representatives from each party, was to evolve policy. Decisions of the bloc were to be unanimous. Bloc committees were to be established in all villages, *Kreise*, *Bezirks* and *Länder* of the SBZ.[15]

Several advantages accrued to the Soviets as a result of this *démarche*. The SBZ was the only zone with legally recognised political life and parties; the four parties, founded in Berlin, were seen as all-German parties; when parties reappeared in the Western zones they bore the same names and found that the initiative of drawing up a manifesto had been seized by the sister party in the East; Central German administrations (DZV) also came into being and were obviously seen as a model for the post-Potsdam all-German administration; the DZV were the only institutions in any zone of Germany headed by Germans. The DZV, which covered the whole range of the economy, sought to attract the co-operation of all non-Nazis with technical expertise. This they achieved with considerable success. A tactic employed was to appoint only three communist presidents out of a total of twelve. However of the seventeen vice-presidents, ten were members of the KPD.[16] Among the presidents Edwin Hörnle headed agriculture, Paul Wandel education and Henry Meyer finance.

KPD and SPD: A pas de deux *But No Union*
Such was the groundswell of goodwill towards the communists on the part of social-democrats[17] in the summer of 1945 that an agreement to

establish a single party representing the working class would have been concluded had it been left to the social-democrats. Erich Gniffke, Engelbert Graf and Otto Grotewohl, leading social-democrats in Berlin, established contact with Arthur Pieck, the son of Wilhelm Pieck, on 14 May and asked for a meeting to discuss the organisational unity of the working class. Pieck agreed to arrange a meeting with leading KPD functionaries on 17 May but no communist appeared at the appointed time. Despite this rebuff further efforts were undertaken towards the end of May to enter into negotiations with the KPD, but without success. The SPD was not so easily put off. On 12 June, Gustav Dahrendorf, a fervent supporter of the concept of 'one party' for the left, made a concrete offer: 'we are prepared to discuss all questions of unity with our communist friends and ask when decisive discussions can take place.'[18] When the SPD reappeared on 15 June, its manifesto called for a 'united political organisation of the working class'.[19] This was a radical departure for the SPD and Dahrendorf, for one, revealed that he was aware of opposition outside Germany when he claimed that: 'this new SPD has no ties with the political practice of the last phase of the old SPD. Nor is it tied to émigré politics. No one abroad has the right to speak for the new SPD'.[20]

At long last, on 19 June, five representatives of the KPD and five of the SPD met to discuss mutual relations. Ulbricht dominated the proceedings and waved aside all SPD requests for a united party. He declared that the moment for the fusion had not yet arrived. A premature unification could lead to the new party breaking up. Hence a period of ideological clarification and co-operation was a prior necessity. Ulbricht made it also clear that the KPD's immediate concern was not socialism, but democracy. However it was agreed to establish a joint committee consisting of five representatives from each party's central committee. Similar committees were to be set up at the local level. Hence the wheels of unification were set in motion by the SPD.

When the manifestos of the two left-wing parties appeared it became apparent that they had reversed the roles they had played in 1933. The KPD no longer restricted its appeal to the working class: the manifesto was addressed to the 'working population in town and country, men and women, German youth'. No mention was made of the dictatorship of the proletariat: 'the creation of an anti-fascist democratic regime, of a parliamentary democratic republic with all democratic rights and liberties for the people'[21] was the declared aim. What 1848 had begun, 1945 was to finish. Key concepts such as revolution, class struggle and socialism do not appear in the document. The statement which aroused greatest enthusiasm read as follows: 'we are of the opinion that it would be wrong to force on Germany the Soviet system since this does not correspond to the present conditions of development in Germany.'[22] The gate was thus opened for a German way to socialism. The immediate task, however, was to clear away the débris, both material and mental, of the Nazi era. This would entail attacking the foundations the fascist state had rested on: militarism, monopoly capital, large landowners. Removing these would not only aid the working class, it would permit the development of a parliamentary democratic republic. The KPD sought to enlist the support of all anti-fascists in this struggle but it went unsaid that views which could be labelled conservative were considered undemocratic. The communists were keen to attract those in the centre of the political spectrum to fight a common battle against the right. Once the right was vanquished the KPD could concentrate its energies on its erstwhile allies. It is instructive that the KPD in its manifesto concentrated on issues which promised to rally support, placing the rebuilding, both physical and political, of Germany, in the forefront. It studiously avoided issues such as nationalisation and collectivisation which would have been divisive in 1945 and which would have concentrated opposition and placed some of the blame for the appalling economic situation squarely on the shoulders of the KPD. To allay the ingrained suspicion of the middle classes, who were well aware of the communist goals of the nationalisation of the means of production, distribution and exchange, the KPD went so far as to state that it favoured 'the completely unhindered development of free trade and private entrepreneurial initiative based on private property'.

The SPD manifesto, which appeared on 15 June, was much less inhibited. It boldly proposed democracy in the state and at the local level and socialism in the economy and in society. The only force capable of carrying out such a policy was the German working class. That working class should be concentrated in and led by a single organisation. Agricultural development should be centred on co-operatives; banks, insurance, mining, raw materials and the energy industry should be nationalised. The SPD's endorsement of the anti-fascist, democratic parliamentary republic, sponsored by the KPD, did not appear to carry much conviction.

An analysis of these two manifestos leads to the surprising conclusion that the KPD and SPD exchanged roles in 1945. The 'social fascists', the 'pillar of state monopoly capital', wanted a socialist economy and society in 1945; whereas the 'advocates of the dictatorship of the proletariat' wanted bourgeois democracy. This was all too much for some communists, labelled 'left sectarians', to imbibe.[23] Ulbricht's statement, when rejecting a united working-class party, that time was needed for ideological clarification, was thus not only directed at social-democrats. The Muscovite leadership, which had flown in to assume leadership of the KPD, obviously needed time to impose its authority on those who had not had the formative experience of living in the Soviet Union. The German road to socialism was acknowledged but it had to join the highway leading to Moscow. This involved co-ordinating plans, in the short- as well as in the long-term.

The KPD and SPD manifestos were drafted in different circumstances. The communists drew theirs up in Moscow and brought it with them to Germany. They altered certain aspects of it in the light of experience after May 1945 but it remained essentially the work of the KPD leadership in exile and reflected KPD thinking since the late 1930s. One of the opponents of a policy which aimed at a parliamentary democratic republic was the Schumann-Engert-Kresse Group in Leipzig, which found expression in the NKFD group there. Schumann and his supporters wanted the Soviet Army, after the defeat of Germany, to launch a war against the Allies so as to secure a 'final peace in Europe and a new socialist order' and to promote world revolution as well. Not all communists in Leipzig shared this view and a group which included Georg Schwarz and William Zipperer linked up with Alfred Nothnagel (SAP) and Richard Lehmann (SPD). They believed that there was no immediate prospect of establishing the dictatorship of the proletariat in Germany and consequently proposed a popular front and total peace in Europe.[24]

Many of the proposals in the KPD manifesto are mirrored in other communist manifestos in Eastern Europe at the same time. Even the German road to socialism was not unique.

The SPD manifesto, unlike the KPD one, was drawn up by party members who had remained in Germany. They had little contact with the SPD leadership in exile. As a result of their experiences in prisons and concentration camps, where they had worked closely with communists, they were in favour of a united party of the left and of socialism in the short-term.

KPD and SPD—A Marriage But Not by Consent
The KPD and SPD got increasingly out of step in the summer and autumn of 1945. The ardent desire of the SPD for a united party of the working class gradually cooled and an air of disenchantment not to say

frigidity, became discernible in the autumn. The SPD complained of many things. As early as June social-democrats in Berlin complained to Erich Gniffke, a CC member, that 'wherever there are positions to be filled, social-democrats [are] pushed aside and communists unfairly favoured'.[25] At an SPD meeting in Berlin Wilmersdorf complaints were voiced that the KPD was 'surrounding' every social-democrat in the administration with communists. The 'unity of action' at the local level seemed to mean that the KPD functionaries made proposals, presumably based on prior consultation with SMAD, then the social-democrats were invited to join the communists in executing the policy. Contumely was poured on those social-democrats who put forward counter-proposals. The position of those who disagreed was traduced and labels such as 'traitor' were frequently stuck on them. The SPD was worried by the resources available to the KPD. Gniffke in September 1945 plaintively pointed out that the SPD could not find the funds to establish an organisation comparable to that of the KPD. 'In contrast the KPD is swimming in money,' he wrote.[26] The social-democratic press was also at a disadvantage. Paper was hard to come by and SMAD not unnaturally favoured the KPD. Gustav Dahrendorf ruefully remarked that at the end of 1945 the SPD had seven daily newspapers with a total circulation of less than 1 million, whereas the communist press had a circulation of 4 million.[27] The SPD press was subject to censorship; for instance it was not possible openly to advocate a socialist economy, and important events such as Otto Grotewohl's speech on 11 November 1945 went unreported.

The first clear call for a united party of the left came from Wilhelm Pieck in a speech on 9 November 1945. He advocated '. . . as soon as possible the complete unification of communists and social-democrats in a single workers' party'.[28] Grotewohl's response was cool and caused consternation among KPD leaders and SMAD functionaries. So confident of his position was Grotewohl that he brushed aside the immediate unification of KPD and SPD. He stated that a decision could only be reached after the clear will of party members had been recorded; no external pressure or indirect force was to influence this decision; unity could come about by increased co-operation and mutual desire for socialist and democratic reconstruction; unification could only take place on an all-German basis. In the words of Henry Krisch he was advocating three steps: united nationwide parties, national unity, and, finally, a decision on unity between the parties.[29] What led the KPD and SMAD to advocate unity in November, thereby reversing their previous policy? The overt change was made known officially in November but covert preparations are discernible from late September. In a speech on 14 September 1945 Grotewohl stated that the moment for the merging of the KPD and SPD had not yet arrived. He went further and spoke of the SPD as a focal point for political mediation on a national scale.[30] He was hinting that the social-democrats, neither bourgeois nor communist, represented the *via media*. The formation of a West German SPD party at Hanover in the British zone in October added a new dimension to the debate. The leading light in Hanover turned out to be Kurt Schumacher. His politics had more in common with the British Labour Party, then in power, than with the East German SPD.[31]

The SPD he led was much more a national party than the SPD of the Weimar era. He was convinced that 'speaking for the nation' should not be left completely to the liberal and conservative parties. Schumacher anticipated the split between the Soviet Union and the USA and so favoured a European alternative, socialism. In retrospect, he underestimated Soviet power and as a consequence overrated the prospects for the SPD on an all-German level.

Schumacher had little sympathy for the KPD, the Soviets or a policy of pandering to their predilections. Despite the allure of Berlin, still regarded as the capital of Germany, Schumacher and his colleagues did not move there. They declared that until a German central government and administration came into being, Grotewohl would represent the East German party and Schumacher, the Western wing. Hence the SPD was split into two segments from its inception and this made it very difficult for the Eastern wing to resist KPD pressure for unification. The open opposition of the Western party to the fusion added fuel to the conviction of SMAD that Schumacher and his colleagues were anti-Soviet and anti-communist. The utterances of West German social-democrats brought down much KPD and SMAD criticism on Grotewohl and his party in September and October. Despite this Grotewohl spoke out on 11 November and obviously felt that the party had considerable room for manoeuvre. Soviet reaction must have shocked him. His speech was not published in the party newspaper nor broadcast as intended. The version which appeared in SMAD's newspaper gave the impression that he favoured unification.[32]

Besides the increasing popularity of the East German SPD and the dangers that it might be unduly influenced by the West German party, other factors motivated the communists to go for unification. The radical stance of many social-democrats who advocated socialism and resented dismantling and reparations led to SPD gains in works' council elections in late 1945. The KPD was however a much more disciplined party than the SPD. Both parties had large memberships but the KPD had proved much more capable at 'schooling' its members in the goals of the party and at integrating 'old' and 'new' members. A complex system of party education had been established. The SPD had nothing similar. Another reason for favouring fusion was the influence of the KPD in the single trade union organisation, the FDGB. Communists were also proving adept at winning support in factories, especially in works' councils. Here again social-democrats were playing second fiddle.

Externally communist parties did poorly in the first postwar elections in Hungary and Austria in November 1945. However, it should be borne in mind that during the pre-election period the communists were very optimistic about their chances and in Hungary the social-democrats did not do very well. Carola Stern makes the point that an SPD victory and a KPD defeat in the local elections to be held in 1946 in all occupation zones had to be prevented if at all possible.[33]

Once they had decided on unification the communists moved with alacrity to put it into effect. The very disturbed CC of the SPD was, however, assured by Wilhelm Pieck that the KPD was not thinking of a fusion before the end of 1946.[34] This appeared to accord social-democrats a breathing space in which to conduct a full discussion about the proposed merger and to devise tactics to ward off a KPD takeover bid. This breathing space turned out to be very short indeed, as the SPD discovered after it had agreed reluctantly to a conference on the merger on 20 and 21 December.

The conference of the sixty – thirty members from each party – met in Berlin amid considerable SPD misgivings, at both zonal and local level. Grotewohl was left in no doubt about the resentment felt by social-democrats, especially in Thuringia, concerning harassment, preferential treatment of communists by SMAD and personal abuse. Grotewohl included some of these objections in his opening speech at the conference. He pointed out that 'deep resentment towards the fraternal communist party had arisen among members' due to the completely uncomradely attitude of middle- and low-ranking KPD personnel and the overt preferential treatment extended to the KPD by SMAD.[35] Grotewohl, in the next breath, drew the teeth of this criticism and exonerated the KPD and SMAD from any blame for this state of affairs. The final conference resolution, based on a KPD draft, stated that the prelude to the realisation of the political and organisational fusion of the KPD and SPD would be the deepening and broadening of inter-party co-operation.[36] No timetable was set for unification and a working group, formed of four members from each party, was set up to work out the framework and programme of the new party. The SPD was not dissatisfied with the outcome, it imagined that it had time to improve its position. The KPD and SMAD read the conference resolution differently. They began a campaign for unity straight away and SMAD encouraged fusion of the two parties at local level, even before a decision had been reached at *Land* or national level. The transformation in Thuringia, for instance, was quite dramatic. The foe of rapid unity, Hermann Brill, resigned and left for Berlin before the end of the year.[37] His successor, Heinrich Hoffmann, was the man most favoured by SMAD.[38] Under his leadership Thuringia became the SPD pace-setter in the race for unity. If Thuringia proved malleable and enthusiastic, the opposite is true of the Berlin organisation. It became the centre of SPD opposition to unity and the fact that Berlin was under four-power control played an important role in making this possible. The KPD pressed the SPD leadership for a firm committal to unity in the immediate future. The social-democratic position was weakened by the hostile reception accorded the December conference in the British and American zones and Kurt Schumacher would hear nothing of a Reich congress of the SPD to discuss the matter. Under pressure from below, the CC of the SPD called a meeting on 10 and 11 February 1946 to debate the issue. After acrimonious debate it was decided to call a party congress for the Soviet zone to decide the matter once and for all. The CC of the SPD divided for the last time on this issue. Those opposed to immediate unity included Gustav Dahrendorf. A fervent supporter of unity in June 1945, he decided to leave for Hamburg rather than submit to the inevitable decision to unite. Two other opponents, Germer and Neubecker, continued their fight in the Berlin organisation until they and it were expelled from the party.

After the decision of 11 February the only thing that remained to be decided was the name of the new party and the date of its birth. The Socialist Unity Party of Germany (*Sozialistische Einheitspartei Deutschlands*, or SED) came into being at a unification congress on 21 and 22 April 1946. Prior to this KPD and SPD had held separate congresses at *Land* and provincial level on 6 and 7 April and separate party congresses on a zonal basis on 19 and 20 April. The unification congress in Berlin was highlighted by a handshake between Otto Grotewohl, approaching from the right of the stage, and Wilhelm Pieck, approaching from the left. This symbolic gesture, both parties compromising and taking up a middle position, made the fusion very palatable to the majority of social-democrats. Many of these may have overlooked something else of more than symbolic significance, the date of the congress: 22 April was the anniversary of the birth of Vladimir Ilich Lenin. The SED at birth was not a 'party of a new type' but it did not take it long to pass from the milk of the German road to socialism to the strong meat of Marxism-Leninism as taught by the Communist Party of the Soviet Union.

How does one account for the rapid shift of opinion within the SPD which transformed the political party with the largest membership in the Soviet zone from one which was becoming increasingly cool *vis-à-vis* the KPD and had all-German ambitions in November 1945, into a malleable and not very demanding partner of the communists in April 1946? The role of Otto Grotewohl is of key importance. As late as the December conference he was equivocal about an immediate fusion with the KPD. Two weeks later he had put these doubts behind him and thereafter pursued a strong pro-unification policy, often in the teeth of opposition from some members of his Central Committee. No convincing explanation for his volte-face has ever been advanced. His supporters would argue that he was following a consistent policy. After all the SPD favoured fusion with the KPD sooner or later. Events, some confined to the Soviet zone, others of an all-German nature, forced the pace of events. Grotewohl, like Wilhelm Külz, the leader of the Liberal Democratic Party, believed that a new page had to be written on German-Soviet relations. The Soviets, so they believed, were in central Europe to stay, if not their army, then their political influence. Grotewohl wanted the resurrection of all-German political parties: only in this way could Germans build a new democratic nation. Since he believed that the SPD was the natural majority party and he its leader, the new Germany would be social-democratic and sympathetic towards the Soviet Union. Kurt Schumacher shattered that dream. He was overtly anti-communist, which to SMAD meant anti-Soviet, and he would not hear of a Reich congress of the SPD to discuss unification with the KPD. Schumacher even suggested that the SPD in the Soviet zone should dissolve itself as a protest against KPD pressure for unification. This would have been self-defeating. Schumacher appeared to prefer being the head of the West German SPD and not to be willing to enter into negotiations with Grotewohl which might enhance the position of the East German SPD. Hence the Eastern SPD felt let down. In the end Grotewohl responded to pressure from below and swam with the rising tide of rank-and-file support for rapid fusion in early 1946.

Grotewohl's detractors would refer to him as vain, weak and too ready to make concessions to the KPD and SMAD. There was abundant evidence to show that local initiative towards fusion was invariably stimulated by SMAD personnel. Grotewohl, despite his conviction that he was trusted by SMAD, did not obtain redress for many of the grievances brought to the attention of the communists. The Central Committee of the SPD was split right up to the moment of unification. Indeed, so strongly did the Berlin organisation feel about fusion in early 1946 that it arranged a referendum among social-democrats in the city on 31 March. At the last moment the Soviets banned it in their sector. However, 23,755 voted in the three Western sectors out of an estimated membership of 33,247. To the question: 'Are you in favour of an immediate merger of the two workers' parties?' 2940 voted yes and 19,529 no. To the question: 'Are you in favour of an alliance which will guarantee co-operation and exclude fratricidal strife?' 14,763 voted yes and 5559 no. Here was clear evidence that the will to co-operate, despite the battles with the KPD and SMAD, was still extraordinarily strong. what was needed was time to iron out the differences between the KPD and the SPD but Grotewohl, far from taking the result of the referendum seriously, brushed it aside as an irrelevance.

Many SPD leaders, especially those who had spent time in concentration camps, wanted a united labour movement after the war. They were unanimous in rejecting the politics of the Weimar era. They all believed that capitalism was finished. Why did men such as Brill and Dahrendorf, fervent proponents of a united left in May 1945, oppose fusion with the KPD in early 1946? The communists they knew and had suffered with, and this created a bond between them, were men with whom they believed they could build a socialist Germany. After 1945 the KPD leadership fell into the hands not of communists who had spent the Nazi era in Germany, but of Moscow émigrés. These men had quite different ideas about the shape of German politics. They had to co-ordinate their policies with the CPSU and with SMAD. The uncertainties of the international situation were such that no one could be certain, not even the Soviets, how events would turn out. Brill, for one, always favoured a united party of the left. However he wanted a party which was distinctly different from the old KPD and SPD. Under these conditions Brill believed that the social-democratic spirit would triumph in a socialist Germany.

SMAD and the KPD handled the difficulties of early 1946 with some skill. The subtle and astute Colonel S. I. Tyulpanov, Chief of the Information and Propaganda Department of SMAD and the head of its party organisation, poured oil on the troubled waters from time to time. Grotewohl was amenable to his influence and Tyulpanov's knowledge of the history of the German working-class movement was effectively used in discussions and interviews with social-democrat and non-social-democrat alike. The KPD's major innovation, agreed in advance with SMAD, was to expound the concept of a German road to socialism. An article on this theme was published, in February 1946, by Anton Ackermann, a leading member of the KPD.[39] He sought to allay fears that Germany would be bolshevised and pointed out that a peaceful transition to socialism was possible. A united workers' party was necessary and Germany's more developed economic and cultural life would make the building of a socialist economy and culture easier. This appeared to indicate that the SED would build socialism with German bricks and on a solid German foundation. Many waverers were won over by this prospect.

PARTY MEMBERSHIP IN THE SBZ

Before examining the membership of the parties of the left in and after 1945, it is worth looking at the impact of the national socialist era, the war and the loss of the territories in the East.

Prior to 1933 some of the key centres of the German labour movement were to be found in the area later encompassed by the SBZ. Cities such as Eisenach, Gotha, Berlin and Halle had a socialist ring to them. In 1932 in the Reichstag election, SPD and KPD together polled a majority of votes in Leipzig and Berlin. Indeed in 1933 about 40 per cent of KPD membership, about 100,000 members, were domiciled in the part of Germany which became the SBZ. The SPD was even stronger, about 60 per cent of its membership — about 581,000 members — resided there.[40] Great social changes took place during the war, notably a decline in the proportion of workers and an increase in the number of women in the labour force. The population expanded from 15,200,000 in 1939 to 16,200,000 in 1945; of these 6,600,000 were male and 9,600,000 were female. The SBZ absorbed 4 million refugees from the lost territories in the East in 1946 and by December 1947 their numbers had risen to 4,200,000, or about a quarter of the total population of 19,100,000.[41] There were 1,100,000 evacuees in Saxony in December 1947 and they made up 24·8 per cent of the population. In Mecklenburg 44 per cent (about 1 million) of the inhabitants were new arrivals. Of the refugees from the east only 27·3 per cent were male and this added to the disadvantageous structure of the SBZ population. About 41 per cent of them had previously been engaged in agriculture, thus underlining the pressure on the land in the Soviet zone.[42]

The structure of the population in 1945 revealed that many young men were still in uniform. In 1946, 440,000 returned and in 1947 about 370,000.[43] However in November 1947 there were still 1,700,000 German prisoners-of-war, 830,000 of whom were in the USSR. Many of these men began returning to Germany in 1948, with a proportion of them settling in the SBZ.[44]

How strong was the KPD in the SBZ in May 1945? Walter Ulbricht calculated that the party lost about half its members during the Nazi era.[45] This would mean that there were about 50,000 communists in the SBZ when national socialist Germany capitulated (see Table 1.1).

TABLE 1.1 Party membership in the SBZ

Date	KPD	SPD	SED
20 November 1945	270000[a]		
3 March 1946	511000[b]		
of which			
Berlin	64000		
Land Saxony	150000		
Province Saxony	120000		
Thuringia	62000		
Brandenburg	60000		
Mecklenburg	55000		
20 April 1946	619256[c]	679,159[c]	1,298,415[c]

Sources: [a] Walter Ulbricht, *Zur Geschichte der deutschen Arbeiterbewegung: Band II: 1933–1946*, 2, Zusatzband (Berlin, DDR, 1968) p. 327.
[b] Walter Ulbricht, *Zur Geschichte der deutschen Arbeiterbewegung: Band II: 1933–1946*, 1, Zusatzband (Berlin, DDR, 1966) p. 359. KPD membership in the American zone was 56000 and in the British zone 104000.
[c] *Bericht des Parteivorstandes der SED an den 2. Parteitag* (Berlin, DDR, 1947) p. 29.

The determined efforts to swell the ranks of the KPD during the unification campaign are reflected in the figures in the table. Ulbricht instructed party members to cover every highway and by-way in the zone in the search for recruiting material. The high membership figures for Brandenburg and Mecklenburg, predominately agricultural areas, demonstrate the attractiveness of the KPD after the land reform.

Why was the KPD so successful in recruiting new members, especially after November 1945? The KPD was, overtly and covertly, closely linked to SMAD. It had the support of the occupying power at its back. This also had its disadvantages. Ulbricht, for one, was very conscious of the fact that KPD economic and political policy had to aim at unifying the population against heavy industry (it had, after all, made the war possible), the military and the large landowners. The KPD had a tough time defending the Soviet Union's right to reparations and the justness of its policy of dismantling vitally needed equipment.

The KPD was not the only party which was very successful at recruiting new members: the SPD kept pace with it. Also the CDU was winning new members in the countryside to add to those in the towns. The LDPD, since it concentrated mostly on middle-class city dwellers, had little impact in the rural areas in 1945. Taken together the number of people organised in political parties in 1945 was surprisingly high. Given the fact that most of the men of military age were still in prisoner-of-war camps, the totals recruited, especially by the KPD and SPD, are exceptional.

The first basic reform carried out in the zone was the land reform in the autumn of 1945. It came under the heading of the denazification and demilitarisation adopted at the Potsdam Conference. The communists saw the large landowners (*Junkers*) as reactionary, which was quite justified in the sense that no large landowner was likely to be pro-communist since this would have meant the nationalisation of his land without compensation. The KPD also saw the *Junkers* as a social class which was closely linked to national socialism and the Prussian conservative tradition. The property of war criminals, Nazi activists and all estates over 100 hectares were transferred to a land fund. This accounted for about one-third of the agricultural land of the SBZ.

Families of agricultural labourers, refugees, small peasants and non-agricultural labourers were the chief recipients. Over 300,000 families benefited from the reform but no family received enough land to become really self-sufficient. For instance, the average agricultural labourer and his family received only seven hectares. At the same time SMAD ordered all the documents referring to the previous ownership of the land to be destroyed. The inspiration behind the reforms was political, not economic. This was admitted by Edwin Hörnle, the KPD specialist on agrarian affairs. The KPD accepted that food production might decrease in the zone as a result. Not only would this mean less food for the SBZ population, but also that less food would be exported to the other zones in West Germany. Those who benefited from the reform were almost certain to vote KPD, if only to retain possession of the land and to obtain vitally needed credits. The land reform turned out to be a great success for the KPD in the countryside.

Another notable success for the KPD was its role in the trade union movement. Order No. 2 issued by SMAD on 10 June 1945 permitted the formation of trade unions. A preparatory committee met in Berlin on 15 June to discuss the problem. For the first time in German labour history, communist, social-democratic, Christian and liberal trade unionists came together, convinced that only an above-party united trade union organisation was capable of making democracy feasible in Germany. The lesson of the Weimar republic was that a divided labour movement smoothed the path for fascism. The KPD, for the first time in labour affairs, was allowed to join the mainstream of the movement. The communists had come in from the cold at last. Their discipline, devotion and training quickly led to the leading role in the movement falling into their hands. Schools for party functionaries, evening classes and the rapid publication of party manuals quickly bore fruit.

The KPD was very careful when selecting candidates for trade union posts. A man who stammered or stuttered would not be elected. Prospective candidates had to stand up to communist questioning beforehand and provide frank and convincing answers while defending the party line. The communists believed that only such candidates would win over the non-committed.

The social-democrats were very much slower off the mark. Their democratic party structure made it more difficult to reach agreement on party goals. SMAD only permitted the establishment of one organisation called the Freier Deutscher Gewerkschaftsbund (FDGB), the Free German Trades Union Association. There were those who would have preferred Christian and liberal trade unions to be established, acknowledging the FDGB as an umbrella organisation. The CDU leaders, Jacob Kaiser and Ernst Lemmer, had considerable union experience behind them. When it came to the foundation of the FDGB in February 1946, the KPD delegates, aided by the pro-unity SPD members, swamped the opposition. KPD success in the trade union movement was of such significance that Hartmut Zimmermann, for one, believes that the fusion of the KPD and the SPD was hardly conceivable without it.[46]

The youth movement followed the same pattern. Youth committees, under strong KPD influence, were established throughout the zone, with a central youth committee in Berlin. This committee applied to SMAD on 26 February 1946 for permission to establish the Freie Deutsche Jugend (FDJ), the Free German Youth Movement. SMAD gave its permission on 5 March and on 7 March the FDJ was founded. Erich Honecker was elected its first leader. Christian and other youth organisations were not permitted to come into existence.

Reforms in the educational and legal spheres (previously worked out in exile in Moscow) provided scope for nominees enjoying the confidence of the communists. Since there were very few specialists available with the requisite qualifications short-term inadequacy had to be countenanced if long-term efficiency was in prospect. Ulbricht, talking about lawyers, put the matter in perspective: 'All active Nazis must be removed. It appears necessary for us to appoint people with sound common sense and an anti-fascist frame of mind. We shall organise courses to provide them with legal knowledge.'[47]

Not every communist favoured the policies adopted by the KPD. Some would have preferred a commitment to socialism in the summer of 1945, others objected to the land reform and looked for the establishment of state farms on confiscated estates, others wanted a communist trade union movement, a communist youth league, and so on. They were easily contained by Ulbricht and the KPD leadership. As Ulbricht said on more than one occasion, the immediate postwar period was the time for the completion of the bourgeois democratic revolution of 1848. Socialism in 1945, from the KPD's point of view, would have split the zone and would have aroused the ire of the Western Allies. This may have cost the KPD a few members to the more openly socialist SPD but as long as Soviet forces stayed in the zone, the KPD represented the *vague de l'avenir*. A KPD party card could be a one-way ticket to success. Recruitment between November 1945 and April 1946 was stepped up on a massive scale and many with only a limited grasp of Marxism-Leninism joined the party. The goal in this period was to achieve at least parity in numbers with the SPD at the unification congress.

THE SED PROGRAMME

The goal of the SED as agreed at the unification congress, was the construction of socialism. If the SPD in 1945 was more openly socialist the KPD caught up with it in April 1946. The document,[48] plotting the future of the zone and of Germany, contained short-term as well as long-term goals, acceptable to ex-KPD and ex-SPD members alike. The long-term goal, everyone agreed, was a socialist Germany; but what were the immediate tasks facing the new party? Under this heading came the need to punish the war criminals; the removal of all fascists and reactionaries from official posts in the administration and the economy; the putting of honest democrats and tested anti-fascists in their place following democratically conducted elections. The systematic training of capable workers and employees to fit them for posts in local government, as teachers, people's judges and enterprise managers, with special attention being paid to women, was to be the order of the day. The monopoly capitalists, large landowners and militarists were to be dispossessed. Enterprises, mineral resources, mines, banks, savings banks and insurance firms were to be placed under the jurisdiction of local government or an all-German government. Economic planning was envisaged and industrial output was to be increased by involving private initiative. The works' councils (*Betriebsräte*) were to be the legal organ for the representation of workers and employees in an enterprise. The councils were to be equal partners when discussing all enterprise and production problems. Agriculture was to be intensified and land reform promoted. A democratic reform was to take place in education. The immediate goal was the creation of a united Germany, an anti-fascist, parliamentary democratic republic, with a central government made up of anti-fascist democratic parties. Leaving aside socialism, the goals presented here are in conformity with the Potsdam Agreement. When it came to implementing the decisions taken at Potsdam, fissures appeared between the various zones. The SED programme stated quite openly that in a bourgeois society the working class is an exploited and oppressed class. Exploitation and oppression can only finally be removed when a bourgeois society is replaced by a socialist society. The SED claimed that it had this goal in view. In order for this to happen the working class, led by the SED, had to seize political power. To do this it allied itself with all employees. Hence the SED was claiming primacy in the political process. Since the combined KPD and SPD party could claim, plausibly, that it represented the majority of the population, it was in a powerful position.

The position of the SED was also greatly strengthened by the nationalisation of large enterprises, the land reform and the taking over of the banks. The previous owners had exercised great political as well as economic influence. Now, after the loss of their social position, they posed no threat. The SED had served notice that it would one day claim to be the only party with the right to shape policy, but that would only happen when the socialist dawn was breaking. Meanwhile the SED had to content itself with the leading but by no means dominant role. A democratic Germany, the fulfilment of the dream of the 1848 revolutionaries, had to be built first. The SED underpinned its claim that the working class should play the leading role during the period of the anti-fascist democratic order by stating that the German bourgeoisie had proved itself incapable in 1848 and 1918 of completing the bourgeois democratic revolution. The responsibility had now passed to the working class.[49] Further, democracy, understood as the rule of the people, places the decisive positions in the state in the hands of the numerically largest group.[50] Also, the working class was the only class led by a party whose policies were guided by scientific knowledge and which was therefore in a position to promote the development of the state in the context of historical progress.[51] This last claim, quite untenable to a non-Marxist, could only be understood by the CDU and LDPD as serving notice that their concepts of a future democratic Germany were out of focus and that they had to learn about progress at the feet of the SED.

The democratic bloc of anti-fascist parties changed its nature after the fusion of the KPD and SPD. Now the new party of the left had 50 per cent of the seats and votes and thus could not be outvoted. Such was its feeling of self-confidence that it did not even bother, in its new programme, to examine the role of the bloc in a parliamentary democratic republic. The immediate future was uncertain but the SED regarded it as a transition period before the advent of socialism. A socialist German state was in the minds of all SED members. At that moment in time, however, the prospect of two German states, one of them socialist, appeared improbable. What was still to be determined was the visage of the new-born state. Was it to be a twin of the first workers' and peasants' state or was it to have a physiognomy that was unmistakably German? The guidelines of this discussion were laid down by Anton Ackermann, in his article in *Einheit*.[52] His conception of a German road to socialism remained official party policy until September 1948.

No very clear image of this route emerged over the period April 1946 to September 1948. Much energy was devoted to analysing contemporary German history and tracing developments in the context of the writings of Marx and Engels. Few authoritative statements were based on the opinions of Lenin and Stalin. The term 'people's democracy' was used but 'anti-fascist democratic republic' was much more popular. Party writers stressed that the SED was a mass party, a party united with others in a common struggle to defeat fascism and militarism and to build democracy. The Communist Party of the Soviet Union is a cadre party inside a mass party and one which takes great care when selecting new members. The SED, after 1946, became more selective too. The organisational structure of the party began to change as preference was given to factory party groups over locality party groups. Recruitment was increasingly directed at workers. The SED needed considerable numerical superiority over other parties before thoroughgoing reforms could be attempted. Then it could place its members in leading positions.

The SED, after the unification congress, was very successful at recruiting new members. For a few months it recorded about 50,000 new members a month but this number dropped in the winter of 1946/47 until only 7000 new members were added in June 1947. In the same month 3385 left the party. Peak membership was recorded in September 1947, when there were 1,799,030 members. This represented an increase of 500,000 or a jump of 38·5 per cent over April 1946, and revealed that in September 1947 8·6 per cent of the SBZ population was in the SED (compared with 3 per cent of the Soviet population in the CPSU at the same time). The social breakdown of SED membership is as follows:

1 in every 5 industrial workers,
1 in every 4 employees,
1 in every 17 farm and forestry workers,
1 in every 10 farmers,
1 in every 7 artisans and tradesmen,
1 in every 8 engineers, technicians, etc.,
1 in every 3 teachers

was in the party.

This meant that the party was made up as follows:

Per cent

47·8 industrial workers
18·4 employees
3·5 farm workers
5·8 farmers
6·4 artisans, etc.
1·0 engineers, etc.
1·7 teachers
1·5 doctors
13·9 housewives

After the IInd Party Congress in September 1947 numbers dropped. In December 1947 there were 1,784,214 members.[53] During 1948 it became more difficult to join the party and a mini-purge was set in motion. It is unlikely that the 1·8 million barrier was ever crossed.

Not all the former SPD members stayed or were permitted to stay in the SED. Those who were disgruntled with the decision to unite and those who actively opposed unification are two groups whom the SED would not be altogether happy to have within its ranks. Coercion, imprisonment and harassment were employed against SPD members who opposed the fusion. Erich Ollenhauer, in April 1961, put the number as high as 20,000. There is no way of telling precisely how many other SPD members refused to join the SED. It was not necessary to use coercion to speed recruitment. Officials in nationalised enterprises and in the state administration could be invited to join the SED as an earnest of their democratic intent and as evidence of their support for developments which had taken place.[54] Job insecurity was very high and living standards very low, hence an official would find it very difficult to refuse the invitation. Those with ambitions and no state job could not fail to notice that membership of the SED, if not a one-way ticket to success was certainly no hindrance to progress. The prestige and influence enjoyed by officials in German society were added stimuli to a career in administration. There was also the tradition of the national socialist era when membership of the ruling party was expected of, though not requested, by all leading officials.

From its inception the SED agreed that communists and social-democrats should enjoy parity in all leading party posts. This meant that at the head of each party organ there were two co-chairmen, one from the ex-KPD and one from the ex-SPD. This principle also applied to section heads, from the Secretariat of the Central Committee down through the *Land* and *Kreis* organisations.[55] The elected Central Committees, at each level, were also composed equally of communists and social-democrats. Social-democrats believed that this inefficient arrangement would make it possible for them to contain the communists, but they soon discovered that they had been greatly mistaken. The communists used a variety of tactics to restrict the influence of social-democrats.[56] A social-democrat could be 'surrounded' by communists, rumours could be spread impugning his integrity, he could be accused of various political inconsistencies, his communist subordinates could ignore his decisions and carry out different policies and a hundred and one other minor irritations could enervate him and make him increasingly ineffective. Some social-democrats capitulated and resigned, others counter-attacked, but fared little better, as they found themselves removed from their positions on some pretext or other and transferred to other, less responsible work. Communists were better prepared for this type of 'administrative tension' than social-democrats. Communist numbers were also swelled by returning prisoners-of-war and from areas such as the Sudetenland where German nationals were being expelled. Those prisoners-of-war who had been through anti-fascist schools or who had shown a willingness to help build a socialist Germany could expect to return home before the more recalcitrant. The National Committee for a Free Germany recruited and trained German prisoners-of-war in the Soviet Union and they played an important role in building up the police and the National People's Army (NVA), or the People's Police in Barracks, as they were called at the time.[57] The SED built up its apparatus as a mirror-image of the state administration. As the zonal administration expanded, so party organs were established to supervise the new responsibilities. The party functionary is, theoretically, not supposed to engage in any administration, since that is the responsibility of the official, sometimes a communist. However the party functionaries are held to be responsible to the party for the manner in which the officials execute their tasks. For example, in an economic sector, the party functionary's job, besides checking to see if any political opposition is being manifested, is to see that the plan is fulfilled. His career depends on many success indicators, but the main one is to record success in quantitative terms. Thus creative tension, if that is not too mild an euphemism, exists between party functionary and state official. There is also a party cell in each administrative unit to which, naturally, only party members belong.

The ability to influence the appointment of officials in the administration and the economy is a key factor in the transformation of any society. The SED, through its personnel departments, actively sought to place its nominees or to prevent the appointment of those who were not very amenable to its influence. The post of personnel director was coveted by the KPD right from May 1945 in all administrations, whether at local, *Kreis* or *Land* level. In the SED there was supposed to be parity in filling personnel departments but as it turned out there were many more ex-communists than ex-social-democrats ensconced in these vital nerve centres of party activity.[58] The personnel departments established close links with the Soviet security police and gradually all posts of any significance in both party and state organisations came under purview. Posts on this list, in Soviet parlance a *nomenklatura*, could not be filled without party consent. Gradually the SED personnel departments linked up with the personnel departments of state organisations and institutions and all in turn linked up with SMAD. Hence the SED party apparatus systematically acquired influence over all appointments, promotions and demotions in the Soviet zone. The personnel departments also carried out investigations and acted as arbitrators in case of disputes. They gave birth to the party control commissions, the sections concerned with security and counter-espionage and the internal party police. (See Figure 1.1)

THE SED: INTERNAL DEVELOPMENTS

The unification congress of the KPD and SPD elected a Central Committee (CC) (*Parteivorstand*) of 80 members. Twenty of these came from the Western zones.[59] At its first meeting on 23 April 1946, the CC elected a central Secretariat, the organising brain of the party. It was composed, in conformity with the parity principle, of seven ex-communists and seven ex-social-democrats. Shortly after the II Congress (September 1947) the number was increased to sixteen.[60]

Wilhelm Pieck (KPD) and Otto Grotewohl (SPD); Joint Chairmen of the SED, responsible for all party decisions and the party newspaper *Neues Deutschland* and the theoretical journal, *Einheit*.

Walter Ulbricht (KPD) and Max Fechner (SPD); Deputy Joint Chairmen and responsible for the following departments of the Secretariat: Ulbricht: the general department, economic activity and finance, *Land* policy and internal affairs, editorial member of *Neuer Weg*, a journal for party functionaries. Fechner: local government politics, justice.

Franz Dahlem (KPD) and Erich W. Gniffke (SPD); responsible for the following departments: Dahlem: personnel, bureau for international co-operation, Western department. Gniffke: organisation.

Anton Ackermann (KPD) and Otto Meier (SPD); responsible for the following departments: Ackermann: party education, publicity, press, radio. Meier: culture and education, youth secretariat. Both were also responsible for the Secretariat library and the party-owned publishing house, Dietz Verlag.

Paul Merker (KPD) and Helmut Lehmann (SPD); responsible for the following departments: Merker: agriculture and co-operative affairs. Lehmann: labour, social security and health.

Walter Beling (KPD) and August Karsten (SPD); responsible for the department for the administration of party enterprises, to which the accounts and business department belonged.

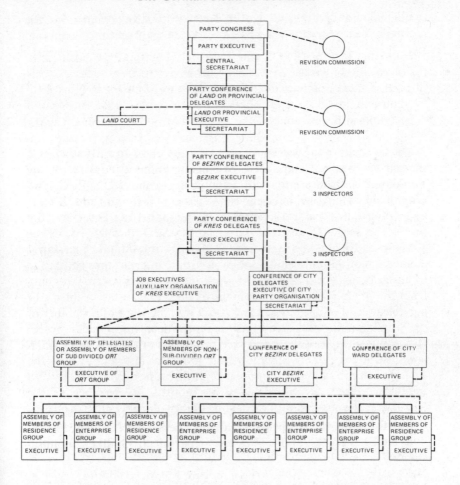

FIGURE 1.1 Organisational framework of the SED according to the Ist Statute (22 April 1946) and the guidelines for the organisational structure of the SED laid down by the Central Secretariat on 24 December 1946

It transpired that the *Bezirks* hindered the implementation of party policy. By the IInd Congress (September 1947), they had disappeared, except for Magdeburg and Anhalt, in favour of direct links between the *Land* and *Kreis* executives.

– – – Sequence of eligibility and accountability

——— Sequence of subordination

Source: Werner Horn *et al.*, *20 Jahre Sozialistische Einheitspartei Deutschlands: Beiträge* (Berlin, DDR, 1966) p. 386.

Elli Schmidt (KPD) and Käthe Kern (SPD); responsible for the women's secretariat and all SED work among women.

Hermann Matern (KPD) and Friedrich Ebert (SPD); both functionaries were elected to the Secretariat as representatives of their *Land* Central Committee (CC), Matern until January 1949 as SED Chairman in Berlin and Ebert until November 1948 as Second Secretary in Brandenburg.

The meetings of the Secretariat always took place on a Monday.[61] If the agenda was not completed, the deliberations continued on the Tuesday. Members sat in twos around a circular table. Pieck and Grotewohl sat together, Ulbricht and Fechner to their right and Dahlem and Gniffke to their left. Richard Gypner and Fritz Schreiber, the former an ex-KPD and the latter an ex-SPD member, acted as secretaries. No minutes were recorded, only resolutions. Secretariat members received the agenda and a multitude of enclosures before the meetings began. An enormous range of questions was covered, ranging from the organisational development of the SED, to the problems of agriculture and refugees. Each enclosure was the work of a member of the Secretariat, the person responsible for the department under review. Occasionally the presidents and vice-presidents of the central German administrations (DZV) and the prime ministers and ministers of the *Land* governments were summoned to address the Secretariat. It soon established itself as a kind of super-ministry. A member of the Secretariat was charged with the responsibility of reporting to the CC of the SED, which met once a month, what problems the Secretariat was discussing, what political decisions had been taken and what had been achieved. Each member took it in turn to deliver this report. The Secretariat meetings were chaired by Pieck and Grotewohl in turn. Business was conducted at a brisk pace but no thorny problem was avoided or discussion was cut short. Gniffke records – he remained in the Secretariat until October 1948 – that it was Ulbricht's proposals which raised the most opposition, even when they were reasonable and necessary.

Some of the 'twins' found it possible to establish amicable working relations in the Secretariat. Others would not or could not work in harness. Pieck and Grotewohl operated well together. Pieck was nominal head of the ex-KPD members but Ulbricht regarded himself as superior to Pieck and as the future leader of the SED. Pieck, because of his age (he was born in 1876) was given to forgetting things and making embarrassing gaffes. Grotewohl, although he did not realise it at the time, was most secure as long as Marshal Zhukov was head of the Soviet Army in Germany. Zhukov was followed, in the spring of 1946, by General, later Marshal, Sokolovsky. The latter was a political general to his fingertips. He went well with Colonel Tyulpanov, the perceptive and prescient head of the army *aktiv*. Grotewohl had cultivated very good relations with SMAD but discovered that although Pieck and he were responsible for contacting SMAD, the person with the best contacts was Walter Ulbricht. Dahlem and Gniffke got on well together. Gniffke harboured a considerable personal animus against Ulbricht, and Dahlem was also an old adversary. This may have influenced their relationship and encouraged both of them to vote against Ulbricht on the same issue. Ackermann and Meier, the one quiet spoken, the other a fighting cock, were never designed to work in tandem. Merker and Lehmann agreed to work apart; they only met at meetings of the Secretariat but there was no co-operation or strife. Ulbricht and Fechner went together like a donkey and a camel pulling a cart. Ulbricht had a fine office, Fechner did not and this riled him. Comrade Walter did not hide his conviction that he was superior to Pieck. Fechner, in Ulbricht's estimation, just did not count. Ulbricht always took it upon himself to speak for both at Secretariat meetings. If Fechner did say something different, Ulbricht observed a studied silence.

Ulbricht made no attempt to cultivate good personal relations with the ex-SPD members. He was ambitious and did not hide it. A man with a phenomenal memory and a formidable appetite for work, he did however devote some of his energy to amorous pursuits. While in the Soviet Union, in emigration, he struck up a friendship with an attractive Frenchwoman. The KPD looked askance at the relationship. It was concerned lest Walter pass on some confidential KPD information in a moment of ecstasy. It was decided that if Walter's wife no longer pleased him at least he should have a German amour, one of course who enjoyed the complete confidence of the party. Thereafter Lotte Kühn became his constant companion. Apparently they went well together: she had an excellent command of Russian and of the ground rules of Soviet politics and was as egotistical as he was. Ulbricht's main defect was that he was born without a sense of humour and this ruled out any small-talk. He had the unenviable gift of being able to kill a swinging party stone-dead just by joining it. His goatee beard and squeaky Saxon voice (he was never able to acquire a standard High German pronunciation) were a godsend to cartoonists and mimics alike. If Walter did not cut a very formidable figure outwardly, he was a doughty opponent in the

Secretariat. He cultivated his own patch and kept encroaching on those of his neighbours. He quickly established good relations with SMAD; Sokolovsky and Tyulpanov and they made a formidable triumvirate. He managed to ensure that any member of the Secretariat wishing to contact a member of SMAD had first to seek his permission.[62] There were only a few exceptions to this rule.[63] Ulbricht also manoeuvred co-operative affairs, the responsibility of Paul Merker, under his own wing by dealing directly over the heads of the Secretariat with Kurt Vieweg, Secretary-General of the association for mutual peasant aid. Through his contacts with Lotte Kühn and Bruno Köhler, the leader of the press bureau of the Secretariat, Ulbricht arranged exposure of his speeches and views in the press of the zone. In this way he circumvented Anton Ackermann, the Secretary responsible for the press.[64] Ulbricht was a great supporter of more and more centralisation in the party. He sought to enlarge his support base among the party functionaries and found many who saw in him the future leader of the SED. His model and mentor was, of course, Stalin. His Soviet experience had given him a formidable insight into party in-fighting. Armed with his ambition and his ruthlessness, he was a redoubtable opponent.

CULTIVATING THE ELECTORATE

The first opportunity the population of the Soviet zone had of expressing its opinions about the course of events was the referendum on the transfer to people's ownership of enterprises owned by war and Nazi criminals in *Land* Saxony. On 25 May 1946 the parties of the anti-fascist democratic bloc and the trade unions proposed a referendum to test public opinion. *Land* Saxony was chosen as the sounding board since the SED felt very influential there. The result was a resounding 77·7 per cent vote on 30 June in favour of expropriation. Of the 4000 enterprises on the official list, 1861 were expropriated and of this number 1002 were placed under *Land* administration.[65]. No further referenda followed in the other *Länder*. Instead SMAD felt strong enough to issue Order No. 124, which concerned expropriation and led to the sequestration of most large and middle-sized enterprises in the zone. The industrial sector of the economy was thus divided into three parts: the private sector; the sector under local state administration; the sector composed of Soviet companies. The sheer economic need led to early thoughts about planning just as it did in the Western zones. The Soviet companies, however, remained outside the plan. SMAD Order No. 103 of 19 October 1945 did require three monthly plans to be drawn up covering 1946. However, Ulbricht, responsible in the Secretariat for the economy, forcefully rejected all proposals for economic planning at a conference on the economy in Jena on 14 July 1946.[66]

Popular support for the SED was to be put to the test in local elections in September and at *Kreis* and *Land* level in October 1946. Other zones had conducted elections, so the Soviet zone could not drag its feet indefinitely. Consulting public opinion was a risk, but there was a feeling that the SED was strong enough to resist the challenge posed by the Christian-democrats and liberal-democrats. The ordinary voter had much to complain about. Hunger, disease and chaos could all be blamed on the war. But what about reparations, dismantling, the misbehaviour of Soviet soldiers, the never-ending arrests and harassment? These could be blamed on the Soviets and by extension on the SED. Action was needed and was forthcoming. Vigorous protests to SMAD led to the discipline of Soviet soldiers improving remarkably during the summer. On 6 July the SED appealed to SMAD to improve rations allocated to the population and improvements occurred a week later. Gniffke states that the decision to increase rations was taken first and then a request backdated to 6 July was made.[67] The unease of the SED was apparent when it proposed that mass organisations should also be allowed to put up candidates. Since mass organisations were to a considerable extent under the influence of the SED, any candidates proposed and elected would most likely vote with the SED faction. After strong opposition from many ex-social-democrats in the central Secretariat, it was agreed that only the association for mutual peasant aid would be permitted to put up candidates. Nevertheless, in Saxony, the democratic German women's association and, in Brandenburg, the trade union organisation (FDGB) and the Free German Youth (FDJ), did put up candidates. The *Kulturbund* also campaigned and won a few seats.

The SED was not the only party in the zone which had socialist aspirations. The Christian Democratic Union (CDU) in its founding manifesto had advocated measures, including the state ownership of natural resources, which were decidedly socialist. Men such as Jacob Kaiser and Ernst Lemmer advocated Christian socialism. The SED sought to counter this line of thought in a handbill entitled 'SED and Christianity' dated 27 August 1946.[68] In it the SED took umbrage at a remark of Jacob Kaiser, who had claimed that two *Weltanschauungen*, Christianity and Marxism, were in direct competition for world influence. The SED objected to the CDU presenting itself as the 'saviour of Christianity.' Indeed the SED did not regard Christian faith and membership of a religious community as obstacles to the acceptance of socialism or membership of a Marxist party. The SED was ready, it declared, to do everything to enable religious communities to play a positive role in the rebuilding of Germany. The fact that the socialist working-class movement had rejected the church in the past did not mean that it rejected the Christian faith. The SED had no heart for a *Kulturkampf.*

It is worth noting that the churches were one of the very few institutions in the SBZ, in this period, which were able to achieve a considerable degree of autonomy. Besides their traditional religious functions, they were also closely involved in social and medical work. The SED was very wary of engaging in polemics with organised religion. Interestingly enough, the commission of the KPD in exile which dealt with religion only considered the problem of Catholicism. Since the vast majority of the SBZ population were Protestants the policies evolved in Moscow were of little relevance. The fact that the Protestant churches in Germany traditionally supported the state may have influenced SED thinking, permitting them much autonomy. The Roman Catholic Church then benefited from the same policy.

The SED was on more certain ground when dealing with the LDPD. Liberal-democrats made no bones about the fact that they regarded private property as the foundation on which a democratic state should be built. Artisans, craftsmen, small businessmen, housewives and students found the LDPD congenial. Liberals complained that they found it very difficult to recruit new members in the countryside. There the SED had cut the ground from under their feet, by pushing through the agrarian reform. Before the *Kreis* and *Land* elections in October the SED claimed that the other parties contained elements who favoured a revision of the reform and that if the peasants wished to keep their newly acquired land only a vote for the SED would guarantee it. This was sharp practice by the SED but every peasant did know that the CDU had favoured some form of compensation for the dispossessed estate owners and had failed to sign an appeal to help the new peasants in the autumn of 1945.

The SED surprised everyone, especially its own members, by coming out in favour of permitting nominal members of the NSDAP to play an active role in the construction of a democratic Germany on 20 June 1946. This was a bitter pill for many socialists who had suffered years of incarceration under the Nazis to swallow. Just how nominal was nominal? Who would decide this thorny problem? Would judgement be based on commitment to democracy? The more ardent the commitment the greater the blemishes forgiven – would this be the norm? Since about 10 per cent of the population were ex-national socialists there were potentially many new members to be enrolled. However no political party, not even the SED, wanted to be known as a haven for ex-Nazis. One former national socialist was so enthusiastic about the new policy that he coined his own slogan: 'Long Live the SED, the Great Friend of Little Nazis'.[69] If this *démarche* promised more votes for the SED, another measure added to the total. Many ex-prisoners-of-war were repatriated at this time. Those who had passed through the anti-fascist schools and had shown a readiness to atone for their past made up the bulk of the returning men.

SMAD also put its shoulder to the wheel. Only those local branches of a political party which had been registered with SMAD could put up candidates. The SED had branches in each of the 11,623 communities in the Soviet zone but the CDU was established in only 4200 and the LDPD in only just over 2200. Nevertheless the CDU was registered in only 2082 and the LDPD in only 1121 communities. Hence about half the Christian-democrat and liberal-democrat candidates were not permitted to stand.[70] The situation would have been worse had it not been for the vociferous protests of Jacob Kaiser, the CDU leader. He claimed that in many areas there were, in reality, no candidates whom SMAD would accept as not having a Nazi past. But this did not appear to apply to SED candidates, some of whom had been Nazis. SMAD relented a little and allowed lists to be handed in after the closing date. This did not mean they were cleared by polling day. SMAD not unnaturally, favoured the SED when it came to the distribution of paper and the provision of travelling facilities. After all, no local SMAD commander wanted to end up with a solidly bourgeois area. This would be a blemish on his record and would not say much for his ability to carry out a 'socialist' occupation.

The local elections, held in the first half of September, brought victory for the SED. Party members were disappointed that the SED had polled only 5·1 million votes (57·1 per cent). The LDPD polled 1·9 million votes (21·1 per cent) and the CDU 1·7 million votes (18·8 per cent). The mass organisations scrapped together 270,000 votes (3 per cent).[71] The SED was surprised at some of the *Land* results. Red Saxony was not so red after all, and only 48·4 per cent voted for the SED there. The highest percentage of votes cast for the SED was recorded in Mecklenburg, a decidedly rural area. One is reminded of Bismarck's quip: when the end of the world comes I should like to move to Mecklenburg since everything there is at least twenty years behind the times! In 1946 Mecklenburg proved itself ahead of the times!

If the SED was dissatisfied with the results of the local elections, it must have been furious when the *Kreis* and *Land* election results, held on 20 October, were made known. The SED polled 4·7 million votes (47·5 per cent) but the LDPD received 2·4 million votes (24·6 per cent) and the CDU 2·4 million votes (24·5 per cent). The mass organisations actually increased their vote to just over 300,000 (3·4 per cent). One reason why the SED lost 400,000 votes and the other parties gained 1·2 million votes was that whereas the local elections were tied to registered party branches the *Kreis* and *Land* elections were not. In the five *Land* parliaments, however, the SED, aided by the mass organisations, were in a minority only in Saxony-Anhalt and Brandenburg. Elections in Berlin on the same day revealed the SPD as the strongest party, the CDU next, the SED third and the LDPD last. That the three Western zones should prefer the SPD to the SED was, perhaps, not surprising but it was a shock to discover that the SPD (permitted in all Berlin as was the SED) was also the leading party in the Soviet sector (43·6 per cent of the votes, compared with 29·8 per cent for the SED). SMAD and the SED learnt a lot from these elections. The principal lesson they drew from the exercise was not to pit one political party against another. Henceforth voting would be on a joint list of candidates. The voter could either accept all the parties of the bloc or reject all of them, but not reveal his favourite party.

The CDU and LDPD quickly discovered that their influence was not proportional, in the elected assemblies, to the number of seats they held. The SED, although often in the minority, managed, by astute tactics, to block much of the legislation it did not favour. It would introduce its own proposals, presented in the context of the anti-fascist democratic revolution, thus making it difficult for the other parties to oppose the measures directly. The CDU and LDPD did not wish to be accused of being in league with fascists and counter-revolutionary elements. SMAD was always ready to call non-socialist politicians to account. If they proved stubborn they could be told that SMAD would withdraw its consent for them to continue as political figures. SMAD sought to differentiate between 'reactionaries' and 'progressives' in the ranks of the CDU and LDPD. By encouraging and flattering the 'progressives', it could drive a wedge into the opposition. The SED ably followed the same course. It was one thing to pass resolutions and even legislation but it was another thing to have them implemented. This affected principally the economic field. By the end of 1945, about 45 per cent of industrial capacity in the Soviet zone was in the hands of the state or the Soviets. The administration contained many SED members. Ulbricht in the central Secretariat of the SED was the person responsible for the whole economy. Christian-democrats and liberal-democrats, in these circumstances, could not significantly affect events in the zone but could, at best, slow down the pace of change.

THE ODER-NEISSE OR NOT

A thorny problem for the SED was the oft-repeated question about Germany's frontiers in the East. In the immediate postwar period the frontier problem reared its head in East and West as it had done after 1918. The French had their eyes on the Saar and the SED could hope for political profit from French manoeuvres in this direction. However the largest claims on the former Reich's territory were made in the east by Poland and the Soviet Union. The invading Soviet Army had forced many inhabitants of East Prussia, Pomerania and Silesia to flee. Those who did not were put in camps to await deportation. Conditions in these camps were often appalling, exacerbated, no doubt, by the dreadful experiences the Poles and Russians had just lived through. Refugees poured into the Soviet zone in a steady stream, full of resentment at their maltreatment and loss of hearth and home. Not all Germans left: some managed to stay behind, no doubt hoping fortunes would change. Polish settlers from the east of Poland, now part of the Soviet Union, took their place. The Potsdam conference did not fix Germany's eastern frontiers, leaving the decision to a future German peace treaty. The Soviets made it plain that they regarded the Oder-Neisse river as the eastern frontier but no political party could espouse such a policy immediately after the war. Besides, not every communist was ready to accept the loss of the Eastern Territories; time was needed to re-educate the recalcitrants. Ex-social-democrats in the SED could be relied upon to put up a fight to keep the territories. Part, if not all, it was hoped, might be salvaged if opposition was strong enough.

The SED had to adopt a stance on the frontier question before the autumn elections of 1946. On 12 August 1946 the Central Committee adopted a resolution entitled: The SED and the Eastern Frontier. It was couched in very cautious language and spoke of a 'provisional eastern frontier' and looked forward to an understanding on that frontier. This did not satisfy everyone but Max Fechner writing in the SED organ, *Neues Deutschland*, on 14 September 1946 articulated the view that everyone wanted to hear: 'I should like to state, as regards the eastern frontier, that the SED will oppose every attempt to reduce the territory of Germany.' V. M. Molotov, Soviet Foreign Minister, weighed in and declared on 16 September that Poland's western frontier had been decided in August 1945.[72] Confirmation at a peace conference would only be of formal significance. Grotewohl replied on 18 September and conceded that Germans would not decide the frontier, others would do that. However, he stated: 'Our policy must be determined by German interests.' The following day the Central Committee of the SED maintained that it would do all in its power to ensure that the voice of the German people was heard at the forthcoming peace conference.[73] The first hint by the SED that it would accept the Oder-Neisse line was given by Anton Ackermann on 2 March 1947 in Berlin-Neukölln when he stated that Germany could live without the territories east of the river Oder. Otto Grotewohl, however, was not of the same opinion. At an editors' conference on 22 March, he maintained that no one could force the SED to recognise the eastern frontiers. On 16 September 1947, Wilhelm Pieck returned to the subject: 'At the forthcoming peace conference the SED is strongly in favour of revising the eastern frontier in favour of the German people.' It was left to Walter Ulbricht to put an end to all these hopes. On 22 October 1948 he declared the Oder-Neisse line to be the peace frontier between Poland and Germany.

THE SED AND THE KPD

Although the unification of the KPD and SPD had been carried out on a zonal basis the goal was to achieve an all-German SED party. The emphatic refusal of the West German SPD leadership to contemplate such a fusion left the KPD and SPD as separate competing parties in the other three occupation zones. Only in Berlin was the SED recognised, and SMAD, in order to gain this concession, had had to permit the SPD in the Soviet sector of Berlin. However certain SPD members in West Germany favoured the fusion of the two working-class parties. At the first congress of the SED, 230 of the 1055 delegates had come from the Western zones and not all were communists. Of the 80 members elected to the Central Committee, 20 were from the West. It was difficult for the SED to keep a close watch on the KPD in the Western zones. No high-ranking KPD émigrés appear to have settled in the Western zones after returning from the Soviet Union. KPD officials regularly attended meetings of the SED central Secretariat when all-German affairs were on the agenda. In order to achieve closer co-ordination an SED-KPD working group was established on 14 February 1947 in East Berlin. An eighteen-man committee was nominated, composed of eight members from the central secretariat, four leading functionaries from the American, four from the British and two from the French zones. Overall responsibility lay with Franz Dahlem and Erich Gniffke. Since the SED was finding it difficult to promote its speakers in the British zone, Konni Zilliacus, a British MP, suggested that the central Secretariat send a letter complaining about discrimination against SED speakers to the British military authorities. This in turn would permit Zilliacus to raise the issue in the House of Commons. Nothing came of this *démarche*. Gniffke approached the American authorities, in the same month, April 1947, and asked about the possibility of the SED being legalised in the American zone. He was informed that General Clay's view was that the SED would be permitted as soon as the SPD was made legal in the Soviet zone. All this activity was linked to meetings of the KPD in West Germany at which it was decided to seek unification with the SED. On 20 April 1947 the KPD in Württemberg in the presence of Franz Dahlem and Elli Schmidt, on 20 April the KPD in Hesse in the presence of Walter Ulbricht; on 25 April the KPD in Bavaria, and on 27 April the KPD in Baden – all voted for unification with the SED, but these intentions were never put into effect.[74] At the second SED party congress in September 1947,[75] 271 SED-KPD delegates from the Western zones attended. The Central Committee elected at the congress numbered 58, of whom 20 represented the SED-KPD working group. It is of some interest that only 2 members of the 840 from the Soviet zone but 11 members of the 271 from the Western zones voted against the Central Committee which was elected. Evidently party discipline was less strict in the West. The SED-KPD working group was dissolved on 3 January 1949 and its members in the Central Committee withdrew. It was felt that the overt KPD connection with the SED was more of a hindrance than a help in the context of the cold war. The KPD's role was that of an opposition whereas the SED was the leading party in the Soviet zone. Covert co-operation still continued, of course, but as time passed the relationship became more and more that of a senior and a junior party.

ONE GERMANY OR TWO?

Once the occupying powers had established themselves in their zones the division of Germany was a reality. Economic unity was to be maintained by the victorious powers, followed later by political unity. No power, with the possible exception of France, wanted a divided Germany. The Soviet Union, ensconced in its own zone, could espouse all-German policies. The Western Allies did not always agree among themselves, except when resisting Soviet initiatives and demands. This had its effect on the reactions of political parties in West Germany when new proposals were floated in the East.

The SED, like all German parties, in East and West, was in favour of a united Germany. In an all-German context the left would be the largest political group. Christian-democrats and liberals knew that they could aspire to a more influential role in an all-German state than as minority parties in the Soviet zone. However there were considerable differences in the thinking of the various parties about the future of Germany. The Free Democratic Party (FDP) and the LDPD did not see eye-to-eye and neither did the CDU/CSU and the East German CDU. On the whole the SBZ parties were in favour of greater social change, and there was always the problem of the leadership struggle.

Since the goal of the KPD, and later the SED, was a socialist Germany, it never confined its horizons to the Soviet zone. The unity of the nation, it could claim, was dear to it. Communists and Social-democrats could point to their opposition, sometimes active, during the Hitler era. As has been said, the SED claimed that since the monopoly capitalists had led the nation into a ruinous war and the bourgeoisie had not stopped them, the responsibility for making Germany a democratic country had now passed to the working class. The land reform, the nationalisation of ex-Nazi industrial concerns, the removal of fascists from the administration, education and the legal profession were an earnest of its intent. The other zones should follow suit. Indeed land reform was mooted in the Western zones and discussions began on changing the ownership of large enterprises. The constitutions of some *Länder*, such as Hesse and North Rhine Westphalia, included a clause to this effect.

The gradual reunification of the American and British Zones, the Bi-Zone, evident in 1946, was a blow. It had come about since the four victorious powers could not agree. Unilateral action was taken therefore by the two who could. Economic considerations were the root cause of this decision. An attempt was made by the Bavarian Prime Minister Dr Hans Ehard, to halt the inexorable process of disunity in German affairs. Prime ministers from all the *Länder*, in East and West, met in Munich in early June 1947. The goal was to discuss ways of relieving distress among the population. The East German delegation proposed

The *Länder* of the SBZ/GDR (May 1945–July 1952) with their capital cities

that Point 1 on the agenda should be the establishment of a central German administration by the democratic parties and trade unions in order to set up a unified state. This was expressly political and furthermore it sought to grasp the initiative in all-German affairs. However, the prime ministers from West Germany, especially those from the French zone, had been expressly warned not to discuss all-German political affairs: that was the responsibility of the occupying powers. Thus the first and last all-German conference of prime ministers was torpedoed before it even began. On 12 June 1947 the SED-KPD working group roundly criticised the West German prime ministers for refusing to adopt a position *vis-à-vis* the restoration of German unity. Two days later, on 14 June 1947, the German economic commission (DWK) was established in the Soviet zone. It was to be the co-ordinating agency of all economic activity in the zone. The economic division of Germany had become reality.

Why did the Soviet zone representatives at the Munich conference put forward proposals which they knew the politicians from the West could not endorse, even if they had wanted to? Was a deliberate decision taken at that time to accept the division of Germany as a *fait accompli* or would concessions have averted this state of affairs? The key figure in the SED was Walter Ulbricht. Far from being despondent after the Munich failure, as were many in the central Secretariat, he was pleased at the outcome.[76] Erich Gniffke is in no doubt about the important role played by Ulbricht:

Ulbricht's rise to his present state and party functions is due more to the West than to the East. Stalin and the Moscow Politburo were willing to make concessions on the German question up to the end of 1947 since they favoured strict adherence to the Potsdam Agreement . . . Ulbricht was isolated until the spring of 1948. However after the so-called Marshall plan was linked with the 'politics of strength' the Soviets also altered their policy towards Germany, although they did not close the door on negotiations straight away. . . . Only in mid-1948 did Moscow open the way for the Soviet occupied zone to develop as a people's democracy, led by a 'party of a new type', headed by Ulbricht.[77]

Since Gniffke was in close contact with Ulbricht in the central Secretariat his opinion must carry much weight. If Ulbricht set himself the goal of primacy in the party, and through that primacy in the state, then it is quite plausible that the growth in power of the SED was his main objective. Since he had little or no prospect of power on an all-German basis, it had to be power in the context of the Soviet zone. In favouring the dominance of the SED in a part of Germany at the expense of communist goals in the whole of Germany, Ulbricht may be linked with S. I. Tyulpanov and A. A. Zhdanov. The other view, of playing for all-German stakes, may be linked with the names of A. Ackermann, Vladimir Semenov, the political adviser to the head of SMAD, and L. P. Beria.[78] Another way of looking at this problem would be to regard the fusion of the KPD and SPD in April 1946 as the moment when the Soviet authorities decided that a bird in the hand was worth two in the bush. Probably a majority of SPD members in the Soviet zone supported the fusion but it is clear that only a minority in the rest of Germany favoured such a move. Hence it cannot be said that the establishment of the SED was the first step on the road to a people's democracy in the whole of Germany. If an all-German policy had been of paramount importance, and winning friends and influencing people the primary object of Soviet endeavours, then the fusion would not have taken place when it did. Some blame must rest with the occupying authorities and the political parties in the West for the increasing gulf between East and West. There was something approaching lethargy in the West when it came to responding to initiatives to further all-German goals when they originated in the East. The lack of warmth between Dr Adenauer, the CDU leader, and Dr Schumacher, the SPD leader, does not altogether explain it.

NOTES

1 Wolfgang Leonhard, *Die Revolution entlässt ihre Kinder* (Frankfurt-am-Main, 1972) p. 271.

2 Ulbricht had previously been KPD secretary in Berlin-Brandenburg and was regarded as being well informed about people and conditions there. The others in the group, besides Leonhard and a young German who served as technical secretary, were: Richard Gyptner, a humourless *apparatchik*; Otto Winzer, a sharp, ice-cold Stalinist functionary; Hans Mahle, a likeable man full of *joie de vivre*; Gustav Gundelach; Karl Maron, who had written the military commentaries for *Freies Deutschland*; Walter Köppe, who quickly proved that he was not suited to a political career; Fritz Erpenbeck. A back-up group of former prisoners-of-war and graduates of Antifa schools followed closely behind and were detailed to render assistance to the Ulbricht Group. The Ulbricht Group landed at Calau, seventy kilometres east of Frankfurt-an-der-Oder on the afternoon of 30 April 1945. See Alexander Fischer, *Sowjetische Deutschlandpolitik im Zweiten Weltkrieg 1941–1945* (Stuttgart, 1975) pp. 148–9.

3 The members of the Ackermann Group were: Anton Ackermann; Hermann Matern, a former KPD political secretary in *Bezirks* Magdeburg-Anhalt, East Prussia and Pomerania; Fred Oelssner, wartime head of the German section of Moscow radio; Kurt Fischer, former KPD secretary in *Bezirk* Mecklenburg and officer in the Soviet Army; Heinrich Greif, German announcer on Moscow radio; Peter Florin; Ferdinand Greiner; Artur Hofmann; Egon Dreger; Georg Wolf. This group was accompanied by ten former German prisoners-of-war 'who had drawn the correct conclusions from the past'. They landed on 1 May 1945 at Sagan in Silesia. See Fischer, op. cit., p. 149.

4 The members of the Sobottka Group were: Gustav Sobottka; Willi Bredel, writer and founder member of the National Committee for a Free Germany; Gottfried Grünberg; Anton Switalla; Karl Raab (also known as Artur Fiedler); Rudolf Herrnstadt, chief editor of *Freies Deutschland*; Fritz Kahmann, Herbert Hentschke; Bruno Schramm; Oskar Stephan. Ten anti-fascists recruited from German prisoners-of-war accompanied them. They landed on 6 May 1945 at Stargard in Pomerania. See Fischer, op. cit., p. 150.

5 *Tägliche Rundschau (TR)*, 9 June 1945. The *TR* was the official organ of SMAD.

6 *TR*, 10 July 1945.

7 *TR*, 11 July 1945.

8 Richard Gyptner has described the work in Berlin: 'removing street barricades and rubble, removing corpses from the streets, destruction of Nazi emblems, restarting traffic, public transport, underground, providing water, electric power and gas again, opening up food stores, etc [Hans Adler, *Berlin in jenen Tagen. Berichte aus der Zeit von 1945–1948* (Berlin, DDR, 1959) p. 32.] See also Fischer, op. cit., pp. 84–5.

9 For example in Malchow the new administration was composed of 'asocial elements from outside the area, adventurers and bandits'. They terrorised the population and discredited the Soviet Army. They were all removed and replaced by another new administration. See Heinz Vosske, 'Über die Initiativgruppe des Zentralkomitees der KPD in Mecklenburg-Vorpommern (Mai bis Juli 1945)', *Beiträge zur Geschichte der Arbeiterbewegung*, 6 Jg. (1964) H. 3, p. 429.

10 Leonhard, op. cit., p. 293.

11 In the weeks immediately after the fall of Berlin the Ulbricht Group was in reality the 'central leadership of the KPD in Germany'. See Siegfried Thomas, *Entscheidung in Berlin: Zur Entstehungsgeschichte der SED in der deutschen Hauptstadt 1945–46* (Berlin, DDR, 1967) p. 30. According to Willy Sägebrecht, later KPD secretary in *Bezirk* Brandenburg, Ulbricht told him, as early as May 1945, to begin setting up the party again in Brandenburg and to put anti-fascists in all important state posts. The Ulbricht Group had overall control. See Karl Urban, 'Die Herausbildung der Aktionseinheit der Arbeiterklasse und der demokratischen Selbstverwaltungsorgane unter Führung der KPD in der Provinz Brandenburg (Ende April bis Anfang Juni 1945)', *Beiträge zur Geschichte der Arbeiterbewegung* 5 Jg. (1963) H. 5/6, p. 887; Fischer, op. cit., p. 218.

12 Carola Stern, *Porträt einer bolschewistischen Partei* (Cologne, 1957) p. 16.

13 At the end of May 1945 a survey in Jena (still under American occupation) of 3000 persons, mostly middle class, about the zone they would prefer to live in, revealed that 76 per cent preferred the American or British zone, 3 per cent the French zone, but only 2 per cent the Soviet zone. See Wolfgang Hoffmann, 'Zur Problematik der nationalen Frage 1945 und der Stellung der Mittelschichten', *Beiträge zur Geschichte der Arbeiterbewegung* 7 Jg. (1965) H. 3, p. 459; Fischer, op. cit., p. 220.

14 *TR*, 10 June 1945. The decision to re-establish political parties appears to have been taken in Moscow on 4/5 June 1945 when Ulbricht, Ackermann and Sobottka paid a flying visit to Pieck in Moscow. See Frank Moraw, *Die Parole der 'Einheit' und die Sozialdemokratie* (Bonn-Bad Godesberg, 1973) p. 94.

15 Hermann Weber (ed.), *Der deutsche Kommunismus Dokumente* (Cologne and Berlin, 1963) pp. 455–6.

16 J. P. Nettl, *The Eastern Zone and Soviet Policy in Germany 1945–50* (London, 1951) p. 117.

17 An attempt by the British military authorities in Schwerin, during their temporary occupation, to establish an administrative organ for *Land* Mecklenburg without communists failed due to the opposition of some SPD functionaries who insisted on unity of action with the KPD. See Robert Büchner and Hannelore Freundlich, 'Zur Situation in den zeitweilig englisch oder amerikanisch besetzten Gebieten der sowjetischen Besatzungszone (April bis Anfang Juli 1945)', *Beiträge zur Geschichte der Arbeiterbewegung* 14 Jg. (1972) H. 6., p. 1000.

18 Henry Krisch, *German Politics under Soviet Occupation* (New York and London, 1974) p. 81.

19 Stern, op. cit., p. 16.

20 Krisch, op. cit., p. 80.

21 Weber, op. cit., p. 435.

22 Ibid., p. 435.

23 In a letter to Wilhelm Pieck, dated 17 May 1945, Ulbricht wrote: 'We must bear in mind that the majority of our comrades have sectarian views and so the composition of the party must be altered as soon as possible by drawing in active anti-fascists who are now proving themselves in the work they are doing.' See Walter Ulbricht, *Zur Geschichte der deutschen Arbeiterbewegung*, Band II. 1933–1946 1. Zusatzband (Berlin, DDR, 1966) p. 205; Moraw, op. cit., p. 93.

Anton Ackermann encountered similar problems in Saxony:

> Arguments with many party comrades and other antifascists were necessary to clarify the situation since many of them still held to the concepts of the pre-1933 era. The red Worker and Peasant Army is in the country – was it not time to establish Soviet power and begin the building of socialism? [Anton Ackermann, 'Der Weg zur Einheit', in *Vereint sind wir alles* (Berlin, DDR, 1966) p. 79].

The Sobottka Group in the north had these problems as well. Gottfried Grünberg relates:

In Waren there was an active group of communists. These comrades had taken up key posts, were publishing a newspaper 'Die Rote Fahne' and had organised a 'red militia' with a 'city commandant' as head. As well as the orders of the Soviet commandant they were issuing regulations and confiscating property. The impact of this policy is obvious. Our 'energetic' comrades clubbed closely together and were isolated from the population . . . My task was to change this and to make the comrades au fait with party policy [Gottfried Grünberg, 'Als Mitglied der Gruppe Sobottka im Einsatz', in *Vereint sind wir alles*, p. 625].

See also Dietrich Staritz, *Sozialismus in einem halben Land* (Berlin, 1976) p. 30.

24 Horst W Schmollinger, 'Das Bezirkskomitee Freies Deutschland in Leipzig', in Lutz Niethammer *et al.*, *Arbeiterinitiative 1945* (Wuppertal, 1976) pp. 224–7.
25 Krisch, op. cit., p. 98.
26 Ibid., p. 89.
27 Ibid., p. 91. Erich Gniffke calculated that for every SPD secretary there were ten KPD secretaries in February 1946. See Moraw, op. cit., p. 185.
28 *Deutsche Volkszeitung*, 10 November 1945; Krisch, op. cit., p. 256, n. 43.
29 Krisch, op. cit., p. 111.
30 *Das Volk*, 18 September 1945; Krisch, op. cit., pp. 104–5.
31 Schumacher studiously avoided political involvement during the years he spent in concentration camps (July 1933–March 1943). He did not share the feeling of solidarity with communists which is so evident among other SPD politicians. See Moraw, op. cit., p. 105.
32 *TR*, 13 November 1945.
33 Stern, op. cit., p. 28.
34 Ibid., p. 29.
35 Krisch, op. cit., p. 136.
36 Ibid., p. 142.
37 Brill, while in Buchenwald, was a fervent apostle of the unity of the left. He signed the Buchenwald Manifesto which regarded the primary tasks of post-war Germany to be: the elimination of fascism; the setting up of a people's republic; the freeing of labour; the socialisation of the economy; peace and the rule of law; a new humanism; the unity of socialism. Brill was against the re-establishment of the SPD in Thuringia and instead the League of Democratic Socialists was set up. On 10 July 1945 he wrote to Ernst Busse, KPD head in Thuringia, proposing 'a complete fusion of the socialist labour movement'. The KPD rejected the proposal on 21 July 1945. Brill also developed the concept of authoritarian democracy. This was needed because of the complete political confusion which reigned in Germany. See Moraw, op. cit., pp. 68, 114.
38 The SPD wanted August Frölich, the honorary president of the party in Thuringia, to succeed him. General Kolesnichenko made it clear that SMAD wanted Hoffman. Kolesnichenko wanted the SPD in Thuringia in January 1946 to set the unification process in motion without waiting for the go-ahead from Berlin. 'Start at the bottom where there is least resistance' was his advice. See Moraw op. cit., pp. 143–4.
39 *Einheit*, 1, no. 1 (February 1946) pp. 23–32.

40 For the KPD: *Bericht über die Verhandlungen des 15. Parteitages der Kommunistischen Partei Deutschlands 19. und 20. April 1946 in Berlin* (Berlin, DDR, 1946) p. 66. For the SPD: *40. Parteitag der Sozialdemokratischen Partei Deutschlands am 19. und 20. April 1946 in Berlin (Protokoll)* (Berlin, DDR, 1946) p. 82.

41 For 1939 and 1945: *Die Volkszählung vom 1. Dezember 1945 in der sowjetischen Besatzungszone Deutschlands* (Berlin, DDR, 1946) p. 44. For 1947: *DDR Handbuch* (Cologne, 1975) p. 147; *Jahrbuch für Arbeit und Sozialfürsorge 1947/1948* (Berlin, DDR, 1948) p. 312.

42 Dietrich Storbeck, *Soziale Strukturen in Mitteldeutschland* (Berlin 1964) p. 223.

43 *Jahrbuch für Arbeit* . . . p. 318.

44 G. W. Harmsen, *Reparationen, Sozialprodukt, Lebensstandard Versuch einer Wirtschaftsbilanz*, Heft 3 (Bremen, 1948) p. 27; Staritz, op. cit., p. 26.

45 Walter Ulbricht, *Zur Geschichte der neuesten Zeit* (Berlin, DDR, 1955) vol. 1, p. 34.

46 In private correspondence.

47 Walter Ulbricht, *Zur Geschichte der deutschen Arbeiterbewegung*, Band II: *1933–1946*, 1. Zusatzband (Berlin, DDR, 1966) p. 269.

48 *Einheit*, no. 2 (1946) pp. 2–5.

49 Max Seydewitz, *Einheit*, no. 1 (1946) p. 4; Stern, op. cit., p. 47.

50 *Einheit*, no. 4 (1946) p. 216; Stern, op. cit., p. 47.

51 Franz Dahlem, *Einheit*, no. 4 (1946).

52 *Einheit* 1, no. 1 (February 1946) pp. 23–32.

53 Moraw, op. cit., pp. 178, 180.

54 Stern, op. cit., p. 53.

55 Ibid., p. 53.

56 Ibid., p. 54. Parity at the top did not extend throughout the apparatus. In the Berlin *apparat*, shortly after the founding of the SED, there were 300 communists among 350 staff. In the secretariat in *Bezirk* West Saxony there were 169 communists and 30 social-democrats. In Thuringia, in the *Land* central committee (*Vorstand*) there were 153 communists and 7 social-democrats. At the *Kreis* and at local level the parity principle was often ignored. In the party administration in *Kreis* Dessau 7 sections were headed by communists and 2 by social-democrats. See Moraw, op. cit., pp. 185–6.

57 K. Schoenhals, 'The "Free Germany" Movement and its impact upon the German Democratic Republic', *East Central Europe*, 1, 2(1974) pp. 115–31. There were more than 1800–2000 front-line representatives of the NKFD. Many of these men became mayors or filled other important administrative posts in towns immediately after they fell to the Soviet Army. Their task was to re-establish authority, restart public utilities and set in motion the anti-fascist democratic transformation of their town. See Willy Wolff, *An der Seite der Roten Armee: Zum Wirken des Nationalkomitees 'Freies Deutschland' an der sowjetisch-deutschen Front (1943 bis 1945)*, 2nd ed. (Berlin, DDR, 1975) pp. 291–2.

58 Stern, op. cit., p. 55.

59 Hermann Weber and Fred Oldenburg, *25 Jahre SED Chronik einer Partei* (Cologne, 1971) p. 55.

60 Stern, op. cit., pp. 56–7; Erich W. Gniffke, *Jahre mit Ulbricht* (Cologne, 1966) pp. 181–2.
61 Gniffke, op. cit., pp. 178–82.
62 Stern, op. cit., p. 58.
63 The political personnel department had close direct contact with the NKVD (Soviet Ministry of the Interior). Ackermann and Oelssner had direct contact on certain issues. See Moraw, op. cit., p. 219.
64 Gniffke, op. cit., pp. 188–9.
65 Ibid., p. 196.
66 Weber and Oldenburg, op. cit., p. 57; Walter Ulbricht, *Geschichte der deutschen Arbeiterbewegung*, Band III: *1946–1950* Zusatzband (Berlin, DDR, 1971) p. 36. Ulbricht stated in May 1946 that socialism could not be built while Germany was occupied.
67 Gniffke, op. cit., p. 191.
68 Weber, op. cit., pp. 459–61 Kaiser's goal, in the context of the CDU, was to move towards a Party of Labour, along Dutch lines, or a Labour Party, as in Great Britain. His socialism was in the Christian tradition but went much further. The CDU, a bourgeois party, had to draw lessons from the Weimar period, and Kaiser for one was committed to radical changes in state and society. The main reason why the CDU did not evolve as Kaiser had wished was the opposition of the occupying power.
69 Leonhard, op. cit., p. 369.
70 *SBZ von 1945 bis 1954.* (Bonn and Berlin, 1964) p. 40.
71 Ibid., p. 43.
72 Idem.
73 Ibid., p. 42. The Potsdam Conference had agreed that the frontiers in the east would be decided at a future peace conference.
74 Weber and Oldenburg, op. cit., p. 61.
75 At the founding conference of the Cominform which met at Szklarska Poręba in September 1947 neither the KPD nor the SED was invited to attend. The only other party of any stature to be ignored was the Communist Party of Albania.
76 According to a former KPD functionary in the US zone, West German KPD functionaries were not pleased at the failure of Munich. During the IInd SED Congress in September 1947 they sharply criticised Ulbricht – the first time this had occurred since the refounding of the KPD. See Moraw, op. cit., p. 209.
77 *Der Spiegel* (Hamburg, 5 March 1958); Hermann Weber, *Von der SBZ zur DDR 1945–1968* (Hanover, 1968) p. 36 Stalin's break with Tito in mid-1948 is obviously of great significance in this context. It hardened Soviet attitudes not only towards the West, but also towards Eastern Bloc countries.
78 All this must remain speculative but Beria's behaviour after Stalin's death, when it would appear he favoured some form of rapprochement with the Western powers on an all-German level, would add credence to the view that he did not favour a communist East faced by a hostile West Germany.

2 A Party of a New Type

THE ALLIES GO THEIR SEPARATE WAYS

The *ad hoc* alliance between the Soviet Union, the United Kingdom and the United States of America did not long survive victory over fascist Germany. France, added after the Potsdam Conference, quarrelled with the UK and the USA as well as with the USSR. The Soviet Union, mindful of the Allied intervention of 1918–20, was distrustful of Western intentions. Germany was unfortunate in that she found herself at the centre of most disputes. This resulted from the fact that Germany was considered to be of crucial importance by both East and West. Compromises could be reached in Austria, even a Soviet withdrawal could be contemplated; but never in Germany. Could not some agreement have been reached to defuse the fear of a revanchist, resurgent Germany ravenously attacking her erstwhile conquerors? Why could the solution for Austria, a neutral, demilitarised republic, not apply to her sister state in the north? This option was never real. Germany was too large, too industrious, too inventive and harboured too much resentment towards her conquerors for them to return home satisfied that the 'German problem' had been solved. Nature abhors a vacuum, so the saying goes; such a power vacuum in central Europe would have been filled by either the USSR or the USA. Neither Great Power was willing to take the risk. A resurgent Germany, playing off East against West, might provoke another catastrophe. Germans could justifiably resent the feeling, in East and West, that if neither side could consistently influence German policy in its favour, then a divided Germany was the lesser of two evils.

Soviet policy was the product of a mesh of concepts – some ideological, some political, some economic. Ideologically, the USSR was convinced that the defeat of fascism was a huge leap forward on the road to socialist revolution in Europe and elsewhere. This was not mere wishful thinking, as communist parties and their allies demonstrated in several parts of Europe between 1945 and 1948. Exhilaration at victory over an economically more advanced country reinforced Great Russian nationalism and the conviction that the Soviet model was indeed viable. The USSR had at last come of age and was a principal actor on the world stage. Economically, and by extension militarily, the Soviet Union was not the power she was politically. The ravished parts of the USSR had to be rebuilt and she found herself physically occupying eastern and much of south-eastern Europe. This demanded expertise and resources which might have been better employed in the USSR proper. Stalin believed that the Soviet Union had caught up technologically with the advanced capitalist world in the 1930s: hence there was then no technological gap; therefore the Soviet Union, capable of autarky in industry and agriculture, did not need to pander to the predilections and *amour propre* of the capitalist West. True, the war years had speeded technological progress in Germany and elsewhere; but the Soviet Union herself had also not been standing still. Since the USSR had suffered grievously during the war years, reparations, sequestrations and indemnity payments were necessary. The more that came from the ex-enemy countries, the faster the Soviet Union would be on her industrial feet again and, given the huge human and material potential of the country, she could outrun the fleetest of foot in the outside world. Soviet political economists soon painted a scenario of crisis-ridden capitalism breaking under the strain of its own internal contradictions. Those like Varga who took a more sanguine view of capitalism's chances of survival were slapped down. Nevertheless Stalin miscalculated. There *was* a technological gap and the Soviet harvest demonstrated an irritating ability to be unpredictable. The gap in optics could not be removed at one fell swoop by carting everything from Carl Zeiss Jena to Moscow. The technical know-how had to be available to carry on improving what had been seized. When the Soviets felt that they needed them, they transported German specialists to Moscow as well.

Did the countries of Eastern and South-eastern Europe represent an economic gain for the Soviet Union? Almost certainly not, in the short-term, since only East Germany was heavily industrialised in 1945. The frantic desire to transport as much as possible back to Moscow in and after 1945 might lead one to the conclusion that Stalin did not expect to stay long in the occupied territories. Politically the area was a gain for the USSR. Stalin, after he had discovered that the Soviet Union could stay, was determined to hold on – and not to take risks elsewhere. The tactics of the communists in France and Italy may be seen in this light; the Soviet Union was not willing to support the aspirations to power of communists there and elsewhere in Europe. Conversely the politics of 'roll-back' failed but the politics of 'containment' succeeded.

Germany found herself at the centre of the East-West conflict. An institutional innovation in one part of Germany was met by a move in the other part of Germany. This continued until 1949, when the inevitable happened: two German states, both claiming to be the heirs of all that was best in Germany history, came into existence. Both sides committed many errors of judgement and policy. One of the potentially most dangerous on the Soviet side was to allow the tension to escalate to such an extent that they decided that a blockade of Berlin was the only card left to play. Heads rolled, notably that of Lieutenant-General V. E. Makarov, Head of the Political Administration of the Soviet occupation forces in Germany, for this piece of political misjudgement.

If any Western statesman believed that the end of the Comintern in May 1943 signalled the end of Soviet interest in revolution abroad he was rudely brought back to reality after the war had been won. Stalin's speech in February 1946 in which he dropped the pretence that the defeat of Germany had eliminated the danger of war, reaffirmed basic communist teachings and lauded the superiority of the Soviet system; Churchill's iron curtain speech at Fulton, Missouri, in March 1946; Byrnes's speech at Stuttgart in September 1946; the launching of the Truman doctrine in March 1947 and the Marshall plan in June 1947; the setting up of the Communist Information Bureau (Cominform) in September 1947; the ending of Allied policy in Germany as a result of the Soviets leaving the ACC in March 1948; the beginning of the Berlin airlift in June 1948 and the establishment of the German Democratic Republic (GDR) in the east and the Federal Republic of Germany (FRG) in the west in the second half of 1949 consummated the division of the Reich into two parts and the world into two camps. The foreign ministers of the Great Powers changed their meeting place from Moscow to London to Paris from time to time between 1946 and 1949, but that was about all they did change.

The Soviet Union appeared content, for the time being, to consolidate her position in her zone of influence. Economically she needed time before she could challenge the United States in the non-socialist world.

Political developments in the SBZ reflected the manoeuvrings of the Great Powers. The gradual binding of East Germany to the Eastern Bloc proceeds gradually from 1945 onwards. As each year passes, so the links connecting the SBZ to the communist camp multiply, until a democratic republic is established, a state not viable on its own but viable with Soviet support. The dominant political party, shaping and transforming the SBZ from an anti-fascist democratic republic to a people's democracy, is the SED. The SED, in April 1946, can be likened to dough, ready for kneading. Beginning in September 1947 it began to take on the shape of 'a party of a new type', a Marxist-Leninist party, modelled on the CPSU. The process was speeded up in the aftermath of Stalin's break with Tito in June 1948, and at the IIIrd Congress in July 1950 it was decided to give even greater impetus to the transformation of the party. By the time of Stalin's death, in March 1953, the SED was a thoroughgoing Stalinist party, a party of a new type. The advent of Beria and Malenkov to power in the USSR and the introduction of the New Course spelled danger for the SED and found Ulbricht loath to follow. The revolt of 17 June 1953 revealed how insecure the new party's foundations were. *En route* to becoming a new-type party some impurities were found in the dough. A *chistka*, or purge, was necessary to remove them before communist leaven would have its desired effect of producing a replica of the CPSU on German soil.

THE REMODELLING OF THE SED

The concept of a party of a new type emanates from Vladimir Ilich Lenin. In his *What Is To Be Done?* (1902) he took issue with the interpretation of Marxism as expressed by the social-democratic parties of the time. He proposed a strictly disciplined party which would be immune to the diseases of revisionism and opportunism. The Russian Social Democratic Labour Party became the first party of a new type. What are the hallmarks of such a party? Such a party is a closed ideological system and this has favoured the development of an authoritarian, hierarchical organisational structure. Otto Grotewohl spelled out the implications for the SED at the Ist Conference in January 1949:[1]

   (i) the Marxist-Leninist party is the *conscious avant-garde* of the working class;
  (ii) the Marxist-Leninist party is the *organised avant-garde* of the working class;
 (iii) the Marxist-Leninist party is the *most developed form* of the class organisation of the proletariat;
 (iv) the Marxist-Leninist party is based on *democratic centralism*;
  (v) the Marxist-Leninist party is strengthened by its struggle with opportunism;
 (vi) the Marxist-Leninist party is permeated with the spirit of internationalism.

Democratic centralism embodies the following concepts:[2]

(a) all leading party organs are elected, from the bottom to the top;
(b) party organs must periodically deliver reports on their activities to the appropriate party organisation;
(c) all members must observe strict party discipline, the minority submitting itself unconditionally to the majority;
(d) the decisions of higher organs are absolutely binding on lower organs.

Opportunism is officially defined as 'placing the interests of the proletariat below those of the bourgeoisie, turning away from the class struggle, from the socialist revolution and the dictatorship of the proletariat'.[3] Social-democratic parties are often the butt of this accusation.

The IInd SED Congress in September 1947 revealed how quickly the party was changing. The information about the convening of the congress was transmitted to party officials by the local Soviet commandant. Soviet political officers played an active role in the preparations before the congress. At meetings held to elect delegates, they advised on the content of speeches and even arranged for speakers to interject their remarks at certain points in the proceedings.[4]

When the list of delegates to the congress was drawn up in the central Secretariat it was discovered that 725 delegates (86 per cent) out of a total of 843 from the SBZ were employees and only 53 (6·3 per cent) were industrial workers. This embarrassing situation was corrected by reclassifying the employees according to the trade they had once practised, thus permitting them to be designated as workers.[5]

At the IInd Congress Ulbricht stated with evident relish: 'we are on the way to becoming a party of a new type'.[6] The speeding up of this process became the order of the day on 3 July 1948 when the CC published a decree containing the sentiment: 'the most important lesson of the events in Yugoslavia for us, German socialists, is to proceed vigorously to transform the SED into a party of a new type which will stand resolutely and without compromise on Marxist-Leninist foundations'.[7] The SED came out unequivocally on the side of the Soviet Union in the struggle against Yugoslavia. The expulsion of the CP of Yugoslavia from the Cominform produced a new term of disapprobation, Titoism. Tito's heresy had been to challenge the primacy of the Soviet model. The SED drew the following lesson from this *démarche*:

the mistakes of the CP of Yugoslavia reveal especially to our party that a clear and decisive attitude *vis-à-vis* the Soviet Union today is the only possible line for every socialist party which wishes to take a resolute stand in the struggle against imperialist war mongerers.

If anyone was in doubt before there was no excuse now. The slightest criticism of the USSR would be construed as anti-communist behaviour which gave succour to the class enemy and contained within itself the seeds of heresy, of Titoism, Trotskyism, revisionism and opportunism. If the Soviet Union was the model, then the SBZ would need to imitate that model. This would take time, for the USSR was the most advanced socialist society and the SBZ was only just beginning its journey towards socialism. The implication was that when the SED had put on its new clothes and was a party of a new type, the SBZ would be a people's democracy.

One other aspect of Yugoslav development caused concern in Moscow and Berlin. The Yugoslav communists had gone furthest in their desire to establish socialism in their country. Wolfgang Leonhard and other young SED members, to speak only of the SBZ, were very impressed by and attracted to the Yugoslav brand of socialism. The SED had to guard against this 'left deviation' and proceed to socialism along the Soviet road.

Adopting Soviet experience as the only guideline for the building of a socialist society meant the death knell for the German road to socialism. It also implied that the SBZ and the other people's democracies would be more closely linked to the Soviet Union politically, economically and militarily. New institutions would be needed to give substance to this trend. Each state would come institutionally more and more to resemble the USSR and bear comparison with a union republic in the USSR. The CPSU has been very successful at devising methods of control in the various parts of the Soviet Union. Eastern Europe would present another challenge but one for which there were many precedents.

The special German road to socialism was abandoned by the SED on 16 September 1948 when it was classified as a 'nationalist deviation' and a means of support for the 'campaign of denigration directed against the Soviet Union and the people's democracies'. Anton Ackermann, the father of the concept in the SED, defended himself before the CC by arguing that attention now as well as in the past should be paid to the historical situation in each country, in working out the programme of the party. He also stated that the theory of the special German road to socialism had not been his but had been devised on the instructions of the CC of the KPD.[8] This was the face he turned to the SED internally, but the face he revealed to the public was quite different: 'The theory of a special German road to socialism has proved to be dangerous and is completely false. From its inception it was fundamentally wrong'.[9]

At the same meeting of the CC it was decided to raise the 'ideological level of the party members' and to stress the 'leading role of the Soviet Union in the struggle for social progress'. A central party control commission and party control commissions in every *Land* and *Kreis* were to be set up. These commissions had the right to expel members from the party and to remove them from their jobs in the state administration.[10] A short time before, Fred Oelssner, in the party newspaper, had declared that permanent purges and criticism and self-criticism sessions were to be introduced into the SED on the model of the CPSU.[11]

Intensive study of Stalin's *History of the CPSU: Short Course* (1936) was ordered by the central Secretariat on 20 September 1948. SED party education was brought more in line with Soviet practice in June 1950. The party training year replaced the educational evenings. Now members were obliged to attend evening seminars twice a month to go through material they had already prepared in their free time. The new party statute in July 1950 obliged every member to extend continuously his political knowledge by studying Marxism-Leninism.[12] There was no way out for the lazy or the recalcitrant – given, of course, that they wished to stay in the party.

The break with Tito heralded a reappraisal of the role played by the KPD and the SPD before 1945. Since the SED acknowledged the absolute primacy of the CPSU and Soviet Stalinist experience, it became necessary to adopt Soviet interpretations of events and to see the world from a sovietocentric position. It was Otto Grotewohl who articulated the new viewpoint.[13] Praise or blame was apportioned according to the extent the KPD and the SPD had acknowledged the leading role of the CPSU and the Stalinist interpretation of events. The SPD was accused of abandoning Marxism in November 1918, of betraying the working class and of preparing the way for fascism and war. Right-wing socialist leaders were lumped together with Trotsky, called the fifth column of American imperialism, accused of wanting to serve Hitler and placed beyond the pale.[14] To defend them, represent their views or propose solutions in any way reminiscent of the years before 1933 or the period between June 1945 and April 1946 was to advertise oneself as a class enemy. The KPD was not let off without a little scolding but the sensitive period before the advent of Nazi rule was glossed over. The KPD's demonologisation of the SPD, its joint action with the NSDAP on certain occasions, the annulling, on Moscow's orders, of a plan to oppose fascist rule should it come and the fact that the KPD contemplated a general strike when the Nazis took over – it remained a general strike only on paper, no action was taken to implement it – these skeletons were discreetly allowed to rest. One of the main reasons for KPD impotence in early 1933 was that it was a party of the unemployed. Without influence in the trade union movement, the numerical strength of the KPD availed it nothing. Against whom can the unemployed strike? This embarrassing interlude in KPD history was better forgotten. A conscious aspect of the new interpretation of German working-class politics was to separate those ex-KPD and ex-SPD members in the SED who baulked at such a radical reinterpretation of the past from the main body, which was willing to accept close alignment with the CPSU. Better that the adversary should declare himself than that he should stay in the corpus of the party.

THE SED BECOMES A CADRE PARTY INSIDE A MASS PARTY

The concept of equal sharing of all functions between ex-KPD and ex-SPD members went unassailed until the IInd Party Congress. It was then presented for discussion. This formula, in party language, can mean either that something hitherto accepted is going to be changed or it can mean that a subject is being quietly buried. The former was true this time. Young members, joining after April 1946, placed in party posts were most likely to be communist nominees. At the suggestion of the central Secretariat the parity principle was abandoned at the Ist Party Conference in January 1949. This led to some ex-SPD functionaries losing their jobs and the central Secretariat elected at the conference revealed a majority of communists for the first time. Following the model of the CPSU the central Secretariat conceded primacy to a Political Bureau (Politburo). This in turn had its own small secretariat. The large secretariats in the *Länder* were also replaced by small secretariats. The centre of gravity of the SED thus moved from the large Secretariat to the Politburo and its small secretariat. All key problems were to pass through the Politburo, with its small secretariat providing information, Intelligence and checking that decisions were being carried out by lower party organs and the administrative apparatus. The prime minister and minister of the interior of each *Land* were members of the corresponding small secretariat. Elections to the new leading bodies of the party revealed how influence had flowed towards the communists and away from former social-democrats. In the Politburo, elected in January 1949, there were five ex-KPD functionaries (Wilhelm Pieck, Walter Ulbricht, Franz Dahlem, Paul Merker and Anton Ackermann) and four ex-SPD functionaries (Otto Grotewohl, Helmut Lehmann, Friedrich Ebert and Karl Steinhoff). The Politburo, elected at the IIIrd Congress in July 1950, revealed only three former social-democrats (Otto Grotewohl, Friedrich Ebert and Erich Mückenberger) among fifteen members and candidate members. The same trend manifested itself in the *Land* and *Kreis* secretariats. Gradually an *apparat* of key functionaries came into being, schooled in strict communist party discipline. They thought almost automatically that the solution to every problem was to be found in Soviet experience and that the SED should become a German twin of the CPSU.

The rank-and-file member was another problem. Many of the almost 2-million-strong party were members more by necessity than choice. The great mass of social-democrats did not take to the concept of 'the party of a new type' like ducks to water. The glorification of the Soviet Union, the loss of the Eastern Territories, the heaping of blame on the SPD for the coming to power of Hitler, the continuing reparations payments and the insistence that every member should study and engage actively in party work in his spare time rankled with many. Life was hard. If party membership made life easier, better stay in the party, so reasoned many. Those who felt they had more to lose by leaving the party were open to party pressure to become more active.

This pressure found expression in the new party statute, adopted at the IIIrd Congress in July 1950. Henceforth every comrade was to extend constantly his sum of political knowledge by studying Marxism-Leninism; he was to observe strict party discipline; he was to participate actively in party life, including regular attendance at party meetings; he was to win over the non-committed; he was to protect people's property and be on his guard against the enemies of the party and the people.[15]

A technique which the SED employed in order to stimulate the recalcitrant was to give members a 'concrete party task'. A central committee decree, dated 29 July 1948, introduced this. Members could be required to find one person who was willing to join the People's Police in Barracks (later known as the National People's Army); report on colleagues; take part in National Front initiatives in West Berlin and West Germany; recruit a party member; and so on.[16] A yet more selective entry to the SED was employed in 1949 when the candidate stage became compulsory. The aim was to build up a phalanx of completely reliable party activists who could be relied upon on all occasions. The term 'party activist' replaced that of 'party functionary' in 1948/49. Ulbricht spelled out the change when introducing the economic plan. Hitherto only members of central committees and leaders of party organisations had been referred to as party functionaries. The term was to be widened to include those party members who held responsible positions in the state, economy, administration, mass organisations, parliaments and cultural life. 'This tightly disciplined staff of functionaries, always ready for action, is to make it possible for party organisations to carry out the concrete tasks allocated to them. . . . These functionaries are to be specially registered and will receive a special pass from the appropriate *Kreis* central committee'.[17]

Ulbricht, in September 1953, called for 150,000–200,000 party activists to be at the disposal of the party leadership.[18] According to Karl Schirdewan there were about 90,000 party activists in April 1954.[19]

Walter Ulbricht's political influence increased in parallel with the rise of the SED in the SBZ. He established close contact with ministers of the interior and police chiefs in the *Länder* and this *ad hoc* group grew into a strictly centralised organ parallel to the NKVD. It in turn co-operated closely with the political personnel department of the central Secretariat. Ulbricht appears to have controlled this 'second apparatus' with the aid of the Ministers of the Interior of Saxony, Kurt Fischer, Thuringia, Ernst Busse, and Mecklenburg, Hans Warnke. Fritz Selbmann of the DWK, Kurt Fischer, who became head of the police in the SBZ in July 1948 and Fritz Lange, head of the central party control commission, rated as Ulbricht's aides outside the party apparatus.[20] Ingo Wachtel, the personal secretary of Erich Gniffke and the source of the above information, had the impression that Anton Ackermann and Franz Dahlem tried to prevent the rise of the 'second apparatus' by engineering the removal of the ministers of the interior in question. Fischer's promotion put an end to that and Dahlem dropped his opposition.[21]

Pieck, Ulbricht and Grotewohl appear to have discussed all important resolutions before they were presented to the central Secretariat. This went some way towards satisfying Grotewohl's vanity and this thirst for status. Ulbricht, for one, was very good at polishing Grotewohl's ego. Grotewohl was the unchallenged leader of the social-democrats in the central Secretariat but he did not pay close attention to the fortunes of his followers and did not ensure that a social-democrat took over from another social-democrat, if the latter was removed from the Secretariat. In May 1948, when Max Fechner was under attack from

Ulbricht on the question of local government, Grotewohl afforded the former little support. Fechner and the other social-democrats recognised that Ulbricht's behaviour could not entirely be explained by the need to satisfy SMAD. Personal political motives were also involved. The social-democrats in the central Secretariat wished to clip Ulbricht's wings before it was too late. Grotewohl was not the man to take the initiative. He even informed Pieck of the planned meeting of the social-democrats. Grotewohl believed that he was secure in his position as joint-chairman of the SED and his supporters found it very difficult to convince him that he had to defend his position in the central Secretariat and not rely only on his popularity with the workers and his oratorical gifts.[22]

Grotewohl could be talked into doing something that he had previously refused to countenance. A prime example of this, and a major breakthrough for Ulbricht, was the question of a party purge in the summer of 1948. Before the meeting of the party CC on 29–30 June 1948 he had refused to endorse a purge. He astonished and dismayed his supporters at the meeting by unreservedly supporting the communist position. The floodgates were opened and the stage set for a purge of social-democrats from leading positions in party and state. Grotewohl, who had not even consulted his colleagues on the volte-face, would not accept that his change of position represented a major victory for Ulbricht. The person instrumental in getting Grotewohl to change his mind appears to have been Colonel Tyulpanov.[23]

THE SED AND THE STATE

The transformation of the SED into a party of a new type was only one aspect of a general development. SMAD and the SED had a common goal: a Soviet-type state on German soil. To play a role comparable to that of the CPSU in the Soviet Union, the SED would have to establish absolute primacy in the state. It would be necessary to restrict more and more the political influence and field of action of the bourgeois parties; the mass organisations would have to be built up; state administration would have to be centralised; the economy would have to be transformed and run from the centre and every aspect of life in the SBZ made amenable to SED influence. This enormous task did not daunt the leading SED functionaries, especially the communists. Rather it stimulated and exhilarated them. After years of waiting in the wings they were now to play leading roles in the transformation of East Germany. They knew that at their backs they had SMAD. This was reassuring but did not make them complacent. The Soviet political officers were demanding task-masters and were ruthless if someone disappointed them. The bourgeois parties often complained of rough treatment by the SED but the same treatment was meted out to the SED by the Soviets.

The Soviets appear to have been the driving force behind the German People's Congress for Unity and a Just Peace, which met on 6–8 December 1947, and the IInd Congress, which took place on 17–18 March 1948.[24] The Ist Congress was to provide Molotov with some back-up on the German question at the conference of foreign ministers in London in December 1947. A seventeen-man delegation, elected at the Congress, was to travel to London but Molotov's request that they be received was rejected and the conference was adjourned indefinitely. The CDU leaders, Jacob Kaiser and Ernst Lemmer, refused to participate in the Ist Congress and this provided the opportunity for Colonel Tyulpanov to dismiss them.

The IInd Congress elected a 400-member German People's Council (300 from the East and 100 from the West) and people's committees and secretariats were set up at *Land* and *Kreis* level. Since the people's congress movement was dominated by persons who supported the SED's views on German unity, greater pressure was put on the bourgeois parties to blame the continuing division of Germany on the capitalist world. The people's congress movement served two functions, one internal, the other external. Arguably the internal function proved more important for the SBZ. Out of it eventually emerged the National Front, on 7 October 1949.

To exacerbate the situation the National Democratic Party of Germany (NDPD) and the Democratic Peasants' Party of Germany (DBD) were set up on 16 June 1948. The NDPD was to appeal to former national socialists and ex-professional soldiers. Professor Heilmann (ex-NSDAP) was the leader but the key man was Lothar Bolz, a communist. The DBD was to win over peasants who were suspicious of the SED. The party leaders were Ernst Goldenbaum and Rudolf Albrecht, both communists. The SED welcomed the founding of these parties and saw them as a means of penetrating the bourgeois front.[25] The founding of the DBD revealed that the SED was not satisfied with its organisational impact on the countryside despite its good electoral performance in 1946. Much to the gratification of the SED, the DBD turned out to be very successful in rural areas.

Both the NDPD and the DBD were admitted to the bloc and this made it easier for the SED to outflank the CDU and the LDPD. The bourgeois parties protested against the formation of these new parties but it availed them nothing.

On the economic front, the German Economic Commission (DWK) was reorganised in February 1948 by SMAD. Some of the central administrations (DZV) were merged with it (only the DZV for the interior, education and justice remained outside it) and it received more authority. The top three men in the DWK, Heinrich Rau, Bruno Leuschner and Fritz Selbmann, were all communists. Social-democrats hardly got a look in. The DWK drew up a plan for the second half of 1948 and a plan for 1949 and 1950. Ulbricht saw the plans as the 'transition to the conscious control of social progress'.[26] The onset of planning is of cardinal importance for the development of the SBZ. A command economy favours the evolution of a Soviet-type system. Hand-in-hand with planning went the removal of those who favoured a market economy or even wanted to slow down the pace of economic change. They could be accused of being enemy agents and tarred with the brush of anti-Sovietism or even Titoism.

The IIIrd German People's Congress, which met on 30 May 1949, was the first to be elected by the population. Only single lists of candidates were permitted by the SED but the result had to be falsified so as to secure a 66·1 per cent yes vote.[27] The Congress elected a second German People's Council which the SED dominated. This Council transformed itself, on 7 October 1949, when the German Democratic Republic (GDR) was founded, into a provisional People's Chamber (*Volkskammer*) of the GDR. It then adopted the constitution of the GDR, which the IIIrd German People's Congress had passed on 30 May 1949, and laws on the provisional *Länderkammer* and the provisional government of the GDR. The SED faction in the provisional *Volkskammer* then asked Otto Grotewohl to form a government. On 11 October 1949 a joint session of the provisional *Volkskammer* and the provisional *Länderkammer* elected Wilhelm Pieck as president of the GDR.[28]

Landtag elections were due in the autumn of 1949 but their legislative sessions were extended by a year and elections were set for 15 October 1950 to coincide with elections to the *Volkskammer*, *Kreistage* and local councils. Extending the legislative period of the *Landtage* was unconstitutional.[29] The CDU and LDPD protested against this but acquiesced when Soviet officers assured them that free elections, with each party putting up its own candidates, would take place as planned. The SED was justifiably nervous about going to the country in October 1949 and bought a year's grace in which to repair its reputation. Elections did take place on 15 October 1950 but only unified lists could be voted upon. This again was unconstitutional, as Clause 51 of the constitution permitted each party to put up its own candidates.[30] The net result was that the CDU and LDPD, who had won 255 out of 520 seats in the *Landtag* elections of October 1946, were now apportioned only 144 seats.[31] From the point of view of the GDR constitution, the *Volkskammer* had been unconstitutionally elected. By extension the GDR government was also not legitimate.

All semblance of unanimity inside the democratic bloc vanished during 1950. The issue which caused the most dissent concerned the legal proceedings against former inmates of the NKVD detention camps at Bautzen, Buchenwald and Sachsenhausen. These camps had been closed down in early 1950 but not all prisoners were freed; 3432 of them were handed over to the GDR authorities for trial. The trials were supervised by the Ministry of State Security (SSD) which had come into being on 8 February 1950. The 'Waldheim Trials', as they became known, took place between April and June 1950. There were so many irregularities, legal and otherwise, that the CDU asked for retrials. The matter was heatedly debated at numerous cabinet meetings and at one of these Walter Ulbricht, then Deputy Prime Minister, lost his temper and bellowed at Otto Nuschke (CDU) that he had been misinformed about the trials. The SED refused to contemplate retrials and the matter was voted upon at a cabinet meeting on 31 August 1950. The result was a foregone conclusion because of the SED majority in the cabinet. This was the first occasion in the history of the GDR that a government decree had not been accepted unanimously.[32]

A major political trial was staged to coincide with the 'Waldheim Trials'. Nine persons, critical of SED policies, were arraigned before the GDR Supreme Court, under the chairmanship of Hilde Benjamin, in Dessau from 24 to 29 April 1950. The chief accused, Professor Willi Brundert (ex-SPD) and Dr Leo Herwegen (CDU), were each sentenced to fifteen years' imprisonment. On 8 August 1950 Günter Stempel, Secretary-General of the LDPD, was arrested by the SSD. He had opposed the unified list of candidates at the October 1950 elections. Despite his parliamentary immunity he was put on trial before a Soviet military tribunal, sentenced to twenty-five-years' forced labour and transported to a camp in the Soviet Union. He was released, however, in April 1956. On 6 September 1950 Dr Helmut Brandt (CDU), State Secretary in the Ministry of Justice, was arrested, sentenced and remained in prison until 1964.[33]

These events put psychological pressure on critics of the SED and they had their intended effect. By the end of 1950 the opposition was broken and the SED had the monopoly of state power. Only dissent within its own ranks could affect its position.

At the IInd Party Conference, in July 1952, the SED unveiled a thoroughgoing administrative reform. The five *Länder* were replaced by fourteen *Bezirks*, with East Berlin making a fifteenth. The former federal system, based on the *Landtage*, was abolished and local administrations were transformed into 'local organs of state power'. *Länderkammer* which, according to the constitution, permitted the *Länder* to participate in the legislative process, continued to exist. They were elected in 1954 and 1958 by *Bezirkstage* but had little influence. The only time the deputies, elected in 1958, met was the occasion on which they discussed the *Volkskammer* decree of 8 December 1958. This decree dissolved the *Länderkammer* but the deputies raised no objection. (See Figure 2.1.)

THE *CHISTKA*

The *Chistka* or party purge is a phenomenon well known in the CPSU. A ruling party attracts, besides idealists, careerists, opportunists and the politically ignorant and immature. A communist party will recruit members from various social backgrounds while it is building up its strength. When the moment arrives to become more selective, the scene is set for the party to slough off the undesirables. In the case of the SED, there was an army of social-democrats within its ranks; there were communists who wanted socialism overnight and those who regarded themselves as German communists, not as executors of orders handed down by Soviet communists; there were artisans, shopkeepers, peasants and small businessmen who looked to the SED for protection; there were also those who were out-and-out careerists and likely to make things even more difficult for the SED among the population; there were former national socialists sheltering from popular hostility within the ranks of the party.

A *chistka* can be carried out in two main ways: by publishing a decree and using this to expel a proportion of the membership or by a renewal of party cards. Only those who meet the changed requirements of the party are given new party cards. The SED, in slimming down, used both methods.

The membership figures, declared by the KPD at the unification congress, aroused some scepticism in social-democratic circles. There was the feeling that there had been some double counting. A member of

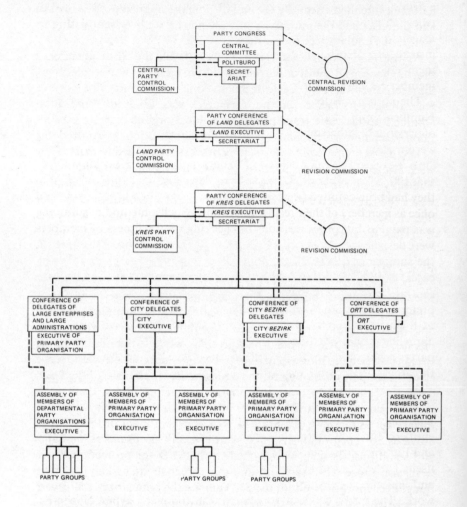

FIGURE 2.1 Organisational framework of the SED in 1950, according to the IInd SED Statute adopted at the IIIrd Congress, July 1950

– – – Sequence of eligibility and accountability
——— Sequence of subordination
Source: Werner Horn *et al.*, *20 Jahre Sozialistische Einheitspartei Deutschlands: Beiträge* (Berlin, DDR, 1966) p. 387

a firm's group was also registered at his place of residence and counted twice. Fritz Schreiber, a secretary in the central committee (*Zentralausschuss*) of the SPD put KPD membership at unification at 325,000 instead of the 620,000 claimed by the communists.[34] He put SPD membership, on 31 March 1946, at 700,700. The SPD claimed 680,000 members at unification.

The party recorded its highest membership in the summer of 1947. Numbers dropped afterwards mainly because of arithmetical corrections of previous membership lists. In the second half of 1947, 54,974 members were written off as a result of closer inspection of membership totals. Otto Grotewohl conceded, at the Ist conference in January 1949, that 140,000 members had been struck off because it was discovered that they had been counted twice, once as members of their firm's group and once as members of their residence group.[35] Such a method of slimming was painless but other methods of checking on the fitness of members were designed to increase anxiety and *Angst*. The position of the party in the summer of 1947 was quite unsatisfactory. The local cell, in many cases, existed really only on paper. The communists wished to concentrate party activity in the enterprise, whereas the social-democrats preferred activity to be centred in the neighbourhood group. A delegate at a party conference in Halle, in August 1947, declared that the appalling economic situation had led to unprecedented passivity within party ranks and that the continued existence of the party was threatened. Pieck and Grotewohl, at the IInd Congress in September 1947, did not disguise the seriousness of the situation.

The SED decided on a purge at a meeting of its CC on 28–9 July 1948. Ulbricht was the prime mover behind this *démarche*. The resolution was entitled: 'Instructions for the Organisational Strengthening of the Party and For the Purging of Hostile and Decadent Elements' and speaks for itself. The resolution was very critical of the passivity of many members and underlined the duty of every member to engage actively in party work. The party was out to remove the following types of person: members who expressed a point of view hostile to the party; members who expressed anti-Soviet views; members who were guilty of corruption, bribery or criminal acts, directly or indirectly; members who had provided false information about their activities during the Nazi era; members who were suspected of working for anti-party bodies (agents of the Eastern Secretariat of the West German SPD) or who were spies or saboteurs in the pay of foreign powers. Commissions of investigation could be set up by party organisations to speed up the expulsion of undesirables.

Social-democrats felt the change in the political climate immediately. Communists had a wide range of charges to bring against those who were holding up the transformation of the SBZ into a Soviet-type socialist state. Anti-Soviet views, opinions hostile to the party and being an agent of the Eastern Secretariat of the West German SPD were very common charges. Thousands of social-democrats were expelled from the party apparatus and from government jobs in the second half of 1948. Grotewohl, in January 1949, put the number of 'active Schumacher people' expelled from the SED at 400.[36] One of those who did not wait to be arrested was Erich Gniffke. He removed himself to West Germany in October 1948 and left his reasons behind. They were presented in a document entitled: 'To the Party of a New Type, Formerly the SED'.

Communists, as well as social-democrats, felt the impact of the purge. The SED was especially industrious in seeking out and expelling those members who had belonged to the various factions which had split from the KPD before 1933. Many of them had found their way back to the KPD during the Nazi era and had played an important role in the resistance. Here again the distinction between those members who were in the party before 1933 and those who joined in 1945 is valid. The former were most affected by the purge. Also the accusation of having had contact with the Eastern bureau of the SPD was made against communists and members of the SED who had had no contact at all with the SPD. Hence the true reason for their expulsion must lie elsewhere.

Grotewohl sounded the death knell of social-democracy in the SBZ at the Ist Conference, in January 1949. He embraced wholeheartedly the Soviet view of the party and the leading role of the USSR. He declared that Gniffke's vain hope that the SED could be influenced by the old concepts of social democracy revealed that not enough attention had been paid in the party to ideological clarification.[37]

In 1949, shortly after the proclamation of the party of a new type, officials of the cadre section of the SED, the state administration, the nationalised enterprises and the mass organisations were informed about Soviet order No. 2. According to this directive, persons who had spent an extended period as a prisoner-of-war in Yugoslavia or the West or who had close relatives (parents, brothers, sisters, children, husband or wife) living in the West or in West Germany were no longer to hold important posts in the above-mentioned institutions. Most émigrés who had spent the national socialist era in the Western world were included in this ban. Such was the fear of agents and spies that the Soviets adopted the easy solution: ban anyone who *could* be an enemy of the party, since it was impossible to verify his *curriculum vitae* while in the West.

This order led to many loyal party members losing their jobs. Since one-third of the SBZ had been occupied by the Americans or British for a short while, many prisoners-of-war had been taken. It was just bad luck for an SED functionary if his unit had surrendered to the 'wrong' enemy forces. It is of more than passing interest that one of the SED officials who should have been put into cold storage as a result of this directive was Walter Ulbricht. He had a sister living in West Germany and a brother, *horrible dictu*, in the USA. Erich Honecker, then the leading light in the FDJ, should also have been under pressure. His family still lived in the Saar.

The campaign against émigrés, communist and social-democrat alike, who had lived in the West can be linked to the show trials in other East European states. There accusations of being Zionists, agents of the class enemy and so on were hurled about. The fact that the SED also turned against communists reveals that the campaign was not merely or primarily aimed at social-democrats. The SED suspected, rightly or wrongly, that many of its communist members who had lived in the 'bourgeois' world harboured independent views and favoured nationally oriented communism.

Order No. 2 was lifted in 1956 in the aftermath of Khrushchev's anti-Stalin speech and those members who had remained true to the party, even in adversity, were gradually re-employed, mostly in more junior positions. As a rule they never again acquired the leading positions which they had once occupied.[38]

The control commissions concentrated, throughout 1948 and 1949, first and foremost, on expelling social-democrats from the SED, without penetrating to the top echelons of the party. However, social-democratic influence at the centre was being systematically restricted and by 1950 had little impact. The CDU and LDPD, by that date, had also been brought into line. Only one group had, as yet, not been affected: top communists. Their turn came on 24 August 1950 when the CC of the SED expelled the following leading functionaries:[39]

Paul Merker, member of the Central Secretariat/Politburo since July 1946 and State Secretary in the Ministry of Agriculture and Forestry since October 1949;

Leo Bauer, deputy chairman of the KPD in Hesse and communist leader in the *Landtag* in Hesse; editor-in-chief of the radio station Deutschlandsender since 1949;

Bruno Goldhammer, editor-in-chief of Berlin Radio in 1945 and afterwards section Head in the Bureau of Information;

Willi Kreikemeyer, Director-General of the Deutsche Reichsbahn (railways) in the GDR;

Lex Ende, editor-in-chief of *Neues Deutschland*, 1946–9;

Maria Weiterer, since 1945 leader of the women's section in the CC, KPD and SED, later member of the secrétariat of the Democratic Women's Association;

Bruno Fuhrmann, leading functionary in the Western section of the CC, SED;

Hans Teubner, since 1945 editor-in-chief of the *Sächsische Zeitung*, later head of the teaching department of the SED Party High School;

Walter Beling, a member of the Central Secretariat, SED until July 1950;

Wolfgang Langhoff, Intendant of the Deutsches Theater in East Berlin.

All these functionaries had held important positions and all were known for their loyalty to the SED. All had been in the KPD, even before 1933. All of them had emigrated during the national-socialist era but not one of them had chosen or been posted to the Soviet Union as his place of exile. The key which locked them together was the fact that they had all known Noel H. Field. An American subject, Field was held to be a spy and was jailed in Hungary. In 1949, he brought down with him Laszlo Rajk in Hungary and Traitscho Kostov in Bulgaria, to name only the most prominent. They were all, in turn, linked with Tito, 'the fascist hangman of the Yugoslav people'. Bauer, Goldhammer and Kreikemeyer were the only ones arrested after being expelled from the party. Merker reverted, for instance, to his former job, that of waiter.[40]

Rudolf Slansky was the most prominent victim of the show trials in Czechoslovakia. He and the other Jewish victims were accused of a new crime, Zionism. They were found guilty of having aided Zionist organisations. The SED, as a result of this, decided to look again very closely at the records of members who had been émigrés in Western countries. Paul Merker and Alexander Abusch were accused of 'defending the interests of Zionist monopoly capitalists' in the pages of *Freies Deutschland* during their exile in Mexico. In December 1952, Merker was labelled a 'hostile agent' and a 'subject of the US financial oligarchy' by the CC, SED.[41] Stalin's death saved him and many others. According to Leo Bauer, Erich Mielke, later Minister of State Security, informed him that a show trial, along the lines of the Rajk and Kostov trials, was to take place in the GDR not later than February 1951. Bauer believes that the trial did not take place because the accused would not make the requisite false confessions and play the roles allotted to them.[42]

Jews, for the first time in the GDR, were under pressure. Erich Mielke ordered security organs, in 1952, to pay particular attention to Jews.[43] In January 1953, all chairmen of Jewish communities in the GDR, fearing arrest, fled to West Berlin. Bauer, one of those most affected by this change of line, afterwards maintained that although anti-Semitism was banned in the GDR, it was resurrected under the guise of anti-Zionism.[44] It is worth noting that an anti-Jewish campaign was being waged in the Soviet Union at the same time, culminating in the Doctors' Plot.

In November 1954, the Hungarian government released Noel H. Field, stating that the accusations made against him had been found to be groundless. It has since come to light that the show trials in Czechoslovakis were also based on false evidence.

Paul Merker, the most prominent SED functionary to fall as a result of the frenetic search for American agents and Titoists, was never completely rehabilitated. Leo Bauer believes that the person behind the witch-hunt in the GDR was Walter Ulbricht, who was using the show trials elsewhere as a pretext for removing some of his political opponents.[45] No show trial was ever held in the GDR nor was any politician shot. The international situation was perhaps too tense for the Soviets to enact another morality play. It is possible that German communists, having seen what was happening elsewhere, were not taken in by promises that nothing untoward would happen to them after they had confessed to imaginary crimes. The purge in the SED had its corollary in the West German KPD. Several leading functionaries were removed from their positions.

Whereas Merker and those tied in with Noel H. Field were judged on their activities before 1945, Franz Dahlem became the first to be condemned as a result of his party conduct after 1945. On 14 May 1953, the CC of the SED accused him of the same shortcomings as Merker while a member of the KPD émigré leadership in France during the war. Further he was found guilty of having demonstrated 'total blindness' towards the attempts of imperialist agents to penetrate the party after 1945. No direct link with Field could be proved but, it was claimed, he had supported the attempts of Field to get a foothold in the SBZ or Czechoslovakia after 1945. Dahlem was removed from the Politburo, the CC and the Secretariat of the SED. He was rehabilitated in 1956 and rejoined the CC in February 1957. Carola Stern sees the removal of Dahlem from the CC as one of Ulbricht's greatest triumphs.[46]

In October 1950, the CC decided on an exchange of party cards and at the same time to test the temper of the membership. To what extent had the SED become a party of a new type? Each member and candidate member was to be subjected to a ten-minute interview to test his suitability for further membership of the SED. About 6000 commissions, embracing the 30,000 most reliable cadres, were set this task. If hostile, immoral or careerist elements were discovered they were to be sacked from their jobs and arraigned before the courts if necessary. Many industrial workers and members of the intelligentsia were expelled by these commissions but the party leadership, in its desire to maintain a certain balance within the SED, countermanded many of these expulsions.

As a result of the exchange of party cards, 150,696 persons were expelled from the SED; 18,180 members were again made candidate members; 4150 candidate members had their obligatory period as candidates lengthened; 406,662 members and 59,631 candidate members declared themselves willing to assume voluntary party obligations. These could be economic, political or cultural. In this way the SED found workers who were willing to spearhead the struggle for higher labour productivity and who put work before material incentives. About 70,000 members were recommended for more important jobs or were judged suitable for training at party schools.[47]

The SED discovered that some members did not share the optimism of the party about the future and many revealed a lack of belief in the strength of the 'world peace camp'. Many opposed the remilitarisation of both West Germany and the GDR. Such was the tension of the time that about 30,000 members and candidate members left the party between 31 December 1950 and mid-1951 either out of dissatisfaction with the purge or because they feared that the answers they had given in their party questionnaire would be discovered to be false. At the same time the SED corrected the fact that about 60,000 members and candidate members had been counted twice.

THE ECONOMIC BASE

'The Germans came to Pskov and stayed to prey'. They did the same in other towns and extracted reparations from the young Soviet state at the treaty of Brest-Litovsk in March 1918. The boot was on the other foot in 1945 and the Soviets could not wait to get their hands on German equipment. They came and demanded reparations to the value of $10,000 million (1938 prices). They acknowledged receipt of $4300 million between 1945 and 1953. Heinz Köhler estimates that they took $17,100 million (current prices) between 1945 and 1953 and $19,300 million (current prices) over the period 1945 to 1960.[48] Reparations caused innumerable disputes and much acrimony in the ACC. The evidence reveals that the USSR did very well indeed out of reparations and received more than she had originally asked for.[49]

Someone had to pay for reparations. It is ironic that the state that was undergoing a socialist transformation should have borne practically the full cost of restitution for Hitler's attack on the Soviet Union in June 1941.

Reparations came in various guises. There was war booty: possibly worth RM2000 million. Bank notes worth RM6000 million were also seized. There was dismantling. Probably about one-half of the 1936 industrial capacity was lost to dismantling. About two-thirds of the metallurgical, chemical and metal working industries and about one-quarter of other basic industries and consumer goods industries were dismantled. The process was most severe in 1945 and 1946 but continued until 1948. The value to the Soviets of much of the equipment seized is debatable. The present writer saw some of it lying, unused, in a field outside Moscow in the mid-1960s. Why go to all the trouble of dismantling factories, railway lines, etc., of transporting them to the Soviet Union and of re-erecting them? Why not leave them in Germany and ship the output to the Soviet Union? The Soviets had plenty of experience of transferring industry from one part of the country to another. They had done it very successfully in 1941. If one accepts the view that Stalin was not certain whether the USSR could remain in Germany, this might explain why the Soviets grabbed everything in sight and sent it back home. Mikoyan was Stalin's deputy on German affairs in 1945. He has always been connected with trade and presumably he had an important say on how the USSR approached the German problem in 1945. The Soviets changed their policy, however, and SMAD issued Order No. 167, dated 5 June 1946. This order set up Soviet companies (SAG). There were 213 of them, enterprises originally designated for dismantling but reprieved. They were to be left in Germany but owned by the Soviets. These enterprises accounted for about one-third of East German industrial output and only about one-third of this stayed in the SBZ. All the SAG had been sold back to the East Germans by 1954 for about 5000 million marks, with the exception of the uranium concern at Wismut which had been entirely developed by the Soviets. Strictly speaking extracting reparations from current production was against the terms of the Potsdam Agreement. The Western Allies, because they had market economies and because of their experience over the years 1918–31, did not want to be compensated in goods. Stalin however did and he had his way, at least in the SBZ.

Reparations out of current production, including deliveries direct to Soviet occupation forces, reached 3000 million marks (current prices) in 1945, according to Köhler.[50] They rose to 4000 million Marks in 1946 and averaged 5300 million Marks (current prices) between 1947 and 1953.[51] Labour services were also rendered by Germans for the Soviet Army. They averaged 460 million marks annually over the period 1945 to 1953.

Table 2.1 shows the effect these payments had on East German living standards and the proportion of real gross national product (GNP) taken up by the reparations. No precise figures are available before 1950 but it is likely that they were higher than 1950. Köhler estimates that

TABLE 2.1 Percentage distribution of the uses of the East German real GNP

	1950	1951	1952	1953
1 Individual consumption	30·9	36·0	42·0	45·7
2 Gross domestic investment	17·7	20·6	20·4	22·7
3 Other	51·4	43·4	37·6	31·6
	100·0	100·0	100·0	100·0
Breakdown of 'other' uses:				
4 Reparation exports	28·6	25·1	23·2	18·4
5 Government	25·7	17·5	16·0	14·5
6 Net foreign investment	−2·9	0·8	−1·6	−1·3
	51·4	43·4	37·6	31·6

reparations accounted for an increasing proportion of real GNP between 1945 and 1947 and then declined to the 1950 level.[52] He puts the 1947 level at 33 per cent. The main consequence of this trend was that living standards dropped precipitiously. In 1950 individual consumption accounted for only 30·9 per cent of real GNP, compared with 60 per cent in 1936, while gross domestic investment remained almost exactly the same. The large decline in domestic consumption did not permit increased investment but the meeting of reparation obligations. Between 1945 and 1950 individual consumption must have been lower than 30·9 per cent. The toughest year for the consumer appears to have been 1947. The burden of reparation exports meant that the real GNP grew slowly. Industry's share in the real GNP in the GDR in 1954 was 51·8 per cent whereas it had been 48·5 per cent in 1936 (see Table 2.2).[54] The structure of industry in the GDR reverted to that of 1944 rather than to that of 1936. The main reason for this was the nature of reparation demands.

TABLE 2.2 Real GNP growth[53]

	1936	*1950*	*1953*	*1956*
East Germany	100	73·4	94·6	108·6
West Germany	100	117·2	151·9	194·7

Foreign trade trends reveal very clearly the reorientation of East German development after 1948. In 1946 only 22 per cent of SBZ trade was with the communist bloc (Poland and Czechoslovakia) and 78 per cent with Western countries, mainly West Germany.[55] In 1947 only 8 per cent was with the communist bloc whereas 75 per cent was with West Germany. All that changed in 1948. To pave the way for the renversement, Pieck and Grotewohl embarked on a grand tour of Warsaw, Prague and Budapest in the summer of 1948 but were accorded a decidedly chilly welcome. Nevertheless the communist world's share rose to 44 per cent and West Germany's share fell to 43 per cent. This trend continued until 1951 when 76 per cent of GDR trade was with the communist world and only 7 per cent was with West Germany. In 1947, 78·9 per cent of SBZ imports came from West Germany and this continued until the summer of 1948.[56] West German trade relations with the SBZ were severed in September 1948. In 1950 the GDR joined the Council of Mutual Economic Assistance (CMEA or Comecon) but their organisation did little to integrate the economics of its member states at that time.

The SED had a difficult row to hoe when it sought to defend reparations. A line constantly adopted was to stress Germany's war guilt. Once this was accepted, it was reasonable to argue that some restitution had to be made. Many Germans in the East, especially in the LDPD, took umbrage at the line adopted by the communists. The strain of reparations began to tell in the winter of 1946/47 and reached breaking point in the summer of 1947. It was the social-democrats in the SED leadership who spoke out against the burden. Grotewohl, in November 1946, put the matter sharply in perspective: 'It is impossible in the long run to sustain the willingness of the working population to pay reparations if we do not succeed to some extent in giving them the feeling that they are producing for their own needs.'[57] A factory representative put the matter thus at an SED conference at Halle in August 1947:

> The [IInd] congress must see to it that the bloc parties, especially the SED, find the courage to tell the occupying powers: you must give us again a breathing space. We can no longer tolerate the fact that we get no coal during the summer for winter, that we never have enough to eat, that workers turn up for work barefoot and that the factories are not in a position to provide the requisite working clothes.[58]

The situation was not eased by the fact that SMAD did not control the Soviet reparation squads. Marshal Sokolovsky assured the SED, in January 1947, that dismantling was at an end. Pieck, at the IInd Congress in September 1947, had to concede that despite this dismantling was still taking place.[59]

The economic difficulties of 1947 prepared the way for Ulbricht to promote the Soviet model. The ground was removed from under the feet of those, especially in the CDU and LDPD, who wished to retain the market economy. The German Economic Commission (DWK) was set up on 4 June 1947 and had the task of preparing plans for the zone. Since West Germany was to receive Marshall Plan aid, it became incumbent on the east to turn in a better performance. Until 1947, economic recovery had been faster in the East than in the West. The Soviet command economy was the only viable socialist alternative to the market economy and there was no guarantee that West Germany's reliance on the market economy would secure her economic recovery. There was also the point that the command economy permitted much closer economic, political and social control than did the market model. Also, at the back of the minds of SMAD and the SED was the gnawing fear that if the West German market economy recovered rapidly this would stimulate trade between the two parts of Germany, and so lend more credence to the views of the CDU and LDPD in their struggle to retain the market economy in the SBZ. No, the framework of a socialist economy had to be evolved before a resurgent West German economy provided a viable model for the recovery of the SBZ – so reasoned SMAD and the SED. Of course the West German economy might fall flat on its face but on the other hand it might not. SMAD and the SED could not, however, wait on events; they had to act and so they adopted prophylactic measures.

Works' councils fell victim to the trend towards a planned economy. Traditionally they were elected by the workers to represent their interests *vis-à-vis* the management. Their functions were gradually usurped by the factory party organisation. These organisations concentrated on raising labour productivity and meeting planned deliveries. In November 1948, the works' councils were merged with the trade union organisation in the enterprise. This removed the last organisation which represented the work force in negotiations on wages and conditions of employment. The trade union organisation (FDGB), dominated by the SED, was responsible to the DWK.

A two-year plan, covering the years 1949 and 1950, drawn up by the DWK, was adopted by the SED in June 1948. A six-month plan, July to December 1948, was also passed. The 1950 goal was to raise production 35 per cent above the 1947 level.

In April 1948 the DWK took over 1800 of the 2800 nationalised enterprises and grouped them into associations of nationalised enterprises (VVB). Economic decision-making was gradually being concentrated in the DWK in Berlin. The DWK was the *de facto* government of the zone until 7 October 1949, when the GDR was founded. It then provided most of the ministers in the first GDR government.

The introduction of the Deutsche Mark in West Germany, in June 1948, obliged SMAD to set in motion its own currency reform. Up to 70 Reichmarks could be exchanged at a rate of 1:1; over that it was 10:1, for new East German marks. Soviet personnel could exchange unlimited amounts at 1:1. This reform dealt the death blow to those who had profited from the scarcity of goods and services in the zone but it also hit savings very hard.

The IIIrd SED Congress, at which Ulbricht became Secretary-General of the party, met in July 1950 in Berlin and proclaimed very ambitious goals for the economy. Industrial production, over the period 1951–5, was to climb to twice that of the year 1936. The SED was in such a hurry to transform the GDR that it did not wait until 1955 before setting new goals. At the IInd Party Conference, in July 1952, Ulbricht declared that socialism was to be systematically built in the GDR. This could now be done, since at the end of 1952 81 per cent of gross industrial production would emanate from nationalised and co-operative enterprises. Heavy industry was to receive the lion's share of investment.

The beginning of collectivisation was also announced. This surprised many delegates, but it was unrealistic, at least in Soviet terms, to expect private agriculture to exist side by side with socialist industry. The agricultural production association (LPG) was the East German version of the Soviet *kolkhoz*. Entry to the LPG was to be voluntary but, of course, entry to the *kolkhoz* had also been voluntary! The beginning of collectivisation in the GDR was not as violent as in the USSR. However, peasants who did not wish to join an LPG or artisans who were reluctant to join a collective were accused of various crimes, such as the non-payment of taxes, political opposition and possessing illegal literature. In April 1953, it was decided that ration cards would no longer be issued to the remaining members of the middle classes.

This animation of endeavour was not to everyone's liking. The GDR lost 10 per cent of her population between 1948 and 1960. They simply voted with their feet and headed westwards. There really was no future for the self-employed in a command economy. True, the collectivisation of agriculture was not completed until 1960. However, peasants were living on borrowed time. Whereas West Germany was not economically attractive before 1948, she became so afterwards as the currency reform provided the spur for economic recovery. If the economic difficulties of 1947 added impetus to Ulbricht's desire to introduce a planned economy, the economic upswing in West Germany, in the early 1950s, acted as a powerful magnet for many in the East. Increasing inability to compete with West Germany economically led the East to step up political pressure on its population. Ironically West German economic success deepened the divide between the two parts of Germany.

THE UPRISING OF 17 JUNE 1953

It poured with rain on 16 June 1953. However, this did not deter an angry crowd of 10,000 workers, spearheaded by construction workers from the Stalinallee, from marching to the House of Ministers on the Leipzigerstrasse to demand the resignation of the GDR government. Their chief complaint was the raising of work norms, which they regarded as an attack on their living standards. Fritz Selbmann (SED), Minister of Heavy Industry and the only top-ranking official to face the crowd, promised at 2 p.m. that work norms would not be increased by administrative order.[60] Nevertheless the crowd challenged Grotewohl and Ulbricht to appear and demanded the resignation of the Government. They threatened a general strike. Then the anger of the crowd subsided, aided by the appalling weather conditions. Gradually they moved back to the Stalinallee, where they heard loud-speaker vans, put on the streets by the government, proclaim that work norms should not be raised by legislative action but only on the basis of conviction and voluntary co-operation.[61] Confusion spread among the striking workers. Had not Selbmann himself stated that the increased norms had been withdrawn? Why were these vans on the streets and just what were they saying? The workers put the worst interpretation on the proceedings and, grabbing one of the microphones, one of them called a general strike for the next day, 17 June.

The demonstrations of 16 June only affected East Berlin and construction workers formed the core of protest. The strikes on 17 June embraced 272 cities and towns and involved 300,000 workers, according to Otto Grotewohl.[62] Western estimates put the totals slightly higher: 274 cities and towns and 372,000 strikers. Only a small proportion of the GDR's work force took part in the demonstrations. Grotewohl's figure represented 5·5 per cent and the Western figure 6·8 per cent of the work force.[63] It was the industrial workers, actively supported by the youth of the GDR, who were responsible for the events of 17 June. The peasants, the middle classes and the intelligentsia played little or no part in the proceedings.[64] The main centres of activity were in the industrial heartland of the GDR. The industries most involved were construction, mining, machine building, chemical and iron-ore extraction – the very cream of the working class who were supposed to be resolutely building socialism. Something had gone desperately wrong, but what?

The SED provided its analysis of the uprising in a resolution of the CC on 21 June. It placed the blame for the trouble fairly and squarely on the shoulders of German and American warmongers. The reactionaries had prepared a 'D-day' plan to provoke unrest in the GDR. The resolution conceded that there were economic difficulties but claimed that measures were being taken to correct them. Then came a momentous admission:

In its capacity as the leader of a Marxist-Leninist party, the Politburo made its findings known in an official announcement, drew attention to the errors committed in the course of the previous year and recommended to the government a number of measures designed to correct those errors. It then began to work out an overall plan for improving the standard of living of the workers prior to submitting it to the CC for its approval.[65]

Not only was it revealed officially, for the first time, that the Politburo was superior to the CC but it was made plain that the government did not play the role assigned to it in the constitution. Later in the resolution, the SED announced wide-ranging measures to improve living standards, the first of which was to reinstate the old work norms. The SED had to concede that the workers had genuine economic grievances. Fritz Selbmann, on 16 June, Otto Nuschke (CDU), deputy Prime Minister, on 17 June, Otto Grotewohl, Prime Minister, in various speeches after 17 June and Max Fechner (SED), Minister of Justice, on 30 June, all conceded that the Berlin construction workers had acted on their own initiative on 16 June and not in response to the appeals of Western *agents provocateurs*.[66] Fechner went so far as to state that the right to strike was written into the GDR constitution. Hence the strikers on 17 June were not guilty of any criminal offence. All this fits uneasily into the framework of the analysis presented in the SED resolution. The party's version of the events was unconvincing and illustrated confusion at all levels. Just why did the party lose control for the first time since the end of national socialism?

It all started at the IInd Party conference, in July 1952, when Walter Ulbricht proclaimed that the moment had arrived when the GDR could start building socialism. This meant, in essence, expanding the industrial base of the country and placing peasants and the self-employed in the co-operative sector. Invest more, consume less was the only feasible policy. Labour productivity was a key issue. Work norms would have to be revised and placed on a 'scientific' basis. Many workers were quick to realise that the new norms meant a drop in wages. The self-employed were also feeling the pressure. In April 1953, all self-employed persons had their ration cards confiscated and were thus obliged to pay much higher prices for anything they bought. This measure affected about 2 million persons. Peasants began leaving the GDR in increasing numbers, thus exacerbating the tight food situation. The mounting crisis was of the SED's own making. As a result more money had to be spent on the police than foreseen.

Ulbricht, when in Moscow for Stalin's funeral, asked for economic relief but received no satisfaction.[67] He repeated the request in a letter to

The *Bezirks* of the GDR with their capital cities (formed 23 July 1952)

the Soviet leadership, in April, but was again rebuffed.[68] He was advised to adopt the New Course, the stepping up of consumer goods production, then under way in the USSR. Ulbricht was reluctant to follow Moscow's advice since the political situation there was still fluid. The return of Vladimir Semenov to Berlin on 5 June, this time as High Commissioner, changed the situation. He told the Politburo that no Soviet aid was in the pipeline and that the SED would have to raise living standards, utilising the resources of the GDR. Semenov brought with him a list of suggestions on how this could be done.[69] On 9 June the Politburo decided on far-reaching concessions. The punitive taxes levied on the self-employed were removed, peasants were invited to return from West Germany and all citizens were to receive ration cards. The Politburo conceded that the SED and the government had 'committed a series of errors in the past' and even *Tägliche Rundschau*, the Soviet newspaper, confessed that the former Soviet Control Commission had 'been responsible to some extent for the mistakes which had been made'.[70] The workers sat back and expected concessions. After all they were the builders of socialism. If the self-employed, the bourgeoisie and the peasants received gifts, why should they, the workers, not receive some too? But no gifts were forthcoming, the higher work norms were to stay. This, confessed Otto Nuschke, 'sparked off the wave of unrest'.

The revolt might never have occurred had Waldemar Schmidt (SED), head of the police in East Berlin, been permitted to disperse the small crowd of demonstrators in the Stalinallee and arrest the ring leaders on the morning of 16 June. The Soviets refused to allow him to do this.[71] Wilhelm Zaisser, the Minister of State Security, called about 700 leading members of the security police to Berlin. He evidently expected trouble only there. The fact that the security police chiefs were in Berlin on 17 June and not available locally to act against the demonstrators, made it easier for the revolt to spread. The Soviets acted late on 17 June. The revolt was not against them nor did they put down the uprising. It had spent itself almost everywhere before they intervened.

The revolt saved Walter Ulbricht's position as top German communist. Semenov, after his return to Berlin on 5 June, had many conversations with top SED functionaries. He appears to have encouraged Rudolf Herrnstadt, editor-in-chief of *Neues Deutschland*, and Wilhelm Zaisser, Minister of State Security, to think of a successor to Ulbricht. Zaisser's immediate superior was none other than Lavrenty Beria. Malenkov and Beria, at that time, were ushering in the New Course and on the crest of a wave. An obvious candidate for the post of Secretary-General was Franz Dahlem, but he was no longer in the

Politburo. Would the Soviets support his return? Beria fell on 26 June. There were many reasons for his arrest but the uprising could not have done him any good. Max Fechner was the first critic of Ulbricht to go. He was dismissed from his post as Minister of Justice, arrested and accused of 'attempting to justify an attempted *coup d'état* and fascist putsch as a strike.'[72] A CC meeting, from 24 to 26 July, expelled Herrnstadt and Zaisser from the Politburo and the party. Anton Ackermann, Hans Jendretzky and Elli Schmidt were not re-elected as candidate members of the Politburo. Ulbricht, thus, had been able to convince Moscow that he was the best man to lead the SED. To drop him would concede victory to the strikers, he could argue. The workers proved to be their own worst enemies and saved Ulbricht instead of removing him. Ulbricht skilfully used the situation to ride out the most serious challenge to his leadership between 1945 and 1971.

NOTES

1 *ND*, 28 January 1949; Hermann Weber, *Von der SBZ zur DDR 1945–1968* (Hanover, 1968) p. 49.
2 Wolfgang Leonhard, *Sowjetideologie Heute II Die Politischen Lehren* (Frankfurt-am-Main, 1972) pp. 38–9.
3 Ibid., p. 29.
4 This information is contained in a report written by Arno Haufe, SPD secretary in *Land* Saxony and in the SED until the IInd Congress. See Frank Moraw, *Die Parole der 'Einheit' und die Sozialdemokratie* (Bonn-Bad Godesberg, 1975) p. 191.
5 Ibid., p. 192.
6 Hermann Weber and Fred Oldenburg, *25 Jahre SED Chronik einer Partei* (Cologne, 1971) pp. 62–3.
7 Weber op. cit., p. 275.
8 Carola Stern, *Porträt einer bolschewistischen Partei* (Cologne, 1957) p. 85.
9 *ND*, 24 September 1948.
10 Weber and Oldenburg, op. cit., p. 69.
11 *ND*, 29 August 1948.
12 Stern, op. cit., p. 87.
13 Otto Grotewohl, *Dreissig Jahre später*, 4th ed. (Berlin, DDR, 1952); Stern, op. cit., p. 88.
14 Stern, op. cit., p. 89.
15 Ibid., pp. 93–4.
16 Ibid., pp. 94–5.
17 Moraw, op. cit., p. 217.
18 *ND*, 22 September 1953; Stern, op. cit., p. 97.
19 *Neue Welt*, 8 (1954) p. 1086; Stern, op. cit., p. 97.
20 Moraw, op. cit., p. 220.

21 Idem.
22 Ibid., p. 223.
23 Ibid., p. 227.
24 Ibid., p. 214.
25 Ibid., p. 215.
26 Idem. Planning also entailed socialist competition, mass schooling, the activist movement and so on: transmission belts for SED influence.
27 Karl Wilhelm Fricke, 'DDR – Gründung und Opposition', *Deutschland Arkhiv (DA)*, 9 (1974) pp. 947–9.
28 Ibid., p. 947.
29 Ibid., p. 951.
30 Ibid., p. 949.
31 Ibid., p. 954.
32 Ibid., p. 952. Some German prisoners were held in the former concentration camps cited here but others, guilty of more serious offences, were removed to the Soviet Union. Before 1953, about 37,000 'Nazi agents, militarists and criminals' were deported to the USSR, while about 10,000 physicists, engineers and technicians signed 'voluntary' five-year contracts to work in the Soviet Union. Most of these people went in 1946 or 1950 and took their families with them. See Heinz Köhler, *Economic Integration in the Soviet Bloc: With an East German Case Study* (New York, 1965) p. 48.
33 Fricke, op. cit., p. 952.
34 Moraw, op. cit., p. 178.
35 Idem.
36 Ibid., p. 228.
37 Ibid., p. 229.
38 Stern, op. cit., pp. 118–9. Order no. 2 was never published.
39 Ibid., p. 120.
40 Ibid., p. 123.
41 Idem.
42 Ibid., p. 128.
43 Hans Lindemann, 'Ein "DDR – Handbuch" ohne Ulbricht', *DA*, 6 (1976) p. 635.
44 Idem.
45 Stern, op. cit., p. 126.
46 Ibid., p. 130.
47 Ibid., p. 134; *Neuer Weg*, no. 10 (1952) p. 5.
48 Köhler., op. cit., p. 29. By late 1951, the Soviets acknowledged that they had received $3658 million (1938 prices). In May 1950, they agreed to cancel one-half of the unpaid reparation debt due after late 1951. This left $3171 million to be collected over a fifteen-year period. After the 17 June uprising it was announced that the GDR would be freed of all reparations as of 1 January 1954. Soviet troop maintenance costs were not to exceed 5 per cent of the GDR national budget. This came to an estimated $700 million annually. In 1957, the costs were cut by half and in 1959 cancelled. Estimates of the cost of all this range from $4000 million (1938 prices) for reparations to $25,000 million (current prices) for reparations, dismantling, troop-maintenance costs, etc. See Marshall I. Goldman, *Soviet Foreign Aid* (New York, 1967) p. 5.

49 The economic value to the Soviet Union of these reparations is quite another matter. There was much waste and destruction during the transfer of equipment to the USSR. See P. J. D. Wiles, *Communist International Economics* (Oxford, 1968) p. 488.

50 Köhler, op. cit., p. 25.

51 Ibid., pp. 25–7.

52 Ibid., p. 33.

53 Ibid., p. 37. According to Werner Bosch every West German received a bonus of DM-West 140 (after taking into consideration reparation payments, Marshall Plan aid, private supplies of food, clothing and equipment) to help rebuild West Germany, while every East German was saddled with a debt of DM-Ost 2500 for reparations, dismantling, etc. Bosch puts the cost of dismantling to the SBZ at DM-Ost 45,000 million. See Werner Bosch, *Marktwirtschaft — Befehlswirtschaft*, 2nd ed. (Heidelberg, 1961) p. 199; Dietrich Staritz, *Sozialismus in einem halben Land* (Berlin, 1976) p. 20.

54 Ibid., p. 39.

55 Ibid., p. 60.

56 Ibid., p. 71.

57 Moraw, op. cit., p. 195.

58 Ibid., p. 199.

59 Ibid., p. 204.

60 Arnulf Baring, *Uprising in East Germany June 17, 1953* (London, 1972) p. 45.

61 Ibid., p. 46.

62 Ibid., p. 52.

63 Idem.

64 Ibid., p. 53.

65 Ibid., p. 162.

66 Ibid., pp. 39–40.

67 Fritz Schenk, *Im Vorzimmer der Diktatur* (Cologne, 1962) p. 182.

68 Victor Baras, 'Beria's Fall and Ulbricht's Survival', *Soviet Studies*, vol. xxvii, no. 3 (July 1975) p. 382.

69 Baring, op. cit., pp. 25–6.

70 *TR*, 13 June 1953; Baring, op. cit., p. 27.

71 Baring, op. cit., p. 79.

72 Ibid., p. 101.

3 The Factious Fifties

THE KREMLIN AND ITS GERMAN POLICY

Germany one and indivisible was the goal of the Allies at Potsdam. Both the Soviets and the Western Allies hoped and expected the whole of the former Reich eventually to fall within their zone of influence. Berlin, under four-power control, was a microcosm which revealed the glaring weaknesses of the arrangements agreed upon. The administration of Berlin was different from the rest of Germany. All the troops of the occupying powers were to move freely in Berlin, although each power was specifically responsible for a sector of the city. This was not so outside Berlin, where zones were strictly delineated. British soldiers, for instance, had no automatic right of entry to the Soviet zone and vice versa. Berlin was the acid test and it fell victim to the rapidly worsening relations between the Great Powers. The introduction of different currencies for East and West Berlin on 23/24 June 1948; the blockading of West Berlin from 24 June 1948 to 12 May 1949; the walkout by the Soviet representative on the Allied Kommandatura on 20 March 1948; the expulsion of the Berlin city council, meeting in East Berlin, by an SED-inspired demonstration on 6 September 1948; and the formation of a separate council and administration for East and for West Berlin – these were the key turning points. The currency reform may be seen as the first step on the road to a divided Germany.

The Soviet Union's policy towards Germany was conducted on two levels. One aimed at building up the East both politically and economically and the other supported the aspirations of all Germans for the unification of their country. This two pronged policy confused the Western Powers. After 1949, they would not acknowledge the legitimacy of the GDR government and made all moves towards German unity conditional on free elections on an all-German level. The USSR regarded the GDR as a successor state of the Third Reich and thus countered the claim of the FRG to 'speak for the whole German people'. Both the FRG and the GDR, as well as the Great Powers, agreed that the inhabitants of all zones shared a common citizenship – German.

A major initiative was taken by the Soviet Union in a note to the Western Powers on 10 March 1952.[1] The Soviets proposed a peace treaty with Germany with an all-German government participating in the negotiations. A united, independent, democratic and peace-loving Germany was the avowed goal. Germany was to be neutral and to be permitted armed forces only for national defence. All occupying powers were to leave the country one year after the conclusion of the treaty at the latest. The SED, in supporting the Soviet initiative, added the demand that the German question should be decided by Germans. Their slogan of 'Germans around one table' became particularly well-known in the FRG.

The Western Powers replied on 25 March[2] declaring that an all-German government could only result from secret, free elections. Preparations for these elections should be examined by a UN commission. The Soviets replied in a note dated 9 April[3] and proposed a four-power conference to arrange the elections but rejected UN participation. The Western Powers turned down this proposal on 13 May.[4] The third Soviet note, dated 24 May,[5] proposed simultaneous negotiations on a peace treaty, the unification of Germany and the formation of an all-German government. A four-power agreement on a non-party commission to look into the preparation of the elections could be agreed. The Western Powers answered on 10 July,[6] rejecting the proposal that the non-party commission should be subject to the four powers. They proposed that a commission should start work at once; then the four powers could discuss the arrangements for the elections. The Soviet Union, on 23 August,[7] rejected the proposal to call a four-power conference to discuss the arrangements for 'free elections'. She wanted to discuss a peace treaty and an all-German government before the subject of 'free elections' was broached. These exchanges illustrate well the nature of Soviet-Western relations in 1952. Neither side could agree on the agenda, let alone get down to serious negotiations.

This particular Soviet initiative was not evaluated by the Western Powers alone. Probably for the first time since its inception the West German government played a vital role in deciding the Western response to a Soviet proposal on Germany. The background to the Soviet initiative was the entry of the FRG into the European Defence Community (EDC). The Soviet Union wished to prevent this and to halt the FRG's gradual integration into the western camp. The West German government wished to join the comity of Western nations and did not relish the thought of a neutral, demilitarised Germany. The

FRG signed the EDC treaty on 27 May 1952, thus making it almost impossible for the Western Allies to negotiate seriously on a unified, neutral Germany.

The SED's thoughts on the Soviet initiative must have been ambivalent. Involved in the gradual transformation of the GDR into a socialist state, the SED could not be challenged as the leading political force. In a united Germany, it ran the risk of being dwarfed by the CDU and SPD. The SED might once again have had to revert to its constituent parts, the KPD and the SPD. Ulbricht, for one, must have been satisfied when Stalin's initiative failed. Just how far Stalin was willing to go to keep the FRG out of the EDC will never be known. The Western Allies and West Germany did not take the Soviet Union's proposals very seriously. On the other hand the Soviet Union misjudged the level of Western scepticism. More substantial concessions in the beginning might have caused the Western side to pause and ponder the possibilities offered.

The death of Stalin in March 1953 opened the way for new moves on the German question. However, the illness of Churchill at a crucial juncture, the uprising of 17 June and the arrest of Beria on or about 26 June intervened. Nevertheless the Western Powers, feeling that Malenkov wished to reduce international tension, proposed, on 15 July 1953, a meeting to consider the organisation of free elections in Germany and the establishment of a free all-German government as preliminaries to a German peace treaty. They also wished to reach agreement on an Austrian peace treaty.[8] The Soviet Union responded in a note dated 15 August 1953 proposing a conference to examine the question of a peace treaty with Germany, the appointment of a provisional all-German government formed from the parliaments of both German states, the holding of free elections and the easing of Germany's financial and economic obligations resulting from the war.[9] This proposal took the SED's breath away. So pessimistic was the SED about its chances in all-German elections that Erich Honecker, then first Chairman of the Free German Youth Movement (FDJ), when asked what would happen if Bonn and the Western Allies took up the Soviet Union's proposals, replied: 'We shall fight and if the worst comes to the worst we shall go under like heroes.'[10] The story going the rounds at that time was that if Honecker came into the office in a foul mood it was because he had dreamt the night before that Adenauer had accepted the Soviet proposals! Honecker received a visit from Alexander Shelepin, his opposite number in Moscow. He told Honecker and the FDJ to send 20,000–30,000 young persons, with over 1 million handbills, to the Federal Republic to add impetus to the Soviet initiative.[11] They were never sent because Bonn reacted negatively to the proposals.

The four-power conference in Berlin, from 25 January to 18 February 1954, ended in deadlock. The USSR refused to discuss secret, free, all-German elections before the formation of an all-German government. Molotov proposed that the EDC be replaced by a fifty-year European security pact which would include both parts of Germany. He also proposed the establishment of joint FRG-GDR commissions to improve economic relations between East and West.[12] The Western Allies rejected all these proposals, seeing them as counter-moves aimed at halting the FRG's entry into the North Atlantic Treaty Organisation (NATO). They also wished to avoid *de facto* recognition of the GDR by agreeing to East German participation in any body. Soviet reaction was swift. On 25 March 1954, the Soviet Union published a declaration on her relations with the GDR.[13] These were to be the same as with any other sovereign state. The GDR government was henceforth to be responsible for all relations with the FRG. The Soviet High Commissioner was no longer to supervise the activities of the state organs of the GDR but was to restric himself to questions affecting the security of the GDR and the maintenance of Soviet relations with France, the UK and he USA as occupying powers.

The FRG, in turn, was declared a sovereign state by the Western Powers on 3 October 1954 and became a member of the Western European Union (WEU) and NATO in due course. Thus the Soviets moved first in declaring the eastern part of Germany a sovereign state. Previously the USSR had allowed the Western Powers to make the running and then followed suit in her zone.

In an attempt to prevent the ratification of the Paris agreements by the FRG, the Soviet Union proposed, on 15 January 1955, all-German elections under international supervision, if the FRG and GDR governments agreed.[14] This Soviet concession was matched by the GDR Council of Ministers on 20 January.[15] The FRG government turned down the proposal on 22 January, stating that although the USSR had (finally) agreed to international supervision really free elections were no longer possible.[16]

The Paris agreements became operative on 5 May 1955. This ended the period of occupation[17] and the FRG joined the WEU. Four days later West Germany joined NATO. The inevitable move did not follow immediately in the East. The USSR favoured GDR membership of the Warsaw Pact, founded on 14 May 1955.[18] However, the Polish and Czechoslovak delegations refused to countenance either the entry of the East German People's police in barracks (the army in the GDR) or to remain passive in the face of the remilitarisation of the eastern part of Germany. They wanted guarantees which would render secure their frontiers with the GDR. The Soviets bowed to this pressure and the Warsaw Pact was founded without the participation of the GDR armed forces.[19] This was a personal blow for Ulbricht and Willi Stoph, Minister for National Defence. They had to face the hostility of the Poles and Czechs, who obviously made no distinction between the old and the new Germany. To them a German was still a German, irrespective of the shirt he was wearing. This unexpected shock brought home to Ulbricht and the SED how wide the divide still was between German and Slav communists. The Poles and the Czechs received the assurances they were seeking and so dropped their opposition. An upper limit was placed on numbers and unlike those of its allies GDR forces were put under the direct control of the pact. This permitted the admission of the GDR as a full member, on the recommendation of the Political Consultative Committee of the Member States of the Warsaw Pact, meeting in Prague on 27–28 January 1956. Willi Stoph then became a deputy commander-in-chief of the Pact forces. This episode underlined the fact that a similar organisation could not have come into being in 1949, when NATO was set up, had the Soviets wanted the GDR as a full member. The same applied, *mutatis mutandis*, to the FRG and NATO. Nevertheless, by early 1956, the FRG and the GDR had become firm parts of the mosaic of their respective worlds.

In the treaty with the USSR on the stationing of troops, signed on 12 March 1957, the GDR came off worse than the other East European states. The question of the movement of troops outside their barracks was dealt with in the treaty. Also, the GDR had no jurisdiction over the movement of Soviet troops into or out of the GDR.[20]

The summit meeting of the heads of government of the Great Powers in Geneva, on 18–23 July 1955, reached apparent agreement on Germany. The 'spirit of Geneva' resulted in foreign ministers being instructed to attempt 'the settlement of the German question and the re-unification of Germany by means of free elections'. The 'spirit' did not last long. On his way back to Moscow Khrushchev changed his mind. In a speech in Berlin he described as 'unreal' the 'mechanical unification of the two parts of Germany'. He refused to solve the 'German question' at the 'expense of the interests of the GDR' and to agree to the 'removal of all her political and social achievements' and her 'democratic transform-ation'.[21] Nikita Sergeevich altered course while in the GDR on his way home from the Geneva Conference. Ulbricht and other SED leaders, therefore, contributed to the reshaping of his opinion. Otto

Grotewohl effectively closed the door on German re-unification in the short-term in a government declaration of 12 August 1955.[22] He looked to re-unification coming as a result of co-operation, proceeding step by step, and the *rapprochement* of the two German states. Grotewohl insisted that the rule of the monopoly capitalists and large landowners would have to be broken if the peace-loving forces among the German people wished to create the preconditions for the unificaton of Germany. In essence this meant that West Gerany would have to tread the path of the 'anti-fascist democratic revolution' which the GDR had already traversed.

The seal of approval of the GDR was appended by Khrushchev on 20 September 1955 when the USSR entered into dipomatic relations with the GDR.[23] The joint Soviet-East German declaration prescribed 'complete equality of rights, mutual respect of sovereignty and non-interference in domestic affairs'. This agreement followed the establishment of diplomatic relations between Moscow and Bonn earlier in the same month. The Soviets thus did not make recognition of the GDR by the FRG a prerequisite for the establishment of diplomatic relations between Moscow and Bonn.

The long period of waiting and uncertainty was thus over for the SED and Ulbricht. Ever since 1945 they had had to live with the possibility that the Soviet Union could reach agreement over their heads with the Western Powers on Germany. Ulbricht, for one, never doubted that a divided Germany, in the short- as well as the long-term, was to his advantage. He and other senior members of the KPD may have been instrumental in motivating SMAD to rush through the fusion of the KPD and the SPD in April 1946. This move restricted Soviet political manoeuvrability in all-German affairs since it added fuel to the West German SPD's suspicions about Soviet motives. The uprising of June 1953 placed the Soviets on the horns of a dilemma. If they had sacrificed Ulbricht to assuage popular resentment at conditions in the GDR, they would have run the risk of weakening the SED. If workers could remove Ulbricht they could remove his successor if he adopted unpopular measures. On the other hand the Soviets allowed Bierut in 1956 and Gomulka in 1970 to be swept away by Polish discontent. Perhaps the Soviets felt that their room for manoeuvre in the GDR was strictly limited, hence there was no change. The explosive Polish situation was unlike that in the GDR. The June uprising had only embraced a minority of the working people and was over by the evening of 17 June. In Poland the situation was quite different and changes had to be made before the crisis ballooned into a complete breakdown of public order.

Had the Soviets shown themselves amenable to local pressure and as a result willing to barter the GDR for concessions elsewhere with the Western Allies after the events of 17 June 1953, they would have greatly weakened their position in Eastern Europe. If the Soviets gave up the GDR after a little revolt, they could presumably be persuaded to leave other people's democracies. This would be the reasoning in the factories and homes of Eastern Europe. No, backing out of the GDR under pressure from the local population would have been a recipe for disaster in Eastern Europe.

Khrushchev's remark to a high-level French delegation in Moscow in 1956 that the reality of 17 million Germans under communist rule was preferable to the imponderables of 70 million Germans in a neutral state[24] sums up the safety-first attitude of the Soviet leaders towards Germany. Although uttered in 1956 the Kremlin may have reached the same conclusion in 1953 as the only viable one in the circumstances.

THE NEW COURSE

The emphasis placed on consumption in the New Course was very welcome to the Soviet consumer. However placing greater stress on consumer goods can, in the Soviet context, only be a short-term policy. Soviet planners prefer the production of 1 million machine tools to 1 million washing machines, if given the choice. Courting the consumer, therefore, was a short-term expediency, necessitated by the need to calm the populace while the CPSU decided on a successor to Stalin. If nation-wide popularity had been the criterion, Malenkov would have won hands down. Ironically this very popularity made his opponents jealous and contributed to Malenkov's defeat at the hands of Khrushchev, by the end of 1954. Malenkov officially resigned as Prime Minister in February 1955 and was replaced by Marshal Bulganin. However, the latter was a political lightweight and proved to be the more refined, articulate and more grammatically correct other voice of Nikita Sergeevich Khrushchev. When the moment proved opportune, in 1958, Khrushchev bushwhacked the actor and took over the role himself.

Ulbricht never took to the New Course. However in the aftermath of the June events he had no choice. Less pressure on living standards, more elbow room for the private sector in industry and agriculture were popular policies. But then Ulbricht had never courted popularity. He and his supporters in the Politburo wanted sacrifices from the population in the short-term, promising great advances in the long-term. In the short-term he would have to soft pedal but if Khrushchev defeated Malenkov the way would be open for a return to the rapid pursuit of socialism. Ulbricht was a Khrushchev man from the outset. They had both fought at Stalingrad, on the same side of course. They were even said to be friends. This takes some believing since, it was rumoured, Walter had no friends, only political contacts.

It is worth noting that after the demise of the New Course, the GDR did not revert to the policies adopted in 1952. Then the transition period to socialism had been viewed as relatively short. Afterwards the period was extended; for example, collectivisation was not completed until 1960.

The GDR required help if she were to get through the difficult period after the uprising. The government's policy was to avoid measures which could lead to renewed demonstrations. The Soviet Union agreed to waive reparations as of 1 January 1954 and troop maintenance costs were not to exceed 5 per cent of the GDR budget. The USSR also came up with credit. In July and August 1953, 485 million rubles was made available at 2 per cent interest. Of this, 135 million rubles was in hard currency. The rest was to be used for commodity imports from the USSR and Poland and 231 million rubles of this was earmarked for food imports.[25]

Economic relaxation was paralleled in the world of culture and religion. The party declared that it wished to normalise relations between the church and the state but warned that opposition groups would not be allowed to use the church as a cover. The possibility of free creative activity for artists, writers and scientists was mooted. Administrative measures were not to be used to force them to convert to Marxism-Leninism.[26] Plans were in the air to extend the rights of representative institutions in the republic.

Such adumbrations of live and let live did not extend to the SED. Indeed just the opposite course was adopted. Ulbricht threw himself into the fray to recover the ground he had lost in June. He engaged in a relentless, skilled battle with his declared opponents in the Politburo and his victory was made public at the XVIIth Plenum of the CC of the SED on 22–23 January 1954, when Rudolf Herrnstadt and Wilhelm Zaisser were expelled from the party, Anton Ackermann, Hans Jendretzky and Elli Schmidt were removed from the CC and Franz Dahlem was barred from holding party office. Along with these adversaries went their counterparts at lower levels of the *apparat*. By 1954, of the members of the fifteen SED *Bezirk* committees elected in 1952, 62·2 per cent had been removed, and 71 per cent of the first and second secretaries of the

SED *Kreis* committees, in office in June 1953; of other members of the committees, 53·6 per cent, were relieved of their duties.[27] At the primary organisational level over half of the functionaries were changed.[28] Nor were the rank and file forgotten. Intensive scrutiny of party members took place between July and October 1953 and resulted in many expulsions and transfers to candidate status. Considerable dissent was found to exist among members who had been in the KPD before 1933. On average about one-third of all those expelled or demoted to candidate status had been in the KPD before that year. In Halle, the proportion was as high as 71 per cent and in five *Kreise* in East Berlin it was 68 per cent.[29] Nor were the remaining members without blemish. The Politburo declared on 22 September 1953 that a great many of the 1·2 million membership had 'no political education or party resolve'. There were many passive members. Social-democratic views were broadcast and there were 'directly hostile and foreign elements who opposed the execution of party policy'.[30] The medicine prescribed itself. The SED had to slim down and imbibe large doses of Marxism-Leninism, as interpreted by the CPSU, before the SED could become a party of a new type, a cadre party. The social structure of the SED changed as a result of the expulsions. Another factor which affected social composition was the campaign which the party waged, and waged successfully, to strengthen its hold on the state apparatus and mass organisations. The net result was, that, whereas the proportion of industrial workers in the party in May 1947 had been 47·9 per cent, and in April 1950 41·3 per cent, it fell to 39·1 per cent in April 1954.[31]

There were wholesale changes in the trade union organisation (FDGB). In the elections held after the June events, 71·4 per cent of the functionaries were changed.[32] The leadership of I. G. Metall, the largest single member of the FDGB, was completely changed[33] and the central committee of I. G. Bau/Holz was also totally replaced.[34] The proportion of SED members in the main FDGB committees dropped from 23 per cent in 1952 to 19 per cent after 17 June 1953.[35] At the IVth FDGB Congress in 1955, 80 of the 101 members elected to the executive in 1950 were not re-elected.[36]

In the Free German Youth movement, the FDJ, the purge was relatively mild, although Erich Honecker was embarrassed by the number of FDJ members who had sided with the rebellious workers on 17 June. Most changes took place at *Kreis* level. The main casualty was Heinz Lippmann, Second Secretary, who avoided arrest by fleeing to West Germany.

Ulbricht was in a confident mood at the IVth Party Congress, which met between 30 March and 6 April 1954.[37] He announced that the SED was once more going over to the building of the foundations of socialism. Great changes in agriculture were in store. This heralded further collectivisation.[38] A new statute, the third, was also adopted. The duration of the candidacy period, stipulated in the new statute, reflected the desired social structure of the SED. Blue-collar workers of five years' standing were required to remain candidate members for six months; other workers, co-operative farmers, for one year; and white-collar workers and members of the intelligentsia, for two years.

The goal of socialism demanded the improvement of the SED's performance in industry and agriculture. The new statute afforded party organisations the right of control of managerial activities. The FDGB had its role in industry enhanced in November 1954. It was to stimulate mass competition, bring about higher labour productivity and reduce waste and inefficiency. The SED had been quite successful in gaining votes in the countryside in the immediate postwar years, especially by claiming that it was the party with the interests of the peasants at heart. Much of this goodwill had however been dissipated. Many peasants preferred to drop out of the political confrontation by moving to West Germany. So great were the losses that a considerable amount of arable land was left untilled in the GDR. The Politburo changed its agrarian policy before the June uprising, inviting peasants to return and giving them back their farms. Quite a few accepted the invitation. Then the procurement levels were lowered and this benefited especially the middle peasants. Hence, although practically no peasants participated in the June events, the ill-advised SED agrarian policy in the preceding year contributed to the crisis.

Collectivisation is never popular with peasants who own or work sufficient land on their own account. Collectivisation is a constituent part of socialism, as interpreted by Marxism-Leninism. The economic argument is that small-scale production units are unviable in the long-run. If a secular rise in food production is the goal then large-scale farming is the more rational. This is because large-scale inputs of machinery, fertilisers, etc., on large units produce greater returns. The labour factor has not been included here. So far socialist agriculture has failed to provide the motivation which drives the peasant proprietor on. There is much truth in the maxim that a farmer farms for his son. The debate on the relative merits of small-scale and large-scale agriculture has a long history. Both the SPD in Germany before 1914 and the Bolsheviks debated it at length. Lenin believed that large-scale enterprises were more efficient and his views were applied in the USSR and later taken over by the GDR. Experience on a world scale does not fully confirm Lenin's convictions.

The SED set about, in January 1954, increasing its 'bases of support' in the countryside and instituted 'rural Sundays' everywhere to provide a focus for mass agitation.[39] Compared with 1960, when collectivisation was completed, collective farmers were thin on the ground in 1954. Only about one peasant in six belonged to a collective farm (LPG) in 1954.[40] The SED was aware that production would suffer during the drive to collectivise. It was willing to accept this in the short-term, believing that in the long-run vastly increased production would result. There was no pressing economic need to phase out private ownership in 1954, so this was essentially a political decision.

Agriculture was one sector where the New Course had little impact. Church-state relations was another. In November 1954 the SED introduced secular confirmation, in the guise of a youth consecration ceremony (*Jugendweihe*), centred on Easter, for fourteen-year-olds. The young were thereby to be solemnly initiated into a *Volksgemeinschaft*, a people's community.[41] Previously the party had resisted such an innovation but it now felt strong enough to challenge the churches on their own ground. The secular ceremony embraced 17.7 per cent of fourteen-year-olds in 1955. This rose to 44·1 per cent in 1958 and to 90·7 per cent in 1962.[42]

The New Course was never popular with Ulbricht but found favour with many SED functionaries and the population at large. Such were the hopes raised that Professor Otto Reinhold placed an article in *Neues Deutschland* on 2 June 1954. He conceded that many state and economic functionaries believed that heavy industry, within the framework of the New Course, was to play a subordinate role. He labelled this view fundamentally false and underlined the fact that the production of capital goods was, as before, to grow faster than gross production. This was out of step with events in Moscow. There was every likelihood that Malenkov, in the summer of 1954, would defeat his adversaries, the Soviet equivalents of Reinhold. Ulbricht, speaking through Reinhold, was siding with Khrushchev. The top economic functionaries in the SED were in favour of the New Course. One of them, Fred Oelssner, made a speech about the transition period from capitalism to socialism in the GDR. Afterwards a conference of GDR economists took place and the participants underlined the fact that the existing planning system was not coping successfully with the economic problems of the day. One can see these criticisms, in 1954, as the beginning of the search for a more sophisticated economic theory and more flexible planning mechanisms.

The New Course was officially abandoned at the XXIVth Plenum of the CC of the SED on 1 June 1955 when Ulbricht claimed: 'It was never our intention to choose such a false course and we shall never choose it.'

THE PARTY AND THE PLAN

One of Khrushchev's most fundamental innovations was his rediscovery of the policy of peaceful co-existence. He formulated his views at the XXth Congress of the CPSU in February 1956. Originally conceived by Lenin, the policy had been engendered by the Soviet Union's economic, political and military weakness. Khrushchev, on the other hand, saw it as a tactic which would permit eventually the demonstration of the USSR's economic superiority. Soviet political and military power was self-evident; all that remained was to catch up and surpass the achievements of the developed capitalist economies. Peaceful co-existence promised to reduce international tension, thus rendering the defence burden less onerous. It also held out the inviting prospect of more trade with the West. This in turn would allow the Soviet Union to close any technological gap which might exist. With competition removed from the military to the economic plane, there could be only one victor – the Soviet Union – thought Khrushchev.

The GDR was a principal benefactor of this new policy. She was already the most efficient economy in the socialist bloc but was now offered the opportunity of entering into a contest with her arch-competitor, West Germany. Communists both looked forward to and dreaded economic competition with the FRG. Of course, there had been competition all along but the opportunity was now presented of evolving an economic model of socialism in the GDR which corresponded to the strengths and weaknesses of East German reality. Since Khrushchev conceived of peaceful co-existence as a contest between political blocs, the GDR would have to knit her economy more closely into those of the Soviet Union and the other Comecon countries. As the technologically most advanced economy, new, inviting vistas would open up for the GDR. The other side of this coin was that the GDR would be expected to provide technical equipment and know-how to the less developed states.

In 1956, the overwhelming proportion of industry was within the public sector in the GDR. Agriculture, employing about one in five of the labour force, was mainly in private hands. Plumbers, electricians and other artisans were predominately self-employed. However, the GDR was unique among Comecon states. Industry dominated the economy, producing over two-thirds of the social product, with agriculture contributing only about 10 per cent. Czechoslovakia was the only other socialist state which had anything approaching these proportions. The GDR had a skilled industrial labour force with limited prospects of drawing additional labour from agriculture. Over half the female population of working age was already in the labour force by the mid-1950s. The GDR had considerable advantages *vis-à-vis* her partners in Comecon. She did not need to rely on the recruitment and training of large numbers of peasants to achieve industrial growth. She had a long tradition in certain industries: chemicals, optics, ceramics, and so on. Her chief task was to discover the correct mechanisms which would release all this potential and channel it towards desired goals. She also suffered disadvantages, the main ones being the lack of indigenous raw materials and energy. Only lignite or brown coal was in plentiful supply, but it is inferior to hard coal. She therefore had to rely on other suppliers for vital raw material inputs, principally the USSR. This economic dependence reflected the political dependence, in force since 1945. Hard questions were bound to be put sooner or later about the economic efficiency of exporting to the Soviet Union. Just what should be imported? A conflict was likely, sooner or later, between the Soviet Union's need for certain exports and the GDR's willingness to go on supplying them, if alternative products promised a higher return to the manufacturer. It was up to the SED to plan the economy efficiently. A Czech, once asked why the GDR's economy was more-advanced than Czechoslovakia's, replied: 'No system has yet been devised to stop Germans working!' More than once, before 1956, one has the impression that the SED was working very hard in that direction!

The first functionary at the centre of economic planning in the GDR was Heinrich Rau (SED). He was the head of DWK, then led the Ministry of Planning when it was set up in 1949 and then transferred to the State Planning Commission (SPK), as chief, when it was established in 1950. Bruno Leuschner succeeded him in May 1952 and for a decade remained the key economic functionary. The SPK was to draw up the five-year plans and the annual plans and to check on their implementation. This format remained with a few alterations until February 1958. The SPK grew over the years from a few hundred specialists, mostly SED members, to over 1000.[43] Most of these were graduates of the High School for the Economics of Planning which had been founded to produce economic specialists trained along Soviet lines. The SPK had a presidium to which, besides the chairman, five to eight heads of sector belonged. One of these had the task of co-ordinating activities with Gosplan in Moscow and Comecon.[44] Until the end of 1955, the SPK attempted to plan economic activity down to the last detail. This Herculean task was beyond the expertise of the SPK, indeed it was beyond the capacity of any planning organ. Administrations of Nationalised Enterprises (VVB) and individual factories were permitted very little say in the framing of their plans. Enterprises (VEB) were responsible to a VVB. It, in turn, received binding instructions from the relevant industrial ministry. Plans changed often. The First-Five-Year Plan (1951–5) was a turbulent period. External factors also led to amendments. The plan was changed four times as a result of decisions taken within Comecon.[45] Then the USSR had, from time to time, the irritating habit of taking a bite, uninvited and unwelcome, out of the GDR economy.

The GDR Council of Ministers set up, in November 1955, three commissions to co-ordinate economic management.[46] The first, for industry and transport, was headed by Fritz Selbmann; the second, for trade and consumer affairs, by Fred Oelssner; and the third, for agriculture, by Paul Scholz. This was the first time, that the three most important sectors of the economy were headed by top SED functionaries who had the power to act when confronted with economic bottlenecks. The next step, to set up a supreme economic body, was taken in April 1957.[47] The new organ, the economic council of the GDR Council of Ministers, was headed by Bruno Leuschner, head of the SPK, and included Selbmann, Scholz, Oelssner, Rau (responsible now for foreign trade) and Rumpf, the Minister of Finance. This body had the power to take decisions in the name of the GDR Council of Ministers. It became in effect an economic cabinet. The political battle waged, over the period 1956–8, between Ulbricht and Schirdewan and Wollweber involved almost all the members of the economic council as well as Gerhart Ziller, the CC secretary responsible for the economy.

THE XXTH CONGRESS OF THE CPSU AND ITS IMPACT ON THE SED

Ulbricht knew about Khrushchev's anti-Stalin speech in advance. The First Secretary of the CPSU had sharply criticised his old mentor in a speech in Sofia in the summer of 1955.[48] Khrushchev, in early 1956, invited several East European leaders, including Ulbricht, to an informal meeting and discussed the forthcoming congress with them.[49]

No hint of this was contained in the greetings of the SED to the congress (14–25 February 1956). They concluded: 'Long live the invincible teachings of Marx, Engels, Lenin and Stalin.'[50] Ulbricht ended his congress speech with the words: 'Long live Marxism-Leninism.'[51] On his return he wrote in the party organ: 'Stalin cannot be regarded as one of the all-time greats of Marxism-Leninism.'[52] Shortly afterwards, at a *Bezirk* conference of the East Berlin SED, he criticised Stalin for 'significant mistakes in agriculture, unpreparedness in the face of Hitler's attack in June 1941, altering in his favour his own biography and for demonstrating towards the end of his life an increasing tendency for personal arbitrariness'.[53] In attacking Stalin, Ulbricht was undermining his own position. Was it not he who had held up the 'coryphaeus of science' as an infallible guide for all progressive mankind? If Stalin was to be removed from his prime position, what about all those who had modelled themselves on him? The average party member, to say nothing of the man in the street, expected Ulbricht to engage in a little self-criticism. The pent-up feeling of the population affected SED functionaries. Bitter anti-party and anti-Ulbricht animosity overflowed and was all the more irresistible because it was expressed, legitimately, under the mantle of anti-Stalinism. SED functionaries had been brought up on the iron law of personal responsibility for failures. If the lower echelons had to pay for mistakes, why not the top leadership? The party newspaper, *Neues Deutschland*, reflected these sentiments. Demands for the secret election of the party leadership and the formulation of party policy by democratic means often made their appearance.[54] So sharp was the cutting edge of criticism that the SED leadership banned the discussion at de-Stalinisation at open party meetings. The party *aktiv*, it transpired, would not defend the leadership.[55] Such was the explosiveness of the de-Stalinisation issue that it was confined to a private meeting during the XXVth Plenum of the CC of the SED (24–27 October 1956). (The subject had been passed over in silence at the IIIrd Party Conference in March 1956). Karl Schirdewan addressed the private meeting and informed the delegates of the contents of Khrushchev's anti-Stalin speech. Party discipline held and the issue was not debated in public. Only the writer Willi Bredel openly criticised Ulbricht at the plenum.[56]

Two events, occurring simultaneously with the plenum – the Polish October revolution and the Hungarian revolution – had considerable impact on the GDR. The former evoked echoes of approval from many segments of East German society. It reinforced the desire of many in the party to sweep away the Stalinist leadership and break new ground in political and economic policy. Among the economists, the philosophers, the teachers and the lawyers it added impetus to the debate on socialism and democracy. The Hungarian revolution, on the other hand, aroused much less sympathy. Both Poland and Hungary, however, caused deep concern in Moscow. The misgivings were not based on any fear of the Soviet population emulating the events, but rather on the revelations about the thinness of the veneer of Marxism-Leninism and the manifest strength of nationalism in Eastern Europe. The events could also be used as a stick with which to beat Khrushchev, who had set the whole thing in motion by denouncing Stalin, thereby undermining the Soviet Union's credibility in the people's democracies. Moscow needed support and Ulbricht was first in the queue. He favoured a conservative stance in Moscow and this appeared to be in the ascendant, in the guise of V. M. Molotov.

The fighting in Hungary aided Ulbricht in another way. His attitude towards the re-unification of Germany was based on the belief that the rejection of the Soviet proposals of 1952 and the entry of West Germany into NATO had fundamentally altered the situation. The distance between the two German states on the political and economic planes was increasing daily. Ulbricht's race towards socialism was speeding up this process. Such was the immediacy of the re-unification issue, however, that Fritz Schäffer (CSU), the West German Minister of Finance, met Soviet Ambassador Pushkin in East Berlin on 20 October 1956. Vincenz Müller (NDPD), Deputy Minister of Defence, was also present. Schäffer wished to explore ways of bringing about the re-unification of Germany. He floated the idea of a confederation of the two parts of Germany along the lines of the Benelux countries but avoiding actual recognition of the GDR. A referendum in East and West would decide the constitutional format of an all-German state. Müller gave the impression that he could not bear the thought of (East) German troops, trained by him, firing on other German troops.[57] Hungary intervened and the Soviets rejected Schäffer's plan. This took some of the wind out of the sails of Ulbricht's opponents on the Politburo, notably Karl Schirdewan and Ernst Wollweber. Later, at the meeting which decided to expel Schirdewan from the Politburo, Erich Honecker referred to a 'refusal to understand those dangers which result from the illusory concept of bringing about the unification of Germany at any price'.[58] This may be *ex post facto* vilification, but Ulbricht's German policy was not the main bone of contention between him and Schirdewan and Oelssner. They disagreed so fundamentally with Ulbricht that they may have sided with his opponents on this issue so as to slow down Ulbricht's 'race towards socialism'. On the other hand their views on economic

growth (see below) would have reduced the gulf in economic management between the two parts of Germany.

If Ulbricht obtained some relief on German policy he was consistently
opposed on internal policy. At XXIXth Plenum of the CC of the SED, in
November 1956, Karl Schirdewan proposed that the 'policy of the
international relaxation of tension should include the relaxation of
tension in our state organs'. He was not in favour of using factory
militias against rebellious students and of taking action, under criminal
law, against the dissident philosopher, Wolfgang Harich.[59] Kurt Hager,
CC secretary for science and further education, and Ernst Wollweber,
Minister of State Security, argued broadly along the same lines. Ulbricht
apostrophised intellectual opposition, in late 1956, as the work of
'hostile agents'. Schirdewan and Wollweber did not share this view.

Internationally late 1956 saw the SED reaffirming its credentials as a
conservative party. It reiterated its sympathy for the Chinese on several
occasions; it criticised Yugoslavia and the condemnation of Stalin;[60] it
stressed friendship with Albania[61] and it agreed with the refusal of the
CP of Czechoslovakia to rehabilitate Slansky and others involved in the
purges.[62] Ulbricht grasped the opportunity of criticising the concept of
a 'special road' to socialism and dismissed the view that the construction
of socialism in the GDR was hindering the unification of Germany.[63]

At the XXXth Plenum of the CC of the SED, from 30 January to 1
February 1957, Ulbricht declared: 'We are going over to the counter-
offensive.' He classified the views of the philosophers Ernst Bloch,
accused of smuggling as much of Hegel into Marx as possible, and
György Lukács, the economist Fritz Behrens and the agricultural
specialist Kurt Vieweg as revisionistic and thereby condemned them.
He directed some barbed criticism at the FRG and announced the
speeding up of socialist construction.[64] The First Secretary scored
another success at the plenum. Alfred Neumann, a supporter of
Ulbricht, joined the Secretariat of the CC. Whereas before and after the
June 1953 events the Secretariat had been Ulbricht's support base and
the Politburo, the centre of opposition, the situation in 1956–7 was
exactly the reverse. Of the seven members of the secretariat in 1956, two
were opponents of the First Secretary: Karl Schirdewan, No. 2 in the
party since he was the secretary responsible for cadres; and Gerhart
Ziller, secretary for the economy. Two others were waverers: Kurt
Hager, secretary for science and further education and Paul Wandel,
secretary for culture and education. Albert Norden, secretary for
agitation and Erich Mückenberger, secretary for agriculture, must rank
as Ulbricht supporters. Ulbricht could go over to the counter-offensive

in February 1957 because precisely at that moment Khrushchev was under attack in Moscow over de-Stalinisation and his plan to abolish most of the central ministries and to devolve a large slice of economic decision-making to over 100 *sovnarkhozy*. The Stalinists appeared to be gaining the upper hand in the CPSU.

For over a year after the dethronement of Stalin, Ulbricht's hard line policies *vis-à-vis* the rebellious intelligentsia did not assume the dimensions he intended. Many decrees handed down by the Politburo to the Secretariat of the CC for implementation were either watered down or rendered ineffective.[65] Karl Schirdewan, Kurt Hager, Paul Wandel, Fred Oelssner, Johannes R Becher (Minister of Culture) and Ernst Wollweber were the key figures in this process. Indicative of their attitude is the following telegram which Paul Wandel sent to Paul Fröhlich, first secretary of the SED in *Bezirk* Leipzig. It was to stop criminal proceedings being instituted against Gerhard Zwerenz, a pupil of Ernst Bloch, and the writer Erich Loest: 'Comrade Fröhlich regarding the matter of Zwerenz and Loest, the secretariat is of the opinion that no administrative measures should be taken. The party should keep young members of the intelligentsia within its ranks.'[66] Ulbricht and Fröhlich had favoured legal action. Paul Wandel remained unenthusiastic about the *Jugendweihe* and the proposed ten-year polytechnical educational programme. He went as far as removing Ulbricht's foreword from the book which was handed to each young person during the *Jugendweihe*. Naturally this infuriated Walter.

Among the intellectuals, the philosopher Wolfgang Harich was an implacable critic. A friend of Ernst Bloch, he formulated sixteen theses 'on the question of the further development of Marxism' in July 1956. His analysis was based on the premise that Marx's analysis was only valid for the nineteenth century. It was therefore necessary to bring it up-to-date. Harich regarded the Stalinist party and government apparatus as 'typically fascist'. He wanted to see the rule of the bureaucratic apparatus over SED members ended. He favoured the expulsion of Stalinists from the party, profit-sharing in enterprises, the raising of living standards and an end to the forced collectivisation of agriculture — the state should favour the middle and small peasant instead. Harich also propagated freedom of spirit, the rule of law, the abolition of the Ministry of State Security and the unification of Germany through free elections.[67] The SED interpreted these views as a direct challenge to its authority and as a result of two trials, in March and July 1957, Harich and his sympathisers were sentenced to long periods of imprisonment.

Jürgen Kuczynski, a noted historian, formulated the role of the working class as follows: 'The working class has the task of overthrowing capitalism, of helping the masses to power and then of merging with the people.' This criticism of the SED's leading role was answered by Ulbricht. He attacked Kuczynski in May 1957. The latter engaged in self-criticism but not abject enough to satisfy Ulbricht. The skirmishing continued and the upshot was that Kuczynski was not re-elected to the *Volkskammer* in the summer of 1958. Thereupon he deemed it wise, in order to avoid further unpleasantries, to set off on a long visit to the People's Republic of China.[68]

The First Secretary was unable to break the opposition before the summer of 1957. Once again events in the USSR provided the springboard for his advance. Ulbricht had repeated every Soviet reform in the GDR. This included decentralisation, inherent in the *sovnarkhoz* reform, and a maize-growing campaign. Khrushchev praised Ulbricht to the skies in August 1957. He referred to him as a 'proven Führer' and a 'true fighter for democracy and socialism'.[69] All this despite the fact that Ulbricht's sympathies had rested with the conservative opposition to Khrushchev, personified by Molotov, during the head-on clash between the 'anti-party group' and Khrushchev in June 1957. Ulbricht, however, was quick to adjust to Khrushchev's victory and his very obsequiousness made him attractive to the First Secretary of the CPSU.

Ulbricht mounted a sharp attack against Kurt Hager and Paul Wandel at the XXXIIIrd Plenum of the CC of the SED, in October 1957. Hager was really being attacked for his hesitant, vacillating attitude in 1956 rather than for any support he had given to the critical intellectuals. He engaged in self-criticism, dissociated himself from the views of Ernst Bloch and put his position in the Secretariat at the First Secretary's disposal. Ulbricht accepted Hager's self-criticism and did not remove him. However Hager had to side uncritically with Ulbricht in his campaign against Paul Wandel and Johannes R Becher. Hager also repaid the First Secretary by playing a leading role in bringing the universities into line. Wandel lost his place in the Secretariat due to 'insufficient hardness in carrying out the cultural-political line of the SED leadership'. He was made Ambassador to the People's Republic of China in April 1958 and remained in that post until February 1961. With Hager now on Ulbricht's side, and Wandel out of the Secretariat, Ulbricht could move against his last adversary there, Karl Schirdewan. Two of Schirdewan's allies in the struggle with Ulbricht passed from the scene in late 1957. Erich Wollweber, Minister of State Security, was dismissed on 1 November 1957 and Gerhart Ziller, secretary for the economy in the Secretariat, took his own life on 14 December 1957. The stage was set for the final showdown which took place at the XXXVth Plenum of the CC of the SED, in February 1958. The resolution on changes in the party leadership, adopted by the plenum, contained the following laconic statements:

> Comrade Karl Schirdewan is expelled from the CC because of his factional activities and receives a severe reprimand; comrade Ernst Wollweber is expelled from the CC in connection with his violations of the party statute and receives a severe reprimand; comrade Fred Oelssner is relieved of his functions as a member of the Politburo because of repeated infringement of Politburo discipline and refusal to become part of the collective of the Politburo.[70]

At the plenum, Albert Norden drew aside the curtain on another issue which divided the leadership. In criticising Fritz Selbmann, Norden openly admitted that there was latent resentment between those members who had spent the national socialist era in Germany and those who had been émigrés. Selbmann was accused of playing up the differences between 'old' communists who had spent the Hitler era in Germany and the émigrés who had repaired to Moscow. The remark: 'Some were in prison, in concentration camps while others spoke on the radio' sums up the sentiment.[71]

This resentment surfaced in personal animosity towards Ulbricht. It may have been fuelled by political differences or, as Schirdewan claimed at his removal, in the case of Herrnstadt and Zaisser the political differences had their origin in the animus harboured towards the First Secretary.[72] Rank-and-file members also bore grudges against Ulbricht. There was considerable political opposition in the Walter Ulbricht Leuna Werke and other large chemical enterprises in *Bezirk* Halle. Ironically, in a factory which bore his name, opposition to the First Secretary personally was consistently voiced. Significantly the number of ex-KPD members of pre-1933 vintage in these chemical enterprises was quite high. In the Leuna Werke, for example, 550 of the SED members fell into this category and they made up about 15 per cent of SED membership.[73] After the Hungarian revolution was crushed, the party moved against these critics and substantial changes in personnel were effected.

The Vth Congress of the SED, which met between 10 and 16 July 1958, saw Ulbricht add substance to his success in the battle against those who wanted more intra-party democracy (Schirdewan) and a more rational economic system (Oelssner, *et al.*). The Politburo was enlarged from 9 to 13 members and the Central Committee from 91 to 111; 21 full members and 16 of the 44 candidate members of the CC were not re-elected. Of these, 12 were agricultural officials, 4 were activists, 3 were members of the presidium of the FDGB, 3 were professors, 8 were leading economic functionaries and factory managers and 4 were teachers. Ulbricht was no longer in any danger of being outvoted in either the Politburo or the Secretariat. With Schirdewan gone, there was no obvious alternative to the First Secretary. Head of cadres and thus of key importance, Schirdewan had been in a position to use his contacts with 'old' communists and Ulbricht's economic critics within the party to good effect. The First Secretary, however, had proved once again that he had no equal as a political in-fighter in the SED.

Promotions and demotions at the top were mirrored in personnel changes in party executive committees in all fifteen *Bezirks* and in *Gebiet* Wismut. There was nothing approaching a full-scale purge. Most officials retained their positions. However in *Bezirk* Gera, 4 of the 11 members were removed, including the second secretary. In *Bezirk* Suhl, 4 were sacked and in East Berlin, Schwerin and Potsdam *Bezirks*, 2 in each fell. In 7 of the 15 *Bezirks*, the official responsible for the economy was changed; in 6, the agricultural secretary had to go and in 4 the head of the state security apparatus lost his job.[74]

The FDGB also felt the draught. I. G. Metall was constantly subjected to criticism, reflecting the view that it was the 'weakest' link in the trade union chain. There were sweeping changes at the Vth Congress of the FDGB, in October 1959. Over half of those elected to the central executive committee at the previous congress in 1955, were not re-elected. The casualty rate in the presidium was even higher. Of the thirty-two members of the old presidium, almost two-thirds were not re-elected.[75]

THE ECONOMIC DEBATE

The economic debate was an extension of the political controversy over de-Stalinisation. Stalin had been condemned, so his command economy could be looked at critically. Two of the most penetrating critics were Professor Fritz Behrens (SED), chief of the Central State Administration of Statistics, and his close collaborator, Dr Arne Benary (SED), head of the Socialist Economy section of the Institute of Economic Sciences of the German Academy of Sciences. Behrens expressed some of his ideas in 1955 but developed and refined them in the course of 1956. He was a frequent visitor to West Germany after 1955 and both he and Benary were well acquainted with Yugoslav views, especially those of Kardelj, on workers' self-management and market socialism. The writings of Wlodzimierz Brus and Oskar Lange, the Polish economists, were another formative influence. The latter especially had considerable impact on the discussions among economists in the GDR. Behrens and Benary had their views ready for the printer in 1956 but publication was blocked. Ulbricht condemned their views out of hand at the XXXth Plenum of the CC of the SED, in February 1957. Since most of the CC members were ignorant of the views being condemned, they demanded and got publication of Behrens's and Benary's proposals.[76] Essentially their programme amounted to a fundamental criticism of the economic role of the bureaucratic-centralist state. They laid stress on the 'spontaneity of the masses' and the 'spontaneous' movement of the law of economic value. This added up to a demand for the self-management of enterprises by workers and as a consequence the gradual withering away of the state, which they thought should start during the transition phase between capitalism and socialism. Socialism, to Behrens, meant the self-management of the economy by the workers: 'Economic management should be the marriage of a minimum of central institutions to a maximum of initiative and independence from below, all based on economic laws, especially the law of value.' This led Behrens to state that wages should not be related to the output of an enterprise but to the profitability of an enterprise. The institution which would co-ordinate economic activity would be an independent central state bank. All this would transform the GDR economy from one in which growth rates were declining and labour productivity and morale were low into one in which economic efficiency was accorded the highest priority.

Another supporter of the view that economic rationality should be allowed full scope in the GDR was Dr Günther Kohlmey (SED), Director of the Institute of Economic Sciences of the German Academy of Sciences. He was especially concerned with the law of value.[77] This led him to the view that the banking system should be independent and should become the regulator of economic activity. It would do this because industrial investment would be channelled through banks. They would be in a position to decide which enterprises should borrow capital and at what rate of interest. Loss-making enterprises would go under, freeing resources for the economically viable. The president of the Deutsche Notenbank, Greta Kuckhoff, was all for the upgrading of her institution.

The agrarian sector produced one notable proponent of the view that economic principles, rather than political ones, should be afforded primacy in agriculture: Kurt Vieweg.[78] A member of the KPD before 1933, he had spent the nationalist socialist era in Scandinavia. He returned to Germany in 1945 and played a leading role in the formation of SED agrarian policy. In 1953 he was appointed Director of the Institute of Agricultural Economics of the German Academy of Agricultural Sciences. Vieweg favoured a variety of co-operatives: machinery co-operatives, wholesale co-operatives, breeding associations, and so on. He did not believe that the LPG (collective farm) should receive preference over the private peasant. He thought that the private peasant should be able to buy machinery from the Machine Tractor Stations and that the latter should be transformed into repair shops. (This did happen in the Soviet Union, except that machinery was sold to collective farms and not to private peasants, of whom practically none remained. The GDR followed suit.) Vieweg wanted the peasant and the LPG to be placed on the same economic footing. No subventions should be paid to weak LPG. Prices should reflect, within limits, demand and supply and there should be profit-sharing for all in agriculture. He put the blame for the agricultural crisis, in 1956, fairly and squarely on the shoulders of the state procurement system. Vieweg's views bore the stamp of his years in Scandinavia. They took production as their starting point. How to satisfy the population's food needs most efficiently – that is, at the lowest possible cost – is a problem which every government has to face. Vieweg's solution for the GDR, outlined above, was an economic one and ignored the SED's claim for the primacy of politics in the state.

The XXXIIIrd Plenum of the CC of the SED, in October 1957, saw a notable success for Ulbricht when Paul Wandel was removed from the Secretariat and Kurt Hager swung completely behind the First Secretary. On the economic front, however, Ulbricht had to concede defeat. The combined criticisms of Fritz Selbmann, Fred Oelssner, Bruno Leuschner and Gerhart Ziller succeeded in lowering the goals of the second Five-Year Plan in the teeth of the First Secretary's opposition.[79] They argued that the economy had to be 'economically managed' and overruled Ulbricht, whose growth rates had been based on political rather than economic desiderata. This was a novel experience for the First Secretary who had been accustomed, through his dominance of the economic commission of the CC, to deciding plan targets. This had been the case until 1956 but the atmosphere had then changed, permitting the first real debate in the GDR on economic rationality. The debate had produced an alliance of academics and top party functionaries which had stopped Ulbricht in his tracks – but not for long. On the agrarian front collectivisation was being slowed down, again against the declared policy of the First Secretary.

The furious debate between Ulbricht and his economic critics spanned the whole of 1957 but the First Secretary's astute manoeuvring won him the day. The XXXVth Plenum of the CC of the SED, in February 1958, put the public seal of approval on the dominant role of the party in economic management. As a consequence Ulbricht's main economic critics were scattered to the winds. Behrens lost his position as chief statistician and engaged in formal self-criticism at the SED High School conference, in February 1958. Benary was dismissed in early 1958. Kohlmey and Kuckhoff were also sacked. Vieweg left the GDR in 1957 when criticism became too pointed but returned in 1958. He was then arrested and sentenced to a term of imprisonment.

The decentralisation of economic management inherent in the establishment of over 100 *sovnarkhozy* (councils of the national economy) in the Soviet Union in 1957 was mirrored in the GDR. In early 1958, about seventy associations of nationalised enterprises (VVB) were established.[80] Unlike the pre-1952 VVB the new variant was essentially an administrative rather than an economic organ. At the *Kreis* level, a plan commission was set up, and at the *Bezirk* level economic councils were formed. They were, together with the VVB, to ensure the proper functioning of the centrally managed enterprises and also to run local industry. Eight industrial ministries were dissolved and their functions passed mainly to the State Planning Commission (SPK). These changes brought conflicts of competence in their wake. There was centrally and locally managed industry; the VVB was subject to the *Bezirk* economic council; it in turn was subordinated to the *Bezirk* council and the SPK, and only the industrial sector of the economy could be integrated from the centre. The enhanced SPK was the central organ of the GDR Council of Ministers for planning the economy and supervising plan-fulfilment. An economic council acted in emergencies in the name of the GDR Council of Ministers. On the party side, the economic commission of the CC was phased out and replaced by an economic commission of the Politburo, in early 1958. This novel move may have been prompted, in part, by Ulbricht's need for first-class economic advice which, presumably, he thought was not being provided by the CC Secretariat. There is also the point that the new commission may have been intended for perspective (long-term) planning, leaving the SPK to devote itself to current planning. The head of the new commission was Erich Apel, a very capable engineer and economist, who had only joined the SED in 1952. The secretary of the commission was Günter Mittag, a very able young technical administrator. The other key figure was Alfred Lange, an industrial economist of great ability. Government and party economic functionaries worked very well together. They instituted conferences for various sectors of the economy, starting in the autumn of 1958, and in so doing achieved a level of co-ordination which helped achieve industrial growth rates of 11 per cent in 1958 and 12 per cent in 1959.[81]

Khrushchev decided that a five-year plan was too restrictive and so decided in 1958 to introduce a seven-year plan. The rest of Eastern Europe had to conform. Buoyed up by economic and political success at home, Khrushchev thought it was time that the USSR caught up with the USA economically and set ambitious goals. If the Soviet Union always measured her achievements in American terms, the GDR always saw herself in competition with her near neighbour, the FRG. So the GDR resolved, in mid-1958, to equal West German *per capita* consumption by the end of 1961 and *per capita* output by the end of 1965. This was referred to as the 'chief economic task'. One aspect of these ambitious goals was never convincingly explained: given that labour productivity in West German industry was about one-quarter higher than in the GDR, how was it going to be possible to achieve West German living standards before West German productivity levels were equalled?

If industrial expansion in 1958 and 1959 was very gratifying, the same could not be said of agriculture. This sector became the real bottleneck of the economy. Over the period 1955 to 1960, agricultural output expanded by 9 per cent, or less than 2 per cent annually.[82] Incomes, however, jumped. Bruno Leuschner, in December 1960, stated that peasant incomes, in the preceding three years, had climbed by 36 per cent (industrial workers' incomes by 25 per cent).[83] Peasants were getting higher state prices for their produce but were not expanding output sufficiently to meet the demand generated by increased money incomes. Ulbricht's solution was political. He set in train the full collectivisation of agriculture in February 1960 and by the end of the year almost all peasants were in collectives. Those who refused joined the increasing numbers crossing into West Berlin.

The Seven-Year Plan, then in operation, had foreseen the completion of collectivisation by 1963–5. Production of tractors, mineral fertilisers, seed and insecticides had been planned accordingly.

The completion of collectivisation was the death knell of the 'chief economic task'. So the subject was dropped, to be replaced by a new one. This one, proclaimed by Ulbricht in September 1960, aimed at making the GDR independent of West German imports. The goal of autarky was economically ill-advised. The SPK was not very enthusiastic. When Ulbricht learned, in mid-1961, of the draft plan for 1962, the sparks flew. To him it did not pay sufficient attention to the problem of making the GDR independent of West German imports. Ulbricht thereupon removed Bruno Leuschner, the head of the SPK. He was replaced by Karl Mewis, who had played an important role during the collectivisation drive in 1960. Although he had spent the national socialist era in Scandinavia, Mewis, unlike Vieweg, had not learnt any economics there. He was quite unqualified for the job of planning chief. The SPK was broken up and was henceforth to concern itself solely with planning. The industrial executive functions, i.e. checking on plan-fulfilment, were transferred to the newly founded economic council of the GDR Council of Ministers (VWR). The VWR was headed by Alfred Neumann, a close collaborator of Ulbricht in the CC, but again someone without economic expertise. The result was economic confusion, to put it mildly. Investment dropped, many projects under construction were abandoned, a fortune of unusable, not to say useless, goods piled up and excess purchasing power reached DM 2800 million.[84] A wage freeze was declared but this led to passivity in the labour force. Attendance at FDGB meetings in *Bezirk* Magdeburg dropped from 88·9 per cent in September 1961 to 58·8 per cent in the first quarter of 1962. The position was similar in other *Bezirk*s.[85]

ULBRICHT THE MASTER

Walter Ulbricht thus revealed himself, after February 1958, as the undisputed leader of the SED. His handling of economic problems revealed him as the dominant goal-setter for the economy. When he found himself being thwarted he was able to break the opposition by administrative reform. He was the prime mover in the race to catch up with West Germany, to achieve full collectivisation, to become independent of West German imports — measures which the purely economic specialist would not have afforded high priority. He needed the economists but if it came to a conflict he was willing and able to sacrifice economic growth for political expediency.

Ulbricht increased his standing in the state in 1960 by two institutional innovations. In February 1960, a GDR national council of defence was established with Ulbricht at its head. Wilhelm Pieck, the first President of the GDR, died on 7 September 1960. The post of president was thereupon abolished. A GDR council of state was set up on 12 September 1960 with Walter Ulbricht as its first chairman. The GDR council of state was similar to the presidium of the Supreme Soviet of the USSR and performed the same function, that of acting in the name of parliament between sessions. Both the council of defence and the council of state carried out functions previously concentrated in the GDR Council of Ministers. Never before had Ulbricht concentrated so much power in his own hands. Others noticed his influence as well. At the XIVth Plenum of the CC of the SED, in November 1961, Otto Schön went so far as to state: 'Walter Ulbricht – he is the party.'[86] Despite this, or perhaps Schön had gone too far, Paul Verner, first secretary in East Berlin, stated the following day: 'Our party was and is a stranger to the personality cult.'[87]

'A SCAR ACROSS THE FACE OF BERLIN'

The opportunity afforded the GDR, in the agreement reached with the Soviet Union in September 1955, of articulating her own foreign policy, was seized upon by Ulbricht to present SED thinking on the German question. Whereas before 1955, the Soviet Union spoke for the GDR at international level, the stage was now set for a second German voice in the councils of the world. The main drawback, however, was that only the USSR, China and the countries of Eastern Europe recognised the GDR as a sovereign state. Ulbricht's chief task, between 1955 and 1971, when the GDR was recognised diplomatically by all major states, was to enunciate a foreign policy which would lead to diplomatic recognition. The GDR was not in a position to adopt an independent policy. She was obliged to lean heavily on the Soviet Union for support. Since the USSR was her chief ally and the only power capable of forcing recognition down the throats of Bonn and Washington, Ubricht did not have much room for manoeuvre. He could influence Soviet thinking on Germany but never determine it. Only once were there major differences between him and Moscow on German policy. That was in 1971 and on that occasion Moscow won hands down.

GDR foreign policy until the 1970s essentially concerned Germany. Ulbricht's first major initiative was launched on 30 December 1956, in *Neues Deutschland*. He proposed, in the interests of the unification of the working class of all Germany, a *rapprochement* of the two German states with differing social systems, so as to bring about·later an interim solution, a confederation.[88] The concept of a confederation remained the hub of the SED's German policy until the mid-1960s.

Ulbricht refined his thinking about the confederation shortly afterwards. The preconditions for the *rapprochement* of the two German states involved such things as a referendum on the nationalisation of key industries, a democratic land reform and an educational reform. Then an all-German council would be elected, with equal representation for East and West. This council, as the government of the confederation, would arrange free all-German elections.[89]

The goal of the SED was, first, diplomatic recognition. Then the FRG and the GDR could have equal representation in a German confederation. Since the SED's avowed future goal was the creation of a 'united, democratic, peace-loving and anti-imperialist German state', the implication was that the confederation would last as long as the FRG was non-socialist. Once the FRG had left capitalism behind the objective conditions were ripe for the creation of a unified socialist German state. Another implication of the confederation was that, at least until the FRG went socialist, the GDR would remain the senior partner – a delicious thought for Ulbricht to savour. It really would have meant the primacy of politics over economics, since the FRG was economically more advanced. Quite another way of looking at the confederation is to regard it as a 1950s version of *Abgrenzung*. By setting the conditions for reunification so impossibly high, Ulbricht was ensuring that the FRG would not enter into serious negotiations about the future of Germany.

In a statement, dated 26 July 1957, the GDR government restated its proposal for a confederation but referred to the all-German council as only having advisory powers.[90] This statement received the full backing of the USSR on 2 August 1957.[91] The Soviets called the GDR initiative a 'serious step on the way to the goal of a united Germany'. This was followed by a Soviet note to the West German government on 8 January 1958 reiterating and strongly recommending the GDR initiative.[92] The FRG government rejected the proposed confederation on 20 January 1958, pointing out that reunification was not the task of two governments but rather the exclusive concern of the German people.[93] Khrushchev's riposte on 29 January 1958 was to state unequivocally that a confederation was the only route which would lead to the unification of Germany.[94] Since Bonn and her allies wished to avoid any measure which would lead to the recognition of the GDR as a sovereign state, they rejected all Soviet and GDR approaches along these lines.

Khrushchev's next move was to propose a peace treaty with both German states. All-German elections would come after the signing of the peace treaty. The GDR followed suit and in a note, dated 4 August 1958, to the FRG government, proposed the convening of an all-German commission whose task it would be to advise the four powers during the negotiation of the peace treaty. The USSR turned out to be the only Great Power interested in a peace treaty with both German states. However Nikita Sergeevich Khrushchev still had a shot in his locker: he would sign a unilateral peace treaty with the GDR and the complexities arising out of that situation would have to be unravelled by France, the UK and the USA in negotiations with the GDR. This was the tenor of his argument from early 1959 onwards. At the back of Khrushchev stood Ulbricht, of course. A peace treaty would have suited the GDR right down to the ground.

The SED went over the head of the FRG government, in April 1960, when it published 'The German People's Plan – An Open Letter to the Working Class of West Germany'. Ulbricht appealed directly to 'social-democratic, Christian and non-party workers, honest patriots in urban and rural areas and progressive businessmen to remove West German militarism in order to create the prerequisites for a confederation of both German states.'[95] The KPD, which had been the mouthpiece of the SED in West Germany, was banned in August 1956. Hence Ulbricht had to project his all-German policy from East Berlin. The SED was serving notice that it intended to influence events in West Germany directly. It reiterated at every opportunity its contention that the GDR was the only 'legitimate German state' and that any intra-German agreement presupposed the recognition of the GDR's sovereignity.

Why did Khrushchev choose to exacerbate international tension at this juncture and why did he select Germany as the place of confrontation? Did the stance he adopted not contravene his declared policy of peaceful co-existence and non-interference in the affairs of states of differing social systems? There are two main reasons for his *démarche vis-à-vis* Germany. One concerns the goal of *de jure* recognition of the frontiers that were drawn at the end of the Second World War, which included diplomatic recognition of the GDR. This would be the last step in the recognition of Eastern Europe as a Soviet zone of influence. The other reason was the weakening economic situation of the GDR. If the USSR wanted a strong economy in the GDR then that country had to have secure frontiers. Without them any citizen who felt disadvantaged could move from East to West Berlin. Given the open frontier in Berlin, socialism could not be built in the GDR. It was as simple as that. In the late-1950s, Ulbricht had set in train policies aimed at making the economy more socialist. The full collectivisation of agriculture was forced through in 1960. This increased the outflow so that by the end of 1960 the point of no return had been reached. Either the frontier with West Berlin was closed or the economic base of the GDR would contract. This would then lead to existing trade agreements with Comecon members being renegotiated and scaled down. Berlin not only affected the GDR and the USSR but the whole socialist camp. A glance at refugee figures will illustrate the situation:[96]

1953	331,390
1954	184,198
1955	252,870
1956	279,189
1957	261,622
1958	204,092
1959	143,917
1960	199,188

About 60 per cent of the refugees were of working age and about half of them were under twenty-five.

Three solutions to this problem suggested themselves. If a peace treaty were signed by the Great Powers, the GDR would gain control of the access routes to West Berlin. Once in control, no GDR citizen could travel legally to West Germany without the permission of the GDR authorities. Given these circumstances, building a wall through the centre of Berlin and around West Berlin would be unnecessary. Even Khrushchev and Ulbricht, in their most sanguine mood, could not forsee this happening. Hence other options had to be pressed into service. One involved changing the status of West Berlin. Declare it a demilitarised, free city; get the Allies out and the access routes would fall into the hands of the GDR authorities. Again there would be no need for a wall. If both these solutions proved inoperative, the only option left was to wall-in West Berlin.

Khrushchev, not surprisingly, played two melodies on the theme of Germany and Berlin. Sometimes one was given prominence, sometimes the other. Ulbricht joined in when the moment was judged opportune. On 27 November 1958, Khrushchev proposed that West Berlin be transformed into a demilitarised, free city and implied, in passing, that if there was no agreement within six months, he would sign a separate peace treaty with the GDR.[97] Hitherto he had always claimed that West Berlin was a part of the GDR. The USSR was certainly innovative in her policy towards Germany. First, between 1945 and 1949, there had only been one Germany. Until 1958, there had been no Germany but two German states. Now there promised to be three: the FRG, the GDR and West Berlin.

The Soviet ultimatum ended in May 1959 but since a foreign ministers' conference was planned for Geneva in May 1959 the matter was not pressed. This underlined the fact that measurements of time when expressed in Russian should not be taken too literally. The time spans given in Soviet ultimata resemble Soviet economic plans: declarations of hope. The Geneva discussions proved inconclusive. However, President Eisenhower extended an invitation to Nikita Khrushchev to visit the US. This he accepted eagerly and the 'spirit of Camp David' promised much. Nevertheless the U2 incident intervened and wrecked the Paris summit in June 1960. Khrushchev and Eisenhower had nothing more of value to say to each other so it was left to the next President, to be elected that autumn, to parley with the First Secretary.

The world congress of communist and workers' parties declared its support for the Soviet Union's stance on Germany at the end of its deliberations in December 1960. Andrei Gromyko, at a meeting of the Supreme Soviet in the same month, indicated that the USSR regarded the solution of the Berlin question as more important than a German peace treaty.[98]

The first half of 1961 resounded to the shrill demands of Ulbricht for a Berlin solution and a peace treaty. He buttressed his argument with the assertion that West Germany was a threat to peace. A peace treaty had to be signed to delineate finally the postwar frontiers, thereby stilling irredentist claims in West Germany. On 17 February 1961, the USSR delivered an *aide-mémoire* to the FRG on a 'German peace treaty and related problems'.[99] So the lines were drawn for the meeting of Kennedy and Khrushchev at Vienna on 3–4 June 1961. At the encounter Nikita Sergeevich played the heavy-handed father admonishing one of his sons. What he said in effect was that if Kennedy did not like the Soviet proposals on Berlin and Germany, he would have to lump it.[100] Kennedy was not so easily browbeaten and later made it clear that the US would stand by her obligations in Berlin. On 15 June, Khrushchev named 31 December 1961 as the last possible date for a settlement. Kennedy remained unmoved. The sabre-rattling in Moscow was answered in kind by Washington. Whose nerve would break first?

Khrushchev had left himself an escape route – build the wall. Ulbricht had been pressing for one, if no diplomatic solution was achieved, ever since 1958. At what moment did Khrushchev decide to back down and grasp his remaining option? A Freudian slip by Ulbricht would indicate on or just before 15 June 1961. On that day, at a press conference, he denied categorically that 'anyone intended building a wall'.[101] On the other hand the meeting of the party leaders of the Warsaw Pact, on 3–5 August, in Moscow, may have been the moment of decision. General Karel Šejna has stated that Khrushchev greeted Ulbricht with the news: 'Yes, you can have your wall, but not one millimetre farther!' At this Ulbricht blanched.[102] If this is so, then he must have come to Moscow hoping to get control over West Berlin.

The flow of refugees to West Berlin turned into a flood in early August. Many in the GDR obviously expected access to West Berlin to be restricted or closed. The Warsaw Pact gave the go-ahead on 12 August 1961[103] and the sealing of the border began during the night of 12/13 August. The date chosen showed that someone in East Berlin had a sense of timing: 13 August 1961 was the ninetieth anniversary of the birth of Karl Liebknecht, one of the founders of the KPD. Kennedy breathed a sigh of relief and remarked that the Berlin crisis was over.[104]

NOTES

1 *Otnosheniya SSSR s GDR 1949–1955 gg: Dokumenty i Materialy* (Moscow, 1974) pp. 200–3.
2 *SBZ von 1945 bis 1954* (Bonn and Berlin, 1964) p. 182
3 *Otnosheniya* . . . , pp. 205–7.
4 *SBZ* . . . , p. 188.
5 *Otnosheniya* . . . , pp. 218–23.
6 *SBZ* . . . , p. 199.
7 *Otnosheniya* . . . , pp. 227–34.
8 *Berlin and the Problem of German Unification* (London: HMSO, no. RF.P. 5869, December 1969) p. 12.
9 *Otnosheniya* . . . , pp. 277–85.
10 Heinz Lippmann, *Honecker Porträt eines Nachfolgers* (Cologne, 1971) p. 163.
11 Ibid., p. 164.
12 *Otnosheniya* . . . , pp. 350–8.
13 Ibid., pp. 377–8.
14 Ibid., pp. 514–7.
15 *A bis Z* (Bonn, 1969) p. 714.

114   *Marxism-Leninism in the German Democratic Republic*

16 Idem.
17 On 25 January 1955, the Soviet Union had declared the state of war with Germany to be at an end. See *ND*, 26 January 1955.
18 *Otnosheniya . . .* , pp. 588–92.
19 Carola Stern, *Portät eines bolschewistischen Partei* (Cologne, 1957) pp. 174–5 and 177, n. 42.
20 Gerhard Wettig, *Die Sowjetunion, die DDR und die Deutschland-Frage 1965–1976 Einvernehmen und Konflikt im sozialistischen Lager* (Stuttgart, 1976) pp. 18, 188–9. The only other treaty which regulated the movement of troops outside their barracks was the one with Czechoslovakia signed on 16 October 1968. Only Hungary, after 1956, had no control over Soviet troops entering and leaving the country.
21 *ND*, 27 July 1955.
22 *ND*, 13 August 1955.
23 *Otnosheniya . . .* , pp. 647–9.
24 Melvin Croan, 'Soviet German Relations', *Survey*, nos 44–5 (October 1962) p. 20.
25 Heinz Köhler, *Economic Integration in the Soviet Bloc: With an East German Case Study* (New York, 1965) p. 310..This was not the first sum advanced by the USSR. In 1949, 100 million rubles had been made available; in 1950, 149 million rubles and in 1950/51, 30 million rubles. See ibid., pp. 309–10. These credits should be seen in the light of economic aid extended by the Allies to West Germany: by 1953 Great Britain had made £208 million available, the USA $3200 million and France $15.7 million. By the German debt settlement of 1953, Great Britain agreed to accept £150 million in full settlement of her claims; the USA agreed to accept $1200 million and France $11·84 million. See *Berlin . . .* , p. 4, n. 1.
26 *Dokumente der Sozialistischen Einheitspartei* (Berlin, DDR, 1954), vol. IV, p. 453; Stern, op. cit., p. 172.
27 Joachim Schultz, *Der Funktionär in der Einheitspartei: Kaderpolitik und Bürokratisierung in der SED* (Stuttgart and Düsseldorf, 1956) p. 259.
28 Idem.; Martin Jänicke, *Der dritte Weg: Die antistalinistische Opposition gegen Ulbricht seit 1953* (Cologne, 1964) p. 39.
29 'Die grosse Gehirnwäsche', *SBZ – Archiv* (20 October 1953) p. 306.
30 *Dokumente . . .* , p. 509. The use of the term 'social-democratic' by the SED does not necessarily mean that the views in question had anything in common with actual or traditional social-democratic values. The term is a political slogan to be used against those who hold views which are at variance with those of the SED leadership.
31 Schultz, op. cit., p. 244. In East Berlin it was only 23·6 per cent in September 1953. *Bezirk* Leipzig with 42·5 per cent had the highest proportion of workers at that date. See ibid., p. 245.
32 Jänicke, op. cit., p. 48.
33 *Die Welt*, 16 October 1953; Jänicke, op. cit., p. 47.
34 *Die Welt*, 31 October 1953; ibid., p. 48.
35 Walter Ulbricht, in *ND*, 26 August 1953.
36 *Die Welt*, 22 June 1955. The figures refer to elected members; the key functionaries in the FDGB in 1953, for instance, were almost all SED members.

37 The composition of the party in April 1954 was as follows:

Politburo and Secretariat	16 persons
Central Committee	91 members and 44 candidate members.
Bezirk committees (*Bezirksleitung*)	1281 members
Kreis committees (*Kreisleitung*)	12,199 members
Enterprise party committees	8399 delegates
Primary organisation committees (*Leitung der Grundorganisationen*)	192,385 members
Primary organisations	1,272,987 members and 140,326 candidate members

See Schultz, op. cit., p. 264.

Ulbricht's confident mood was misplaced, at least as far as the economy was concerned. The Congress decrees were not successfully implemented. Various CC plenums were held in 1955 and the economic crisis in the GDR is evident in the debates. Attempts were made to make planning and management more flexible and the debate on prices and profits also started in earnest in 1955. Such a discussion would have been unthinkable in 1952.

38 Anastas Mikoyan called the continuation of collectivisation in the GDR 'the first task of the SED'. See *ND*, 2 April 1954.

39 *Dokumente der Sozialistischen Einheitspartei Deutschlands* (Berlin, DDR, 1956) vol. V, p. 50; Peter C. Ludz, *The Changing Party Elite in East Germany* (Cambridge, Massachusetts: MIT Press, 1972) p. 72. The original German edition is *Parteielite im Wandel* (Cologne and Opladen, 1968).

40 The SED was also backward in the countryside. Of the 4617 LPG, at the end of 1953, only 2461, or 53·3 per cent, had an SED primary organisation or candidate group. At the same date 11·7 per cent of all rural communities had no SED party organisation. See Schultz, op. cit., p. 252.

41 *ND*, 8 January 1955; Hermann Weber, *Von der SBZ zur DDR 1945–1968* (Hanover, 1968) p. 97.

42 Ludz, op. cit., p. 73, n 11. These figures should be interpreted with caution. Participation in the *Jugendweihe* was so high because the churches adopted the view that participation in the secular ceremony and continued church membership were not mutually exclusive. The churches, however, did object to the atheism which was underlined during the ceremony. The flexible reaction of the churches to this challenge is another illustration of their considerable political skill. They have been able to secure and maintain a surprisingly high level of autonomy and to make their influence felt. The role of the church in political and social life is much wider than the activities of the CDU.

43 Ernst Richert, *Macht ohne Mandat*, 2nd ed. (Cologne and Opladen, 1963) p. 129.

44 Idem.

45 *A bis Z* (Bonn, 1969) p. 474.

46 Richert, op. cit., p. 130.

116   *Marxism-Leninism in the German Democratic Republic*

47 Ibid., p. 131.
48 Jänicke, op. cit., p. 72.
49 Idem.
50 *ND*, 14 February 1956.
51 *ND*, 17 February 1956.
52 *ND*, 4 March 1956.
53 *ND*, 18 March 1956.
54 *ND*, 29 April 1956, 31 May 1956, 21 June 1956.
55 Jänicke, op. cit., p. 76.
56 Ibid., p. 74.
57 Ibid., p. 82.
58 *ND*, 8 February 1958.
59 Jänicke, op. cit., p. 83.
60 *ND*, 20 November 1956.
61 *ND*, 29 November 1956.
62 *ND*, 21 December 1956.
63 *ND*, 30 December 1956.
64 *ND*, 5 February 1957. Here again the economic difficulties of 1956 should be borne in mind. Ulbricht was seeking ways of improving economic performance but the views of Oelssner, Vieweg, Behrens and Benary, who were also very concerned about the situation, were regarded by Ulbricht as a threat to the dominance of the party and the central planners.
65 Jänicke, op. cit., p. 87.
66 Gerhard Zwerenz, 'Immer noch stalinistische Terrorjustiz', *SBZ – Archiv*, no. 2 (1959).
67 'Die politische Plattform Harichs und seiner Freunde', *SBZ – Archiv*, nos 5/6 (1957).
68 Jänicke, op. cit., p. 121. Kuczynski's criticisms were only the tip of the iceberg. Most of the staff and students in the country's universities were in a volatile mood in 1956–7. Kuczynski was in quite a strong position from which to launch his arrows at the SED leadership. He had worked closely with the Soviet embassy in Berlin in the late 1930s and thus had some Russian connections. During the war he was a leading KPD figure in England and hence had good contacts in the party. His voice was an important one during the troubled time under review and his influence was by no means restricted to academic circles.
69 'ZK Tagung der SED im Schatten Moskaus', *SBZ – Archiv*, no. 14 (1957).
70 *ND*, 8 February 1958.
71 *ND*, 26 February 1958. Selbmann's views should be seen in the context of the debate on economic reform.
72 Jänicke, op. cit., p. 84.
73 Fritz Selbmann, in *ND*, 17 July 1957.
74 Jänicke, op. cit., p. 94.
75 Ibid., p. 103.
76 *Wirtschaftswissenschaft*, Sonderheft 3 (1957). This did not mean that Ulbricht was against reforming the economy. In all the plenums in 1955 he consistently supported the view that new forms of economic organisation were necessary to rescue the GDR economy from the crisis it was in. However, he was determined that the central planners should set the goals

and success indicators. He wished to retain the command economy with its emphasis on heavy industry, collectivisation and price formation at the centre.

77 Jänicke, op. cit., p. 108.
78 Ibid., pp. 110–2.
79 The original plan (1956–60) foresaw gross industrial production rising by 55 per cent. This was reduced to 34 per cent, then raised to 38 per cent. See Richert, op. cit., pp. 119–20.
80 *A bis Z*, pp. 690–1. Two critics of this reform were Fred Oelssner and Fritz Selbmann. They thought it viable in a country as large as the USSR but irrelevant to a country as small as the GDR. After all, one could traverse the GDR from north to south in a day and from west to east in half a day. Most industrial enterprises could be reached in half a day from Berlin. Oelssner categorised the decentralisation as a 'regression to the pre-monopoly stage of capitalism'. See Jänicke, op. cit., p. 88.
81 *Statistisches Jahrbuch der DDR 1972* (Berlin, DDR, 1972) p. 114.
82 Richert, op. cit., p. 144.
83 *ND*, 22 December 1960.
84 Richert, op. cit., p. 137.
85 *Die Tribüne*, 16 May 1962.
86 *ND*, 29 November 1961.
87 *ND*, 30 November 1961.
88 This was not the first mention of the concept of a confederation. The GDR Council of Ministers had broached the subject in *ND*, 30 October 1955.
89 *ND*, 3 February 1957.
90 *A bis Z*, p. 715.
91 *Pravda*, 3 August 1957.
92 *A bis Z*, p. 715.
93 Idem.
94 Ibid., p. 716.
95 Ibid., p. 717.
96 Ibid., p. 212.
97 *Pravda*, 28 November 1958.
98 *Pravda*, 24 December 1960.
99 US Congress Senate Committee on Foreign Relations, *Documents on Germany 1944–1961* (Washington, DC, 1961) p. 635.
100 James O' Donnell, interview on West German television, 12 August 1976.
101 Anita Dasbach Mallinckrodt, *Propaganda hinter der Mauer* (Stuttgart, 1971) p. 32.
102 Interview on West German television, 12 August 1976.
103 *ND*, 13 January 1961; Mallinckrodt, op. cit., p. 73.
104 James O'Donnell, interview on West German television, 12 August 1976.

4 Socialism with a German Face

The Wall is the symbol of the GDR. Its building marks the turning point in the evolution of the first 'socialist state on German soil'. Had Ulbricht had his way it would have been built earlier. The longer the frontier to West Berlin remained open, the greater was the economic loss to the eastern part of Germany. Between 1956 and 1959 the number of the departing dropped steadily but the introduction of the Seven-Year Plan in 1959, the collectivisation of 1960, the sharp increase in the number of artisan co-operatives (membership jumped from 8000 in 1957 to 144,000 in 1960), the severe cut-back in the number of privately owned retail outlets and the sharp reduction in the proportion of industrial output emanating from the private sector (8 per cent in 1958 but 3·8 per cent in 1960) motivated an increasing number to leave peremptorily the GDR. In an interview in *Pravda*, on 30 December 1961, Ulbricht put the cost to the GDR of the massive flight of labour at 30,000 million Marks. The impact of the departed was immediately noticeable, forcing changes in the Seven-Year Plan. Half of the refugees were under twenty-five years of age and three-quarters under forty-five. Then there was the expense of building a 45·9-kilometre wall through Berlin and a 114-kilometre barrier round West Berlin. Besides this the East-West German border would have to be strengthened and all frontiers more carefully guarded. To cope with these new demands, national service was introduced by a law passed by the *Volkskammer* on 24 January 1962. Men between the ages of 18 and 26 years were to serve 18 months and be members of the reserve afterwards until they were 50. This law complemented the 'Law on the Defence of the GDR', passed by the *Volkskammer* on 20 September 1961. This latter law provided Ulbricht, as chairman of the Council of State of the GDR, with wide-ranging powers in an emergency. The tense internal situation after the building of the wall put such a strain on the existing police and armed forces that more men had to be recruited to maintain law and order and security. The SED, before 1962, had shied away from national service, although it was in operation in the FRG. It was a useful propaganda point that only West Germany had national service but that was not the main reason why this option was not seized upon in the GDR. National service in the GDR before August 1961 would have increased the flow of refugees and would have run the risk of arming opponents of the regime. Hitherto the police and army had had to rely on volunteers to serve short periods to supplement the regular forces. SED party organisations and mass organisations were often presented with the task of recruiting a given number of men. Pressure was sometimes applied by hinting that refusal could lead to the loss of a job or the barring of the route to technical or higher education.

More resources then would have to be devoted to defence and border control. The SED calculated that the money was well spent if the flow of refugees was reduced to a trickle. How many refugees represents a trickle depends on the Politburo in East Berlin. Any attempt to make it absolutely impossible to leave the GDR without permission would be prohibitively expensive.

If more young men were to serve in the armed forces, gaps in the labour force would be exacerbated. There was only one source of new labour left in the GDR to plug the holes left by the refugees and the national servicemen: those females who were not yet gainfully employed. Correspondingly a campaign was launched to recruit more women. A communiqué of the Politburo on 24 December 1961 entitled 'Women and Peace and Socialism' summed up the situation. However there was no great army of unemployed women waiting for the call: 68·4 per cent of all able-bodied women between sixteen and sixty years were already in work, making up 43·9 per cent of the labour force. What was of paramount importance was the raising of the skills of the employed women. More than ever before women would be needed to fill highly skilled jobs and managerial posts. Women made up 28 per cent of the student body but were concentrated in the non-engineering and applied science fields. They dominated pharmacy, for example, making up 71 per cent of the student body but in technical high schools only 6 per cent of students were female.[1]

The SED also put its house in order. An exchange of party cards was carried out between 1 December 1960 and 31 January 1961. This was paralleled by the removal of those functionaries who were regarded as qualified supporters of the First Secretary. Between 1958 and 1961, 105 top functionaries were removed from the 15 *Bezirk* party organisations; 7 first secretaries and 16 other secretaries were voted out. The purge was especially thorough in *Bezirk* Dresden, where 16 functionaries were replaced, and in *Bezirks* Halle and Cottbus, 10 officials were removed in each.[2]

Party and FDJ members dealt summarily with those GDR citizens who were openly critical of the wall. Those voicing opinions at variance with the official line that the construction of the wall was an historic victory for peace often received a knuckle sandwich as a reward. The *Leipziger Volkszeitung* wrote: 'Some may have doubted lately if it is right to seize and beat enemies of our republic' and concluded that fists had to be used to make clear to enemies the real state of affairs.[3] One worker was beaten up so badly that he had to be taken to hospital. The go-ahead however had been given by the party organ *Neues Deutschland*, in a leading article on 9 August 1961. It had praised the action of a worker who had rammed his fist ' into the cakehole of a warmonger'. No attempt was made to convince critics of the correctness of building the wall by rational debate – elemental violence was found more communicative. It is difficult to resist the conclusion that the SED felt itself incapable of convincing doubters by logical argument. In October, Werner Krolikowski, first secretary in *Bezirk* Dresden, and Paul Fröhlich, first secretary in *Bezirk* Leipzig, threw their weight against the 'iron fist' policies of the period.[4] By the end of 1961 the violence had died down.

The SED was in no danger from any other political party in the GDR. The CDU accepted that it and the other democratic forces in the country were subject to the leadership of the 'party of the working class', the SED. The CDU glorified Soviet experience and looked forward to the victory of socialism in the GDR. It had long since ceased to function as a party with a viable political alternative to Marxism-Leninism in the GDR. The LDPD was also hitched to the bandwagon of the SED. It recommended its members, many of them artisans, private retailers and owners of small firms, to join the co-operative sector and condemned the 'daydreamers' who believed that it was possible to introduce a system which was neither capitalist nor socialist. The NDPD and the DBD had always been closely allied to the SED. So the National Front, which embraced all political and mass organisations, was firmly under the leadership of the SED. The GDR was one of the few countries in which all the political parties, other than the SED, consciously aimed at political suicide. Since they all welcomed socialism they were becoming more and more irrelevant as socialism matured.

The mass flight of the period before August 1961 revealed much more convincingly than the results of local or *Volkskammer* elections that only a minority of the population was devoted to the 'party of the working class' and the goal it proclaimed – socialism. Having bolted all the doors, the SED was politically master in its own house; now it was up to it, in the short-term, to neutralise and, then, in the long-term, to win over the majority who were agnostics.

THE NEW ECONOMIC SYSTEM OF PLANNING AND MANAGEMENT OF THE ECONOMY

On the economic front, the late 1950s and early 1960s were a chastening time for the SED. The 'chief economic task' of catching up and surpassing the FRG in the important economic arena petered out; becoming free of the need to import from West Germany was not a feasible policy; growth rates were slowing down and concomitantly the return on investment was contracting. The stark reality of the situation was underlined by the fact that between 1951 and 1955 an investment of 32,000 million Marks had produced an increase in national income of 21,000 million Marks. Between 1956 and 1960, 63,000 million Marks were invested but the increase in national income was only 21,000 million Marks. Between 1961 and 1964, 66,000 million Marks were invested, to produce an increase in national income of only 10,700 million Marks.[5] The great spurt of the 1950s was over. A similar phenomenon is observable in the development of industry on the present territory of the GDR between 1933 and 1944. If 1936 is taken as 100, 1933 production was equivalent to 64 and that of 1944 to 168. The fastest-growing sectors were machine, vehicle and steel construction, electrical equipment, and precision and optical instruments, which expanded their output more than sixfold between 1933 and 1944 and over threefold between 1936 and 1944.[6] By the early 1960s, a new economic strategy had to be developed. A quantitative or extensive growth pattern was no longer adequate: a qualitative or intensive growth pattern had to be evolved. The USSR was also casting around for a new industrial approach. There, the early years of the Seven-Year Plan (1959–65) had not come up to expectations. Of course there was a model ready to hand, one which had set in motion a *Wirtschaftswunder* – the West German market economy – but it was officially out of bounds to socialist economists. However it did have some impact on socialist thinking. The most rapid slow-down in economic growth, by the early 1960s, was recorded in the two most industrially advanced socialist states, Czechoslovakia and the GDR. The two countries had to act quickly before the situation became too critical. With the Soviet economy also slowing down there was a community of interest in introducing economic reforms. Khrushchev's decentralisation of economic decision-making, inherent in the *sovnarkhoz* reform of 1957, was not producing the desired results. Economists such Evsei Liberman were advising greater autonomy for the enterprise as the way out of the growth dilemma. He wanted the factory to respond more positively to consumer demand and thereby reduce the production of goods which no one wanted to buy. Plant profitability was to become an important yardstick. Since a market economy was not being contemplated – prices were to be set by the central planners and not by the interplay of demand and supply – communist party involvement in the economic process would have to increase. Communists would have to make a greater contribution to the solution of technical problems in enterprises and supervise the whole functioning of the enterprise. This required a greater emphasis on technical expertise from party and non-party members alike. If this was true of the Soviet Union it was even more true of the industrially more mature GDR. A reform had to be initiated which would tap the latent resources of the labour force in such a way as to enhance the economic viability of the country without at the same time endangering the dominant position of the SED in state and society.

It is apposite here to consider the managerial structure of a socialist enterprise. The managing director has the task of managing an enterprise according to the principles of one-man management. He is aided by the all-round collaboration of the work force. As the representative of socialist state power he has two functions: he is an economic manager and an ideological teacher. His position is embedded in a 'system of social management' which is composed of four elements. The key element is the enterprise party organisation which helps the director to 'recognize and deal with the needs of the work force'. (See Table 4.1.) There is also an economic *aktiv* in the enterprise and in large enterprises a production committee (formed in 1963). The production committee concerns itself with basic technical and economic questions. Its membership is recruited mainly from the above four groups. Commissions of the Workers' and Peasants' Inspectorate (ABI) were set up in enterprise in May 1963. They had ten to twenty members, depending on the size of the enterprise. The ABI is supervised by the enterprise party organisations. It has mainly control functions and supervises the implementation of party and government directives.

Ulbricht spent August 1962 in the USSR and returned to Berlin

TABLE 4.1 System of social management[7]

SED	State	Trade union	FDJ
Executive of enterprise party organisation	Enterprise director	Enterprise union executive	Enterprise FDJ executive
Departmental party organisation	Departmental manager Departmental assistant managers	Departmental union executive	Departmental FDJ organisation
Party group organiser	Section head foreman	Trade union shop steward	FDJ group leadership

brimming with ideas. Essentially he wanted to promote a thoroughgoing decentralisation of the GDR economy. Many of the ideas of the New Economic System of Planning and Management of the Economy (NES), which was introduced in 1963 and disappeared into oblivion with Ulbricht, owe their genesis to the wrangling with the 'revisionist' economists of the 1956–8 period. There was one major difference: now the economic reform was being promoted from above whereas in the 1956–8 confrontation all the innovative thinking had stemmed from below.

Before turning to the reform some other events are of immediate relevance. Evsei Liberman published his article 'The Plan, Profits and Premia' in *Pravda* on 9 September 1962. This meant that the Soviet Union had legitimised economic policy changes throughout the socialist bloc. Just how radical these reforms could be without incurring Soviet wrath was unknown at this stage. Ambitious economists began attempting to marry aspects of the market economy to the planned economy. Some were very radical but economic ideas were not the main bone of contention between eastern Europe and the USSR. Only if the economic changes involved a risk of the communist party losing its monopoly of political power woud Moscow intervene. Czechoslovakia, possibly because she had the most miserable economic record of the early 1960s, raced ahead and in so doing endangered the power of the communist party. This brought the retribution of 21 August 1968. Hungary launched her New Economic Mechanism (NEM), which was just as radical as that of Czechoslovakia, in 1968, but was able to convince Moscow that the reform meant no loss of power by the communist party. The NEM is still in operation. The GDR ran ahead, took fright at the excesses of the Czechoslovaks, and withdrew into her shell. The NES was gradually dismantled.

In order to concentrate the minds of party officials on a particular task, Khrushchev split the CPSU apparatus into industrial and agricultural wings in late 1962. This momentous decision was testimony to his frustration at the inefficiency of the party in coping with economic tasks. In a region which had an industrial and an agricultural sector, the erring official when upbraided for not meeting planned goals in, say, agriculture, could plausibly argue that he had not been able to devote much time to agriculture since he had been overstretched in the industrial sphere. Now Khrushchev cut the ground from under this argument and there was understandably a stampede of party officials trying to leave the agricultural sector for the industrial, where it was much easier to fulfil planned goals. The same argument was used by the SED when it split the apparatus in 1963. At the VIth Congress, Erich Honecker, then CC secretary for security, quoted the example of *Bezirk* Halle, which makes a valuable contribution to industry and agriculture in the GDR. There the argument had some credence but in some other regions, where one needed a pair of binoculars to find any industry, the argument had little validity.

The VIth Congress, which met between 15 and 21 January 1963, set in motion fundamental political and economic reforms. The aim was to go further than the victory of socialist production relations, to a fully integrated, efficient socialist economy. The SED was to be the instrument for fashioning this breakthrough to economic cornucopia. In order to gear the party for this task it was split down the middle according to the 'production principle'. In February 1963, four new bureaux or commissions were established in the Politburo: the bureau of industry and construction; the bureau of agriculture; the ideological commission; and the commission for agitation. These organisations appeared also at CC level. At *Bezirk* level, a bureau of industry and construction, a bureau of agriculture, and an ideological commission were set up. At *Kreis* level, either a bureau of industry and construction or a bureau of agriculture, according to the dominant form of economic activity, and an ideological commission were established.[8] (See Figures 4.1 and 4.2.) Hitherto the party had been organised along territorial lines, i.e. a party organisation covered all activities in a given area. Now, without jettisoning the territorial principle, party economic endeavour in a given area was split in two. SED *Bezirk* and *Kreis* executives were

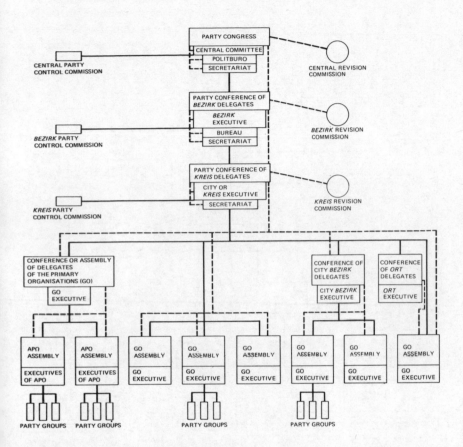

FIGURE 4.1 Organisational framework of the SED in 1958 according to the IIIrd SED Statute adopted at the IVth Congress, as amended by the Vth Congress

--- Sequence of eligibility and accountability
—— Sequence of subordination

Source: Werner Horn *et al.*, *20 Jahre Sozialistische Einheitspartei Deutschlands: Beiträge* (Berlin, DDR, 1966) p. 388.

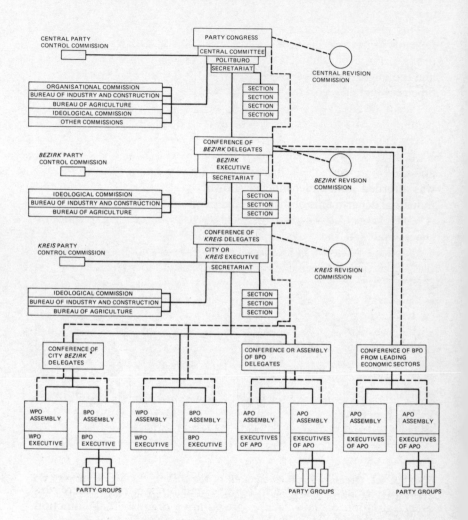

FIGURE 4.2 Organisational framework of the SED in 1963 according to the IVth SED Statute adopted at the VIth Congress
– – – Sequence of eligibility and accountability
——— Sequence of subordination

Source: ibid., p. 389.

responsible for the leadership of all bureaux and commissions in their area.

This reform also embraced the state and economic bureaucracy. Officials were to be brought directly into contact with the concepts of profit, price, profitability and so on. This put a premium on technical and economic expertise and tended to favour the younger generation of officials who had seized the opportunity of further education. The army of the middle aged, who had fought for the revolution with a rifle in one hand and a Marxist-Leninist primer in the other, faced a bleak future.

The most important institution in the new economic system was the VVB. Previously it had been midway between the Council of Ministers and the enterprise, the VEB. Now it acquired economic functions and was afforded some independence. Power was devolved to it from the industrial departments of the National Economic Council and the SPK. A VVB concentrated on a particular industrial branch, e.g. plastics or shoes, and had the task of advancing that branch technically and economically. The decision-making power of the managing director of the VVB was widened and his sphere of operation increased. He was to supervise his accountants, check the profit-and-loss account, engage in some marketing, introduce consumer research studies and establish closer relations with scientific research institutes. Labour was to be given a new deal, with material incentives being afforded priority. Wages and bonuses were to be tied to the profitability of the enterprise. Bonuses were to be based on real gains in productivity, eliminating waste and increasing efficiency. Extra time off could be granted fo meritorious achievement. This switch to material incentives underlined the optimism of the leadership that the NES would bring about a revolution in efficiency.

Initially the NES reforms applied to the following branches of industry: chemicals, electrical engineering, metallurgy, machine building, energy and transport. Then they were extended to building and construction, agriculture and domestic and foreign trade. There was even legislation on how local representative organs should function under the NES.[9]

The concept of profit and profitability, without a fundamental price reform, is only a bookkeeping one. If the GDR economy was to become efficient and internationally competitive then prices had to reflect relative scarcity. GDR prices for machinery, equipment and buildings had been laid down between 1948 and 1953 and they had been based on 1944 prices for machinery and equipment and 1913 prices plus a 60 per cent mark-up for buildings.[10] The price structure in the early 1960s was such that raw materials were priced too low, leading to waste and a neglect of substitutes, which were often priced too high. All this in a country which was desperately short of raw materials. Output measured in terms of volume was the chief plan indicator. This led to the production of goods whose cost to the economy was higher than enterprise costs. Economic and technical progress was restricted in that investment, based on existing prices, promised handsome returns but a rational price structure would have revealed this to be false.[11]

The first stage, revaluing fixed capital, was completed on 30 June 1963. The value of gross fixed capital in the GDR was increased by 52 per cent, on average, 105,000 million Marks (47,000 million Marks of buildings and 58,000 million Marks of machinery and equipment).[12] The next step, the key one, reforming industrial prices, was carried out in three stages: Stage 1 began on 1 April 1964 and affected coal, energy, iron, steel and basic chemicals and raised prices, on average, by 70 per cent; Stage 2 began on 1 January 1965 and affected the paper industry, leather, skins, building materials and the chemical industry and raised prices, on average, by 40 per cent; Stage 3 started on 1 January 1967 and involved machinery, electrical goods, electronics, final products of the chemical industry and the light and food industries and increased prices, on average, by 4 per cent.[13] Profits were to be calculated on fabrication costs, i.e. value added by the enterprise. Previously the cost of materials had been added when calculating profits. The new formula prevented an enterprise from gaining large profits by manufacturing goods with a high input of expensive raw materials. The reform also introduced a production fund tax, a charge on the gross fixed and circulating capital of the enterprise. This 'interest' charge worked out at 6 per cent.[14]

NES also introduced the product group and made it subject to the VVB. Product groups are groups of enterprises, whether nationalised, semi-private or private, within a given industry which produce technologically similar or related products or semi-fabricates. The goal was for the VVB to unify economic and technical management in the various types of enterprise, to discover and utilise all productive and research capacities, to raise labour productivity through specialisation and standardisation and to increase control over semi-private and private enterprises. A glance at the electrical appliance industry will illustrate how the product group functioned. This branch of the electrical industry produced about 10,000 products in 1963 and was structured as follows: the VVB Electrical Appliances embraced 18 VEB which were divided into 10 product groups involving 31 other VEB (under the VVB), 38 locally managed VEB and 270 semi-private and private enterprises and co-operatives.[15] The communication problems must have been formidable!

The blueprint for the NES was published in July 1963.[16] How long would it take for the NES to become fully operational? Ulbricht, at an SED economic conference, declared: 'It will take two to three years to elaborate and introduce the NES.'[17] However, six months later, at the IXth Plenum of the CC of the SED, in April 1966, he revealed that the NES had not been fully introduced and that it would take another two years to complete the job.[18] However it was still not complete by 1968 when recentralisation set in. The SED, therefore, discovered that reforming economic management, which was only the first step towards a fundamental reformation of GDR society, was more complex than had been imagined.

What were the major innovations between 1963 and 1968? The genesis of the NES was the desire to remove the weaknesses and shortcomings of the centrally directed economy. It was hoped that an increasingly self-regulating mechanism would evolve which would reduce drastically direct intervention from the centre. The centre would still set the national economic goals but the local entity, essentially the VVB, would put flesh on the bare bones of the plan by solving the economic tasks more efficiently than the centre could ever do in pre-NES days. This assumed that the interests of the VVB and the national interest coincided. What was good for the VVB was good for the GDR. From the beginning, the central authorities kept something in reserve. The prices for raw materials were set at a lower level than market forces would have dictated.[19] This implied that some sort of administrative allocation was envisaged.

Walter Ulbricht, at the XIth Plenum of the CC of the SED, from 15 to 18 December 1965, drew up an interim balance sheet and launched the 'second stage' of the NES reform.[20] The National Economic Council (created in 1962) was abolished and its departments transformed into seven ministries. Two new ministries, the Ministry of the Material Economy and the Ministry for *Bezirk*-managed Industry and Food, were set up. The State Planning Commission (SPK) was again made responsible for drawing up and supervising annual and perspective plans. The *Bezirk* economic councils were made responsible for all previously locally managed industrial enterprises. A State Bureau of Labour and Wages and a Bureau of Prices were also established. (See Figure 4.3.) The SPK was to reduce the number of plan indicators but to liaise more closely with enterprises. The VVB and the VEB were gradually to go over to more and more self-financing. Parallel to this,

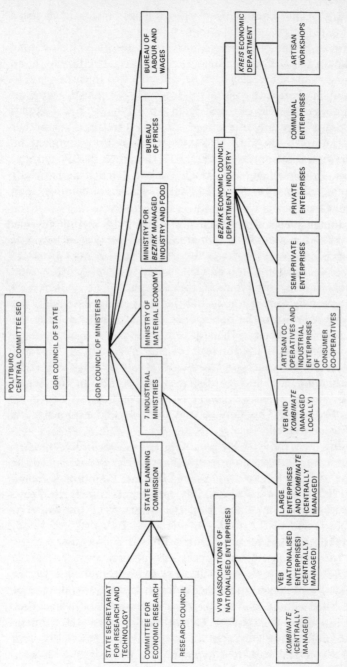

FIGURE 4.3 The organisation of GDR industry after 1965 (simplified)

Source: Fünfter Tätigkeitsbericht 1965/1969 (Bonn and Berlin, 1969) p. 75:

financial control by the Ministry of Finance was to increase. The net result was that the effective powers of the VVB director were curtailed. Evidently enterprises had been quick to elaborate plans which were advantageous to themselves but detrimental to the national economy.

Labour morale was given a boost after the plenum. The five-day week, every other week, was introduced in 1966 and a year later, after the VIIth Congress, every week became a five-day week. Some bank holidays disappeared, however, as a result. Later the minimum holiday period was increased by a further three days to fifteen days.

The shortage of labour and capital and the low technical level of many enterprises led to the concept of rationalisation being given great prominence. Great stress was placed on the need to switch over from extensive to intensive growth. Discussion of the NES in 1966 revealed the enormous task facing GDR industry in its uphill task of becoming internationally competitive. It was found that huge investments were necessary to replace obsolete and obsolescent machinery and equipment. Success overnight was out of the question.

The SED put a brave face on the industrial price reform, arguing that it would only affect industrial prices. However it was soon evident that consumer goods would also be affected. Rents for new flats also increased.

Stage 2 of the NES lasted just over a year. It was overtaken by a 'new phase of development'. This was proclaimed in a book by Walter Ulbricht with a preface by Günter Mittag, CC secretary for the economy, a key figure in the genesis and development of the NES. The First Secretary revealed that the NES was to embrace more than economic goals: 'We intend to elaborate and introduce the NES not only in the economy but also in all social development.'[21] Shortly afterwards the NES was rechristened. It became the Economic System of Socialism (ESS).

THE POLITICAL THAW

The economic reforms, begun in 1963, were accompanied by a political thaw. A feeling of optimism was abroad and the licence afforded the economists and technicians to question party-sponsored solutions spilled over into other walks of life. One of the first to test the temperature of the new dispensation – and one of the first to discover its sharp edges – was Professor Robert Havemann. A Professor of Physical

Chemistry at the Humboldt University in East Berlin, Havemann had already, in 1962, in Leipzig, raised eyebrows by asking the question: 'Has philosophy [meaning dialectical materialism] been of help to modern science in solving problems?' His answer was that far from helping it, it had been hindering it. He even came up with names of Soviet and GDR scientists who had suffered for their scientific views. Nothing untoward befell the outspoken professor but, in October 1963, he began a series of lectures at the Humboldt University on 'Scientific Aspects of Philosophical Problems'. They were extremely popular with students. Then Havemann broached the question of morals and politics. This was going too far since the SED ideologues regarded this territory as their own. The seminar on 7 February 1964 was Havemann's last. He was expelled from the SED and lost his professorship just over a month later. He was not jailed but his professional career was effectively at an end. The SED was willing to do without an outstanding physical chemist because his political views were considered subversive. Since he maintained that he was a convinced communist and was not challenging Marxism, the dispute must have concerned the interpretation of some of Marx's writings. It did; it concerned dialectical materialism. Essentially Havemann wanted an end to dogma about the dialectic. He wanted the dialectic to be left entirely in the hands of scientists, whom he believed had discovered an objectively dialectical character in reality, a real self-contradictoriness, but that this character (as well as the other features of reality) was being misrepresented by the official philosophers of dialectical materialism.[22] In other words, leave the dialectic to those who understand and use it: the scientists. He was serving notice that the professional philosophers were redundant and what is more that their continued employment was actually hindering the advance of science. This was heady stuff but not something that the SED was likely to find palatable. Another irritant for the SED was that the Italian Communist Party (PCI) took up Havemann's case. The PCI's main point seemed to be that it should be possible for Havemann to disagree publicly with the SED without being expelled. Or perhaps the PCI was using the Havemann case to rile the SED. The PCI could hardly have accepted Havemann's views on the dialectic since they were only revealed to practising scientists. It is worth noting that no scientist since 1964 has argued that he has made a fundamental discovery by exploiting the special insights gained from Havemann's teachings on the dialectic.

Havemann's downfall in 1964 was exceptional. Generally speaking intellectual life was more relaxed than before, with writers and film directors seizing the opportunity of criticising the Stalinist past. East

German writers began to take part in discussions in the FRG. Western life-styles and clothes were no longer taboo. West Berliners could once again visit their relatives in East Berlin on public holidays. All this made the more conservative figures in the Politburo apprehensive. Men such as Erich Honecker – seen by many as the heir-apparent and called the *Kronprinz* – Paul Fröhlich, Alfred Neumann, Albert Norden and Alfred Kurella argued that the relaxation, instead of strengthening the role of the party, was in fact eroding it.[23] Their hand was strengthened by the changes in the Soviet Union. There the new collective leadership was feeling its way and wanted support. Given the chance, the Kremlin wished to mend its fences with China. It certainly wanted nothing in Eastern Europe which the Chinese could point to as a complete denial of Stalin's legacy.

Honecker and the conservatives launched an attack on the permissive ideological climate at the VIIth Plenum of the CC of the SED, in December 1964. They called for stricter controls by the party, demanded a tougher line towards West Germany and criticised the drift of the regime's foreign policy away from the East.[24] For the time being these demands fell on deaf ears. However the following year provided even more ammunition. The Soviet Union was so concerned about its trade with the GDR that Brezhnev flew to Berlin, in November 1965. Prices appear to have been a sticking point and Hans Apel chose to commit suicide on 3 December 1965 rather than sign the trade treaty. The XIth Plenum of the CC of the SED followed soon afterwards and marks a return to tried and trusted formulae. Ulbricht made it clear that the new economic system was to stay but with minor alterations. It was left to Erich Honecker to launch the major attack against the artists and writers. Two films under attack were screened at the plenum to add impetus to the argument. Writers such as Stefan Heym and Wolf Biermann were labelled traitors for having published in West Germany. A stream of dismissals followed the plenum. The most prominent casualty was the Minister of Culture, Hans Bentzien.

The other sector of society castigated at the plenum was youth. FDJ leader Horst Schumann went so far as to admit that his organisation had been employing 'totally erroneous ideological guidelines'. The only correct policy, now, according to Schumann, was to revert to past practices. This was qucikly put into effect and a determined effort was made to wean youth away from West German radio and television and Western life-styles. Schumann later underlined the leadership role of the party, admitting that many young people had challenged and openly rejected that role.

THE ESS

The VIIth Congress, from 17 to 22 April 1967, set the new guidelines for
the country. Whereas the VIth Congress had declared the main task to
be the 'all-round construction of socialism', the VIIth Congress
proclaimed the 'completion of socialism' to be the order of the day. 'The
formation of the developed social system of socialism begins with the
VIIth Congress. . . . Developed socialist society utilises to the full the
economic system of socialism in the context of the scientific-technical
revolution.'[25] Thus the GDR was the first country in the socialist bloc to
attempt to consolidate a socialist economic model, embedded in a
developed socialist society. Other countries of the bloc were experiment-
ing with new economic mechanisms at the same time, but the GDR
officially declared that the experimental stage was over and that
something higher was being evolved. If the GDR had little political
impact inside and outside the socialist world, she could gain respect and
international recognition if she could evolve a successful socialist
economic model. Ulbricht also made it abundantly clear that the ESS
would be a centrally planned socialist economy but some aspects of the
market economy would creep into it:

> The socialist planned economy is neither an administered economy
> nor a so-called market economy which functions spontaneously. The
> socialist production of goods and thereby the market plays quite an
> important role in it. However the determining factor of its organic
> unity is and will remain social planning.[26]

Although marked economic progress was recorded between 1963 and
1967, the SED was not satisfied. Research, rationalisation and com-
petitiveness in foreign markets all had to be increased rapidly. Erich
Apel sketched in the expanding horizons of the GDR economy: 'Our
sights are set on world standards. If in any given field the Soviet Union
achieves world leadership we shall model ourselves on that pattern; if
West Germany or Japan achieves a similar distinction, then we shall
follow that example.'[27] Apel was as good as his word. GDR-USSR trade
turnover between 1962 and 1965 dropped from 49·3 per cent of total
GDR foreign trade to 43·4 per cent, and trade with the East Europeans,
between 1963 and 1966, slipped from 78 per cent to 73·7 per cent.[28]
However old habits die hard. GDR firms, isolated from foreign
competition, were used to receiving subventions to cover losses.[29]
Ulbricht quoted Marx to the effect that the capitalist had to think in
terms of the world market. The First Secretary caustically reminded

everyone that the GDR economy was not a nature reserve for poorly functioning enterprises.

Another administrative reform was launched in the course of 1967. The SPK was elevated to the role of the economic general staff of the Council of Ministers.[30] Some of the duties of the SPK were, at the same time, transferred to the Council of Ministers. This upgrading of the Council of Ministers and ministries is evidence of further recentralisation. The VVB were apparently to have their wings clipped even more.

Günter Mittag, at the IIIrd Plenum of the CC of the SED, in November 1967, revealed that the GDR had now entered a higher stage of development. 'The formation of the developed social system of socialism, with its economic system as its core, permits us now to enter the second phase of the socialist revolution in the GDR in which socialism will henceforth develop on its own base.'[31] In this second phase business management became a respectable socialist discipline and lost its appellation as a 'capitalist pseudo-science'.

As of 1 January 1968 the ESS was extended. Not only the whole of industry but also trade and agriculture were more closely enmeshed. The VEB were to become more and more self-financing. In order constantly to revise prices due to changing technologies, the VVB were made responsible for the initiation of dynamic price changes.[32] VVB profitability was watched closely by the centre. If it exceeded 15 per cent (ratio of profits to capital – fixed and stocks) prices were reduced to cut profitability to about 10 per cent.[33]

Data processing was also given a boost. The State Secretary for Data Processing was accorded the rank of a member of the Council of Ministers and his field of competence expanded. The number of computer outlets was to be expanded rapidly and a whole army of computer experts trained. Of course the success of this initiative depended on sufficient data being available for processing. Given the increasingly tense relations between Czechoslovakia and the USSR, at this time, the prospects of GDR enterprises gaining any more real autonomy were slim. Indeed one can see the sudden emphasis on data processing as an attempt to recentralise more and more decision-making. The SED's hope was that the computer would make possible what manual methods had proved incapable of doing – making central planning efficient.

Considerable success was recorded by GDR industry throughout the 1960s but by the end of the decade a crisis was looming. As of 1968/69 certain branches of industry, classified as structure-determining, were given priority. These included chemicals, machine- and vehicle-building and electronics. These sectors of the economy accounted for half of industrial output by 1970 (their proportion in 1955 had been 36 per cent).[34] By 1969/70 it was clear that the economy had not developed the potential to attempt higher growth rates during the period of the 1971–5 plan. Some of the reasons stemmed from the vagaries of the weather, others from the obtuseness of man. The winters of 1968/69 and 1969/70 were long and hard and were followed in both cases by hot, dry summers. These abnormal conditions placed a strain on the GDR economy which it could not bear. Energy, transport and the water supply had been constantly neglected by the planners. Agriculture was in an even worse state. It could not match the performance of industry during the 1960s. Compared to industry's 4·4 per cent real annual growth between 1960 and 1965, agriculture could only manage 0·3 per cent; between 1965 and 1970 industry recorded 5·8 per cent annually, while agriculture limped behind with 1·7 per cent.[35] Summer droughts cut back fodder supplies and only expensive imports of fodder prevented a significant reduction in the animal population. This helped to increase the foreign trade deficit to over 1000 million Valuta Marks in 1970. Added to this came the revelation that enterprise behaviour often conflicted with the goals set by the state for the structural development of the economy. It became more and more difficult to balance financial and material plans. False price relationships led enterprises to produce goods which conflicted with the planned goals for the economy.[36] The state was faced with a choice: either allow the economy to develop disproportionately and thereby risk a slow-down in growth, or intervene directly to restore plan discipline. A decree of the GDR Council of Ministers, dated 23 September 1970, revised the goals of the 1970 plan.[37] Then the whole future of the ESS was thrown open for discussion and the deficiencies of the system laid bare. The XIVth Plenum of the CC of the SED, in December 1970, was devoted to the problem. The result was a restriction of decision making by the VEB, the ending of price formation by the VVB, a price freeze, more direct government intervention and an increase in the number of plan indicators handed down by the central planners.[38] The NES and its Mark II model, the ESS, were thereby laid to rest.

THE SCIENTIFIC-TECHNICAL REVOLUTION[39]

If James Watt's improved steam engine was one of the breakthroughs which fathered the first industrial revolution, Norbert Wiener's cybernetics was a legitimate offspring which presaged another industrial revolution, the scientific-technical revolution (STR). The STR implies an enhanced role for science in all spheres of human activity. Advances in research lead to new machinery, new production processes and new technology. Cybernetics and computers remove much of the repetitive work from research. The advances in the natural sciences spilled over into the social sciences and furthered the use of mathematics in the conceptualisation of concrete social phenomena. Industry, based predominately on machines, passed to automation, with production directed by cybernetic control systems. Synthetic materials took their place alongside natural raw materials.

A natural step was to search for a more rational approach to the organisation of labour. Greater and greater demands were being made on everyone, from the unskilled worker upwards, in the production process. A whole new range of specialities came into being: computer programming, data processing, systems analysis, and so on. Science became a key weapon in the struggle for higher labour productivity. Indeed it became so important that it was elevated to the status of a force of production in the GDR and elsewhere. The way forward to the abolition of the distinction between physical and mental labour appeared to be beckoning.

As the STR was a universal phenomenon, it spilled over national boundries. The GDR could look forward to closer economic and scientific integration in Comecon and more contact with the advanced capitalist economies, if only to take cognisance of what was going on.

THE GDR AND THE STR

The GDR and Czechoslovakia welcomed the STR with open arms. Despite the fact that they were the industrially most advanced societies in the socialist bloc, they had to acknowledge the primacy of the Soviet Union. What was Soviet dominance based on? Essentially subjective factors: the USSR was the land of the Great October Revolution; she enjoyed a higher level of consciousness and the CPSU had a greater experience of the class struggle; she was a world power and hence a force in international relations. The STR circumvented all these factors. It legitimised theorising and the challenging of accepted viewpoints. Since scientific research was conducted on a world-wide scale there was no need to regard the Soviet Union as the fount of all scientific wisdom. On a more practical political level the SED leadership used the STR to overcome popular disbelief and to justify the role of the party. Since the GDR and Czechoslovakia enjoyed the highest living standards and recorded the highest labour productivity in Comecon, they had a head start on the others.

The NES/ESS and the STR went together like a horse and carriage. Both promised to boost self-confidence in the future of socialist industry in the GDR. The prospect of a socialist economy which reflected objective conditions in the GDR was very inviting. The country might be able to slough off its pygmy image in international political affairs and put on the cloak of a thrusting, innovative, economic force in the socialist bloc and outside.

The Soviet Union, at the XXIst Congress of the CPSU, in 1961 adopted a new party programme which looked forward to communist society. It boldly declared that science was a force of production and spelled out the meaning of the scientific-technical revolution. The use of atomic energy, man's probing of the cosmos, the developments in chemistry, the automation of production, were merely the harbingers of greater successes. Only socialism, declared the party programme, was capable of bringing the STR to its full fruition. In the worldwide contest, within the context of peaceful co-existence, great emphasis, during the period of socialism, would be placed on economic criteria such as accounting, money, prices, costs, profit, trade, credit and finance. The SED classified science as a force of production in the programme adopted at the VIth Congress in 1963. Further, the empirically oriented social sciences, planning, management and the natural sciences which are of immediate relevance to production were all classified as forces of production. Although the expressions 'technical revolution' or 'scientific-technical revolution' are not to be found in the SED programme, both were employed by Ulbricht in a speech on 6 October 1964 to mark the fifteenth anniversary of the founding of the GDR. Both expressions co-existed side by side until, in 1966, the STR gained the upper hand and at the VIIth Congress, in April 1967, the STR was adopted as a matter of course.

The STR implied greater consultation, more contact between workers and management, more information for everyone, greater technical proficiency from everyone including party functionaries and the need to appeal to self-interest to a greater degree than hitherto. The SED's response was to expand 'socialist democracy'. Permanent production councils, production committees, social councils at VVB level, more commissions of representative institutions at local level and increasing responsibilities for mass organisations, especially the FDGB, were responses to the problem. Political pressure from above was not an efficient way of meeting the challenge of the STR. Precisely that stratum which harboured reservations about the SED, the intelligentsia, had to become more involved in setting the goals of GDR society.

The party was not abdicating its key position. Marxism-Leninism was to remain, as before, the well from which to draw correct answers and scientific guidelines. The SED however was conceding that empirical data, amassed by social scientists, were relevant and could be used when measuring the effectiveness of the guidelines laid down for society. Social contradictions and social conflicts, non-antagonistic of course, were recognised within society. Henceforth things would be more difficult for the SED since it could not merely rely on ideological postulates to justify its policy preferences.

Education was one field in which great successes were recorded. The technical level of the work force was raised significantly and there was a great expansion of trained scientists, engineers and economists. Almost every science received a stimulus and the universities and technical high schools were besieged by aspiring students.

The extravagant hopes held out for the STR in the 1960s were not realised. It was discovered that the whole operation was much more complex than imagined. For example, industrial price reform, a key element in the rationalisation of economic decision making, was not completed. A part of the planning mechanism, the input-output table, was never satisfactorily drawn up. Scientific advance did not of itself guarantee a more socialist society. The driving force behind the STR was the intelligentsia, and instead of breaking down the differences in society and the division of labour it enhanced and hardened them. It did nothing to reduce the gap between mental and physical labour. In socialist industry, in 1971, the level of mechanisation of direct production was 61·4 per cent but that of indirect production (enterprise transport, repairs, packaging, quality control) was only 33·4 per cent.[40] Those employed directly in production dropped from 74·4 per cent in 1962 to 67 per cent in 1970; those involved in research and development rose from 3·2 per cent in 1962 to 5 per cent in 1970; and those classified as belonging to management rose from 6·5 per cent in 1962 to 10 per cent in 1970.[41] Not surprisingly the incomes of production workers rose noticeably faster than those of the working population as a whole between 1965 and 1974.[42] The rush to acquire better qualifications produced too many skilled workers. In one heavy industrial concern, in 1976, 28·6 per cent of jobs intended for semi-skilled workers were being done by skilled workers. In the GDR economy as a whole, in 1976, about 7–10 per cent of skilled workers were doing jobs which did not correspond to their qualifications.[43]

The STR made greater demands on workers. It led to more night shift work to make full use of automatic equipment, and to pollution of the environment, greater nervous strain, boredom and tiredness setting in more quickly as machines reduced the number of operations required of the worker, and resistance to work on the assembly line. Increasing labour productivity often meant worse working conditions and social side-effects such as a decreasing birth rate and an increasing divorce rate. These side-effects might have come about without the STR but it speeded them up.

A more sober approach towards the STR became evident in the late 1960s. The first flush of enthusiasm gave way to a realisation that scientific advance created a host of new problems, some of them completely novel to the SED. The other factor which slowed down the process was the headlong rush of Czechoslovakia to disaster. The SED carried sufficient weight in the GDR to rein-in its more impetuous spirits just when it wanted to.

THE EVOLUTION OF THE PARTY

Although the population of the GDR declined during the 1960s, the SED expanded during the same period:[44]

members and candidate members

December 1957	1,472,932
December 1961	1,610,769
December 1963	1,680,446
December 1966	1,769,912
June 1971	1,909,859

The social composition of the party was as shown in Table 4.2.[45]

TABLE 4.2 The social composition of the party

	1957	1961	1966	1971
Workers	33·8	33·8	45·6	56·6
Peasants	5·0	6·2	6·4	5·9
Employees	42·3	32·6	16·1	13·0
Intelligentsia		8·7	12·3	17·1
Others	18·9	18·7	19·6	7·4
	100·0	100·0	100·0	100·0

A determined effort was made by the party in the 1960s to redress the balance between workers, employees and members of the intelligentsia. The abnormal phenomenon of a workers' party being numerically dominated by non-workers had to be changed. This situation had arisen due to the after-effects of the June 1953 uprising. In 1947, 48·1 per cent of members were workers, 17·6 per cent employees and 4·4 per cent members of the intelligentsia but this ratio changed dramatically after 1953. The party made a concerted effort to recruit skilled workers during the NES/ESS. The party grew by just over 150,000 between 1961 and 1966. Even if all new recruits had been workers the percentage of workers in the party in 1966 would not have climbed to 45·6. A possible explanation would be that large numbers of employees and members of the intelligentsia left the party, but there is little evidence to support this. Indeed the SED was keen and successful in recruiting members from the burgeoning technical intelligentsia. It would appear that some members were reclassified as workers partly due to the STR. The usual practice is for a member, throughout his party career, to be classified according to his job when entering the party. Hence Ulbricht was down as a worker even though he was a full-time party functionary. The more active and ambitious members of worker origin quickly left the workbench and rose to positions of responsibility in the party, government and mass organisations. There is no way of telling how many of those listed as workers have done this and what proportion have remained on the factory floor. At the VIth Congress, in 1963, it was stated that 55·5 per cent of the delegates were workers but that almost half of these were performing 'leading functions' in party, government and mass organisations.[46] Further details were given about workers in the party at the VIIth Congress, in 1967:

The character of our party as a party of the working class is expressed by the fact that 61·6 per cent of all members and candidate members were workers on joining the party. A large proportion of these comrades now occupy leading functions in the party, state, economy, police and armed forces; many are acquiring qualifications to become members of the intelligentsia or technical employees.[47]

Does this mean that when workers join the intelligentsia they cease to be classified as workers in party statistics?

Conscious recruitment of skilled workers afterwards pushed up the proportion of workers in the party. Between the VIIth and VIIIth (1971) Congresses, 296,720 candidate members were accepted and of these

211,899 were workers (71·4 per cent).[48] What happens if a non-worker wishes to join the SED and the party does not wish to recruit him? He is advised to try one of the other parties, especially the NDPD.

The proportion of workers in the SED given by Honecker at the VIIIth Congress, in June 1971, was the highest ever attained by the party and has been falling slowly ever since. The brand-new First Secretary also stated that 76·8 per cent of all members were of worker origin.

The term employee is also a floating concept. It includes party and government officials. Workers and employees made up 81·3 per cent of the labour force in 1963 and 84 per cent in 1971.[49] The proportion of workers and employees in the party has never exceeded 70 per cent.

There is no precise definition of intelligentsia as used by the SED. Nevertheless these key individuals almost doubled their proportion within the party during the 1960s. This was partly due to recruitment policies but also to the great expansion of technical education. The increased opportunities were seized by many already in the party. At the VIth Congress, in 1963, the number of members who had graduated from universities and technical colleges was put at about 190,000. This represents just under 12 per cent of the membership. In 1966, there were 283,000 graduates (just over 16 per cent).[50] Honecker stated, also in 1966, that the number of graduates was 372,655 but this may have included some who were soon expected to graduate.[51] Since 12·3 per cent of party members, in 1966, were classified as belonging to the intelligentsia this means that about 4 per cent of graduate members were still being counted according to their original classification.

An increasing number of graduates in the GDR were either in or were joining the ranks of the party. The number of graduates was 437,000 in 1963, and 557,000 in 1966.[52] Hence, in 1966, just over half of all graduates were in the SED. This trend continued during the late 1960s.

The age structure of the party, in 1966, was as shown in Table 4.3.[53]

TABLE 4.3 The age structure of the party, 1966

25 years and under	8·2
26–30 years	12·1
31–40 years	25·1
41–50 years	17·2
51–60 years	16·2
61–5 years	8·3
66 years and over	12·9
	100·0

It was also revealed that 41·2 per cent of members had been fifteen to twenty years in the party and that 6·9 per cent had previously been in the KPD or SPD. The SED was thus a party not yet dominated numerically by those who had become politically active in the context of the SBZ/GDR. It would take another decade before the majority of party members' experience of political life was restricted to the SBZ/GDR.

The Educational Level of Party Functionaries

Party veterans who made and defended the revolution with a rifle in their right hand and a copy of Lenin's writings in their left are splendid performers when it comes to anniversaries or when someone is needed to address the local primary school or youth group. However good they are at winning hearts with their stirring tales it is the party official who can win minds who takes precedence. The SED actively recruited graduates in all disciplines and these new members were often attached to work groups and commissions to provide the local party *apparat* with skilled advice. Gradually some of these graduates moved upwards and became members of the local party executive. The guidelines laid down for selecting the executive of the primary party organisation in 1968 read as follows:

> The new tasks require that special care be taken when deciding the party leadership. Besides comrades who have proved themselves in political work with the masses and with years of experience in the leadership of primary organisations, preference should be given to comrades with scientific knowledge, to engineers, pacesetters and innovators. Party executives will thereby be enabled to solve their problems in a comprehensive manner.[54]

A trend is discernible in the composition of party executives and their work groups and commissions. There are three main groups: party functionaries, technically qualified where possible; representatives of the state and economic administration — some of these are members *ex officio*; and specialists in industry, science and education.[55]

Members of executives and those in the party *apparat* are required, as a matter of course, to enlarge the compass of their political and technical knowledge. There are multifarious ways of doing this. Primary and *Kreis* executive members have the *Kreis* and enterprise schools of Marxism-Leninism. *Bezirk* and large enterprise executives have special 'educational centres' or party schools. The Central Committee has its own party schools and the zenith is the Karl Marx Party University.[56]

In 1967, over 100,000 executive members of primary organisations were graduates.[57] If one estimates five to six executive members, on average, for each of the 52,800 primary organisations, about one-third of executive members of primary organisations were graduates. This is in line with the statement that 33·7 per cent of the executive members of primary organisations, elected in 1966–7, were graduates.[58] Hermann Axen, however, stated, in 1968, that 29.6 per cent of the 321,660 executive members of the 52,827 primary organisations and 15,177 subsections were graduates.[59]

There is a wide gulf between the qualifications of executive members of primary organisations in different parts of the country. *Kreis* Döbeln, with a considerable amount of industry, appears to be one extreme. There, in 1967, only 4 per cent of 'comrades had advanced political and technical qualifications and long experience of party work'.[60] On the other hand, graduates made up 50 per cent of the executive members of primary organisations in *Kreis* Berlin-Pankow.[61] One has also to bear in mind that executive members of primary organisations and *Kreis* executive members, with the exception of full-time secretaries, are usually gainfully employed and sit on executives without remuneration.

Considerable stability among party *apparatchiki* was evident, in 1967, from the statement that 77·7 per cent of the first secretaries and 57·5 per cent of second secretaries of *Kreis* executive committees had been over ten years in the party *apparat*.[62] Also 83 per cent of all *Kreis* secretaries (usually 5 to 6 per *Kreis*) were graduates and 64·2 per cent had passed successfully through the Karl Marx Party University.

The same level of academic achievement is not reproduced at the *Bezirk* level. In 1967, of the first secretaries of the 15 *Bezirk* executive committees and *Gebiet* Wismut only 6 were graduates (or 37.5 per cent). Few data are available on the other 79 *Bezirk* secretaries. All *Bezirk* first secretaries are members of the Central Committee. A further 13 secretaries are either members or candidate members. Of these only 2 are graduates.

The Central Committee
The Central Committee elected at the VIth Congress (1963) was much younger than that elected at the previous Congress (1958). The average age of 1963 members was 56 years and that of candidates 40 years. The technical and professional qualifications were also noticeably superior to those of the 1958 CC. Of the 121 members elected in 1963, 27 were graduates. (See Table 4.4.) Another five were at that moment enrolled at

TABLE 4.4 Members and candidates of the CC in 1963 according to the function they were performing when elected; and the proportion of graduates[63]

	Members		Candidates	
	Total	of which graduates	Total	of which graduates
		%		%
Party *apparat*	49	13 (26)	13	6 (46)
State *apparat*	30	8 (27)	12	6 (50)
Leading position in the economy	15	3 (20)	14	10 (70)
Mass organisations	11	3 (27)	6	3 (50)
Education, Culture, Science, Free professions	10	5 (50)	13	10 (77)
Others	5	–	2	–
No information	2	–	–	–
Total	121	32 (26%)	60	35 (58%)

the Karl Marx Party University and later graduated. Hence 32 of the 121 can be considered graduates. Among the 60 candidate members elected in 1963, there were 35 graduates. Candidate members were noticeably better qualified than full members, especially those concerned with the economy and with education, culture and science. Table 4.5 shows that, as in 1963, the 1967 candidate members are better qualified, but there is a

TABLE 4.5 Members and candidates of the CC in 1967 according to the function they were performing when elected; and the proportion of graduates[64]

	Members		Candidates	
	Total	of which graduates	Total	of which graduates
		%		%
Party *apparat*	54	29 (54)	15	10 (67)
State *apparat*	39	18 (46)	13	9 (69)
Leading position in the economy	14	11 (78)	9	8 (89)
Mass Organisations	8	4 (50)	5	5 (100)
Education, Culture, Science, Free professions	11	8 (73)	8	6 (75)
Others	5	–	–	–
Total	131	70 (53%)	50	38 (76%)

marked improvement among full members, most noticeably among those with key economic posts. Some full members acquired academic qualifications between 1963 and 1967. Of the 13 members elected to the CC for the first time at the VIIth Congress (1967), 11 were graduates. Among the 25 new candidates, 19 were graduates. Of the 38 new admissions (13 candidate members were promoted to full membership as well), 16 were employed in the party *apparant*, 14 in the state *apparat*, 2 were leading economic functionaries, 2 were involved in the mass organisations and 2 were in education, culture and science. The overall effect was again to lower the average age of the CC. The average age of members was 51 years and that of candidate members 43 years. Table 4.6 shows the figures for 1971. Again the emphasis the party places on professional qualifications is clear. This is most marked among the young candidate members, where those engaged in economic affairs, the mass organisations and in education, culture and science are all graduates. The average age of members rose to 54 years and that of candidates to 45 years. Hence just over 50 per cent of members and candidates were under 50 years of age.

TABLE 4.6 Members and candidates of the CC in 1971 according to the functions they were performing when elected; and the proportion of graduates[65]

	Members		Candidates	
	Total	of which graduates	Total	of which graduates
		%		%
Party *apparat*	58	36 (62)	16	13 (81)
State *apparat*	41	18 (44)	14	11 (78)
Leading position in the economy	10	10 (100)	13	13 (100)
Mass organisations	9	6 (67)	5	5 (100)
Education, Culture, Science, Free professions	12	9 (75)	6	6 (100)
Others	5	–	–	–
Total	135	79 (59%)	54	48 (89%)

An examination of the composition of the CC between the VIth and VIIIth Congresses reveals the following:

The largest group in the CC has remained the party functionaries. The 10 CC secretaries are the core of this group. Then there are the 15 *Bezirk* and *Gebiet* Wismut first secretaries. Other *Bezirk* secretaries, sectional heads of the CC *apparat* and *Kreis* secretaries account for most of the rest.

High officials in the government *apparat* make up the second largest group. The tendency has been for the Council of Ministers to have an increasing proportion of its members in the CC.

There is a sprinkling of directors of VVB in the CC.

The heads of all mass organisations are in the CC.

No Sorb has yet been elected to the CC. This is curious since the Sorbs are an officially recognised Slav minority, numbering about 100,000 and living in and around Bautzen. They held Wilhelm Pieck in high regard, but Walter Ulbricht never concerned himself much with them, let alone addressed one of their Congresses. Given the official recognition of the German minority in Romania, with their representation in the Romanian Council of State and the CC of the Romanian Communist Party, one would have expected at least one Sorb to have been guaranteed a place on the CC of the SED.

The Secretariat

The Secretariat of the Central Committee is the brain of the party through which all the threads of decision-making in the state pass. The Politburo and the Secretariat are the key institutions in the GDR. Between them they take all major decisions. The Secretariat is headed by a First Secretary (or Secretary-General since 1976). Walter Ulbricht filled this role until May 1971.

The other secretaries elected at the VIth Congress in 1963 were:

Gerhard Grüneberg, (born 1921)	agriculture
Kurt Hager, (born 1912)	ideology
Erich Honecker, (born 1912)	security
Günter Mittag, (born 1926)	economic affairs
Albert Norden, (born 1904)	agitation
Paul Verner, (born 1911)	West German affairs

Hermann Axen (born 1916) became a secretary, responsible for international relations, in February 1966. Werner Jarowinsky (born 1927) joined in November 1963 and was made responsible for domestic and foreign trade and supply. Werner Lamberz (born 1929) was elected secretary responsible for agitation and propaganda at the VIIth Congress, in April 1967. On 3 May 1971 Walter Ulbricht was replaced as First Secretary by Erich Honecker. Paul Verner took over Honecker's responsibilities for security.

A striking factor is the stability of membership of the Secretariat. Another is the division between the mature members (4 over 50 years old in 1963, Axen was almost 50 years old when he joined in 1966) and the

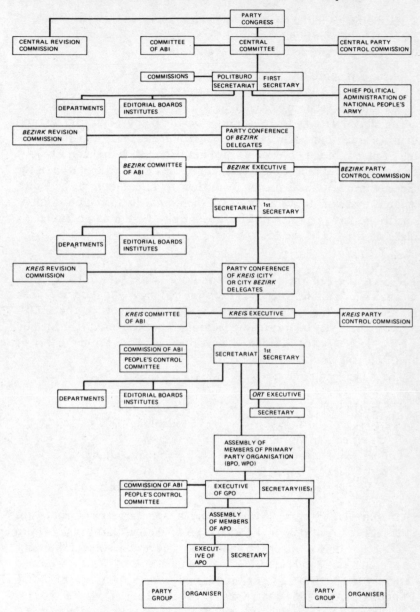

FIGURE 4.4 Organisational framework of the SED in 1971

ABI = Workers' and Peasants' Inspectorate
GPO = Primary Party Organisation
BPO = Enterprise Party Organisation

youthfulness of the others. Mittag was 37 years old in 1963 – he became secretary for economic affairs in June 1962; Jarowinsky, 36 when he joined in 1963; Lamberz 38 on joining in 1967.

There are about forty departments of the Central Committee, with about 2000 key functionaries, and all are responsible to a secretary of the CC. The departments mirror all the functions covered by the government and the party. They range from agitation, health, trade unions, Comecon affairs, science, to sport, legal questions, mechanical engineering and metallurgy. These departmental heads are sometimes promoted to a secretaryship of the CC.

The CC departments perform the everyday tasks.[66] They collect information, prepare papers on current problems and may on occasion suggest possible solutions. In this way they can influence discussions in the Politburo and the Council of Ministers. The CC departments maintain contact with their CPSU and other communist party opposites. They even have their own primary party organisation.

The Secretariat of the CC meets, it is believed, every Thursday under the chairmanship of its First Secretary. All party work is planned in advance and co-ordinated by the Secretariat. In 1971, all secretaries were either members or candidate members of the Politburo with the exception of Horst Dohlus, secretary for party organs. Hence these top functionaries have the greatest influence on party and state decision-making. They have at their elbow the technical information, provided by the CC departments, so that they marry in their person ideological and technical expertise. This leads, doubtless, from time to time, to friction with the other competing bureaucracies.

It is not easy to distinguish clearly between the competence of the Secretariat and that of the Politburo. The Secretariat is mainly concerned with party affairs – party elections, cadres policy, party schooling, directives to *Bezirk* and *Kreis* executives, and supervision of all lower-level party *apparats* by means of work groups and commissions. The Politburo takes the decisions which affect state and society as a whole. The Politburo has its own bureau which acts as a go-between between it and the secretariat. Its head has the rank of a CC

WPO = Residence Party Organisation
APO = Departmental Party Organisation
A primary party organisation is formed when three party members are to be found. If more than 150 members are enrolled in the GPO, departmental party organisations (APO) may be formed. Party groups may be formed embracing workers doing the same job in an APO or a GPO with less than 150 members. See IVth SED Statute, Articles 56–61.

Source: *DDR-Handbuch*, p. 760

departmental head. It prepares the agenda for Politburo meetings. It is also responsible for organising top-level conferences, running the party's own courier service and guiding the technical and administrative departments of the CC.

The Secretariat is not only immediately responsible for party organs but also includes under its wing the state and economic apparatus and all social institutions. A secretary or CC departmental head cannot formally issue instructions to a minister or state secretary but, due to the leading role of the party, the minister or state secretary may find it very difficult to ignore party recommendations or suggestions. Generally speaking a CC departmental head is the equal of any minister. The legislative activity of the *Volkskammer* is set in motion by suggestions and draft decrees emanating from the Secretariat, revealing once again its all-embracing role.

The Secretariat's key role is illustrated by the fact that all leading positions in party and state are filled by nominees of its cadres commission. It has also a decisive say in the election of new members to the CC.

Each secretary has his own bureau, with a head and, on average, three to five assistants. The head of the bureau enjoys the rank of a CC departmental head and takes part in discussions with CC department heads on an equal footing.

Party decrees and their significance for *Bezirk* and *Kreis* party organisations are analysed and explained by secretaries of the CC at conferences and meetings with *Bezirk* and *Kreis* first secretaries at the CC's special school in Brandenburg. Leading central functionaries may also address in person certain *Bezirk* or *Kreis* party organisations, e.g. at times of crisis, during party elections, etc. Printed information from the centre to the local party organisation and vice versa also plays an important role in making clear the party line. If the Secretariat believes that deficiencies have become evident in the work of a *Bezirk* or *Kreis* organisation then work groups or instructor brigades are despatched to remedy the situation. This action has also been taken in large enterprises.

The Politburo

According to the party statute, the CC elects the Politburo as political head of the work of the CC between plenary sessions. These should take place at least once every six months. The effective power of the Politburo is hardly discernible from such phrasing.

The Politburo elected at the VIth Congress, in 1963, consisted of 14 members and 9 candidates. Besides Walter Ulbricht, the full members were Friedrich Ebert, Paul Fröhlich, Otto Grotewohl, Kurt Hager, Erich Honecker, Bruno Leuschner, Hermann Matern, Erich Mückenberger, Alfred Neumann, Albert Norden, Willi Stoph, Paul Verner and Herbert Warnke. The candidate members were: Erich Apel, Hermann Axen, Karl-Heinz Bartsch, Georg Ewald, Gerhard Grüneberg, Werner Jarowinsky, Günter Mittag, Margarete Müller and Horst Sindermann. By the VIIth Congress, in 1967, the scythe of time had removed Otto Grotewohl and Bruno Leuschner; Erich Apel had taken his own life; Karl-Heinz Bartsch had been unmasked as a former member of the Waffen-SS; and Gerhard Grüneberg and Günter Mittag had become full members, in September 1966. Horst Sindermann became a full member at the Congress. Walter Halbritter and Günther Kleiber became candidate members. Between the VIIth and VIIIth Congresses, Paul Fröhlich and Hermann Matern, chairman of the Central Party Control Commission, died.

Hermann Axen became a full member in December 1970, replacing Paul Fröhlich. Werner Lamberz was promoted to candidate member at the same time. The VIIIth Congress, in 1971, saw some changes. (See Table 4.7.) Erich Honecker had replaced Walter Ulbricht just before the Congress. Ulbricht stayed in the Politburo but he passed all his party functions to Honecker. Werner Lamberz became a full member, as did Werner Krolikowski, first secretary in *Bezirk* Dresden, without ever having been a candidate member. Harry Tisch, first secretary in *Bezirk* Rostock and Erich Mielke, Minister of State Security, became candidate members.

Each Politburo member is responsible for a specific area of policy and the Politburo has its own commissions, e.g. the commission on national security, headed by Paul Verner.

Compared to the 1950s, the 1960s were a period of remarkable stability. No one left the Politburo as a result of policy differences with the First Secretary. Young, competent, educated cadres were drawn in and the SED's image thereby improved. As one would expect the candidate members are better educated than full members of the Politburo. Exceptions among full members are Werner Lamberz and Günter Mittag. Lamberz exhibits great skill in creatively interpreting Marxism-Leninism and the emphasis placed on ideology by the CPSU underlines the importance of his position as secretary for agitation and propaganda. Mittag unites considerable economic expertise with hard-headed political realism. Although often described as a technocrat, he came out, for example, in 1968, with an uncompromising demand for all questions to be resolved from an unequivocal Marxist-Leninist viewpoint.

TABLE 4.7 Members and candidates of the Politburo and the CC Secretariat (elected at the VIIIth Congress, June 1971)[67]

Name	Date of birth	Party member since	Politburo member (CC member)	Politburo candidate (CC candidate)	CC Secretariat	Other party or state function
Honecker, Erich	1912	1929 KPD	1958 CC 1946	1950	First Sec. (sec. 1958)	Chairman, National Defence Council; member of Council of State; member of *Volkskammer*
Axen, Hermann	1916	1942 KPD	1970 CC 1950	1963	Int. Relations 1966	Member of *Volkskammer*
Ebert, Friedrich	1894	1913 SPD	1949 CC 1946	—	—	Deputy Chairman of *Volkskammer*; member of Council of State
Grüneberg, Gerhard	1921	1946 KPD	1966 CC 1958	1959	Agriculture 1958	Member of *Volkskammer*
Hager, Kurt	1912	1930 KPD	1963 CC 1954	1958 CC 1950	Ideology, Science, Education, Culture 1955	Member of *Volkskammer*
Krolikowski, Werner	1928	1946 SED	1971 CC 1963	—	—	First Sec. *Bezirk* Dresden; member of *Volkskammer*

Lamberz, Werner	1929	1947 SED	1971 CC 1967	1970 CC 1963	Agitation 1967	Member of *Volkskammer*
Mittag, Günter	1926	1946 SED	1966 CC 1962	1963 CC 1958	Economic Affairs 1962	Member of *Volkskammer*
Mückenberger, Erich	1910	1927 SPD	1958 CC 1950	1963 CC 1950	–	Chairman, Central Party Control Commission; 1971; member of Presidium of *Volkskammer*
Neumann, Alfred	1909	1929 KPD	1958 CC 1954	1954	–	First Deputy Chairman of Council of Ministers; member of *Volkskammer*
Norden, Albert	1904	1920 KPD	1958 CC 1955	–	Propaganda and bloc parties 1955	Member of *Volkskammer*
Sindermann, Horst	1915	1945 KPD	1967 CC 1963	1963 CC 1958	–	First Secretary of *Bezirk* Halle; member of *Volkskammer*
Stoph, Willi	1914	1931 KPD	1953 CC 1950	–	–	Chairman of Council of Ministers; Deputy Chairman of Council of State; member of *Volkskammer*
Verner, Paul	1911	1929 KPD	1963 CC 1950	1958	Security 1971	Member of Council of State; member of *Volkskammer*
Ulbricht, Walter	1893	1912 SPD 1919 KPD	1946 CC 1946	–	–	Chairman of Council of State; member of *Volkskammer*

TABLE 4.7 (continued).

Name	Date of birth	Party member since	Politburo CC member candidate	CC Secretariat	Other party or state function
CANDIDATES					
Ewald, Georg	1926	1946 SED	– CC 1963	1963	–	Chairman of Council of Agriculture and Food; member of *Volkskammer*
Halbritter, Walter	1927	1946 SED	– CC 1967	1967	–	Head of the Bureau of Prices; member of *Volkskammer*
Jarowinsky, Werner	1927	1945 KPD	– CC 1967	1963	Trade and Supply 1963	Member of *Volkskammer*
Kleiber, Günther	1931	1949 SED	– CC 1967	1967	–	Deputy Chairman of Council of Ministers; member of *Volkskammer*
Tisch, Harry	1927	1945 KPD	– CC 1963	1971	–	First Secretary of *Bezirk* Rostock; member of *Volkskammer*
Mielke, Erich	1907	1925 KPD	– CC 1950	1971	–	Minister of State Security; member of *Volkskammer*
Müller, Margarete	1931	1951 SED	– CC 1963	1963	–	Member of Council of State; member of *Volkskammer*

Women in the Party

Women have always been in the majority in the GDR. A very heavy burden was placed upon them immediately after the war. As almost all men of military age were prisoners-of-war women had to take over most jobs. The SED paid great attention to party work among women. The Democratic Women's Association of Germany (DFD) was very active and women quickly made up a substantial proportion of trade union (FDGB) membership. In the 1960s women made up more than 50 per cent of the population, just under 50 per cent of the labour force and trade union members. Despite this, female membership of the SED has always lagged far behind the proportion of women and the roles they play in society. There has been a constant increase in the proportion of women in the party over the years but in December 1966 it was only 26·5 per cent. By the VIIIth Congress, in June 1971, it had risen to 28·7 per cent. However this was a higher proportion than in the CPSU. In it women made up only 19·5 per cent of members and candidates in 1961, but this had risen to 22·2 per cent by 1971.

What role do women play in the SED *apparat*?

In the 15 *Bezirk* executive committees, elected in May 1971, 24·9 per cent of members were women and 42·7 per cent of candidate members were women. However of the 90 *Bezirk* secretaries only 4 were women and of the 195 *Bezirk* secretariat members only 9 were women.[68] Among the 121 members of the CC, elected at the VIth Congress in 1963, 15 were women (12·4 per cent); 5 of the 60 candidate members were women (8·3 per cent). At the VIIth Congress in 1967, 16 women were among the 131 members (12·2 per cent) and 6 of the 50 candidates were female (12 per cent). Women increased their representation at the VIIIth Congress in 1971. Of the 135 members, 18 were members (13·3 per cent) and of the 54 candidates, 7 were women (13·0 per cent). No woman has ever been elected a full member of the Politburo since its inception in January 1949. However, Margarete Müller was made a candidate member in 1963 and has remained so ever since. There were no women among the 10 secretaries of the CC in 1971.

Women were as underrepresented in the state *apparat* as they were in the party *apparat* in 1971. Of the 15 *Bezirk* councils, only 1 was headed by a woman, Irma Uschkamp in Cottbus. There was only 1 woman in the Council of Ministers: Margot Honecker, wife of the Secretary-General, as Minister of Education. Margarete Wittkowski, President of the State Bank was the only other woman to occupy a key post in the state. Both women were members of the CC in 1971. Among the 150-odd state secretaries and deputy ministers only 3 were female; 5 of the 25 members of the Council of State, in 1971, were women. One woman who was a member between 1967 and 1971 was Maria Schneider. Her unique distinction is that she was the first Sorb to be elected to a leading GDR institution.

Hence the limited representation of women in the upper echelons of the SED is also mirrored in the centres of decision-making in the government. This phenomenon is also present in other socialist countries, notably the USSR. There are no women in the Politburo, no secretaries of the CC and few in the CC of the CPSU. So the GDR is not an exception. How is this to be explained in a country which claims that women have the same opportunities as men? Traditional prejudice against career women, the close link between key positions in the SED and the government, a shortage of suitably qualified women for leading positions, the concentration of women in certain political and economic fields, the burden of work, children and the home (76·3 per cent of women of working age were employed in 1967[69] and this figure continued to rise afterwards), the fact that top jobs require more travel and more time spent away from home and the lack of organisations which will effectively promote the political interests of women – these are some of the reasons which explain the position women find themselves in in the GDR. Why are women not joining the party in greater numbers? It is true that the proportion of women in the party is steadily rising but there does seem to be some reluctance to join the SED. Perhaps the prospect of party responsibilities, including the need to attend evening meetings, is too daunting for many women, who are over-occupied as it is. Or perhaps the key is that the percentage of women in the SED reflects the role they play in the GDR. If half the leading positions in the country were filled by women perhaps half the membership of the party would be female. That day may be a long way off, for as Gabriele Gast pithily puts it in her book *Die politische Rolle der Frau in der DDR* 'Where there is power – you will find no women.'

RELATIONS WITH THE FEDERAL REPUBLIC

The Berlin Question
West Berlin was always a thorn in the flesh for the GDR. Not only did it represent a capitalist island in a red sea but it was also a base for Western troops. The Four-Power Agreement meant that the Western Powers had rights of access by land and air. This was a further irritant for the GDR. However, in 1955, the Soviet Union handed over control of civilian

traffic to and from West Berlin to the GDR. Nevertheless the Western Powers still regarded the USSR as holding jurisdiction in these matters.

Prior to 1958 the GDR had never objected to the presence of West German representative institutions in West Berlin. Indeed the GDR had welcomed the convocation of the *Bundesversammlung*, held to elect the Federal President in 1954 and the *Bundestag*, or lower house, in 1955. Why then was there a change of policy in 1958? Challenging the legitimacy of the West German presence in West Berlin promised to enhance the prestige of the GDR. If the GDR could undermine the foundations on which the West German presence in West Berlin rested, the USSR would benefit also. By bringing successfully into doubt the legal position of the West German presence, the legal position of the Western Powers could also be questioned. This could only be done successfully by the Soviet Union. By allowing the GDR to act as a stalking horse, the USSR was accepting the risk that at a future date, when the interests of the GDR and the USSR diverged, the GDR might be able decisively to influence policy on Berlin. This the GDR could do by launching an initiative which was not fully in accord with Soviet policy. In such a case the USSR might find it difficult to dissociate herself from the GDR move.

When a plenary session of the *Bundestag* was scheduled for 7 April 1965 in West Berlin, the USSR and the GDR swung into action. The latter published a decree stating that participants would be refused permission to cross GDR territory during the session. This was not only a challenge to Bonn but also to the Western Powers. They had already stated that civilian as well as military access to West Berlin was the result of Allied victory. Until the Four-Power Agreements were abrogated, the GDR could not act unilaterally in such matters. The anomalous situation existed that whereas the access routes were on GDR territory, the Western Powers did not need to acknowledge the existence of that state since the arrangements arrived at in 1945 were still valid. Only a German peace treaty or the Western Powers giving up West Berlin could fundamentally change the situation.

Transit traffic was disrupted. Army manoeuvres across the routes led to the halting of all traffic to West Berlin on several occasions, Soviet Air Force planes crossed the flight path of air traffic to West Berlin and traffic on the waterways stopped for a week. It all suddenly came to an end on 10 April 1965 when the Soviet High Command called off the army manoeuvres. The GDR had stated they were due to end on 11 April. The reason for the abrupt change of heart? The US began to send armoured units to Berlin for the first time on 10 April. The implication was clear. The GDR and the Soviet Union had been playing a diplomatic game but at the first sign of trouble they backed down. The GDR did not take the diplomatic rebuff lying down. At the Xth Plenum of the CC of the SED, on 24 June 1965, Otto Winzer, the newly appointed Foreign Minister, claimed complete and unrestricted sovereignty over the land, water and air of the GDR. He pointed out that the USSR exercised 'control over the flights necessary for communication purposes and the supplying of the three Western Powers in West Berlin'[70] only by virtue of the fact that this right had been conceded to her by the GDR. Furthermore, if the Western Powers wished to overfly the GDR they would have to apply to the GDR government for permission to do so. This was a nice piece of cheek.[71] The picture of Brezhnev, Kosygin and Podgorny entreating the GDR government to concede them one of the rights which they had previously handed over is almost too delicious for words. If one takes Winzer at his word, the GDR had, for the first time since 1945, managed to out-bargain the Soviets! Possibly it was not only the Western Powers which were having their rights of access challenged. If the GDR had made a concession to the Soviet Union presumably at some future date this concession could be withdrawn. Perhaps the Western Powers could have offered the USSR support in their common struggle to preserve their 1945 agreements *vis-à-vis* the increasing power and ambition of the GDR!

The establishment of diplomatic relations between the FRG and Romania, on 31 January 1967, was a nasty shock for the GDR. She had assumed that the Bucharest Declaration of 6 July 1966 was fully binding on all Warsaw Pact countries. The Declaration called for pressure to be brought to bear on the FRG to force her to recognise the GDR as a second German state within her existing frontiers. Romania broke ranks and it appeared that Bulgaria, Hungary and Czechoslovakia were preparing to follow. The GDR pressed very hard at the Warsaw meeting of foreign ministers, in February 1967. She conjured up the picture of the FRG devouring the GDR first and then proceeding to nibble away at the sovereignty of the other Pact states, if a united front was not presented. Ulbricht got his way at the Karlovy Vary conference of European communist parties, in April 1967. Henceforth diplomatic relations with Bonn would depend on the FRG first recognising the GDR.

It may be coincidence but at the same time the GDR decided to underline her unique identity. The State Secretariat for All-German Affairs was renamed the State Secretariat for West German Affairs, on 2

February 1967. A new citizenship law was passed by the *Volkskammer*, on 20 February 1967, repealing the Reich and State Citizenship Law of 1913 and annulling the claim in the GDR constitution which stated that there was only one German citizenship.

Towards a Dialogue with the SPD

In 1966, with the SPD in opposition, the SED decided to launch an initiative to test feeling in the FRG about German unification. The Central Committee of the SED therefore addressed an open letter, on 7 February 1966, to the delegates of the SPD congress, scheduled for Dortmund, in June 1966, and to party members and supporters. This was nothing new. The SED had forwarded twelve open letters to the SPD during the years since 1951 but not one of them had been directly answered. Likewise the SPD had also sent twelve open letters over the period 1951–63.

The latest SED *démarche* appears to have been motivated by three factors: the new Soviet strategy towards social-democracy; the self-confidence of the SED in internal GDR affairs; and the belief that a possible crisis was looming in West Germany.

The new Soviet line, articulated by Academician A. A. Arzumanyan at a conference in Moscow in September 1964, on the occasion of the 100th anniversary of the founding of the First International, was that state monopoly capitalism had arrived and that consequently small private entrepreneurs had transferred some of their economic functions to the state. The crisis capitalism was in had forced the state to act to stabilise the capitalist system. There was a danger that the state might be successful in maintaining the monopolies in power but there was also the possibility that the state, by regulating the economic activity of the nation, was preparing the way for socialism. Arzumanyan believed that the working class in the West could now become a real force since it was no longer solely subject to the monopoly capitalists but was now likely to clash head-on with the state. Whereas previously the confrontation had been mainly economic it would now become political. To gird the working class for battle Arzumanyan called for the unity of all sections of the working class. It followed that communists should now seek to co-operate closely with social-democrats, excluding, of course, the leadership of social-democratic parties.

Water Ulbricht echoed these sentiments on his return from Moscow at a meeting on 25 September 1964, likewise to celebrate the 100th anniversary of the founding of the First International. He called for the 'greatest possible co-operation and unity of communists and social-democrats' without however foregoing the right to criticise 'SPD revisionism and opportunism'. This policy resulted in the SED going to great lengths to stress its desire for a united, democratic Germany. One of the tangible products was the setting up of the State Secretariat for All-German Affairs, headed by Joachim Herrmann, on 17 December 1965.[72]

In its latest missive the SED proposed that the two parties should work together to bring about a German peace treaty and a unified democratic Germany. This time the SPD leadership replied, on 18 March 1966, although technically the SED letter had not been addressed to it. The SPD proposed a wide-ranging discussion about German unity, with all the parties in the two parliaments participating. The SED reacted, on 25 March, proposing that only the SED and SPD should provide speakers. Two joint meetings, one in the GDR and one in the FRG, could be held. The SED wanted the meetings before the Dortmund congress, but the SPD insisted on their taking place afterwards.

The timing of the initiative is significant. The SED had started a propaganda campaign to mark the twentieth anniversary of the fusion of the KPD and the SPD in April 1946. Then *Neues Deutschland*, on 26 March 1966, published the SPD reply to the SED proposals. This was a bold step since it was the first occasion for twenty years that social-democratic views were given prominence in the SED official organ. The result was predictable: all 800,000 copies printed were sold in a few hours. Enormous interest was aroused in the GDR and hundreds of meetings were held to expound the SED position. However the wall and the order to fire on anyone attempting to cross the GDR-FRG border were two very sticky problems for party speakers. The response on the other side of the border, in West Germany, did not come up to SED expectations and this fact, allied to the unwillingness of many GDR citizens to accept SED views at face value, led the XXth Plenum of the CC of the SED, on 28 April 1966, to postpone the proposed dialogue from May to July 1966. Meanwhile the second SPD letter, dated 15 April, had arrived, but it was not publicly acknowledged until 30 April, when *Neues Deutschland* only published extracts, with little attention paid to comments about the wall, border shootings and travel restrictions. The SPD called for the full publication of its second letter on several occasions but this request was not acceded to until 29 May.

The writing was on the wall. The SED multiplied the number of conditions which had to be met before it would send speakers, thus effectively terminating the initiative. The SPD, for its part, entered the Grand Coalition with the CDU/CSU, in December 1966, thus ending any lingering SED hope that a wedge could be driven between the SPD and the CDU/CSU on the preconditions necessary for Germany unity.

Back to Berlin

Talks between Andrei Gromyko and Egon Bahr aimed at improving Soviet-German relations got under way in Moscow on 30 January 1970. The USSR wanted the FRG, above all, to recognise the existing borders in Europe and to renounce force in international relations. Not only did the Soviet Union want the territorial *status quo* to be recognised, but she also wanted the FRG to accept the irrevocability of existing frontiers. This implied that existing frontiers could never be changed and negated the prospect of a future unified Germany. Moscow also shared the GDR's view that Bonn should recognise the GDR in international law. Hence the West Germans found that in negotiating with the Soviets they were once again face-to-face with the thorny problem of intra-German relations.

However, Bahr came up with a counter-argument which won him some room for manoeuvre. In his view neither the FRG or the GDR was a fully sovereign state. Only when a German peace treaty was signed would they become so. Hence in international law the FRG could not recognise the GDR and vice versa. The reason was that the four powers, as victors, had assumed control over Berlin and the whole of Germany in 1945. This made them competent to negotiate matters which extended beyond the frontiers of their respective zones. There were two German states, and Chancellor Willy Brandt had recognised this for the first time on 28 October 1969, but they existed under the umbrella of the Great Powers. Hence, as Brandt pointed out, they were not foreign to each other. The FRG could not recognise the GDR in international law and thereby settle the problem of Germany's division and Germany's future since this would imply rejection of four-power responsibility. Neither the FRG nor the GDR could act unilaterally in these matters. The problem could only finally be solved by a peace treaty with all interested parties participating. These points did not fall on deaf Soviet ears and the talks made such progress that a draft treaty was ready by 22 May 1970.

While these negotiations were going on in Moscow, Bonn was attempting to improve relations with East Berlin. Willy Brandt sent Willi Stoph, Chairman of the GDR Council of Ministers, a note on 22 January 1970 suggesting discussions on the future nature of relations between the two German states. The GDR was hesitant about entering into talks and acted defensively. One of the demands made was that

Brandt should not pass through West Berlin on his way to East Berlin, where talks could take place. How could Brandt, a former ruling *Bürgermeister* of West Berlin, accept such a precondition for talks? Clearly East Berlin was not keen on an exchange of views on its own territory. However a compromise was reached and Erfurt was chosen as the first meeting place, on 19 March 1970. Stoph took a hard line at Erfurt. One of his demands was that the FRG should recognise the GDR in international law, something that Moscow had already agreed with Bonn could not be done at that moment. A second meeting was arranged for Kassel, just across the border in West Germany, on 21 May. Stoph maintained his unyielding position and asked for 100,000 million Marks compensation for the damage done to the GDR economy before the building of the wall in 1961. His demands implied rejection of Brandt's twenty-point programme. The stance adopted by Stoph at the two sessions demonstrates that the GDR leadership was opposed to the meetings. An event occurred at Erfurt to convince them that publicised meetings in the GDR of East and West German statesmen were inadvisable. Brandt was given a tremendous reception by the crowds in Erfurt. Shouts of 'Willy, Willy' filled the air. When reproached by police the local people insisted that they had been shouting 'Willi, Willi' (Stoph). Since there is no phonetic difference between the two names it was a point nicely made. Why then did the meetings come about? There appears little doubt that the prompting came from Moscow. Stoph's conduct was calculated to produce a frosty atmosphere but not to lead to a breakdown of the talks. Indicative of this was an incident, in Kassel, when the GDR flag was torn down and burnt. The GDR Prime Minister did not break off talks but merely stated that a 'pause for thought' was necessary before the next meeting.

The Moscow Treaty was signed by Chancellor Willy Brandt and Foreign Minister Walter Scheel for the FRG and by Alexei Kosygin and Andrei Gromyko for the USSR, on 12 August 1970. While in the Soviet Union Brandt had discussions with Leonid Brezhnev. He pointed out to the Secretary-General of the CPSU that without a satisfactory Berlin settlement it would not be possible to secure a majority for the ratification of the treaty in the Federal Parliament.[73]

Four-power negotiations on Berlin had begun on 26 March 1970. The USSR and the Western Powers were poles apart in their attitudes. The USSR considered East Berlin an integral part of the GDR, so only West Berlin was the subject of four-power control. The Soviet Union wished to separate West Berlin from the FRG and have this recognised in international law. The West regarded the whole of Berlin as under four-power control and wished to discuss transit rights. The Soviet answer was that these should be discussed with the government of the GDR, over whose territory they ran.

Walter Ulbricht, on 8 November 1970, speaking for the GDR, insisted that a transit agreement could only be concluded when the special political status of West Berlin had been acknowledged.[74] He underlined once again that the GDR would not accept any restriction of her sovereignty over access routes to West Berlin. Arrangements could be reached with the Federal government and the West Berlin senate. However the USSR, in the meantime, had changed her position. She was no longer insisting that acceptance of a special political status for West Berlin had to precede a transit agreement. So the GDR was again out of step and what is more Ulbricht wanted 'all activities by other states' in Berlin to cease.[75] This implied that the Western Powers had no rights in West Berlin. Since the Soviet Union was keen to reach an agreement with the Western Powers on West Berlin and thereby improve her image in Bonn there was bound to be conflict with the GDR, who only wanted an agreement on her own terms. Whereas the GDR could wait to kingdom come to win the day, the USSR could not. Moscow was hoping that the treaty with the FRG and a mutually acceptable Berlin solution would lead to the FRG gradually loosening her close ties with the Atlantic alliance.

The covert dissent between Moscow and East Berlin became overt dissent at the Xth Congress of the Hungarian Socialist Workers' Party, in Budapest, at the end of November 1970. Brezhnev had hoped to meet Ulbricht to iron out the differences between them but the SED First Secretary sent Friedrich Ebert, a former social-democrat, as head of the SED delegation. Ebert was only on the periphery of the SED leadership, so it was certain that anything he might say to Brezhnev would not be regarded as binding on Ulbricht. During the Congress Gromyko turned up in East Berlin but got no change out of Ulbricht.[76] At a Warsaw Pact summit, in Berlin on 2 December, Brezhnev and Ulbricht clashed head-on.[77] It would appear that Ulbricht's views on the whole prevailed. This meant that the four-power talks at ambassadorial level made little progress in early 1971. However, the atmosphere changed in May 1971 and the negotiators began to pencil-in a draft treaty. It was no accident that Soviet flexibility increased after the departure of Walter Ulbricht as First Secretary of the SED, on 3 May. The vital breakthrough came on 11 August. American commentators see a link between this and Henry Kissinger's visit to Peking and the announcement that President Richard Nixon was to visit the Chinese capital.[78] The text was ready for signing on 2 September but just beforehand it was discovered that the German translation (and interpretation) of the four-power agreement by the GDR was at variance, on several points, with the West German version. Under pressure the FRG and GDR agreed an official translation but a low-ranking official signed for the GDR. The Berlin Agreement was then signed on 3 September 1971. Straight away *Neues Deutschland* published a translation of the text which reverted to the original translation and ignored the one signed the day before.[79] It translated the Russian *svyazy*, the English *links* and the French *liens* as *Verbindungen* – an imprecise term in German – instead of the agreed and stronger *Bindungen* between West Berlin and the FRG. Another complication was that whereas the English and French terms imply that West Berlin may develop political ties which do not conflict with the supreme authority of the Western Powers, the Russian term implies that no political ties between West Berlin and the FRG are permissible.[80]

It was never made clear, because of differing interpretations, whether the Four-Power Agreement applied to the whole of Berlin or merely to the Western sectors. *Pravda* referred to it as the Four Power Agreement but in its editorial spoke of an agreement on West Berlin.[81] There was agreement that West Berlin did not form part of the FRG and was not to be governed by her. However the FRG could represent West Berlin abroad, although all questions concerning security or status were to remain the prerogative of the Western Powers. The GDR, however, refused to countenance the view that Bonn could represent West Berlin's interests in matters affecting transit between the FRG and West Berlin. The GDR negotiators maintained that only the West Berlin senate was competent in these matters.

The GDR had no particular interest in the proper functioning of the Four-Power Agreement on Berlin but the USSR had. The Soviet Union wanted the Moscow Treaty to be ratified by the West German parliament, the Berlin Agreement to become operational, the Conference on Security and Co-operation in Europe to meet and Washington to be wooed away from its flirtation with the Chinese.

Brezhnev reverted to his habit of dropping into East Berlin for a chat on his way home from distant parts. On 30 October 1971 he flew in *en route* from Paris to Moscow. Honecker proved less obdurate than Ulbricht and GDR negotiators suddenly revealed a willingness to discuss access to and from West Berlin with the FRG. The GDR had to accept, also, that the negotiations between the two German states formed part of the Four-Power Agreement. Eventually accord was reached and a document was signed on 17 December 1971.

Brezhnev's keen interest in a European security conference, sooner rather than later, meant that the USSR wanted speedy ratification of the Moscow Treaty and the Berlin Agreement. The Western Powers made it clear to the Soviet Union that Helsinki could only come after Moscow and Berlin. Since East Berlin was the main stumbling block, Brezhnev had to prevail on Honecker to make the vital concessions. This he was able to do and the way was open for the passage of the Moscow Treaty through the *Bundestag* and *Bundesrat*. This was achieved on 17 and 19 May 1972 respectively. The Berlin Agreement, together with the supplementary FRG-GDR accords, came into force on 3 June 1972 with the signing of the final protocol.[82] The last barrier on the road to Helsinki had been removed.

A NEW VIEW OF SOCIALISM

Walter Ulbricht used the occasion of the 100th anniversary of the publication of Karl Marx's *Das Kapital*, in September 1967, to amend the master's definition of socialism. Marx understood socialism as the first, lower phase on the road to communism. To him socialism did not possess any completely new qualities, it would bear the birthmarks of the old society from whose womb it had emerged. Ulbricht, on the other hand, stated that socialism was not 'a short transition phase in the development of society . . . but a relatively independent socio-economic formation during the historical epoch of the transition from capitalism to communism'.[83] Only one further step was needed to anchor socialism in the present and relegate communism to the distant future: declare that socialism developed on its own base. The man who took this step was, appropriately enough, Günter Mittag, the leading economic brain behind the economic reforms of the 1960s. What led Ulbricht, ably abetted by Mittag, to introduce such a radical revision of Marx?

The fundamental reason was that socialism had not been victorious on a world scale. Given the fact that advanced capitalist industrial states still existed where the forces of production were more developed and labour productivity was higher, it was necessary to stretch the definition of socialism to allow time for the socialist states to catch up and outstrip the capitalists. When that happened, as Vladimir Ilich Lenin had pointed out, the victory of socialism over capitalism would be secure.

Why not follow the Soviet example and accept the orthodox Marxist definition of socialism? The SED did not go along with one particular strand of the Soviet view. The CPSU argued that the foundations of communism could be built in a socialist state even before the forces of production and labour productivity had attained the levels prevailing in advanced capitalist states. It based its contention on the argument that the forces of production and labour productivity in the USSR, although behind at the present time, would eventually outstrip capitalist levels. Why should this happen? It would happen because the rates of growth achieved under capitalism would slow down due to the inherent contradictions of the system. The SED did not go along with this sanguine interpretation, it believed that socialism had to be more industrially advanced than capitalism before the foundations of the communist society could be built. Given this view it is a short step to the opinion that socialism will be a long march on the road to communism.

Ulbricht had previously accepted that the victory of the socialist relations of production, in 1961, had signified the beginning of the phase of the completion of the construction of socialist society and simultaneously the gradual transition to communism. At the XVIIth Plenum of the CC of the SED, in October 1962, the First Secretary referred to the new phase as the all-round construction of socialism. This had to be attained before the construction of the foundations of the communist society would commence. The construction of socialism meant 'a new increase in the forces of production, based on a complete and rigorous use of the fundamental laws of socialism'.[84] Then at the VIIth Congress, in April 1967, Ulbricht declared that 'the all-round construction of socialism' incorporated 'the formation of the developed social system of socialism'.

An important event occurred at the XXIInd Congress of the CPSU in 1961. Science was reclassified as a force of production, thus transferring it from the superstructure to the base. This added impetus to the scientific-technical revolution and meant that business and management techniques, in use in capitalist economies, could be employed. It also meant that cybernetics, referred to as the 'fundamental science of the coming age' by Khrushchev at the Congress, could be applied to a socialist society. This science, which also includes systems theory, can be defined as a theory of dynamic self-regulating systems. Its main proponent in the GDR was Professor Georg Klaus. One of his aims was to express historical and dialectical materialism in mathematical terms. He understood systems theory to be a force of production of the first order which would provide the rationale for automation. Klaus developed a cybernetic theory of society in which social organisations were to administer themselves in a rational, optimally efficient fashion. Eventually the central organs of state and party would be 'controlled' via feedback by the working population.

Naturally such a theory aroused strong passions, especially among those at the centre who were to be gradually phased out. The battle for cybernetics was fought and won between 1962 and 1965. A major factor in its success was that Ulbricht threw his full weight behind it.

Under the NES the chief activity of the SED was to raise labour productivity but under the ESS the beginnings of a general theory of the planning and management of social processes was evolved.

The state's task was to guide the development of the forces of production (people, the means of production, management, technology and the organisation of production and science) and to promote the socialist human community. This community was possible since the socialist relations of production had produced a completely new class structure. The SED extended the definition of the working class to embrace an increasing number of persons engaged in mental work. It was running the risk of diluting the definition so much that practically the whole working population could squeeze into the working class.

Why did Ulbricht not claim that the GDR was building communism, since labour productivity was highest there?

The First Secretary felt himself in a stronger position *vis-à-vis* the new Soviet collective leadership which took over from Khrushchev, in October 1964. He had been angered by Khrushchev's flirting with Bonn in the summer of 1964 when the First Secretary had attempted a political *rapprochement* with the FRG. This was clear from the message sent to the CPSU by the Politburo of the SED, on 17 October 1964. It referred to the ousted First Secretary's initial implementation of Marxist-Leninist policy, as elaborated by the Central Committee of the CPSU as successful, and contrasted this with his 'final failure' and the fact that 'he was no longer capable of fulfilling his duties'.[85] None of this appears in the CPSU's condemnation of Khrushchev. It became clear, after 1964, that the SED First Secretary was determined to defend the GDR's interests in the international socialist community with more resolution and vigour than in the days of Stalin and Khrushchev. Ulbricht could only do this within certain limits however. He could not claim, for instance, that the GDR was building communism, since primacy had to be afforded the CPSU and the Soviet Union.

Of special concern, besides the FRG, were Poland and Czechoslovakia. This 'northern tier' or 'iron triangle' was closely interlinked, with events in one country rapidly affecting the others. There was one event in

Czechoslovakia which continued to rankle with the SED — the coming in from the cold of Franz Kafka. This had taken place at the Liblice literary conference, in May 1963. There was little the GDR could do to halt the re-emergence of this literary figure who had written exclusively in German. In the post-Dubček era, the SED always came back to the rehabilitation of Kafka as the initial fatal step on the road to revisionism.

The redefinition of socialism underlined Ulbricht's self-confidence. By creatively interpreting Marxist-Leninist theory, he was declaring that the SED could play a leading role in this field. The fact that no other ruling party took up the new definition and that the CPSU, into the bargain, waited until 1970 to rebut this ideological innovation, reveals the extent to which Ulbricht and the SED acted on their own initiative. As the SED First Secretary never failed to remind the others, Karl Marx was German. With the long history of the German labour movement behind it, the SED felt justified in asserting its understanding of the master. There were those in Marx's day who disparagingly referred to his doctrines as German socialism, seeing them as too authoritarian. His latter-day heirs also ran into the same problem.

By stressing the scientific in scientific socialism, Ulbricht reasoned that the party stood a very good chance of winning over a stratum of the population which was vital for the future development of the GDR — the technical intelligentsia. Now that science was part of the base, the scientists and technologists could be given their head to the mutual benefit of party and state. There was a real chance that the legitimacy of the party would gradually be enhanced among this stratum, given that the goal of the SED was now the scientific management of society.

The SED was very conscious of the fact that socialism in the GDR had been built on a solid industrial foundation, inherited from capitalism. This marked the GDR off from the other socialist countries, especially the USSR, which had built socialism on agrarian foundations. This was spelled out thus: 'The developed socialist society has been achieved in a country which was already a highly developed industrial country under capitalism. This in itself is an objective reason for the increasing attractiveness of the GDR in the eyes of the progressive forces in West European capitalist countries.' The GDR went so far as to claim that she was making an increasing contribution to the building of communism in the USSR. The SED prided itself that the GDR was the first country to demonstrate that socialism could also be built in a highly developed industrial state. There were benefits for the USSR as well. Soviet specialists could and did point to the GDR as proof that the 'capitalist criticism that socialism is a form of social organisation only suitable for countries with a low level of industrial development was untrue'.

On reflection, 1967 was Ulbricht's best year. The economic system of socialism, with its increasing emphasis on centralisation, guaranteed the hegemony of the party in economic planning. The redefinition of socialism put the ideological icing on the cake. Karlovy Vary made sure that no East European state would negotiate with the FRG over the head of the GDR. The GDR also signed bilateral treaties of 'friendship, co-operation and mutual assistance' with Poland, Czechoslovakia, Hungary and Bulgaria – additional insurance against Bonn's *Ostpolitik*.

Looked at purely pragmatically, the GDR should have supported Czechoslovakia in 1968. Ulbricht was asserting himself internationally in Eastern Europe and defending the GDR's interests *vis-à-vis* the Soviet Union more vigorously. Arguably, since he wished the GDR to have a greater say in deciding her own model of socialism, he should also have supported Alexander Dubček, who was seeking ideological latitude as well. However several factors led to Ulbricht turning against the Czechs and Slovaks. First their democratisation of socialism was anathema to the SED. It implied a less centralised leadership, more local initiative and the loss of the communist party's monopoly of political power. The SED could not survive in such an environment. The economic system of socialism implied that the monopoly of political and economic power would remain with the SED and that democratic centralism would be strengthened. Even so the SED's position could be undermined if the Czechoslovak model of socialism proved extremely attractive to the citizens of the GDR.

Another major factor was the fear of increasing West German influence in Czechoslovakia. This in turn would undo the 'iron triangle' and nullify the GDR's success at Karlovy Vary. The fact that the USSR was as alarmed as the GDR at the turn of events in Czechoslovakia provided Ulbricht with the opportunity of playing the role of being the USSR's most reliable ally in Eastern Europe.

The vituperative nature of the propaganda directed against Czechoslovakia by the GDR was only surpassed in one other case – the polemics directed against the FRG. This reveals the depth of unease felt *vis-à-vis* Prague. Ulbricht was not the instigator of the invasion. True he did meet Dubček, ironically at Karlovy Vary, on 13 August 1968. On his return to Berlin he seized the opportunity of reporting negatively on Czechoslovak developments. The catcalls which visibly annoyed him only compounded his resentment at Czechoslovak developments. His point of view, however, was well known – he cannot be accused of proceeding to Karlovy Vary with an open mind – and his report was only one of several assessed by the CPSU leadership.[86]

Two other points underline the independent thinking of the SED. Historically it was claimed that the SBZ/GDR had passed through two revolutions, unlike the other people's democracies. Between 1945 and 1949–52, because of national historical circumstances, the SBZ/GDR had experienced the antifascist-democratic revolution. With this revolution completed, the GDR then passed to the second revolution, the socialist revolution. This was quite different from the experience of the other people's democracies. There, it was maintained, there had been only one revolution, the socialist revolution. It had begun in 1945, with the socialist elements in each country playing the key role. This national distinctiveness of GDR history was only given up after the removal of Ulbricht. At the beginning of the Honecker era, the GDR fell in line with all the other people's democracies and agreed that the socialist revolution really began in 1945 because of the leading role played by socialist elements.[87] The antifascist-democratic revolution, as elsewhere, has been downgraded and is now classified as a stage on the road to socialism.

The concept of the people's state was also understood differently by Ulbricht and the SED. The CPSU programme speaks of a state of the whole people which is a characteristic of a developed socialist society. During the transition period of the construction of developed socialism the state gradually loses its oppressive characteristics, evident during the dictatorship of the proletariat, and becomes the expression of the will and interests of the whole people. Just when the Soviet Union passed from the first to the second stage is a matter of dispute. The state of the whole people is not considered to be a *new* type of state, merely as a stage *en route* to communism. The state of the whole people is doomed to extinction as communism is built, the goal of which being self-administration. This concept of the people's state has never penetrated SED thinking very deeply. True, between 1963 and 1967 it gained some significance.[88] The 1963 SED programme speaks of the 'gradual development of the worker and peasant state, the dictatorship of the proletariat, into a people's state'.[89] However, according to Otto Reinhold, only the 'conditions' for the transformation of the dictatorship of the proletariat are created during the construction of developed socialism.[90] The CPSU, on the other hand, regards the transformation process as being under way during the construction of developed socialism and as being completed once developed socialism has been achieved. The SED tends to ignore the two stages and to link the socialist state to the dictatorship of the proletariat.[91] The GDR presumably feels less secure as a state than the USSR and correspondingly continues to underline the class nature of the state.

In line with the SED's views on the socialist state, as of 1968 scientific socialism was taught at GDR universities not, as in the Soviet case, scientific communism. The latter classifies state organs as the most important political organisations of a socialist society, with the communist party in second position. In the GDR the position is the exact reverse. The SED claims primacy in state and society. In 1972, the concept of scientific socialism gave way to scientific communism, thus bringing the GDR into line once again with the Soviet Union.

DROPPING THE FIRST SECRETARY

Walter Ulbricht did not step down as First Secretary of the CC of the SED: he was pushed. Given the choice, only the undertaker's hearse would have removed him from office. In his resignation speech to the XVIth Plenum of the CC of the SED, on 3 May 1971, Ulbricht admitted that the decision to go had not been easy for him to take. However he was only resigning as First Secretary; he was still holding on to two other key posts: chairman of the Council of State and chairman of the Defence Council. However he was soon eased out of the chairmanship of the Defence Council. To sugar the pill of losing the top party post, the CC elected him chairman of the party 'in honour of his services'. The only other chairmen the SED had ever had were Otto Grotewohl and Wilhelm Pieck, who had been co-chairmen between April 1946 and April 1954. Whereas Grotewohl and Pieck had been co-chairmen of the CC, Ulbricht became chairman of the SED, a vague office not mentioned in the party statute. Although he remained in the Politburo, Ulbricht's days of real influence were over. This was underlined by his role as chairman of the Council of State. By the time of his death on 1 August 1973 the job amounted to little more than shaking hands.

Given that a First Secretary of the CC of the SED cannot be removed and replaced without the consent of the First Secretary of the CC of the CPSU, what factors led Brezhnev to initiate or acquiesce in the ousting of Ulbricht? Who made the initial move? There is little evidence to sustain an argument that it was taken by the East German side. True, Ulbricht had his detractors in the Politburo of the SED but his consummate mastery of intra-party tactics doomed the overt appearance of an 'anti-party group' to almost certain failure. Anyway Ulbricht was approaching his seventy-eighth birthday, in the spring of 1971, so the scythe of time was going to remove him in due course. There were already signs that old age was creeping on: a speech uncompleted here, an address in which he forgot completely what he was talking about there, provided pointers. Why should his obvious successor, *Kronprinz* Erich Honecker, take any risks? A little more patience and all the waiting since 1958 would bear its reward. So it would appear that Moscow made the first move. Another possibility is that since Ulbricht could not be outvoted in the Politburo of the SED, Honecker approached Brezhnev and Brezhnev seized the opportunity of setting the whole train of events in motion. The whole operation· was made easier by the fact that Ulbricht spent seven of the nine weeks between early February and early April in the Soviet Union.

What led the Soviet leadership to part company with Ulbricht? Or expressed in another way, why did the man who had over the course of half a century demonstrated such dazzling doctrinal footwork *vis-à-vis* the CPSU leadership suddenly stumble and fall victim to the axe? Why should Ulbricht's almost legendary flexibility desert him towards the end of his career?

Strange as it may seem, the man who has been labelled Moscow's most faithful lieutenant in Eastern Europe, developed late in life into a national communist: a national communist in the sense that he began to put German interests ahead of Soviet and international communist interests.

The erection of the Berlin wall provided the GDR with the possibility of economic development within firm frontiers. The upsurge of confidence in the party was reflected in the adoption of the new economic system and from then on Ulbricht grasped every opportunity of underling the uniqueness of the GDR experiment. The fall of Khrushchev enhanced Ulbricht's position. He passed from economic to ideological innovation. Socialism was reshaped and Ulbricht began to talk of the socialist people's community in the GDR. The invasion of Czechoslovakia presented the SED with further opportunities of extending its authority. The GDR was held up as a model to be emulated not only in Eastern Europe, but also in Western Europe. Ulbricht made the point that since the GDR was already a highly developed industrial state before the transition to socialism, the path to socialism had been different from the one taken by the Soviet Union. The GDR example was the one for the developed countries of Western Europe to follow. He also claimed that in forming the developed social system of socialism certain elements necessary for the transition to communism were already coming into being. Ulbricht certainly regarded the GDR as the junior partner of the USSR, a far cry from 1945. Indeed his admonitions, his pretentiousness, his pedantry and his 'Vladimir Ilich said to me' style might lead one to the assumption that the GDR regarded herself as at least the equal of the Soviet Union on many issues. In Eastern Europe, Ulbricht found it difficult to break the habit, endemic to some Germans, of going round pointing out ways of improving things to the natives.

The goatee-bearded Saxon also had all-German ambitions. His drive to demonstrate to the world that the GDR was the true heir of German democracy culminated in the description of the GDR in the 1968 constitution as the 'socialist state of the German nation'. Ulbricht always wore bifocals when looking at Germany. To him the German nation still existed but was unfortunately divided into two states. His most fervent wish was to see the FRG recognise the GDR before the conclusion of a Berlin Agreement. He wanted the Western Powers out of West Berlin and a special political status conferred on that part of the city. In GDR parlance there is no East Berlin; that part of the city is referred to as Berlin, capital of the GDR. In other words, Greater Berlin, which had existed in 1945, has passed away and would only be resurrected when West Berlin requested unification with Berlin, capital of the GDR. If the FRG had recognised the GDR before a Berlin settlement was signed the position of the Western Powers would have been considerably weakened. West German and West Berlin traffic account for over 90 per cent of the traffic on the transit routes. With diplomatic recognition the GDR could have imposed any terms she cared to name. She could have prevented all meaningful FRG contact with West Berlin. Since West Berlin's lifeblood comes from the FRG and the city is economically unviable on its own, the Western presence in West Berlin would soon have become a political and economic embarrassment. The First Secretary knew what he was doing. With the Western Powers out of West Berlin, the GDR could unite the two parts of the city. Berlin would no longer only be the capital of the GDR, it would be the potential capital of a unified Germany – a united socialist Germany, of course. This would not only have enhanced GDR influence in all-German affairs, it would have given the GDR more leverage *vis-à-vis* the Soviet Union.

The GDR could only attain these goals if the USSR supported her unconditionally. Whereas GDR foreign policy until the early 1970s was essentially concerned with the German question, Soviet foreign policy embraces the whole world. The Soviet Union decided that the Moscow Treaty, a minimum of conflict with the Western Powers over West Berlin and the prospect of a Helsinki conference took precedence over the wishes and goals of GDR foreign policy. The GDR was willing to wait to kingdom come for diplomatic recognition and the right Berlin settlement but the USSR was in a hurry. She needed Western, including West German, technology and US grain – the two main reasons for détente. She also found the prospect of a Helsinki conference putting the final stamp of approval on the territorial *status quo* in Europe too appealing to be sacrificed. By 1970 it was clear that the interests of the GDR and the USSR diverged considerably. Given the relationship between the two countries, the interests of the Soviet Union were almost certain to prevail. Ulbricht's self-confidence made Brezhnev's task more difficult. This peaked at the XXIVth Congress of the CPSU, in March/April 1971. During his speech Ulbricht said that he was reminded of Vladimir Ilich Lenin and his speech at the IVth Congress of the Comintern on 13 November 1922. Ulbricht declared that Lenin had made an indelible impression on his memory. He had stated that 'after five years of the Russian revolution we must above all learn and then learn some more'. Lenin then added: 'Russian comrades must learn in their own way.' After this bit of Lenin one-upmanship Ulbricht completely omitted to mention China.[92] To underline the fact that the First Secretary was not speaking for the SED, Erich Honecker put the matter right in a speech at Magnitogorsk on 4 April in which he castigated the Chinese in no uncertain manner.[93]

The decision to unseat Ulbricht was probably taken in Moscow during the Congress. A clear sign of how the wind was blowing was provided by the telegram of congratulations sent by the CPSU to the SED on its twenty-fifth birthday, on 21 April 1971.[94] Instead of Brezhnev, as Secretary-General of the CPSU, sending greetings to Ulbricht, as First Secretary of the SED, the telegram was unsigned and was from the CC of the CPSU to the CC of the SED. It praised the roles played by Pieck and Grotewohl in building up the SED. Ulbricht was not even mentioned. In the world of reality, compared to Ulbricht, Pieck and Grotewohl were political pygmies. When Ulbricht stepped down,[95] Brezhnev and the Supreme Commander of Soviet Forces in Germany sent telegrams to Ulbricht and Honecker. Pyotr Abrasimov, the Soviet Ambassador in East Berlin, however, only sent one to Honecker, praising his career in detail and omitting all mention of Ulbricht's role in the communist movement.[96] This is indicative of the frustration which

Abrasimov must have felt, since he had been at the receiving end of Ulbricht's ire at Soviet diplomatic moves for some time.

To the outside world the changeover in the SED leadership appeared smooth and without any overt recriminations between the old and the new First Secretaries. The mask of urbanity, however, slipped on the morning of the opening of the VIIIth Congress of the SED, on 15 June 1971. Walter Ulbricht refused to appear at the Congress to deliver the opening address. The SED responded by making available to the *New York Times* an abrasive account of Ulbricht's resignation, one which contradicted the official version.[97] The leadership took it that Ulbricht was not ill, only 'sick with rage'. The final straw for the former First Secretary was the speech which he was to deliver. It had been handed to him the evening before. He was also given the text of Honecker's speech. This infuriated him since there were many overt criticisms of his political style in it: unreceptiveness to criticism, lack of regard for the collective, and overweening self-confidence. This contrasted sharply with the blithe words which Honecker had uttered at the XVIth Plenum. Ulbricht took umbrage at being expected to listen to such language about his career. His speech, an anodyne one, was read for him, just as it had been written for him. Three main reasons for removing him were given in the leaked report: conducting a policy on West Germany which was independent of the Russians; his creation in the previous four years of a personal apparatus which was above the Central Committee apparatus; and his insistence on a great leap forward, in the Chinese communist pattern, leaving out phases prescribed by the Soviet leaders.[98] The first point is understandable, Ulbricht was in the way of a Berlin settlement. Next the complaint of the Secretariat that Ulbricht, since the VIIth Congress in 1967, had created a personal Secretariat which had, in effect, reduced the influence of the CC Secretariat. This may have put Honecker's position as successor in jeopardy. Certainly promotions to the Politburo at the VIIIth Congress favoured CC secretaries. Then the mentioning of Ulbricht in the same breath as the Chinese – a greater insult would have been hard to find. It refers to his views on socialism, which Honecker dissociated himself from at the Congress.

Why was it not possible for Ulbricht to resign formally at the Congress? It would have provided a fitting platform for the departure of the only First Secretary the party had ever had. However there is little sentiment in politics just as there is little sentiment in business. Ulbricht had intended to deliver his main speech on the 'developed social system of socialism in the 1970s'. The new leadership, however, wanted to change the direction of party and state policy and wished to use the

Congress to publicise this. Had Ulbricht dominated the Congress, Congress resolutions would have borne his unmistakable imprint; so he had to go, gracefully or ungracefully, before the Congress.

NOTES

1 *ND*, 10 February 1962.
2 Martin Jänicke, *Der dritte Weg: Die antistalinistische Opposition gegen Ulbricht seit 1953* (Cologne, 1964) p. 185.
3 *Leipziger Volkszeitung*, 23 August 1961.
4 Hermann Weber, *Von der SBZ zur DDR 1945–1968* (Hanover, 1968) p. 159.
5 Walter Ulbricht, *Die Wirtschaft*, no. 37 (1966) p. 12; Manfred Melzer, 'Das Anlagevermögen der mitteldeutschen Industrie 1955 bis 1966', *Vierteljahrshefte zur Wirtschaftsforschung*, Jg. (1968) Erstes Heft, p. 106.
6 Alfred Zauberman, *Industrial Progress in Poland, Czechoslovakia and East Germany 1937–1962* (London, 1964) p. 33.
7 *Fünfter Tätigkeitsbericht 1965–1969* (Bonn and Berlin, 1969) p. 76.
8 *Dokumente der Sozialistischen Einheitspartei Deutschlands* (Berlin, DDR, 1965) vol. IX, pp. 331–5; Peter C. Ludz, *The Changing Party Eute in East Germany* (Cambridge, Massachusetts, 1972) pp. 97–8.
9 *Fünfter . . .* , p. 43.
10 Melzer, op. cit., pp. 105–6.
11 Manfred Melzer, 'Preispolitik und Preisbildungsprobleme in der DDR', *Vierteljahrshefte zur Wirtschaftsforschung*, Jg. (1969) Drittes Heft, p. 314.
12 Ibid., p. 315.
13 *Fünfter . . .* , p. 99.
14 Manfred Melzer, 'Der Entscheidungsspielraum des VEB in der DDR', *Vierteljahrshefte zur Wirtschaftsforschung*, Jg. (1970) Zweites Heft, p. 145.
15 *A bis Z* (Bonn, 1969) p. 175.
16 *Gesetzblatt der DDR*, II (1963) no. 64, pp. 453–98.
17 Walter Ulbricht, 'Probleme der Ausarbeitung des Perspektivplans bis 1970', *Die Wirtschaft* (14 September 1965).
18 Walter Ulbricht, *Die nationale Mission der DDR und das geistige Schaffen in unserem Staat* (Berlin, 1966) p. 44.
19 Dorothy Miller and Harry Trend, 'Economic Reforms in East Germany', *Problems of Communism*, vol. XV, no. 2 (March/April 1966) p. 34.
20 Walter Ulbricht, *Probleme des Perspektivplans bis 1970* (Berlin, DDR, 1966) p. 15.
21 Walter Ulbricht, *Zum neuen ökonomischen System der Planung und Leitung* (Berlin, DDR, 1966) p. 9.
22 Neil McInnes, 'Havemann and the Dialectic', *Survey*, no. 62 (January 1967) p. 33. Havemann's lectures are reproduced in Robert Havemann, *Dialektik ohne Dogma? Naturwissenschaft und Weltanschauung* (Hamburg, 1964).
23 Ilse Spittmann, 'East Germany: The Swinging Pendulum', *Problems of Communism*, vol. XVI, no. 4 (July/August 1967) p. 15.
24 Ibid., p. 16.

25 *ND*, 23 April 1967.
26 *ND*, 18 April 1967.
27 *ND*, 21 February 1964.
28 Ilse Spittmann, op. cit., p. 16.
29 Before the industrial price reform, subventions to industry amounted annually to about 13,500 million Marks; after the reform to about 7500 million Marks. In 1967, the raw materials sector was to receive subventions amounting to 900 million Marks, agriculture 1700 million Marks, and transport 1100 million Marks. See Günter Mittag, *Die Wirtschaft*, no. 38 (1966); Beilage, p. 7.
30 Just how complex the task of economic administration was can be gleaned from the fact that the SPK received new statutes in 1962, 1964, 1966 and 1967.
31 *ND*, 24 November 1967.
32 Michael Keren, 'The New Economic System in the GDR: An Obituary', *Soviet Studies*, vol. xxiv, no. 4 (April 1973) p. 568.
33 Idem.
34 Peter Mitzscherling *et al.*, *DDR-Wirtschaft Eine Bestandaufnahme* (Frankfurt-am-Main, 1974) p. 67.
35 Ibid., p. 117.
36 Ibid., p. 68.
37 *ND*, 24 September 1970.
38 Mitzscherling *et al.*, op. cit., p. 69.
39 Unless otherwise stated this section is based on Hartmut Zimmermann, 'Politische Aspekte in der Herausbildung, dem Wandel und der Verwendung des Konzepts « Wissenschaftlich-technische Revolution » in der DDR', *DA*, Sonderheft (1976) pp. 17–51.
40 Christoph Ziegenrücker, 'Wissenschaftlich-technischer Fortschritt und Partizipation in der DDR', *DA*, Sonderheft (1976) p. 80.
41 Idem.
42 Frank Grätz and Dieter Voigt, 'Der Einfluss materieller Stimuli auf sozialstrukturelle Veränderungen im Verlauf der wissenschaftlich-technischen Revolution in der DDR', *DA*, Sonderheft (1976) p. 128.
43 Ibid., p. 87.
44 *DDR Handbuch* (Cologne, 1975) p. 762.
45 Ibid. For 1971 See *Protokoll der Verhandlungen des VIII. Parteitages der SED* (Berlin DDR, 1971) vol. i, p. 100.
46 *ND*, 21 January 1963; Eckart Förtsch, *Die SED* (Stuttgart, 1969) p. 104.
47 'Bericht des ZK an den VII. Parteitag der SED', in *Protokoll der Verhandlungen des VII. Parteitages der SED* (Berlin, DDR, 1967) vol. iv, p. 226; Förtsch, op. cit., p. 104.
48 *DDR Handbuch*, p. 762.
49 *Statistisches Jahrbuch der Deutschen Demokratischen Republik 1976* (Berlin, 1976) p. 15.
50 *Protokoll der Verhandlungen des VII. Partitages* . . . vol. iv, p. 225; Förtsch, op. cit., p. 105.
51 *ND*, 19 September 1966; Förtsch, op. cit., p. 105.
52 *Statistisches Jahrbuch der Deutschen Demokratischen Republik 1962*, vol. iv, pp. 226–7; Förtsch, op. cit., p. 105.

53 *Protokoll der Verhandlungen des VII. Partitages* . . . ,vol. IV, pp. 226–7; Förtsch op. cit., p. 105.
54 *Neuer Weg*, no. 2 (1968) pp. 60–1; Förtsch, op. cit., p. 106.
55 Förtsch, op. cit., p. 106.
56 Idem.
57 *Neuer Weg*, no. 7 (1967) p. 319; Förtsch, op. cit., p. 107.
58 *Protokoll der Verhandlungen des VII. Parteitages* . . . , vol. IV, p. 212; Förtsch, op. cit., p. 107.
59 'Bericht des Politbüros as das 6. Plenum', in *Volksarmee*, no. 6 (1968) Beilage; Förtsch, op. cit., p. 107.
60 *Neuer Weg*, no. 2 (1967) p. 57; Förtsch, op. cit., p. 107.
61 *Neuer Weg*, no. 4 (1967) p. 163; Förtsch, op. cit., p. 108.
62 *Neuer Weg*, no. 7 (1967) p. 319; Förtsch, op. cit., p. 108.
63 Förtsch, op. cit., p. 111. Here and elsewhere Hochschule is regarded as a university, Fachschule as a technical college and the Karl Marx Parteihochschule as the Karl Marx Party University. Those who successfully complete courses at all these types of institution are counted as graduates.
64 Ibid p. 112.
65 *SBZ Biographie: Ein biographisches Nachschlagebuch über die sowjetische Besatzungszone Deutschlands* (Bonn and Berlin, 1965); Günter Buch, *Namen and Daten: Biographien wichtiger Personen der DDR* (Berlin, Bonn and Bad Godesberg, 1973).
66 *DDR Handbuch*, p. 332.
67 *A bis Z*, p. 222.
68 *DDR Handbuch*, pp. 766–8.
69 Ibid., pp. 650–5; Förtsch, op. cit., pp. 116–20; Buch, op. cit.
70 Gerhard Wettig, *Die Sowjetunion, die DDR und die Deutschland-Frage 1965–1976 Einvernehmen und Konflikt im sozialistischen Lager* (Stuttgart, 1976) p. 24. Part of this book appeared as *Community and Conflict in the Socialist Camp The Soviet Union, East Germany and the German Problem 1965–1972* (London, 1975).
71 The Soviet leadership took umbrage at these remarks by Winzer. The account of the Xth Plenum published in *Pravda* and *Izvestiya* on 26 June 1965 omitted all mention of the GDR Foreign Minister's speech. The SED also avoided the subject for the next three years. See Wettig, op. cit., p. 190.
72 After the failure of the SED-SPD dialogue to get off the ground its name was changed to the State Secretariat for West German Affairs.
73 Wettig, op. cit., p. 83.
74 Ibid., p. 90.
75 Ibid., p. 91.
76 Ibid., p. 92.
77 Ibid., p. 93.
78 Ibid., p. 109.
79 *ND*, 4 September 1971.
80 Wettig, op. cit., p. 112.
81 *Pravda*, 4 September 1971.
82 Wettig, op. cit., p. 118.

83 Walter Ulbricht, *Die Bedeutung des Werkes Das Kapital von Karl Marx für die Schaffung des entwickelten gesellschaftlichen Systems des Sozialismus in der DDR und den Kampf gegen das staatsmonopolistische Herrschaftssystem in Westdeutschland* (Berlin, DDR, 1967) p. 38.
84 *Dem VI. Parteitag entgegen* (Berlin, DDR, 1962) p. 21.
85 *ND*, 21 November 1964; Wettig, op. cit., p. 12.
86 Melvin Croan, 'Czechoslovakia, Ulbricht and the German Problem', *Problems of Communism*, vol. xviii, no. 1 (January/February 1969) p. 1.
87 Waltraud Falk, 'Der Beginn des planmässigen Aufbaus des Sozialismus in der DDR – Bestandteil des revolutionären Weltprozesses' *Beiträge zur Geschichte der Arbeiterbewegung*, no. 6 (1972) p. 962; Völkel, op. cit., p. 71.
88 Völkel, op. cit., p. 72.
89 *Programm der SED Protokoll des VI. Parteitages der SED* (Berlin, DDR, 1963) vol. iv, p. 374; Völkel, op. cit., p. 72.
90 Otto Reinhold, 'Der historische Platz der entwickelten sozialistischen Gesellschaft', *Einheit*, no. 11 (1972) p. 1471; Völkel, op. cit., p. 72.
91 'Zur Dialektik der Entwicklung der sozialistischen Gesellschaft', *Deutsche Zeitschrift für Philosophie*, no. 5, (1972) p. 602; Völkel, op. cit., 72.
92 *ND*, 1 April 1971.
93 *Pravda*, 5 April 1971; Stoph also attacked the Chinese.
94 *Pravda*, 21 April 1971.
95 According to one GDR source 'Ulbricht went down fighting, trying to the very end to assert his old authority.' See *New York Times*, 22 June 1971.
96 Myron Rush, *How Communist States Change Their Rulers* (Ithaca and London, 1974) p. 200.
97 *New York Times*, 22 June 1971; Rush, op. cit., p. 208.
98 Ibid; Rush, op. cit., p. 210.

5 The Honecker Era

Ulbricht was born a Saxon and Honecker a Saarlander. The first SED First Secretary was at home in the East but the first SED Secretary-General was an outsider whose contact with the East before 1945 was practically non-existent. His formative years were spent in the Saar, an area which was the object of Franco-German rivalry after 1918 and which was only incorporated into the Reich in 1935. It was again severed from Germany in 1945. Honecker, sentenced to ten years' imprisonment in 1937, absconded from a Berlin prison in March 1945. He laid low until he made contact with the Ulbricht Group in early May. Not surprisingly the ambitious thirty-two-year-old, a roofer and member of the KPD since 1929, decided to stay in Berlin and not to return to the Saar. Visits home confirmed his conviction that a successful political career could only be built up in the Soviet zone of Germany; the French were in no mood to countenance autonomous political activity among the German population. On his last visit in 1948 a French official tore up his papers on entry, thus underlining the fact that Honecker had no future in the Saar as long as the French were there.

Before his arrest in 1935, Honecker's party activities had been concentrated in the youth movement. After attending a course at the Lenin School in Moscow in 1930 he was appointed secretary of the communist youth movement (KJV) in the Saar in 1931. What was more natural than a return to youth work in the SBZ in 1945? He was straight away made secretary for youth in the CC of the KPD. The FDJ was built up by Honecker and he remained its chairman until May 1955. Then, after study in the Soviet Union, he became CC secretary for security.

Hence Ulbricht and Honecker spent their formative years in the party in quite different environments. Ulbricht was accustomed to thinking in all-German terms and to regarding Germany as economically and militarily more powerful than the USSR (1918–41). Honecker, on the other hand, was constrained, from 1945 onwards, to think only in terms of the SBZ/GDR and to regard the Soviet Union as Germany's economic, political and military superior. Ulbricht's long experience of dealing with Soviet communists was, from time to time, astutely used to benefit the GDR. By over-dramatising the situation, he secured Soviet aid on occasions and was flexible in responding to Soviet initiatives until 1970. Ulbricht was an autocratic First Secretary who possessed considerable self-confidence *vis-à-vis* the Soviets in the 1960s and even more *vis-à-vis* the other socialist countries. This made relations with some East European leaders a trifle difficult, especially where Gomulka was concerned.

Honecker, when he assumed Ulbricht's mantle, did not assume his authority. True the new First Secretary enjoyed overt Soviet support and inside the SED he was Ulbricht's 'natural' successor. However his experience in the SED was restricted to two main areas: youth policy and security. He had never held a government post and had little knowledge of economic and technical questions. Willi Stoph, an able and experienced administrator, was then Prime Minister and appeared an important rival. Then there was Günter Mittag, probably the best economic brain in the party leadership, and the driving force behind the NES/ESS. Some observers spoke of a collective leadership similar to that existing in the CPSU after Khrushchev's removal in October 1964. However, just as Brezhnev quickly manifested his ascendancy over Kosygin, the technocrat, so too did the party leader take precedence over the government leader in the GDR. This was made clear to all on 3 October 1973 when Stoph was kicked upstairs to become chairman of the Council of State, succeeding Ulbricht, who had died on 1 August 1973. Under the ESS the Council of State was developing into the leading institution for the formation and implementation of policy but it had been declining in significance under Honecker. Could Stoph make the post a politically significant one just as Podgorny had done with his position as chairman of the presidium of the USSR Supreme Soviet? As for Günter Mittag, he ceased to be CC secretary for the economy, also in October 1973. He became First Deputy to the new Prime Minister, Horst Sindermann. Mittag's place in the Secretariat went to Werner Krolikowski. Honecker thus proved himself an able politician and dispelled all talk about a collective leadership in the GDR. He was developing into a statesman and was pursuing a policy of cautious continuity. There were no dramatic moves, no open confrontations. No one left the Politburo, except in a hearse. Lacking the personal vanity of his predecessor, he nevertheless developed an appetite for political office. By late 1976 he headed three of the key institutions in the GDR: the party, the National Defence Council (he became its chairman on 24 June 1971) and the Council of State (he was elected chairman by the *Volkskammer* on 29 October 1976).

By nature a conciliator, he set out to win the trust of the GDR population. He is approachable and by all accounts has the knack of coming up with solutions to knotty personnel problems. Long years in the youth movement, first reserve for future SED cadres, and in military and security affairs brought him into close personal contact with a whole GDR generation. Not given to ideological innovation, his forte is the ability to express the prevailing party view without ostentation, while adding his own nuances. He set out deliberately to simplify party and government jargon. This is very marked when one compares one of Honecker's speeches on the economy with one by the previous First Secretary. Walter Ulbricht could never resist the temptation to pick up and use the latest neologism. However, Honecker does develop his own phraseology. If the term the 'economic system of socialism' was used by Ulbricht to characterise the last years of his influence, Henecker in turn has coined the phrase 'real, existing socialism' to underline the down-to-earth attitude he employs when dealing with day-to-day problems. He is enamoured of the word *real*, real or realistic, and it appears often. There is the realistic plan, the realistic view and so on.

Along with his simple, direct manner goes credibility. Part of this is due to the fact that he evidently believes what he is saying. His faith in the Soviet Union and in Marxism-Leninism is clear for all to see and contributes to his popularity among young workers. His uncomplicated manner and speech make others feel at ease in his presence. This is in marked contrast to his predecessor. Party workers can invite Honecker to a social evening knowing that he will contribute to the *Gemütlichkeit*. They know where they are with him and he makes himself available for *tête-à-tête* on specific party problems. To underline his approach-ability, Honecker went so far as to have a magazine withdrawn from circulation which contained an article about him, by Jürgen Kuczynski, which the First Secretary regarded as too laudatory.[1]

The SED under Honecker has re-emphasised the primacy of Marxism-Leninism and the dominant role of the party. Actually the decision to change the direction of party policy was taken in the wake of the XXIVth Congress of the CPSU and consequently before Walter Ulbricht was removed from office. A Politburo decree of 15 April 1971 signalled the demise of the 'developed social system of socialism', socialism as a 'relatively independent socio-economic formation' which was to develop on its own base and of the concept of a 'socialist human community'. The decree underlined the binding nature of the guidelines, agreed on at the CPSU Congress, for the formation of the 'developed socialist society in the GDR'.

The VIIIth Congress of the SED confirmed this change of course. The ESS had seen the rise of disciplines which were difficult to reconcile with the traditional values of the party. Kurt Hager, at the Congress, did not mince words: 'The clear meaning and content of the policy of the SED was lost in a jumble of concepts borrowed from systems theory.' Whereas the term system had dominated the ESS, it became taboo under Honecker. *Partiinost*, or party-mindedness, under the ESS, had consisted of achieving the greatest possible effectiveness in the work of party organs, state organs and social organisations in fulfilling the decrees of the party and the demands of the scientific-technical revolution. The demands of the scientific-technical revolution, however, as expressed in cybernetics and systems theory, had proved too much for the mass of party workers. GDR society became once again a 'class society of a special type' and left the harmonious aspirations of the 'socialist human community' far behind. Under the latter it had been claimed that the 'socialist relations of production do not eliminate classes but produce a completely new class structure'. The state, in turn, was based on a democratic alliance and the amicable co-operation of the working class and the other classes and strata. Into the bargain, the working class had been redefined very generously to include as many persons engaged in mental work as possible. Hager, again, had something acerbic to say about these developments at the Congress: 'When an attempt is made to define the content of society using the systemic concepts of cybernetics, the result is that the socio-economic and class content of socialism is positively undermined.' The advent of Honecker signalled the return to Soviet-type orthodoxy when thinking about class.

Philosophy reasserted itself anew. Hager, once again, put the matter in sharp perspective:

The function of historical and dialectical materialism is seriously endangered when Marxist-Leninist philosophy is robbed of its *Weltanschauung* and partly deideologised by the uncritical acceptance of views and concepts drawn from various disciplines. Dialectical and historical materialism should not and cannot be replaced by individual sciences or transformed into an appendage of such sciences. (Kurt Hager, '*Die entwickelte sozialistische Gesellschaft Aufgaben der Gesellschaftswissenschaften nach dem VIII. Parteitag der SED*', *Einheit*, No 11/1971, p. 1207.)

One of the things Hager had in mind was the attempt by Georg Klaus to elaborate a cybernetics of society which would replace historical materialism. Klaus, however, had conceded the inadmissibility of such an undertaking in 1970.

Economic policy was also brought down to earth at the Congress. Whereas the ESS had emphasised planning and management, with the stress on perspective planning, the new Five-Year Plan spoke of management and planning, underlining short-term planning. The ESS, with its emphasis on structure-determining industries, had led to imbalances, so the goal now became planned, proportional growth.

Another outgrowth of the late Ulbricht era was the gulf which had developed between social groups, especially between those who possessed the requisite skills to play a major role in the scientific-technical revolution and those whose lack of expertise condemned them to a lowly supporting role. The technical intelligentsia expanded very fast in the 1960s and its members were favoured in the allocation of new flats, as well as in employment. Admissions to further education peaked in 1971 when over 44,000 entered the portals of the tertiary sector, but this number had dropped to about 32,000 in 1976. The wild optimism of Ulbricht has given way to the sober reasonableness of Honecker. The ESS flattered to deceive: there were simply not enough jobs to go round. Social policy, to repair the neglect of the 1960s, has paid particular attention to the low-paid, old-age pensioners and mothers.

Relations with the USSR have been somewhat easier than during the last years of Ulbricht. Honecker possesses neither the self-assertiveness nor the self-confidence which marked the old First Secretary's handling of the Soviets in the 1960s. Gone is the concept of a socialist German state held up as a model for all advanced states to contemplate. Gone is the inflexibility over Berlin. In their place has come a closer relationship between the CPSU and the SED. The latter has sought to become the most reliable ideological ally of the CPSU. In this way it seeks to influence Soviet thinking and policy. This again reflects Honecker's preference for a low-profile, private approach rather than the staking out of an SED view in public. Presumably the Soviets are happier with an undisputed leader in the GDR, instead of a collective leadership. The latter is much more unpredictable and is always subject to shifting alliances.

The signing of a Basic Treaty with the FRG in 1972 was a long-sought-after achievement for the GDR. Satisfaction and pleasure multiplied in East Berlin as the GDR won diplomatic recognition on a world scale, followed by entry into the United Nations. By 1976 the GDR had diplomatic relations with 121 countries and was actively engaged in many international bodies. Whereas previously GDR foreign policy had almost exclusively been concerned with Germany, the 1970s saw the GDR taking a more active part elsewhere, especially in the Middle East and Africa.

The GDR economy recorded a considerable number of successes during the early 1970s. Living standards rose visibly and the GDR reinforced her position as the socialist country with the highest standard of living. However all this changed with the Yom Kippur War of October 1973. The massive increase in the price of hydrocarbons, followed by other raw materials, hit the West straight away, but the impact on Eastern Europe was only delayed. The USSR began to move towards charging world prices for these commodities, but not in one fell swoop. Rolling five-year averages are to bring Comecon prices up to those on the world market by 1980. It was a bitter blow for the GDR, which imports so much of its raw material needs. The only way the GDR could counterbalance the price increases was to raise the prices of her exports to the USSR. This she failed to do. Increasing international indebtedness has been the result. This has forced the GDR to attempt to sell more to the Western world – this at a time of economic recession in the advanced capitalist countries. Economic difficulties in the second half of the 1970s have cast their shadow over the cultural scene. The more relaxed cultural atmosphere of the early Honecker years has given way to a less tolerant attitude. More and more artists and writers have found that the only course open to them is to leave the GDR. The party does not wish to enter into a dialogue with the critical cultural intelligentsia and thereby reflects its own unease at their criticisms. Possibly the party ideologues would prefer an open dialogue but officials responsible for security may have had the upper hand. Hand-in-hand with the outspokenness of some GDR intellectuals has gone an increasing boldness on the part of the ordinary GDR citizen. Basing themselves on the Helsinki Final Act, over 100,000 persons have requested permission to surrender their GDR citizenship and emigrate to the FRG.

CHANGES IN PERSONNEL

Continuity was the order of the day at the Ist Plenum of the CC elected at the VIIIth Congress, at its first meeting after the congress. All sitting Politburo members were re-elected but two new full members were added: Werner Lamberz and Werner Krolikowski. Harry Tisch, first secretary of *Bezirk* Rostock, and Erich Mielke, Minister of State

Security, were made candidate members. All the CC secretaries, except for Horst Dohlus, who only became a member of the Secretariat at the congress, were thus in the Politburo. Lamberz, CC secretary for agitation since 1966, was already known as a close collaborator of Honecker. Krolikowski was the real surprise. He jumped from membership of the CC to full membership of the Politburo without going through the candidate stage. He retained his position as first secretary of *Bezirk* Dresden. Mielke's close personal ties with the First Secretary dated from the days when Honecker had been CC secretary for security.

If the turnover at the top was modest, it was certainly not so at the *Bezirk* level. Of the 15 first secretaries, 5 changed shortly after the congress. [2] The hand of Honecker in these appointments is very evident: 4 of the 5 new appointments had played important roles in the FDJ; 3 of these had been close collaborators of the new First Secretary during his FDJ days: Konrad Naumann (East Berlin) had been second secretary of the FDJ between 1957 and 1967; Werner Felfe (Halle) had been second secretary of the FDJ between 1954 and 1957: Hans-Joachim Hertwig (Frankfurt/Oder) had been secretary and deputy chairman of the Ernst Thälmann pioneer organisation between 1960 and 1966. Horst Schumann should be added to the list although he became first secretary of *Bezirk* Leipzig in November 1970. He had been first secretary of the FDJ between 1959 and 1967.

It was not until the Xth Plenum of the CC of the SED, in October 1973, that decisive personnel changes at the top were made. Walter Halbritter lost his position as a candidate member of the Politburo. Heinz Hoffmann, Minister of National Defence, became a full member and Werner Felfe, Joachim Herrmann (chief editor of *Neues Deutschland*), Ingeborg Lange (who also became CC secretary for women), Konrad Naumann and Gerhard Schürer (chairman of the State Planning Commission) became candidate members. At the same meeting Willi Stoph replaced Walter Ulbricht as chairman of the Council of State. The new Prime Minister was Horst Sindermann, previously Stoph's First Deputy. Günter Mittag became the new First Deputy Prime Minister, with Werner Krolikowski replacing him as CC secretary for the economy.

Halbritter's demotion was not altogether unexpected. He had been responsible for the price reform of the NES/ESS but since that had come to an end with Ulbricht, Halbritter's position had always been in doubt under Honecker. His departure removed another economic specialist from the ranks of the Politburo. An even more significant demotion for the proponents of the NES/ESS was the departure of Günter Mittag, Halbritter's former mentor, from the ranks of the CC secretaries. The first indication that Mittag's position under Honecker was insecure was his failure to secure re-election to the Council of State in 1971. The new CC secretary for the economy, Krolikowski, was a man of quite a different hue. Lacking any formal qualifications in economics, his task was apparently to weld the party more closely to the goals of the Five-Year Plan. Krolikowski's promotion reveals that an official can make good even after having blotted his copybook. He had been dismissed, in 1952, from his post as first secretary of *Kreis* Ribnitz-Damgarten for infraction of the party statutes. His successor as first secretary of *Bezirk* Dresden was Hans Modrow, head of the CC department of agitation. Modrow's previous career was almost a blueprint for success under Honecker: a student at the Komsomol School in Moscow in 1952–3, then first secretary of the FDJ in *Bezirk* Berlin until 1961, while at the same time being a member of the Central Council of the FDJ. Although another technocrat of the Ulbricht era, Günther Kleiber retained his position as a candidate member of the Politburo, his star was on the wane. Responsible for the spread of data processing under Ulbricht, he saw his state secretariat dissolved in 1971. A few days before the Xth Plenum he was named Minister for General Machine Building.

Joachim Herrmann also had worked closely with the First Secretary during his FDJ days. Herrmann had been chief editor of the FDJ newspaper *Junge Welt* between 1952 and 1962. Ingeborg Lange, too, had been an FDJ secretary between 1952 and 1961.

Horst Dohlus, head of the CC department for party organs since 1960, became a fully fledged secretary of the CC, presumably for party organs and cadres, at the Xth Plenum. However he was not elevated to the Politburo at the same time. As such he was the only CC secretary not in the Politburo. This anomaly was removed at the IXth Congress, when he became a candidate member of the Politburo. Since he occupied a very important post, his very slow progress to the Politburo must presumably be ascribed to the fact that he had enemies in high places.

The changes also increased the influence of the party in the state apparatus. Never before had so many key figures in government and state been simultaneously members of the Politburo: Willi Stoph, chairman of the Council of State; Horst Sindermann, chairman of the Council of Ministers; Günter Mittag, first deputy chairman of the Council of Ministers; Alfred Neumann, first deputy chairman of the Council of Ministers; Erich Mielke, Minister of State Security;

Heinz Hoffmann, Minister of National Defence; Günther Kleiber, Minister for General Machine Building; Gerhard Schürer, deputy chairman of the Council of Ministers and chairman of the State Planning Commission. Thus about one-third of Politburo members held leading positions in the state apparatus.

The election of the new *Bezirk* and *Kreis* party executive committees, in early 1974, produced a few changes. Of the 95 *Bezirk* secretaries, 24 were not re-elected and of the remaining 124 members, 39 were replaced. At the *Kreis*, city and city *Bezirk* level about one-third of the executive committee members were changed. Of interest is the fact of the 263 *Kreis* first secretaries only 9 were women; 3 of these were to be found in *Bezirk* Leipzig.

Shortly after becoming chairman of the FDGB, Harry Tisch was promoted to full membership of the Politburo at the XIVth Plenum of the CC, of the SED, in June 1975.

There is a parallel between some of these promotions and the composition of the Politburo of the CC of the CPSU. In the Soviet case the Minister of Defence, the head of the KGB and the Foreign Minister were all made full members in April 1973. In the GDR, the Minister of National Defence became a full member in October 1973, the Minister of State Security (the equivalent of the KGB in the GDR) was then already a candidate member, but Otto Winzer, the Foreign Minister, was not promoted to the Politburo. This was in spite of the fact that he had been a member of the Ulbricht Group and a member of the CC of the KPD in 1945 and of the CC of the SED since 1947. Honecker may not have been influenced by the Soviet precedent since the upgrading of defence and security matters accords closely with his own background and the decision to render the frontiers of the GDR as impassable as possible. Erich Mielke, Yuri Andropov's opposite number in East Berlin, became a full member of the Politburo at the IXth Congress in May 1976.

The changes effected at the VIIIth Congress and the Xth Plenum significantly increased Honecker's authority. He had proved himself capable of picking his own team and of getting it ensconced in the Politburo and the Secretariat. Worthy of note is the fact that if Herrmann Axen, Werner Lamberz and Paul Verner – all previously connected with Honecker and the FDJ – are added to those newly promoted, the new First Secretary in just over two years was able to build up a group amounting to about one-third of Politburo members who were personally linked to him. The other side of this coin is that the demotion of the economic specialists revealed that the economy presented few worries for the First Secretary. The Yom Kippur War and the resultant huge increase in hydrocarbon and other primary product prices would change all that.

SOCIAL AND ECONOMIC DEVELOPMENTS

Great emphasis was placed on the desire to improve living standards for all in the GDR during the Five-Year Plan which began in 1971. Groups, such as the old-age pensioners, who had been neglected during much of the NES/ESS period, again found favour. The more obvious inequalities which a policy of rewarding those with the necessary technical and scientific skills must produce were softened. The primacy of economic growth gave way to a more egalitarian approach to social rewards. It was always stressed, however, that higher living standards for the ordinary worker were dependent on higher labour productivity. The old maxim that one could only consume what had first been produced was still valid.

Old-age pensioners were given a boost in 1971 and again in 1972, when their pensions were increased by 20 per cent – the largest ever jump in the GDR. This moved their pensions up to 200–240 Marks per month or about one-quarter of the average wage. The maximum pension was set at 367 Marks per month. The net result was to reduce the gulf between the various pensions paid by the state. The 1972 increases were enjoyed by about 4 million pensioners. All in all the income of old-age pensioners, over the years 1965–72, increased at an annual rate of 6·5 per cent, faster than any other group in society.[3] The minimum pension was again raised on 1 December 1976 to 230–300 Marks. Whereas the average pensioner had received about 199 Marks in 1970 he received about 300 Marks in 1976.

Minimum wage levels for workers were also raised in 1972. Hand-in-hand with these went restrictions on the self-employed and on artisan co-operatives. Semi-state and private industrial and building firms and some of the artisan co-operatives were transformed into VEB. This reduced the number of self-employed plus family helpers to 2·7 per cent of all employed in 1972. The self-employed have always been at the top of the incomes tree in the GDR. In 1960, they earned 3·4 times as much as those employed in the public sector but in 1972 this was down to 2·8 times. The tenor of the SED's policy in 1972 indicated that this would be a continuing trend.

Collective farmers were also given a boost in 1972. After three bad harvests they were in need of financial help from the state.

The 1971–5 Plan foresaw an increase of 4 per cent annually in the net income of the population. This compares with an average annual increase in the gross income of the population between 1961 and 1965 of 2·5 per cent and between 1966 and 1970 of 3·9 per cent. The comparable figure for 1971 and 1972 was 4·3 per cent.[4] Things went even better in 1973 and 1974.

The basic wage was raised from 350 to 400 Marks on 1 October 1976, with smaller increases for those earning between 400 and 500 Marks. About 1 million workers and employees benefited from these measures, revealing that about one worker and employee in seven had been on these very low rates. Higher wages with correspondingly higher work norms are to be introduced by 1980 for about 1,500,000 workers in key industries. Further social improvements are contained in the new labour code which became operative on 1 January 1978. Among the benefits are: payment for work time spent consulting a doctor; greater job security; and increased care taken to place a worker in a job with similar pay when rationalisation has phased out his previous employment.

The next generation was also not forgotten. To halt the decline in the birth rate generous allowances were paid to mothers and longer paid leave was granted. Mothers received 1000 Marks on the birth of a child and to help large families 80 million Marks was disbursed in 1974 to families with four or more children. Interest-free loans were made available to young couples to buy flats and furniture. The declining birth rate can be ascribed to the increasing divorce rate (higher than in the FRG), to the fact that 83 per cent of all women aged between fifteen and sixty were in employment (76 per cent if old-age pensioners are excluded) in 1972 – something which affords women greater economic independence – and to the declining influence of religion.

Considerable resources were devoted to improving the living conditions of the population. The 1971–5 Plan called for an increase in the housing stock of 500,000 dwellings – 383,500 of these to be new. Although this appeared very ambitious in 1971 it was in fact achieved by the middle of April 1975. An even higher target, 750,000 dwellings – 560,000 of them new – was set for the 1976–80 plan period.

Improvements in the medical care of the population and the amelioration of the working conditions of medical staff were outlined in a decree dated 25 September 1973. The goal was one doctor per 500–520 citizens by 1980. There was one doctor per 596 citizens in 1972 but wide regional variations were observable. East Berlin had one doctor for every 308 citizens but Mecklenburg had to be satisfied with one doctor per 758 citizens. Some hospitals were to be renovated and a beginning made to the building of polyclinics, old people's home and sanatoria during the 1971–5 plan period. All this activity was to be supplementary to existing building commitments.[5] The reason for this extra-plan activity was the need to retain medical staff who had prospered under Ulbricht but who were revealing a disturbing propensity to move to the FRG under Honecker.

YOUTH

A striking facet of the Honecker era is the increased emphasis placed on the military training of children and young people. This policy can be traced back to 1968 but it has been pursued with renewed vigour since 1971. The ideological justification is the 'sharper struggle between imperialism and socialism on German soil the ruthless use of force by imperialism and its increased aggressiveness and danger'. This reading of intra-German relations leads to a greater need for every citizen to be prepared militarily to defend the GDR. In order to do this he must be politically and ideologically committed to his socialist state. This involves not only intensive instruction in Marxism-Leninism but also implies creating in his mind a credible image of the enemy on whom he can focus his hatred. Hence all the military expertise in the world is of little consequence if the soldier does not believe that the man on the other side of the frontier is his enemy.

In a Politburo decree of 7 November 1972, on agitation and propaganda, it was stated that 'socialist patriotism and proletarian internationalism express themselves now in the strengthening of the defence of the GDR and the socialist commonwealth. Internationalism and patriotism are fusing more and more together.' The decree also stated that on the ideological front there could be no peaceful co-existence and that the meeting of huge numbers of people with different *Weltanschauungen* and life-styles was producing a sharpening of ideological confrontation, requiring greater class awareness and activity. Here was a clue to the new line of thought. Détente, the signing of the Berlin Agreement, the negotiation of a Basic Treaty between the GDR and the FRG and the resultant stream of visitors from West Berlin and West Germany (1·54 million West Germans visited the GDR and 1·06 old-age pensioners from the GDR visited the FRG in 1972) far from breaking down ideological barriers were seen by the SED as a challenge which had to be resisted and overcome. The impact of these new developments on the young people of the GDR can be assessed from a speech by Margot Honecker, Minister of Education and wife of the First Secretary, made at a conference of head teachers in May 1973. She warned that although the Brandt government's foreign policy contained 'certain realistic aspects' in the end its measures were increasingly anti-communist. She called for greater importance to be given to the development of a resolute class point of view. Not only was political and ideological instruction to be increased but 'our whole military-political, military sporting and pre-military training and education at the school level must be conducted with more rigour and at a higher level'.[6]

The core of this type of training is the Hans Beimler competition organised by the FDJ for Classes 8–10 of the ten-year general polytechnic high school. Although organised by the FDJ it involves all schoolboys and girls. The competition was introduced in June 1967 but new directives were issued in May 1972. It was then declared to be the chief method of socialist military training in Classes 8–10 in high and special schools. The competition includes military-political round table discussions; running a special wall newspaper; the reading and discussion of socialist and Soviet war and memoir literature; finding the strongest schoolboy; cross-country running; overcoming obstacles; throwing hand grenades and firing an air gun; a ten-kilometre march involving the surmounting of obstacles; camouflage and the setting-up of field kitchens. Teachers, especially of German history and civic affairs, were to relate their material to the goals of the competition.

New regulations covering the military training of boys and girls in Classes 9 and 10 came into effect on 1 September 1973. Shooting and field training take up most of the time: 100 hours are to be spent on these – 60 in Class 9 and 40 in Class 10. Four hours one afternoon every other week is the recommended mix.[7]

The pre-military training of pupils in Class 11 of the expanded high schools was laid down in legislation dated 12 February 1973. Pre-military training for boys and medical training for girls are obligatory and are to take place during a twelve-day exercise in the summer holidays. Girls are to be trained by the German Red Cross in addition to the instruction they receive in civil defence.[8]

Apprentices are also to receive pre-military instruction as part of their all-round training. Pre-school children were also not forgotten. The five- to eight-year-olds are to develop friendly relations with soldiers and are to visit them and to be visited by them in their kindergartens. They are to collect photographs of soldiers and to talk about them. Children are to be encouraged to simulate the discipline, bearing and readiness for action of the soldier.[9]

A key element in preparing young people for military service is sport. The Society for Sport and Technology plays a leading role in this respect. Thus the emphasis placed by the GDR on sport over the last decade or so serves two goals: the winning of international recognition through sporting success and the preparation of GDR youth for military service.

How do young people react to this emphasis on military affairs and training during their formative years? Most of them accept it as a necessary evil, a social duty which they must perform in order to advance educationally and professionally. Some of them take to it like ducks to water but not in sufficiently large numbers to provide adequate recruitment levels for the armed forces. Many youngsters are not aware of the 'danger of an imperialist attack by the West Germans'. They do not believe that 'West German imperialism could be as barbaric as US imperialism' and for many 'West German imperialism is not conducting a visible war'. One of the reasons for this, and the GDR authorities lament the fact, is that GDR youth has access to West German television programmes and thus finds that its perception of West German reality conflicts with the image put out by the SED. There is still the widespread belief among young people that time spent on military service constitutes an irreparable loss to their own development. An important reason why young men are not willing to serve longer periods in the National People's Army (NVA) is the influence which their girlfriends are able to exert. To counter their negative attitude girls are to be more closely involved in political and defence training.[10]

The new emphasis placed on pre-military training places an even greater burden on teachers. Besides preparing their pupils for the workbench and the university they now have to get them ready for the army as well. To prepare the teachers for their new tasks special political instruction is to be made available.

What will be the effect on GDR youth of all this martial training? The NVA party organisation in listing the desirable character traits of a soldier states that 'an NVA soldier hates imperialism and its paid agents and resolves to annihilate any aggressor resolutely while putting his own life at stake'.[11] The consequences of fostering this level of aggressiveness in young men will be felt within GDR society in the years to come.

A draft youth law was published just before the Xth World Festival of Youth which took place in East Berlin during July and August 1973. It appeared just in time to provide material for discussion for young GDR people when they met foreigners at the festival. It stressed proletarian internationalism and the validity of the Soviet example and underlined the increased responsibility of the FDJ for raising the material and cultural level of life. Working and living conditions of young people received considerable attention. The military obligations of youth were not forgotten: 'The defence of the socialist fatherland and the socialist state community are the honourable duty of all young persons.' Youth was also active on the economic front. Between 1971 and 1973 youth brigades increased by 2500 to over 16,600, and 35,000 youth projects were completed. In honour of the Xth Festival over 8000 building projects were started. Then there were the fairs of the Masters of Tomorrow and the innovation movement among young workers in the scientific-technical field.[12] The new youth law was passed by the *Volkskammer* on 28 January 1974. It was stated that 5,400,000 GDR citizens had expressed their point of view and that this had resulted in about 200 changes being made in the draft text. These alterations underlined even further the responsibility of parents for preparing their children for life and work under socialism.[13]

FOREIGN POLICY

Relations with the USSR and Comecon

The Berlin Agreement, the Basic Treaty with the FRG, the worldwide diplomatic recognition of the GDR (121 states in June 1976) and the entry of the GDR into the UN were tangible results of the relationship beteen the GDR and the USSR. Although the GDR would have preferred fewer concessions on Berlin, she could feel satisfied at the successes her Soviet connection had brought her. She knew that it had been the Soviet Union which had forced the developed world to recognise her and to accord her equal status with the FRG in the councils of the world. By tenacious policies, eventually crowned with success, the USSR had displayed her trust in the SED and the East German population. Naturally the Soviet Union would expect the trust to bear tangible fruit – on the ideological and economic fronts.

Ideologically the SED wanted close links with the CPSU. Partly due to a divided Germany and an industrially more developed state on the other side of the minefields and watch towers, the SED lacked the national self-confidence of the other East European parties. SED policy was to cleave close to the CPSU and attempt to transform the

Abgrenzung, its policy *vis-à-vis* the FRG, into general communist party policy. The SED and the CPSU saw eye-to-eye on détente: it was necessary because of the economic gains it would bring but it increased the need for ideological watchfulness.

The desire of the USSR and the GDR for closer relations among the member sates of Comecon not only in the economic sphere, but also in the political and social ones, gradually bore fruit as the 1970s progressed. Co-operation and integration were the avowed objects of many Comecon meetings. A list of the goals declared would include: exact co-ordination of economic plans; inter-state specialisation and co-operation in production, especially in the sectors which play a key role in technical progress; extending links between scientific and technical research institutes; expansion of intra-Comecon trade; active use of international credits; and expansion of contacts between ministries, economic agencies and enterprises.[14]

There has been considerable movement on some of these objectives. Some, however, are easier to put into effect than others, e.g. expansion of contacts between ministries, enterprises, research institutes and so on. Especially at the enterprise level the GDR and the USSR are developing close relations; there are even SED cells now in some Soviet factories. Joint investment ventures have become common. The GDR has committed herself to investing 7000–8000 million Marks in Comecon, the lion's share in the USSR, between 1976 and 1980. The Orenburg-Uzhgorod natural gas pipeline is a joint Comecon venture with all evental users building a section (except Romania which supplied equipment instead). This trend towards joint investment in the USSR, especially for the exploitation and transport of raw materials to Eastern Europe, will continue.

Is it feasible or even desirable for Comecon members to increase thier trade with one another? Is there a limit to this incestuous economic relationship? Only Romania and Poland come anywhere near meeting their own energy needs; countries such as Hungary and the GDR have to import most of their energy and this dependency will increase in the future. Only in 1980 will the Soviet Union charge the world price for hydrocarbons, hence it is in the interests of those who import Soviet oil and gas to continue to do so. However the USSR has made it clear that increased energy needs, especially of oil, will have to be met by imports from the Third World. Comecon, especially the USSR, is a huge market and not as competitive or demanding as the rest of the world. Thus a country which is capable of turning out products which are reasonably reliable (and here long production runs are very important) but not up to the latest world standards, will find a ready market in the East. This is fine if you have no ambitions to be a world leader or any need to import from the developed world and the Third World. However since the USSR cannot satisfy the demands of her Comecon partners for certain goods, these states must trade with the West and the developing world. In order to acquire hard currency, since their own currencies are inconvertible, they must export or borrow from Western banks. To export successfully they must be competitive; to be that they must first import Western technology to raise the quality of their goods. Hence technological backwardness is a millstone round their necks.

The GDR's position in Comecon is understood by the SED to be unequivocally of benefit to her. It provides a ready market and, since GDR industry is a leader in some sectors, the GDR has the opportunity of long production runs for certain products. Hence closer co-operation is sought in structure-determining sectors: machine-building, chemicals, electronics, electrical engineering, optics and glass and ceramics. Three of the twenty-three permanent Comecon commissions (1975) have their headquarters in East Berlin: building, chemicals and standardisation. The GDR is now the main trading partner of the USSR in Comecon. How has this relationship been developing during the 1970s?

The goal set for GDR trade turnover in 1975 was 63,000 million Valuta marks (VM). Of this, trade with Comecon was to account for 47,000 million VM and the remaining 16,000 million VM was to be achieved in trade with the West and the Third World. This implied an increase of about 70 per cent in Comecon trade and an increase of about 42 per cent in trade with the 'capitalist industrial countries' and the 'developing countries'. The plan between 1971 and 1975 did not turn out to be a very accurate prognostication as far as trade with Comecon was concerned. It increased (1970 = 100) from 105·7 (1971) to 149·4 (1975) or just short of 50 per cent.[15] Turnover with the non-socialist world rose from 105·8 (1971) to 143·3 (1975) or just over the planned level.[16] The often-repeated goal of raising trade with Comecon countries to 75 per cent of all trade was also not achieved. In 1975 it was only 66·2 per cent in current prices but 69·2 per cent in fixed prices.[17]

GDR trade turnover calculated in current prices reveals a different story. Turnover almost doubled over the Five-Year Plan period, from 39,600 million VM in 1970 to 74,400 million VM in 1975. Of this, trade with Comecon countries jumped from 26,700 million VM in 1970 to 49,300 million VM in 1975. Trade with the USSR rose almost as fast, from 15,500 million VM in 1970 to 26,600 million VM in 1975. Over half of this increase (6500 million VM) was registered in 1974/75. Trade turnover with the developed world and the Third World doubled between 1971 and 1975. The wide discrepancy between fixed and current prices is mainly due, of course, to the price increases which followed in the wake of the Yom Kippur War in October 1973. This affected GDR trade with the non-socialist countries in 1974 and 1975. The momentous decision taken by the USSR to break the agreement on fixed trade prices between 1971 and 1975, followed by all other Comecon countries, raised GDR trade turnover with Comecon from 39,100 million VM in 1974 to 49,300 million VM in 1975. Put into context the increase in trade was 26·1 per cent in current prices but only 7·1 per cent in fixed prices. In other words the terms of trade had turned against the GDR.[18] Compared with the price increases in Western markets those in Comecon were modest in 1975. However the USSR made it known that world market prices would apply as of 1980. Between 1976 and 1980 rolling five-year averages would gradually raise prices to world levels.

GDR foreign trade has been in deficit since 1973. Prior to that date GDR trade with socialist countries and the Third World was always in surplus but trade with the West has been in the red since 1969. Over the period 1960–72 the GDR recorded a healthy surplus of 6800 million VM on her trade with the world. The deficit in 1973 was 1200 million VM, in 1974 it reached 3100 million VM and it climbed to 4200 million VM in 1975 – the highest trade deficit ever recorded. Hence the 1960–72 surplus of 6800 million VM had turned into a 1960–75 deficit of 1700 million VM. 1975 was a depressing year, GDR trade with Comecon, the West and the Third World were all in the red. The deficit with the West in 1975 reached 3600 million VM, causing total indebtedness with the Western world (including GDR-FRG trade) to climb to 14,000 million VM over the years 1970–5.[19] An additional reason for the weak 1975 performance was the poor harvest, in common with most European countries, and the subsequent need to import grain and feedstuffs from North America.

The increased price of Soviet oil in 1975 raised the GDR's import bill by about 1500 million VM. Soviet oil cost 14 transferable rubles (TR) in 1974 but 35 TR in 1975. The GDR imported about 15 million tonnes in 1975.[20] Over the plan period 1976–80, 88 million tonnes of oil are to be imported from the USSR, an annual increase of about 5 per cent. Another 14 million tonnes are to come from the Persian Gulf.[21]

Despite the problems with the balance of payments, the GDR consumer has not been forgotten. Exports of consumer goods declined from 20.8 per cent of all exports in 1971 to 15.6 per cent in 1975. Imports of consumer goods, on the other hand, rose from 4·7 per ent in 1971 to 5·8 per cent in 1975 (8·4 per cent in 1973).[22]

The decision by the USSR to take advantage of world prices and to introduce them gradually from 1975 means that Comecon trade has now to be planned without using fixed prices. Most of the benefits accrue to the USSR since the prices of raw materials have risen faster than those of finished products. One may ask whether world prices, based on the market economy, should be used for Comecon trade, where in most cases prices are determined by central planners. World prices can be volatile, so if an economy such as the GDR or Hungary makes structural changes based on existing world prices and those prices fall in the future, considerable losses may be incurred. It all means that planned economies must become more flexible in their approach to foreign markets. Windfall profits should be reaped wherever possible. This in turn will cause disruption in domestic and intra-Comecon trade.

This can be illustrated with reference to GDR estimates of trade turnover with the USSR during the 1976–80 Plan period. Expressed in 1974 prices, the volume of trade is to amount to 28,000 million TR over the period. In current prices it is expected to reach 40,000 million TR – an increase of 43 per cent. The comparable figure for the rest of Comecon is 26,000 million TR and 34,000 million TR – an increase of 30 per cent. However these price increases are simply inspired guesses.

GDR trade accounted for about one-quarter of Soviet trade with Comecon and about one-eighth of all trade between 1971 and 1975. Thus the GDR was of primary importance to the Soviet Union during the above plan period but will this continue to be the case in the future? Until the 1960s some sectors of the GDR economy, notably chemical plant, were on a par with the world's best. This is no longer the case. It is still true that GDR industry, on the whole, is more advanced than Soviet industry. Nevertheless, much to the chagrin of East Berlin, the USSR now finds that West Germany is a more important source of new technology and know-how. The recognition by the USSR that she was suffering from technological lag occurred in the late 1960s. She took the decision, in 1969, to import vast quantities of Western technology as a means of overcoming that lag. This gave rise to détente and the signing of the Final Act at Helsinki. So long as détente lasts, and it is of vital economic significance that it should last indefinitely, the role of the GDR as an industrial innovator in the Soviet economy is restricted. Even so the GDR still has some influence on the course the Soviet economy takes. The reason for the termination of the discussions in 1976 between West German firms and the Soviets on the building of a nuclear power plant at Kaliningrad (formerly Königsberg) appears to owe much to East German pressure. The Soviets were planning to export some of the energy to West Germany via West Berlin.

Along with closer co-operation among Comecon countries in industrial and trade matters has gone an expansion and deepening of co-operation in foreign and defence policy and in ideology. At the XXVth Congress of the CPSU, Leonid Brezhnev revealed that the Politburo seldom met without discussing the 'strengthening of the unity and the development of co-operation with the fraternal countries and with the building up of our common international position'.[23]

If the intensity of party contacts is taken as a measure of the development of contacts in state and society then there is a special relationship between the USSR and the 'iron triangle' of Poland, Czechoslovakia and the GDR. There has also been a rapid increase in contacts at all levels among the three countries. These countries, the most developed, are the key to a more integrated Comecon. Of particular importance is the fact that the USSR appears to be willing to afford the GDR a special status among the three. Pointers in this direction in 1975–6 were: the GDR-USSR Treaty of Friendship, Co-operation and Mutual Aid dated 7 October 1975; the important role the SED played in arranging the second conference of communist and workers' parties, which was held in East Berlin on 29 and 30 June 1976; and the signing of a series of model bilateral co-operation and integration agreements affecting the economy, science, technology, culture and other fields.[24]

The new treaty of support and co-operation, according to Leonid Brezhnev, aims at 'a further *rapprochement* of both countries and peoples'.[25] It replaced the twenty-year treaty of 12 June 1964 ahead of time but without completely invalidating it. The new treaty altered the legal status of the GDR *vis-à-vis* the USSR. It makes no reference to all-German affairs except that the GDR/FRG border is stated to be 'inviolable'. West Berlin again appears as an independent political entity. Several of the statements give the impression that the Soviet goal is to make the GDR an additional guaranteeing power of the Four-Power Agreement on Berlin signed on 3 September 1971.

The military obligations of the GDR have been increased. There is now no longer any regional limitation to the theatre of operations the GDR armed forces could be involved in. In the case of a Sino-Soviet border conflict the GDR would be duty bound to render military aid if requested. The treaty also makes it clear that it is the 'international duty' of every socialist state to 'defend socialist achievements' in the 'socialist commonwealth of nations' whenever they appear to be under threat. This acceptance of the 'Brezhnev doctrine' is spelled out in an Article which states that it is the 'mutual responsibility of the GDR and the USSR' to render such aid. The duties involved in Warsaw Pact membership have also been incorporated into the new treaty, as have a very detailed list of duties and obligations arising from membership of Comecon, including the goals of 'socialist economic integration'. The treaty is for twenty-five years with automatic extentions for ten-year periods.

Pyotr Abrasimov, Soviet Ambassador to the GDR between 1962 and 1971, and the negotiator of the Berlin Agreement, returned as Ambassador in March 1975. The able and experienced Abrasimov was evidently regarded by Moscow as the man most capable of coping with the problems thrown up by the complicated relations between the GDR and the FRG and West Berlin.[26] The new Ambassador arrived at a time when substantial price increases in Soviet hydrocarbons and coal were causing problems of adjustment, to put it mildly. Into the bargain the increasing bilateral military co-operation between the GDR and the Soviet Unon was increasing defence bills. Abrasimov, heading a Soviet delegation at a meeting of an East German-Soviet commission on 20 December 1975, apparently asked the GDR for a larger contribution towards defraying Soviet military costs.

There has been an intensification of contacts between the CPSU and the SED of late. Between June 1971 and June 1976 Leonid Brezhnev and Erich Honecker met at least twenty-two times. According to the press, in 1974 and 1975 there were also a further fourteen meetings or conferences of the CC secretaries of the CPSU and the SED for international relations, ideology, propaganda, party organs, the economy and agriculture; and over the same period eleven party delegations, below the level of CC secretary, met for working sessions and fourteen mixed consultative groups held meetings.

In the field of ideology there has been especially close contact. The ideology agreement signed by the CPSU and the SED on 29 November 1973, buttressed by the treaty of friendship of 7 October 1975, has produced a closely enmeshed network of contacts and common programmes. This embraces also all the Warsaw Pact and Comecon countries with the exception of Romania.

A 'plan for cultural and scientific co-operation between the GDR and the USSR between 1976 and 1980' was signed on 25 June 1976 by Foreign Minister Andrei Gromyko and Oskar Fischer, GDR Foreign Minister. The ideological stimulus for such an agreement was provided by the meeting of CC secretaries of all Warsaw Pact and Comecon countries in Prague in March 1975. The new plan provides for closer co-operation between mass organisations in the two countries, more contact between scientific institutions and universities, more sharing of experience at primary educational level, in professional training, in health care, in the realm of law, television and radio, and art and culture. There are to be 'GDR days of culture' in the Soviet Union, to commemorate the thirtieth anniversary of the founding of the GDR, in October 1979, and 'USSR days of culture' to mark the thirty-fifth anniversary of the victory of the Soviet Army over the German Wehrmacht, in May 1980.

Relations with the FRG

The Berlin Question. The Four-Power Agreement on Berlin paved the way for negotiations between the FRG and the GDR on the normalisation of their relations. The goal of both was membership of the UN. How soon this would occur would depend on the Basic Treaty. The GDR, supported by the Soviet Union, would be in no hurry to reach agreement, especially concerning the FRG's position in West Berlin, if membership of the UN could be obtained first. The FRG, backed by France, the United Kingdom and the USA, was determined that a treaty should be concluded before both states were sponsored for UN membership. The United States, for instance, feared that if the GDR were admitted to the UN without acknowledging four-power responsibility for Germany, she would treat membership as a declaration of full sovereignty and withdraw from her obligations under the Berlin Agreement.[27] Berlin was one sticking point because it involved four-power responsibility for Germany and the unity of the German nation was another.

State Secretary Egon Bahr's instructions in negotiating the Basic Treaty with State Secretary Michael Kohl were to strengthen the concept of the German nation, not to agree to anything which would make a future unification more difficult and to achieve good neighbourly relations with the GDR.[28] The East German side aimed at achieving full sovereignty, i.e. divesting itself of the Berlin connection and avoiding any recognition of four-power responsibility for Germany, denying the existence of one German nation, one German citizenship, preventing the reunification of Germany at any future date (except on its own terms) and forcing the FRG to recognise the GDR as a foreign country, thereby obliging the FRG to amend her constitution. It was clear that there had to be compromise, if agreement was to be reached. Both sides won concessions; a useful way round the impasses was to add letters and statements, making concessions to the official treaty which did not find their way into the text.

On the national question, since the GDR refused to accept the concept of one German nation, the compromise reached was to include in the preamble the words: 'proceeding from historical circumstances and irrespective of the differing views of the FRG and the GDR on fundamental questions, including the national question'.[29] In order to underline the FRG's commitment to the concept of the unification of Germany, Egon Bahr, on the day the Basic Treaty was signed, 21 December 1972, sent a letter to this effect to Michael Kohl.[30] The GDR conceded the FRG's right to hold to the concept of one citizenship for all Germans. The West German view that permanent representatives should be exchanged and not ambassadors, since the FRG and the GDR were not foreign countries, was also conceded. In separate negotiations, the four powers agreed that the eventual entry of the FRG and the GDR into the UN would not invalidate the four-power agreements. Bahr and Kohl agreed too that the Permanent Representative of the FRG in the GDR could also represent the interests of West Berlin.

The West German elections also played a part in speeding up agreement on the treaty. It was initialled on 8 November 1972 in Bonn and signed on 21 December 1972 in East Berlin: that is, after the SPD/FDP coaltion had been returned to power in the FRG. The Basic Treaty became effective as of 21 June 1973. Both German states entered the UN on 18 September 1973.

The GDR, backed up by the USSR, has attempted to restrict the presence of the Federal government in West Berlin ever since the Basic Treaty. The ultimate aim is to sever every governmental link between the FRG and West Berlin and to transform West Berlin into a separate political entity. Despite the terms of the Berlin Agreement, GDR authorities intervene, from time to time, to turn back some travellers on the access routes.

The German nation

Until 1955 both German states agreed that there was one Germany and one German nation. Then Otto Grotewohl, in September 1955, speaking on the occasion of the signing of the treaty with the USSR expressly referred to the existence of 'two German states'.[31] In 1956–7 came Ulbricht's concept of a confederation of the two German states and this is also to be found in the SED programme of 1963. A specific GDR citizenship was first introduced on 20 February 1967. However, right up to 1970, Ulbricht held to the idea of the unity of the German nation, although Albert Norden had stated in late 1967 that West Germany's entry into NATO had finally severed the bonds of German national unity.[32] Ulbricht, in 1970, then counterposed the 'socialist German national state' in the GDR to the 'capitalist NATO state' with its 'limited sovereignty' in the FRG.[33]

Erich Honecker, on the occasion of the VIIIth Congress of the SED, in June 1971, made his position very clear. 'All talk of the unity of the German nation' is 'twaddle', he proclaimed. Instead a new type of nation, the socialist nation, had come into existence in the GDR. In the FRG the bourgeois nation existed. The parting of the ways had commenced in 1945–6, when the proletariat, in the course of building socialism, gradually became the standard bearers of the 'socialist' German nation. Over the decades the proletarian class had become the 'national' class. Just when the working class became the 'national' class has never been decided. Neither is it clear if the socialist nation has come fully into being or if is it still developing. The socialist nation is held to be the heir of all that is good in German history and represents 'historical progress'. The future therefore belongs to it.

The concept of class, according to the First Secretary, is of paramount importance in any assessment of the national question. The nation is linked to class, class content, class struggle and class contradictions. The historical dimension is introduced when Honecker insists that the German bourgeoisie led Germany into two disastrous wars and thereby forfeited leadership of the nation. 'Only the working class was called to renew the nation on the basis of democracy and to secure its unity in an anti-fascist democratic German state,' he has declared.[34]

The reason for the sudden attention lavished on the idea of the nation, since 1970, is not difficult to discern. Willy Brandt's *Ostpolitik*, which made its appearance in late 1966 and developed momentum in late 1969, the negotiations leading to the Berlin Agreement, the approaching normalisation of relations between the FRG and the GDR, including the first face-to-face meetings of government leaders, Brandt's concept of the unity of the German nation on the basis of a common culture – all called for the clarification of the SED's views on the German nation. Since the SED refused to countenance the view that there were two German states in one German nation, it had to come up with a counter-argument; hence the two German states and the two German nations argument. However the SED went further than this and claimed that the nation in the GDR was the heir of the German nation which had been shattered in 1945. Why introduce this complication, why not argue that the German nation had expired with the Reich in 1945 and that the nation in the GDR was something quite new? Apparently because the SED felt that it needed to boost its own legitimacy, to demonstrate to itself and to the population that it was the heir and protector of all the best traditions in German life and culture. Here again it was on the horns of a dilemma since it claimed that the working class in the GDR, with the SED at its head, was the true standard bearer of the interests of the German nation. This also implied the right to defend the true interest of the German nation in the FRG. Only the working class, led by the SED, and not the bourgeoisie, could decide what truly served the German national interest. The SED was coming perilously close to being tarred with the brush of nationalism. The last thing the SED wanted was to become involved in an argument with West German poltical parties over what constituted German national interest. The SED added to the complexity of the situation by maintaining that citizens of the GDR and the FRG share a common nationality – German. Hence the argument that there are two nations of one nationality.[35] It follows that, as far as the SED is concerned, there is no 'national question': it has been resolved.

Since 1971 the SED has avoided using the adjective German. Article 1 of the Constitution, 'The GDR is a socialist state of the German nation', has become, 'The GDR is a socialist state of workers and peasants';[36] the German Academy of Sciences has become the Academy of Sciences of the GDR, and so on. Interestingly enough, one institution has retained its name, the SED. Strictly speaking the party should now be called the Socialist Unity Party of the GDR.

The SED is faced with quite a legitimacy problem. Apparently in 1975 over two-thirds of the GDR population did not regard the Federal Republic as abroad. Only about a quarter of GDR citizens were firm supporters of the regime, while about one-fifth of them rejected it, also in 1975.[37]

Abgrenzung

Relations between states having differing social systems fall within the ambit of peaceful co-existence. This concept has three aspects: a form of class struggle; non-nuclear competition with the capitalist world; and co-operation, especially with the West.[38]

Class Struggle
The SED has repeatedly underlined the fact that there can be no reconciliation between 'socialism' and 'capitalism', between the 'socialist' GDR and the 'imperialist' FRG. Indeed

> peaceful co-existence is not akin to class peace between socialist and imperialist states since there can be no class peace and no class harmony between the working class and the bourgeoisie. The policy of peaceful co-existence, as a form of class competition between socialism and capitalism, abolishes neither classes nor the class struggle. Therefore it is always accompanied by sharp, ideological struggle.[39]

The class struggle between the two German states is not confined to Germany, it is conducted on a world-wide basis. The SED sees itself in the front line, and as having a special role to play in this regard, in defending the border between socialism and capitalism. Erich Honecker, at the VIIIth Congress of the SED, stressed the fact that the contradictions between the GDR and the FRG were increasing since the FRG was proceeding along a capitalist path of development. This was producing a situation where the 'process of *Abgrenzung* between both states was gathering pace in all areas of social life'. Hence *Abgrenzung* is understood to be something which started after the war and will eventually lead to contact between the two German states only at governmental level.

Peter Ludz makes a distinction between intervention and intercession in intra-German affairs.[40] Intervention in the internal affairs of another sovereign state is contrary to the UN Charter and to the Helsinki Final Act. Intercession is acceptable under international law, permitting one country to influence events in another and lying somewhere between intervention and non-intervention.

Until the revision of the constitution in 1974, the SED legally held to the reality of one German nation and was thereby able to justify certain of its activities in the FRG. The 1968 constitution declared that the goal of the GDR and her citizens was to overcome the division of Germany and to bring the two German states closer and closer together until eventual unification on the basis of democracy and socialism was achieved. The 1974 constitution dropped all this and merely refers to the duty of the GDR and her citizens to observe the rules of international law.[41] Since then the situation has been unclear. Presumably the SED would regard it as legitimate, in a time of crisis, to aid economically, politically and possibly militarily those forces whose goal it was to establish a Marxist-Leninist state in the FRG. The SED would not classify this as intervention, merely as aiding the class struggle in the FRG, thereby doing its international class duty. The SED can also work through such parties as the SEW (the SED in West Berlin) and the German Communist Party (DKP) in West Germany.

Co-operation

The Basic Treaty, effective as of 21 June 1973, made it encumbent on both states to negotiate a whole series of agreements to improve mutual relations. Among those which have been negotiated so far are: the accreditation of journalists in East Berlin and Bonn; the protection of the frontiers and the development of frontier waterways; the exchange of permanent missions (the missions began functioning on 20 June 1974); a health agreement; the development of the transport routes to West Berlin; a post and telecommunications agreement; an agreement to exploit lignite deposits on the frontier. Negotiations are continuing in several other fields. There are also three permanent commissions: on the frontier, transit and traffic.

These agreements do not contradict the concept of *Abgrenzung* since they were all negotiated at governmental level. Indeed more and more categories of people in the GDR are being banned from direct contact with citizens of the FRG.

The number of West Germans visiting the GDR has jumped since the travel agreement was signed in 1972. It reached 3,120,000 in 1976. The flow from the GDR (almost exclusively pensioners) has risen by a quarter since 1971. It stood at 1,330,000 in 1976. In the same year 14,850,000 West Germans and West Berliners used the transit routes in both directions.[42] The flow of so many West Germans into the country poses certain problems for the SED and the security police as well as the opportunity of recruiting agents and gathering Intelligence. However the problems far outweigh the opportunities. The average East German has direct contact with the average West German; thus contrasting the image of West Germany drawn by the SED with the one the average West German makes in the East. It makes *Abgrenzung* that little bit more difficult to enforce. The GDR government must have a compelling reason for concluding so many agreements and for allowing so many 'foreigners' to wander around the republic. It has: it is called money.

Each West German visitor has to spend a minimum amount every day during his stay. Another powerful stimulus is the need to develop intra-German trade. It was first regulated by the Berlin Agreement of 1951 and since then GDR trade with the FRG has developed faster than GDR trade with other Western industrial nations. The EEC founding members, in 1957, afforded a special status to GDR trade with the FRG. The GDR, until the signing of the Basic Treaty, always denied the special status of intra-German trade and was wont to classify trade with the FRG as foreign trade. The Basic Treaty appears to recognise its special status.[43] The FRG has always been interested in expanding this trade on political and especially on all-German political grounds. On the other hand the GDR has been politically wary but has expanded trade on economic grounds. However, given the economic potential of the GDR, she has not achieved a level of foreign trade as a proportion of gross domestic product commensurate with her economic ranking in the world.[44] In other words she does not trade enough with the rest of the world, including the FRG. Given her resource base and the small home market, she might have achieved greater growth if she had expanded her foreign trade turnover more rapidly.

What advantages does the GDR draw from intra-German trade? She can export agricultural produce without any dues or charges; she can buy Cuban sugar at a low price and export it at a high price; she can raise the price of her exports since turnover tax is reduced; due to calculating imports from the FRG in constant units, price rises in the FRG have practically no effect. Quantifying the advantages is much more difficult. However, Reinhold Biskup has put the value of the waiving of import charges to the GDR at some DM 230 million and the financial advantages of being a 'supernumerary member' of the European Community in 1970 at DM 500 million.[45] Added to this is the saving or interest-free credit enjoyed by the GDR, since she is in deficit on intra-German trade. In 1974 the credit stood at DM 660 million, in 1975 it had risen to DM 790 million and in 1976 it hit the ceiling imposed by the FRG in 1974, DM 850 million. The overall trade deficit has been growing; at the end of 1970 it amounted to DM 1400 million but it had climbed to DM 2400 million by the end of 1975.

The structure of the trade is quite different. The GDR imports predominately investment goods, especially for the chemical industry. In 1974 over one-third of GDR exports were made up of food and textiles, while about three-quarters of FRG exports were composed of production and investment goods.[46] The GDR, already in substantial deficit, will need to diversify her exports if only because the developing world will become increasingly competitive, especially where textiles are concerned. However, the GDR has no choice, she must continue to import investment goods and technological know-how. Intra-German trade is much more important to the GDR than to the FRG. In 1973 it came to less than 2 per cent of total West German trade turnover but to 9·2 per cent of total GDR trade.[47]

Relations with the third world

Until April 1969, the GDR was recognised by only thirteen states, all socialist. Then came the breakthrough; between 1969 and 1971 seventeen more states recognised the GDR; afterwards the rush became an avalanche and the GDR enered the UN and at last established diplomatic relations with the USA, in September 1974.

During the 1950s and 1960s the GDR displayed great ingenuity in overcoming the refusal of the Western world to extend diplomatic recognition to her. The first step on the road to full diplomatic recognition was the acceptance of trade missions by most developed countries; other countries accepted trade missions at governmental level and others permitted the establishment of general consulates. With the exception of Finland, countries falling into these two categories belonged exclusively to the developing world. Hence in 1971, even though the GDR exchanged ambassadors with only thirty states, she had representatives in sixty-one countries. Altogether the GDR has used twelve routes to full diplomatic recognition – ranging from the direct establishment of an embassy to the setting up of a chamber of foreign trade, upgraded to an office, then a mission and finally into an embassy.[48]

Thus trade paved the way for political recognition, especially in the Third World. However a price had to be paid. Large credits had to be extended and aid programmes arranged. Egypt[49] set the pace, closely followed by Syria. Between 1953 and 1965, the GDR signed thirty agreements with Egypt. In the 1970s the GDR expanded her diplomatic and economic activities to all parts of the Third World.

Relations with countries regarded as socialist are governed by the precepts of socialist internationalism. Relations at party level come under the heading of proletarian internationalism. The SED regards it as its international and proletarian duty to support all those states and parties which are struggling for national independence and striving to build a socialist tomorrow. This involves aid in all its forms, including military aid. The GDR has been playing an active role in Africa ever since President Nimeiri of the Sudan became the first African head of state to visit the GDR in 1970. Today it is rare for a month to go by without a delegation from an African country visiting the GDR. Of particular interest to the GDR are Mozambique and Angola. An SED delegation, headed by Werner Lamberz, attended the IIIrd FRELIMO Congress, in Maputo, in February 1977 and Lamberz assured President Samora Machel that the 'SED and the socialist German state would also in the future be found at the side of FRELIMO to help carry through the people's democratic revolution and to vitiate all imperialist attacks against the young people's republic.'[50] In Mozambique the GDR Ministry of State Security is actively involved in developing the National Service for People's Security (SNASP). In Angola, according to Holden Roberto, head of the FNLA, GDR specialists head the Section for Information and Security (DISA).[51] Both these organisations are responsible for re-educating political prisoners in labour camps. Aid to Angola exceeded 10 million Marks in 1976.[52]

The GDR is directly involved in the guerrilla war with Rhodesia. Solidarity gifts are regularly sent to the African National Congress (ANC) and during the handing-over ceremony in Lusaka of one such delivery, Hans Scharf stressed the 'close ties of the people of the GDR with the freedom struggle of the Zimbabwe patriots'.[53] Besides providing instructors in guerrilla warfare, the NVA has many radio operators in guerrilla camps in Mozambique. One estimate of GDR involvement puts the number of officers and NCOs at 430.[54]

The policies pursued by the GDR brings her into conflict with some of the African governments with whom she has diplomatic relations. On 2 May 1977 Zaire expelled GDR diplomats, accusing them of involvement in the invasion of her southern province, Shaba. On four other occasions diplomatic relations have been severed. Ghana, in 1966, the Central African Empire and Zambia, in 1971 and Morocco, in 1975, all broke with East Berlin but diplomatic relations have been restored with all these states.

All this diplomatic activity provides the SED with a wider platform on which to conduct its ideological offensive against the FRG. One of the SED's goals is to draw the German question out of its European context and to internationalise it. It has been doing this successfully during the late 1970s.

The GDR needs to import raw materials and energy, especially oil, from the Third World so she is keenly interested in developing trade. However the lack of convertible currency and the shortage of hard currency will restrict economic relations with the developing world. The demands, issued after the IVth UNCTAD Conference, that the Third World should be allowed to participate in East-West trade, that trade between Comecon and the developing world should not be conducted in non-convertible currencies and that aid should be stepped up to at least 1 per cent of the social product will all have an effect on the GDR. The Third World has shown its gratitude for the political support which it has received from the socialist world; now it is asking for a large increase in economic aid. The GDR, as the most developed economy in Comecon, will be expected to play an increasing role in Comecon-Third World aid programmes. The political and economic opportunities for the GDR in the developing world are considerable: will she be able to grasp them fully?

THE IXTH CONGRESS

The XXVth Congress of the CPSU which took place in Moscow in February/March 1976 was a triumph for Leonid Ilich Brezhnev. The proceedings were stage-managed very well and the Secretary-General exuded confidence and optimism, especially in the realm of foreign policy. Nevertheless no innovatory policies emerged from the congress. In Berlin, the impressive new glass-and-concrete edifice, the Palace of the Republic, played host to the IXth Congress of the SED which sat between 18 and 22 May 1976. Thus it took place after the CPSU Congress and in its shadow. It was even better stage-managed and Erich Honecker rose to the occasion and looked and acted every inch the dominant force in the SED. The Secretary-General, for so he was renamed in the new party statute, gloried in the trimmings of power. There were the torchlight processions, the delegation of the NVA and the border troops who marched right up to the rostrum, accompanied by military music, to declare the fealty of the armed forces, and the several hundred children from the Ernst Thälmann Pioneer organisation who sang his praises. The whole Congress grew into a convention of declaration and acclamation.[55] There were no new turnings in social or economic policy and the openness of a Brezhnev in criticising the shortcomings of the economy was missing. Indicative of the uncritical mood of the occasion was the unanimous acceptance of the new party programme and statute, without a word of discussion being offered. The whole show was superbly ordered, arranged and transformed into an event which had impact not only in the GDR but abroad, thanks in part to the exemplary facilities afforded foreign journalists at the congress. The only jarring notes for some journalists were the images which flashed through their minds of similar, brilliantly enacted political conventions of yesteryear.

The self-confident SED was on show and it had plenty to boast about. The years since the VIIIth Congress in 1971 had brought something which the SED had been struggling for in vain for over two decades — the entry of the GDR on to the international stage as a sovereign state. On the economic and social fronts the years had been very good; indeed it all added up to the best five years the GDR had ever experienced. As Erich Honecker exclaimed to the 2500 delegates: 'We have chosen the right road' and 'it has all been worth while'. There were no doubters among the delegates on these points.

A closer look at the proceedings reveals differing shades of emphasis. The Minister of National Defence, Heinz Hoffmann, gloried in the increased battle-readiness of the NVA occasioned 'above all by the introduction of modern Soviet weapon systems and the increase in the fire power and manoeuvrability of the land and sea forces'. Concomitant to this was a violent attack on the objectives of the 'all-German Wehrmacht'. Oskar Fischer, the Foreign Minister, on the other hand presented the GDR as a state which was 'open to the world and keen to co-operate'. The FRG was referred to as 'our immediate neighbour' and Fischer expressed the desire of the GDR for further co-operation. Margot Honecker, Minister of Education, pointed out that the SED would have to give more weight to the claims and needs of young people.[56] The Secretary-General, on the other hand, stressed the need for hard work, order, discipline and strength of mind when referring to young people.

Although the equation increase in labour productivity equals increase in living standards appeared in many guises the population clearly expected improvements to be announced at the congress, especially as the new draft programme spoke of improvements in living standards. Over 1,200,000 requests were forwarded to the SED during the run-up to the congress. An increase in old-age pensions appears to have been a constant theme in these letters. The new Five-Year Plan directives, passed by the congress, contained nothing about raising pensions. However, on 27 May 1976, five days after the end of the congress, it was announced that old-age and disability pensions were to go up as of 1 December 1976. Minimum wages were also to be increased from 350 to 400 Marks per month, from 1 October 1976; 1,200,000 three-shift workers were to have their working week reduced to 40 hours as from 1

May 1977; shift workers were to qualify for an extra three days' holiday from 1 January 1977; teachers and educationalists were to receive a thirteenth month's pay; mothers were to have their maternity leave extended to twenty-six weeks and the working week was to be reduced for mothers with two or more children under sixteen years of age.[57] The Secretary-General, speaking at the Xth Parliament of the FDJ, put the cost of these measures, over the period 1976–80, at 14,000 million Marks. It would appear that these improvements were wrung out of a reluctant SED as a result of popular disappointment. Had the SED had a choice it would have introduced them piecemeal and over a longer period of time.

These changes illustrate once again the Secretary-General's concern for the less well off and the importance he attaches to the social demands made by workers. Put another way he has a sharp eye for possible sources of unrest. Security is now afforded more weight than under Ulbricht.

The 90,000 or so private artisan firms received a fillip in the form of tax changes which were backdated to 1 January 1976. This was not all. Whereas the draft programme had spoken of involving the artisans in solving the problem of services, the programme finally adopted at the congress stated that 'the private provision of services would be systematically promoted . . . '. This was a change in direction for the SED. Prior to the congress life had been getting more difficult for self-employed plumbers, electricians, etc., especially since the national-isation of private and semi-private industry in 1972.

Harry Tisch, chairman of the FDGB, was also a bearer of glad tidings; in the name of the trade unions, he promised 100,000 extra dwellings for 1980. The Five-Year Plan envisaged 550,000 newly constructed dwellings and a further 200,000 renovated homes. It was not made clear how many of the extra 100,000 would be newly built and how many would be merely refurbished dwellings.

CHANGES IN PERSONNEL

The Central Committee

The CC elected at the IXth Congress was the largest ever: 145 members and 57 candidates, 202 in all. Of the 135 members of the 1971 CC, 13 died between Congresses and 8 were dropped. Of the 54 candidates elected to the 1971 CC, 23 were promoted to full membership and 9 disappeared. There are only 8 entirely new members of the 1976 CC but 35 new candidates.

Among the new candidates, those employed in the party and state *apparat* and in the economy make up the lion's share: 3 are functionaries of the mass organisations, 3 are involved in education, culture, etc., and 1 is the deputy chief of the political administration of the NVA. The diplomatic service and foreign trade have been upgraded, with three ambassadors and a state secretary becoming candidates. Others involved in foreign affairs in the CC are Oskar Fischer, the Foreign Minister; Herbert Krolikowski, his First Deputy; Peter Florin, GDR Permanent Representative at the UN and Harry Ott, GDR Ambassador to the Soviet Union. Horst Sölle, Minister for Foreign Trade, and Gerhard Weiss, GDR Representative in Comecon, are also full members of the CC. These changes reflect the entry of the GDR on to the world stage.

Not surprisingly the educational level of CC members is on the rise. (See Table 5.1.) It is most marked among candidate members. About one-third of the members are now in the 50–9 age range. This has raised the average age of members to 55 years. The average age of candidates has also increased, compared with the 1971 CC, to 47 years.

TABLE 5.1 Members and candidates of the CC in 1976 according to the function they were performing when elected; and the proportion of graduates

	Members		Candidates	
	Total	of which graduates	Total	of which graduates
		%		%
Party *apparat*	59	37 (63)	15	13 (87)
State *apparat*	46	23 (50)	13	11 (85)
Leading positions in the economy	12	12 (100)	16	16 (100)
Mass organisations	13	10 (77)	7	7 (100)
Education, Culture, Science, Free professions	11	9 (82)	5	5 (100)
Others	4	–	1	–
Total	145	91 (63%)	57	52 (91%)

The Politburo

The first plenary session of the CC after the IXth Congress elected a Politburo composed of nineteen members and nine candidate members.

This made it the largest Politburo ever to have been assembled. One reason for the growth of the supreme policy-making body was the desire of the Secretary-General to underline continuity. No member of Ulbricht's Politburo has been removed except to the other world. Newcomers to full membership after the congress were: Werner Felfe, a candidate member since 1973 and first secretary of *Bezirk* Halle since 1971; Erich Mielke, a candidate member since 1971 and Minister of State Security since 1957; Konrad Naumann, a candidate member since 1973 and first secretary of *Bezirk* Berlin since 1971. New candidate members were: Horst Dohlus, a secretary of the CC since 1973; Joachim Herrmann, who also became a secretary of the CC after the congress; Egon Krenz, first secretary of the Central Council of the FDJ since 1974; and Werner Walde, first secretary of *Bezirk* Cottbus since 1969.

The milieu from which these promoted men emanated mirrors the Secretary-General's own career. Of the new members Felfe and Naumann acquired their political skills in the FDJ and Mielke in security matters. Of the candidates, Herrmann was in the FDJ and Krenz still is. This leaves Dohlus, who has been in the CC Secretariat a long time, and Walde, who has been in the party *apparat* in Cottbus since 1953. Why Walde gained preference over other first secretaries is not apparent to an outsider. The FDJ connection is now very pronounced in the Politburo, with nine of the twenty-eight members and candidates having had experience in it.

Later in the same year, in October 1976, Willi Stoph reverted to his previous position as Prime Minister, replacing Horst Sindermann, who became President of the *Volkskammer*. At the same time Günter Mittag ceased to be First Deputy Prime Minister and returned to his pre-October 1973 position, that of CC secretary for the economy. Werner Krolikowski moved to Mittag's former position and became First Deputy Prime Minister. Stoph's successor as chairman of the Council of State was none other than Erich Honecker. Hence the SED Secretary-General became head of the party and head of state one year ahead of his mentor, Leonid Brezhnev. This was a mere acknowledgement of his true power. Not formally being head of state had not prevented Honecker from signing the treaty of friendship with the USSR and the Final Act at Helsinki. Here again he took after the CPSU leader.

THE SOCIAL STRUCTURE OF SED MEMBERSHIP[58]

In his report to the congress, Erich Honecker, proudly announced that SED membership had topped the 2 million mark. As of May 1976, there were 1,914,382 members and 129,315 candidate members or 2,043,697 persons in the party. Thus the membership level achieved by the SED before the tumultous events of June 1953 had again been equalled. The 1976 figure represented a larger proportion of the population since the number of GDR citizens had dropped since 1953. 'Every sixth GDR citizen over 18 years of age and every eighth GDR citizen between the ages of 18 and 25 is a party member or a candidate member,' declared the Secretary-General.

He put the proportion of party members who were workers at 56·1 per cent but claimed that 74·9 per cent of members and candidate members were of working-class origin. Both figures were lower than those quoted in 1971. Then 56·6 per cent were workers (the highest ever recorded) and 76·8 per cent were of working-class origin. Collective farm peasants made up 5·2 per cent in 1976 (5·9 per cent in 1971), the intelligentsia amounted to 20 per cent (17·1 per cent in 1971) and the employees made up 11·5 per cent (13 per cent in 1971); 7·2 per cent of members went unclassified in 1976.

As regards the age structure, the party is in a very healthy state: 43·4 per cent of members and candidates are under 40 years of age, 20·1 per cent are under 30 years of age and 12·2 per cent are under 25. It appears that, compared with 1971, the number of under-25s has increased markedly, with a reduction in 25—30-year-olds and the 31—40-year-olds remaining constant. The sudden influx of under-25s is connected with the campaign to recruit new members – over 100,000 FDJ members joined the SED as a result of it. The age structure of the SED is now much more favourable than that of the GDR population.

The level of education of party members has also risen appreciably. In 1976, 27·4 per cent of members and candidates were graduates. As recently as 1973 it had only been 22·5 per cent. This indicates that the proportion of graduates in the party is higher than in the population as a whole. Further, all secretaries of *Bezirk* and *Kreis* committees and 93·7 per cent of party secretaries in *Kombinate* and large enterprises were graduates in 1976. The party now expects a considerable number of its new candidate members to be graduates. Into this category fall those who have been through the party schools. To progress in the party now, a young functionary must, almost without exception, be a graduate.

The number of women in the SED has increased and the percentage of females in the party rose to 31·3 per cent in 1976 (28·7 per cent in 1971). Nevertheless women are still underrepresented, compared with their numbers in the population and in the labour force, where they are in the majority.

THE NEW PROGRAMME[59]

The original idea of the party leadership had been to revise the first programme, passed in 1963, as a consequence of the decisions taken at the VIIIth Congress. However it soon turned out that a thorough revision of the language and concepts which the excitement of the early NES period had thrown up was needed. A commission, chaired by the First Secretary, consisting of forty-two persons, was set up at the VIth Plenum of the CC of the SED in July 1972.

The new programme bears the imprint of the Honecker era. Gone are the concepts borrowed from systems theory and cybernetics, gone is the convoluted Marxist-Leninist language; a real effort has been made to present the goals of the SED in terminology which is accessible to the average citizen. To this end the document is about half the length of its predecessor.

In order to popularise it, the new programme was published in draft form in *Neues Deutschland* on 14 January 1976 and 'presented for discussion'. Two days later the new draft statute was published. These two documents together with the directives for the Five-Year Plan 1976—80 aroused enormous interest and the man in the street jumped at the opportunity of adding his comments. He had much to say about the desirability of reducing the working week to forty hours, about raising wages and pensions and about his wish to enjoy longer holidays. So much so that the First Secretary, speaking at a *Kreis* party conference in Weisswater on 14 February 1976, was led to criticise the critics: 'The tenor of the discussion so far makes it necessary for *Kreis* executives and primary organisations to conduct it more strictly and more resolutely. Discussion must not be allowed to take its own course.'[60] This took the steam out of the discussion but, according to Kurt Hager, there were still 1905 proposed changes to the draft programme. Of these 442 were accepted and the result was 125 changes or additions.

The new programme reflects the changes in SED thinking about the German nation which have occurred since 1971. *Abgrenzung* is the declared policy and the flowering of the socialist nation in the GDR is linked to the 'development of closer links with the other nations in the socialist commonwealth'. The provisions of the Soviet-GDR treaty of October 1975 have been worked into the text but the Basic Treaty between the FRG and the GDR, signed on 21 December 1972, is not mentioned. One of the reasons for the scrapping of the twenty-year Soviet-GDR treaty, signed in 1964, was the wording of Article 7, which bound both sides to work towards the 'creation of a peace-loving, democratic, unified German state'. The 1975 pact has no all-German ambitions.

The goal of the SED, in the new programme, is a 'developed socialist society'. Gone is Ulbricht's formulation: 'the developed social system of socialism'. The party thereby underlines the fact that it has abandoned the GDR model of socialism, promoted by Ulbricht, and has returned to the Soviet way of thinking. However even within the framework of CPSU orthodoxy, the SED underlines the uniqueness of its own experience of building socialism in a developed industrial state. Interestingly enough the term 'socialist internationalism' does not appear in the programme. This expression was used to justify the invasion of Czechoslovakia in August 1968 and has become a stumbling block in relations with West European communist parties. Instead 'proletarian internationalism' is included, referring to relations between ruling and non-ruling communist parties. In international relations the only time the word socialist appears is in the expression socialist patriotism.[61]

The end goal of communism again appears on the horizon after having been pushed out of sight by Ulbricht in the years immediately prior to 1971.

THE NEW STATUTE

To go with the new programme, a new Statute, the Vth, was adopted on the last day of the IXth Congress, 22 May 1976. It replaced the IVth, Statute which had been valid since 1963. Paul Verner, chairman of the twenty-two-man commission set up in July 1972, reported that no fewer than 2445 proposals had been made to improve the draft statute. Of these 251 had had an impact and 51 changes had been made as a result. These alterations are all, however, of a minor nature.

Conditions of entry remain as before. A newcomer who must be at least eighteen years old, remains a candidate member for one year. Two testimonials are needed, from persons with at least two years' full membership of the SED. In addition they must have known the applicant personally for at least one year. A primary organisation may accept a candidate or member but his registration is only effective when it has been confirmed by the relevant *Kreis* executive. It is possible once again for a member to resign from the party. Between 1950 and 1976 he had to be struck off or expelled in order to leave the party while alive.

The supreme party organ is the congress, which is to meet every five years. Extraordinary congresses may be called but the SED has never convened one. The Central Committee is to meet at least once every six months and it is the supreme organ between congresses. Its sessions are private. The CC elects the Politburo, which 'guides politically the work of the CC between congresses'. The CC also elects the Secretariat, which 'is responsible for day-to-day business, chiefly the execution and control of party decrees and the selection of cadres'. Between congresses the CC may convene party conferences to discuss 'pressing questions of policy and tactics'. So far there have been three conferences, in 1949, 1952 and 1956.

The post of Secretary-General appears in the statute after a long absence and is based on the example of the CPSU. Between 1950 and 1953 the SED also referred to its top man as Secretary-General.

The SED is organised at *Bezirk*, city, *Kreis* and city *Bezirk* level depending on the territorial location. These bodies 'provide the political leadership of social development in their area, basing themselves on the party statutes'.

A primary organisation may have as few as three members and as many as 150. Honecker stated at the congress that there were 74,306 primary organisations. These organisations, besides having political-educational and organisational functions also have wide-ranging control duties. Whereas the 1963 Statute had stated that party organisations had no control functions 'due to the particular conditions of work of the state apparatus' the new Statute gives them the right to exercise 'control over the activities of the [state] apparatus in its implementation of party and government decrees and the maintenance of socialist legal norms.'

THE SED AND THE BERLIN CONFERENCE

As long as Stalin was alive there was little need for international conferences of communist party leaders. It was enough to be invited to spend a vacation in the Soviet Union for most communist party leaders to forget their differences. The dominating figure of Stalin ensured that the Soviet viewpoint prevailed. True there was Szklarska Poręba, the Cominform and the expulsion of the Yugoslavs – even Stalin could not enforce complete uniformity of interpretation. Khrushchev's attack on Stalin at the XXth Congress of the CPSU broke the seal of infallibility which had surrounded the CPSU. If the Soviet party could criticise its own record so could the other communist parties and even their relations with the CPSU before 1956 could be looked at in a new light. Things would never be the same again. Discipline would be very difficult to enforce especially in those countries where there was no Soviet military presence.

Conferences of communist and workers' parties, on a world scale, took place in Moscow in 1957, 1960 and 1969. At the last one the Basic Document went so far as to say:

All parties have equal rights. At present, when there is no leading centre of the international communist movement, the voluntary co-ordination of the parties' actions in the interests of the successful accomplishment of the tasks confronting them, acquires increased importance.[62]

On a European level the first meeting was at Karlovy Vary, in Czechoslovakia, in April 1967. The rapid changes of the 1970s made it more and more necessary to convene another European conference to arrive at a consensus which would be binding on all participants. Herbert Mies, chairman of the German Communist Party (DKP) expressed himself along these lines in November 1973.[63] At a meeting in Warsaw, in October 1974, it was decided to hold a conference in Berlin not later than mid-1975.[64] The second European conference of communist and workers' parties did not convene until 29 June 1976. Why did it take twenty months to get twenty-nine national parties (Albania and Iceland refused to attend) to sit down at the same table?

Détente, the unhealthy state of Western economies after 1973 and the increased status of some parties, especially the Italian and the French, added to the self-confidence of the non-ruling parties. Then came the Romanians and the Yugoslavs and it was clear from the beginning that they were not going to sign a document which reduced their auto nomy.

The CPSU had hoped, originally, to hold the conference some time after the signing of the Final Act in Helsinki in August 1975, and before the XXVth Congress of the CPSU in February 1976. French, Italian, Spanish, Romanian and Yugoslav opposition at various stages frustrated this plan. They were objecting to the contents of the final document. The editorial committee, set up at Budapest in December 1974, met sixteen times in East Berlin before a document which satisfied all parties was agreed upon at the last meeting on 10–11 June 1976. The SED played a leading role in reaching a compromise. This involved top-level meetings with those parties which had reservations about the text.

Apparently five versions of the final document were prepared by the SED between October 1975 and May 1976.[65] The main stumbling block was that the CPSU wished to go further than the Basic Document of 1969. It favoured an agreement which would be binding on all parties and which would provide a basis for action within the context of proletarian internationalism. This would have underlined the hegemonial position of the CPSU and was therefore a non-starter for the Romanians and the Yugoslavs and some West European parties. The key question was what concessions the CPSU would be willing to make just to have the conference convene. Just as at Helsinki, Leonid Brezhnev and his colleagues decided that the holding of the conference was their prime objective. That the Albanians did not come surprised no one. The CPSU would have had to abjure all developments since 1956 and adopt a *mea culpa* attitude towards the Albanians to have got them to Berlin. This was just not Leonid Ilich's style! Why the Icelanders did not come is not clear. Nevertheless to get Ceausescu (who had ignored Karlovy Vary), Tito (attending his first international communist conference since 1948), Berlinguer, Carrillo and Marchais around the same table with Brezhnev and the other East European leaders was quite a feat. It could only be done at considerable cost to Soviet ambitions. The final document was accepted but not signed and it was not binding. There was no argument over the document, it had been agreed before the conference. That the meeting took place at all was due to Soviet concessions but also to the skill and persistence of the SED in searching out and finding areas of agreement.

The conference was a feather in the cap for the SED. It underlined the international significance of the party and the trust placed in it by the CPSU. The SED represented a highly developed industrial society and its experience was of direct relevance to parties in Western Europe. Also it was tactically beneficial to the CPSU if the SED portrayed the Soviet party as *primus inter pares*.

At the conference the position of the CPSU and the SED were very similar. Both stressed proletarian internationalism, democracy and socialism *à la sovietique*, the validity of the East European socialist model for West European parties and the heretical nature of Maoism. The final document, referred to as the result of an exchange of views, avoided intra-socialist polemics and omitted all references to proletarian internationalism. This phrase has come to be associated with the claim that the CPSU was the dominant communist party. Instead the document spoke of 'international, comradely, voluntary co-operation and solidarity'.[66] This bore some resemblance to Brezhnev's concept of proletarian internationalism at the conference. He had viewed it as the solidarity which bound all communists together in their common struggle. Honecker, on the other hand, kept to the traditional meaning of the phrase.

The conference was a great success for the SED. It was superbly organised and the image of the party in the GDR was thereby enhanced. It also established links between the SED and the West European parties which were developed afterwards. The conference did not annul the 'Brezhnev Doctrine' but underlined its validity as far as the socialist bloc was concerned.

RELATIONS WITH THE YUGOSLAVS AND THE EURO-COMMUNISTS[67]

As long as Walter Ulbricht remained party leader, the SED found it very difficult to establish close relations with the League of Communists of Yugoslavia (LCY). The acrimonious exchanges of the 1948–55 period, exacerbated by the tensions of the 1958–62 years and the occupation of Czechoslovakia in August 1968, were too closely linked with the persona of Walter Ulbricht for the LCY and the SED to forgive and forget and start anew. It was only with the arrival of Erich Honecker that a fundamentally new relationship between East German and Yugoslav communists can be said to have come into being.

Tito visited the GDR in November 1974 and his visit was returned by Honecker in Belgrade in January 1977. These exchanges were possible because the SED had blunted its ideological campaign against Yugoslavia. The communiqué which followed Tito's visit spoke of co-operation based on the principles of sovereignty, independence, equality, non-intervention and mutual benefit, bearing in mind the particularities of internal development and the international situation. Honecker, in Belgrade, went further. He praised Tito's role in convening the European communist conference and called the Yugoslav policy of non-alignment a positive factor in international relations. He even went so far as to call Tito a 'model of a true communist for our youth'. But this was only for Yugoslav ears, the eulogy was not included in the version of the speech which appeared in *Neues Deutschland*. The official communiqué spoke of the 'high level' of party relations. If party contacts have been rewarding, so have economic relations. Trade turnover between 1971 and 1975 reached $1400 million, over twice the 1966–70 figure. Trade turnover is to double again between 1976 and 1980 and is to reach $2800 million. This is a part of a trend – Yugoslavia has been very successful in expanding trade with the Comecon countries, especially the USSR, during the 1970s.

Ideologically the SED now has less to fear from the LCY than formerly. The attractiveness of the Yugoslav model has been reduced by the economic difficulties of the country; especially inflation, unemployment, the need for so many workers to find employment abroad and the balance of payments deficits, leading to repeated devaluations of the dinar. Workers' self-management has lost some of its shiny appeal. The LCY has also reasserted its authority from the centre, especially since 1971–2. Whereas the SED, in early summer 1969, dismissed the LCY as a party which was 'gradually transforming itself into a party of a social democratic type', the verdict in the early 1970s was quite different. The SED is now cultivating better releations with all communist parties, ruling and non-ruling alike, and has not forgotten the services the LCY rendered the SED in the Third World during the 1960s. There is also the point that the better relations are with Belgrade the more likely the LCY is to lend a sympathetic ear to the SED's views on West Germany.

Since 1973–4 there has been a noticeable mildness in the SED's commentaries on developments within the Italian Communist Party (PCI), the French Communist Party (PCF) and the Communist Party of Spain (PCE) – the leading Eurocommunist parties. Heinz Timmermann has traced three phases in the SED's relations with the West European parties: the first, which extended to the mid-1960s, reveals very little dissent, since the West European parties were very flattering to the SED, regarding the GDR in many respects as the model of their own future socialist society – indeed the PCF held to this view until the end of the 1960s; the second phase, which lasted until the mid-1970s, was characterised by SED attacks on developments within the Eurocommunist parties and this led to less cordial relations; the third phase, the present much more cautious and understanding approach to the Eurocommunists, is geared to maintaining good relations with them.

West European communist parties were of great importance to the SED before the full diplomatic recognition of the GDR. They provided a platform for the SED's views in their respective countries and set in motion bilateral exchanges on a party and state basis, especially in France and Italy. The move towards a more critical attitude to the 'real socialism' of Eastern Europe, fuelled by the invasion of Czechoslovakia, alarmed the SED. There was the real danger of 'socialism with an occidental face' turning out to be very like 'socialism with a human face'.

This would increase its potential attractiveness to GDR citizens, not to speak of SED members.

The SED's approach to the problem of dampening the fires of 'revisionism' varied from party to party. In the case of small parties, such as the CP of Austria, it actively supported critics of the leadership and provided a mass of literature to back them up. The pro-Soviet faction eventually triumphed, much to the gratification of the SED. At a time when the Portuguese Communist Party (PCP) was under attack from the PCI and the PCF, the SED demonstrably expanded its contracts with the PCP, and Hermann Axen, CC secretary for international relations, visited Cunhal several times to express the solidarity of the SED and to agree on measures which aimed at strengthening the position of the PCP. As Heinz Timmermann says the SED was probably acting there as the surrogate of the CPSU.

An SED delegation visited the CP of Greece (pro-Moscow), in 1977, the first visit by a fraternal party from the socialist world. Visits were also paid, simultaneously, to the CP of Denmark and the CP of Norway, in June 1977. Here the removal of Reidar Larsen in November 1975, and his replacement by the pro-Soviet Martin Gunnar Knutsen, removed the CP of Norway from the ranks of the Eurocommunists, at least for the time being. One presumes that the SED did all it could to promote the chances of Knutsen becoming party chief.

The approach of the SED to the PCI and the PCF has been more cautious, especially since the Berlin Conference. However, the SED was very critical about the PCF's dropping of the concept of the dictatorship of the proletariat from its statute at the XXIInd Congress, in February 1976. Towards the Eurocommunists the SED has a sharply differentiated internal and external approach. Internally the SED rejects all manifestations of Eurocommunism and this came to a head in November 1976 when Wolf Biermann was deprived of his GDR citizenship. All the Eurocommunists joined Biermann and the GDR intellectuals who protested against the action of the GDR authorities. This led Kurt Hager, in a speech to social scientists, to refer to Eurocommunists in the same breath as social-democrats. He stated that there existed 'only the alternative of the revolutionary Marxist-Leninist path or the Eurocommunist social-democratic path of Biermann and Havemann'. These words were missing when the speech was printed in *Neues Deutschland*.[68] Evidentally internally the SED would have no truck with the ideals and goals of the Eurocommunists; no debate was permissible, only outright condemnation.

Externally the SED has drawn in its claws since the Berlin Conference.

The close contact which was built up during the preparations for the conference has been developed further. Relations between the SED and the PCF were very close until just before the conference. The hard line pursued by the SED and the changes in the orientation of the PCF appear to have led to mutual recrimination. Since the conference, however, the SED has been at pains to repair its fences with the PCF and there has been much to-ing and fro-ing between Berlin and Paris.

Relations with the PCI have been of great importance to the SED. To speak of a special relationship between the two parties might be going too far, but both the PCI and the SED are very keen to study and understand developments in their respective countries. Relations took a nose-dive, however, when Benito Corghi, a lorrydriver, was shot dead at the GDR-FRG border crossing at Rudolfstein-Hirschberg by GDR border guards on 5 August 1976. It transpired that Corghi was a member of the PCI and had fought in the Resistance. The SED was acutely embarrassed when asked for an explanation by the Italian government. Afterwards the SED redoubled its efforts to improve its relations with the PCI and ideological differences have been played down in the GDR media.

Contacts with the PCE have been close and, despite the disagreements between Santiago Carrillo and the CPSU, the SED has been engaged in an intensive round of discussions with Spanish Communists.

The SED lined up with the Hungarian, Polish and Romanian parties, at the conference of CC secretaries in Sofia in March 1977, to frustrate open criticism of the Eurocommunists as desired by the Soviet, Bulgarian and Czechoslovak parties. The SED is particularly keen not to forgo the close contacts developed before the Berlin Conference and, besides acting as a go-between for the CPSU, it pursues its own interests. The experience of the GDR, as a developed industrial state, is of particular relevance to West European parties. The prospect of the PCF and PCI participating in government is inviting for the SED as it would permit the expansion of contacts at all levels. Hence the SED plays down ideological differences and is the only East European party to have published in full the final document of the Brussels Conference of West European parties in January 1974, the speeches at the Berlin Conference in June 1976 and the Madrid declaration of the Eurocommunists in March 1977. However, it did not go so far as to published the civil rights charter of the Eurocommunists. Although *Neues Deutschland* did publish Moscow's attack on Carrillo and his book *Eurocommunism and the State*, which appeared in *Novoe Vremya* on 24 June 1977, it offered no commentary of its own.[69] An article by Hermann Axen on the historical significance of the Berlin Conference, published in August 1977, makes no mention of the ideological differences between the CPSU and the Eurocommunists.[70]

The open-mindedness *vis-à-vis* Eurocommunists contrasts starkly with the SED's attitude towards its own critics. Since the Berlin Conference Robert Havemann has been under house arrest, Wolf Biermann, Sarah Kirsch, Reiner Kunze, Manfred Krug, Katharina Thalbach, Eva-Maria and Nina Hagen, to name only a few, have left the GDR, many of them against their will, and Rudolf Bahro, author of the most penetrating critique of the party by one of its members, languishes in prison.[71] One explanation of this contradictory approach is that in the GDR those who speak for security have greater sway than those ideologists who favour a debate with the party's critics. Externally, since security is only marginally involved, it is the ideologists who have had their way. This does not mean that everyone in the upper echelons of the party favours a dialogue with the Eurocommunists, just that a significant number do and this group includes the Secretary-General.

NOTES

1 Jürgen Kuczynski, 'Mein Genosse Erich Honecker', *Die Weltbühne*, no. 24 (1971).

2 Details of these and other personnel changes will be found in: *DDR Handbuch*; Günther Buch, *Namen und Daten*; Heinz Lippmann, *Honecker Porträt eines Nachfolgers* (Cologne, 1971); Peter C. Ludz, *Die DDR zwischen Ost und West Politische Analysen 1961 bis 1976* (Munich, 1977).

3 Heinz Vortmann, 'Einkommensverteilung in der DDR', *DA*, no. 3 (1974) p. 274.

4 Idem.

5 Peter Probst, 'Verbesserungen im Gesundheitswesen', *DA*, no. 10 (1973) pp. 1020–1.

6 *Deutsche Lehrerzeitung*, no. 20 (3 May 1973) p. 27.

7 *Rahmenprogramm für Arbeitsgemeinschaften der Klassen 9 und 10– Wehrausbildung* (Berlin, DDR, 1973); Hartmut Vogt, 'Wehrerziehung der Kinder und Jugendlichen in der DDR', *DA*, no. 12 (1973) pp. 1289–90.

8 *Bildung und Erziehung*, C/1c/57, pp. 1–4; ibid.

9 *Bildungs – und Erziehungsplan für den Kindergarten* (Berlin, DDR, 1967) p. 173.

10 Vogt, op. cit., pp. 1284–5.

11 Klaus-Dieter Uckel, 'Probleme der Persönlichkeitsentwicklung aus der Sicht des Militärwesens', *Pädagogik*, 28, no. 4 (1973) p. 398.

12 Gisela Helwig, 'Entwurf für ein neues Jugendgesetz', *DA*, no. 7 (1973) pp. 687–8.

226   *Marxism-Leninism in the German Democratic Republic*

13 Manfred Rexin, 'DDR – Jugendgesetz in dritter Auflage', *DA*, no. 3 (1974) pp. 228–30.
14 Ludz, op. cit., p. 165.
15 *Statistisches Jahrbuch der DDR 1976* (Berlin, DDR, 1976) p. 264.
16 Idem.
17 Maria Haendcke-Hoppe, 'Betrachtungen zur aussenwirtschaftlichen Entwicklung der DDR 1976 und 1975', *DA* no. 3 (1977) p. 264.
18 The terms of trade is the index of export prices expressed as a percentage of the index of import prices. In this case the terms of trade had turned against the GDR since the prices of raw materials had increased faster than the prices of finished products.
19 Maria Haendcke-Hoppe, 'Aussenhandel – Integration – Planung 1971–75', *DA*, no. 3 (1976) p. 300.
20 *Leipziger Volksstimme*, 17 August 1975, for the 1974 price; and *Deutsche Aussenpolitik*, no. 4 (1976) p. 528, for the 1975 price. See also Haendcke-Hoppe, 'Betrachtungen . . . ', p. 265 (1 Transferable ruble = 5 Valuta Marks; 1 Valuta Mark = 1 Deutsche Mark); as of July 1976 1 Transferable ruble = 4.05 Marks.
21 *Beilage zur Tribüne*, no. 20 (20 January 1977) p. 4; Haendcke-Hoppe, 'Betrachtungen ... ', p. 265. Between 1971 and 1975, 12 million tonnes of oil were imported from hard currency countries.
22 *Statistisches Jahrbuch der DDR 1976*, p. 264.
23 *Pravda*, 25 February 1976.
24 *Sowjetunion 1975/76 Innenpolitik, Wirtschaft, Aussenpolitik Analyse und Berichte* (Munich, 1976) pp. 210–14.
25 *Pravda*, 7 October 1975.
26 Soviet views on the FRG and West Berlin did not always mirror those of the GDR. This resulted in *Pravda* toning down or reproducing articles from *Neues Deutschland* in abbreviated form. Compare the polemics against Hans-Dietrich Genscher, the FRG Foreign Minister, in *Neues Deutschland*, 30 May 1975, and the report in *Pravda*, 31 May 1975.
27 *Die Welt*, 9 and 30 October 1972; Wettig, *Die Sowjetunion . . .* , p. 212, n. 471.
28 *Wettig*, op. cit., p. 127.
29 *Dokumentation zur Entspannungspolitik der Bundesregierung* (Bonn, 1977) p. 190.
30 Ibid., p. 194.
31 Ludz, op. cit., p. 287.
32 Ibid., p. 288.
33 Ibid., p. 233.
34 Ibid., pp. 223, 227–31.
35 The Sorbs, of course, are an exception. They are GDR citizens of Sorbian nationality. Hermann Axen in an article in *World Marxist Review* (March 1976) refers to the GDR as a 'socialist nation of German nationality'.
36 This change was effective as of 7 October 1974. It is instructive that the 1974 alterations to the constitution were passed by the *Volkskammer* without any public debate although Article 65 of both the 1968 and 1974 constitutions states that fundamental changes should be presented to the population for debate. The 1974 changes underline the uncertainty of the SED on the

national question. It did not want an exchange of views with the public on this sensitive issue. The situation was quite different in 1968 when the constitution was confirmed by referendum.

37 Ludz, op. cit., p. 224.
38 Ibid., p. 200.
39 *Einheit*, no. 2 (1971) p. 223; Ludz, op. cit., p. 201.
40 Ludz, op. cit., p. 201.
41 Dietrich Müller-Römer, *Die neue Verfassung der DDR* (Cologne, 1974) p. 82.
42 *Jahresbericht der Bundesregierung 1976* (Bonn, 1977) p. 445.
43 Ludz, op. cit., p. 315.
44 Throughout the postwar era, *per capita* trade volume in the GDR has ranged from 50 to 60 per cent of that of the FRG. See Gert Leptin, *Die deutsche Wirtschaft nach 1945 Ein Ost-West Vergleich* (Opladen, 1971) p. 59; Paul Gregory and Gert Leptin, 'Similar Societies under Differing Economic Systems: The Case of the Two Germanys', *Soviet Studies*, vol. xxix, no. 4 (October 1977) p. 523.
45 Reinhold Biskup, *Deutschlands offene Handelsgrenze: Die DDR als Nutz-niesser des EWG – Protokolls über den innerdeutschen Handel* (Berlin, 1976) pp. 203, 206; Ludz, op. cit., pp. 315–6.
46 *DDR Handbuch*, pp. 423–4.
47 Ibid., p. 425.
48 Jürgen Radde, *Die aussenpolitische Führungselite der DDR* (Cologne, 1976) p. 36.
49 The breakthrough came with Ulbricht's visit to Egypt in 1965. The invitation from President Nasser was in part due to the preparatory work done by the Yugoslavs. Relations between the GDR and Yugoslavia had taken a turn for the better after the East Germans had agreed to pay reparations to the tune of about 100 million Marks in early 1963.
50 *ND*, 10 February 1977; Henning von Löwis of Menar, 'Solidarität und Subversion: Die Rolle der DDR im südlichen Afrika', *DA*, no. 6 (1977) p. 647.
51 *Süddeutsche Zeitung*, 3 November 1976; Henning von Löwis of Menar, op. cit., p. 644. Apparently East Germans are to be found among President Machel's personal bodyguard.
52 *ND*, 27 April 1977; Henning von Löwis of Menar, op. cit., p. 644.
53 *ND*, 26 January 1977; Henning von Löwis of Menar, op. cit., p. 645.
54 *Die Welt*, 10 November 1976; Henning von Löwis of Menar, op. cit., p. 645. The ANC newspaper *The Zimbabwe Review* is printed in the GDR, as is *Sechaba*, the official organ of the ANC of South Africa.
55 Karl Wilhelm Fricke, 'Der IX. Parteitag der SED', *DA*, no. 6 (1976) p. 561.
56 Ludz, op. cit., p. 168.
57 Dieter Heibel 'Zu den neuen sozialpolitischen Massnahmen der DDR', *DA*, no. 7 (1976) pp. 680–2; Gisela Helwig, 'Verstärkte Förderung der berufstä-tigen Mütter', *DA*, no. 7 (1976) pp. 683–6.
58 Ludz, op. cit., pp. 192–4.
59 Based on Karl Wilhelm Fricke, *Programm und Statut der SED vom 22 Mai 1976* (Cologne, 1976).
60 *ND*, 16 February 1976.

61 Fred Oldenburg, 'Die konservative Revolution. Das Parteiprogramm der Honecker-Ära', *DA*, no. 2 (1976) pp. 114–5.
62 *Pravda*, 18 June 1969; *Current Digest of the Soviet Press,* vol. xxi, no. 28, p. 24.
63 Ludz op. cit. . . . p. 264.
64 Karl Wilhelm Fricke, 'Die SED und die europäische KP-Konferenz', *DA*, no. 7 (1976) p. 673.
65 Ludz, op. cit., p. 265.
66 *ND*, 1 July 1976.
67 Heinz Timmermann, 'Ost-Berlins Beziehungen zu Jugoslawien und Euro-kommunisten', *DA*, no. 9 (1977) pp. 949–65; Jürgen Rühle, 'Euro-kommunismus – Arzt an wessen Krankenbett?', *DA*, no. 4 (1977) pp. 344–6; Manfred Steinkühler, 'Machiavellismus heute: Zum Verhältnis zwischen SED und IKP', *DA*, no. 2 (1974) pp. 121–4.
68 *Der Spiegel* (Hamburg), no. 51 (13 December 1976) p. 20. The words missing from *ND*, 26 November 1976, were also excised from the speech in a published brochure: *Der IX. Parteitag und die Gesellschaftswissenschaften: Reden auf der Konferenz der Gesellschaftswissenschaftler der DDR am 25 und 26 November 1976 in Berlin* (Berlin, DDR, 1976); Timmermann, op. cit., p. 960.
69 *ND*, 26/27 June 1977. The article was printed at the back of the newspaper, on p. 10.
70 Hermann Axen, 'The Historic Significance of the Berlin European Communist Conference', *World Marxist Review* (August 1977) pp. 11–20.
71 Rudolf Bahro, *Die Alternative Zur Kritik des real existierenden Sozialismus* (Cologne, 1977). Bahro's thesis is that the SED is redundant and should therefore be abolished and replaced by a new communist party. The moment has also come, according to him, to do away with the planned economy and the state bureaucracy which is needed to run it. He favours the introduction of the free economic associations described by Marx.

Appendix: Short Biographies

ACKERMANN, Anton (né Eugen Hanisch) Born 25 December 1905 in Thalheim, Erzgebirge. Member KPD 1926. Graduated from Lenin School, Moscow, 1928. Worked in German section of Comintern 1932. Member of CC, member of Politburo, KPD 1935. Fought in Spanish Civil War 1936–7, afterwards in USSR. Co-founder of NKFD 1943. In Saxony as member of Matern Group 1945. Member of Secretariat of CC, KPD 1945. Member of Saxon *Landtag* 1946. Author of special German road to socialism 1946–8. Member of Central Secretariat of SED 1946. State Secretary, Ministry of Foreign Affairs October 1949–October 1953. Member of CC October 1950–January 1954. Candidate member of Politburo October 1950–July 1953. Member of VK 1950–4. Supporter of Zaisser-Herrnstadt 'faction'. Expelled from CC 23 January 1954. Rehabilitated 29 July 1956. Head of Film Section, Ministry of Culture 1954–8. Member, Head of Culture, Education and Health Section, State Planning Commission 1958–. Died 4 May 1973.

APEL, Erich. Born 3 October 1917 in Judenbach, Thuringia. Mechanical engineer 1939, then soldier. Engineer in USSR 1946–52 Member of SED 1952. GDR Deputy Minister of Mechanical Engineering 1953–5. Minister 1955–8. Head, economic commission of Politburo February 1958. Candidate 1958–60. Member of CC 1960–5. Member of VK 1958–65. Candidate member of Politburo 1961–5. Secretary of CC July 1961–June 1962. Named Minister July 1962. Chairman of State Planning Commission and Deputy Chairman of Council of Ministers January 1963–65. Committed suicide 3 December 1965.

AXEN, Hermann. Born 6 March 1916 in Leipzig. Member of KJV 1932. Sentenced to three years' imprisonment 1935. Moved to USSR 1939. Member of KPD 1942 (according to GDR sources in prison in France and in Auschwitz and Buchenwald 1940–5). Co-founder of FDJ 1946. Secretary for organisation, then for agitation and propaganda, Central

229

Council of FDJ 1946–9. Secretary for agitation, CC, SED 1950. Member of CC, SED 1950–. Second SED secretary, *Bezirk* Berlin 1953–6. Member of VK 1954–. Chief editor *Neues Deutschland* 1956–66. Candidate member 1963–December 1970. Member of Politburo December 1970–. Secretary of CC, responsible for relations with fraternal parties February 1966–.

BARTSCH, Karl-Heinz. Born 25 November 1923 in Löblau, Danzig. Member of Hitler Youth Movement (HJ) 1932–9. Member of SS July 1940. Member of Waffen-SS April 1941. Member of SED 1949. Member of SED *Bezirk* Erfurt executive 1954–60. Professor of Animal Husbandry, Humboldt University November 1960–February 1963. Worked in, then Head of agricultural section of CC, SED 1960–2. Deputy Minister of Agriculture, early 1963. Member of CC January–February 1963. Candidate member of Politburo January–February 1963. Chairman of Agricultural Council of Council of Ministers and member Presidium of Council of Ministers 7–9 February 1963. Expelled from CC and relieved of all his government functions because he 'concealed his membership of the Waffen-SS and thereby greatly damaged the party' 9 February 1963.

BAUMANN, Edith. Born 1 August 1909 in Berlin. Member of SPD 1927, 1945. Member of SAP 1931. Imprisoned 1933–6. Member of CC, SED 1946–73. Deputy Chairman of FDJ 1946–9. First wife of Erich Honecker. Secretary of CC, then of SED *Bezirk* Berlin 1949–53. Candidate member of Politburo 1958–63. Member of VK 1950–73. Secretary of East Berlin city council 1963–73. Died 7 April 1973.

BECHER, Johannes R. Born 22 May 1891 in Munich. Member of KPD 1923. Emigrated to USSR 1935. President of League of Culture 1945–58. Member of PEN centre in GDR 1948–53. Member of VK 1949–58 Member of CC, SED 1946–58. Wrote words of GDR national anthem. Minister of Culture 1954–8. Author of many books. Died 1958.

BELING, Walter. Born 19 May 1899. Member of KPD 1924. Lecturer, Reich Party School of KPD, until 1933. Afterwards two and a half years in prison, then emigrated to France. Member of KPD 1945. Member of CC, SED 1946–. Member of Central Secretariat of SED 1947–50. Relieved of his functions in August 1950 in connection with Field affair. Rehabilitated 29 July 1956 Chief section Head, Ministry of Foreign Affairs 1957–9. Permanent GDR Representative in Economic Commission for Europe 1959 until retirement on pension.

BENJAMIN, Hilde (née Lange). Born 5 February 1902 in Bernburg. Member of KPD 1927. Lawyer in Berlin 1928–33. Reinstated by SMAD as lawyer in Berlin-Steglitz May 1945. Head of personnel department, Central Administration of Justice 1947–9. Vice-President, Supreme Court of GDR 1949–53. Member of VK 1949–67. Minister of Justice 1953–67. Member of CC, SED 1954–. Professor of Law 1967–.

DAHLEM, Franz. Born 13 January 1892 in Rohrbach, Lorraine. Member of SPD 1913–7. Member USPD 1917–20. Member of KPD 1920. Member of Reichstag 1928–33. Member of CC, KPD 1928–. Head of section on trade unions in CC, KPD 1928–. Illegal work for KPD in Berlin 1933–summer 1934. Emigrated to Paris. Member of KPD committee abroad. Political Head of International Brigade in Spain 1937–8. Fled to France 1938. In Vernet concentration camp 1939–42. In Mauthausen 1942. Returned to Germany October 1945. Member of KPD 1945. Member of CC, SED 1946–53. Member of Politburo 1950–3. Member of Secretariat of CC 1950–3. Member of VK 1949–54, 1963–. Relieved of all his functions for 'political blindness' by CC decree of 14–15 May 1953. Head of Section in state secretariat for Higher Education March 1955. Later first Deputy State Secretary for Higher Education, Deputy Minister of Higher and Technical Education 1967–74. Rehabilitated 29 July 1956. Co-opted on to CC January 1957. Member of CC 1958–75. Died 1975.

DOHLUS, Horst. Born 30 May 1925 in Plauen, Vogtland. Member of KPD 1946. Member of VK 1950–4, 1971–. Candidate member 1950–63. Member of CC 1963–. Second Secretary SED *Gebiet* Wismut 1953–4. SED Secretary of Schwarze Pumpe Kombinat, Hoyerswerda 1956–8. Second Secretary *Bezirk* Cottbus 1958–60. Head of Party organs section of CC 1960–. Head of Politburo commission on party and organisational questions 1964. Member of secretariat of CC June 1971–3. Secretary of CC 1973–. Candidate member of Politburo May 1976–.

EBERT, Friedrich. Born 12 September 1894 in Bremen, son of the first German President. Member of SPD 1913. Soldier 1915–8. Editor of *Vorwärts* and *Sozialdemokratischer Pressedienst* 1919–25. Member of Reichstag 1928–33. Imprisoned for eight months in 1933; under police surveillance until 1945. Soldier 1939–40 then employed by Reich publishing board. Member of SPD 1945. Secretary of SPD *Bezirk* Brandenburg-*Land* executive. Member of CC, SPD 1945–6. Member of CC, SED 1946–. Member of Central Secretariat/Politburo 1946–.

Oberbürgermeister of East Berlin November 1948–July 1967. Member of VK 1949–. Member of State Council of GDR September 1960–71. Deputy chairman 1971–.

EWALD, Georg. Born 30 October 1926 in Buchholz, *Kreis* Stralsund. Member of SED 1946. Student at SED Party High School 1953–4. First Secretary of *Kreis* Doberan 1954–5. First Secretary of *Kreis* Rügen 1955–60. First Secretary of *Bezirk* Neubrandenburg 1960–3. Member of CC 1963–73. Candidate member of Politburo 1963–73. Chairman of Agricultural Council of Council of Ministers and member of Presidium of Council of Ministers February 1963–73. Member of VK 1963–73. Minister of Agriculture, Forestry and Food November 1971– September 1973. Killed in road accident 14 September 1973.

FECHNER, Max. Born 27 July 1892 in Rixdorf bei Berlin. Member of SPD 1911–7, 1921. Member of USPD 1917–21. Imprisoned several times between 1933 and 1945. Chairman of CC, SPD 1945. Deputy chairman of SED 1946. President of Central Administration of Justice 1948–9. Minister of Justice 1949–53. Member of CC, SED 1950–3. After June 1953 uprising arrested and expelled from the SED on 26 July 1953 as an 'enemy of the state and party,' then amnestied. Re-admitted to SED June 1958.

FELFE, Werner. Born 4 January 1928 in Grossröhrsdorf. Member of KPD 1945. Instructor for SED in *Land* Saxony 1949–50. First Secretary of *Kreis* Flöha 1950–3. Second Secretary of Central Council, FDJ 1954–7. Member of VK 1954–8, 1971–. Candidate member 1954–63. Member of CC 1963–. Chairman of council of *Kreis* Zschopau 1957– 60. Chairman of council of *Bezirk* Karl-Marx-Stadt 1960–3. Deputy Section Head in CC, SED 1965–6. Secretary for agitation 1966–8. Second Secretary 1968–71. First Secretary *Bezirk* Halle May 1971–. Candidate member 1973–6. Member of Politburo 1976–.

FISCHER, Oskar. Born 19 March 1923 in Aš, Czechoslovakia. Soldier of Wehrmacht 1941–4. Prisoner-of-war in USSR 1944–6. Member of SED 1946. Worked in Czech factory 1946–7, then expelled from Czechoslovakia. Member of Central Council of FDJ 1949–52. Secretary of Central Council of FDJ 1951–5. GDR Ambassador to Bulgaria 1955–9. Head of Section, Ministry of Foreign Affairs 1959–65. Deputy Minister of Foreign Affairs 1965–73. State Secretary and Permanent Deputy Minister of Foreign Affairs 1973–5. Minister of Foreign Affairs January 1975–.

FLORIN, Peter. Born 2 December 1921 in Cologne. Grew up in Moscow. Graduate of Comintern School in the USSR. Member of KPD 1945. Deputy *Landrat* of *Kreis* Wittenberg 1945, then chief editor of *Freiheit* in Halle. Departmental Head, Ministry of Foreign Affairs 1949–53. Head of department of international relations of CC, SED 1953–67. Member of VK 1950–. Candidate member 1954–8. Member of CC 1958–. GDR Ambassador to Czechoslovakia 1967–9. State secretary and First Deputy Minister of Foreign Affairs 1969–73. Deputy Minister of Foreign Affairs and Permanent Representative of GDR in UN 1973–.

FRÖHLICH, Paul. Born 21 March 1913 in Niederplanitz, *Kreis* Zwickau. Member of KPD 1930, 1945. KPD secretary for agitation in Glauchau 1945. SED secretary for propaganda and culture, *Kreis* Dresden 1946–9. First Secretary *Kreis* Bautzen 1949–50. First Secretary *Kreis* Leipzig 1950–2. First Secretary *Bezirk* Leipzig 1952–70. Candidate member 1954–8. Member of CC 1958–70. Secretary of CC 1958–70. Candidate member 1958–63. Member of Politburo 1963–70. Member of VK 1954–70. Died 19 September 1970.

GNIFFKE, Erich. Born 14 February 1895 in Elbing. Member of SPD 1913. Secretary of General Free Employees' Union Braunschweig 1926. Owner of company and simultaneously in SPD opposition 1933–. Imprisoned 1938–9. Co-founder of SPD in Berlin 1945. Member of the CC, SPD 1945–6. Member of Central Secretariat of SED 1946–8. Fled to West Germany in October 1948. Later joined SPD. Died 4 September 1964.

GROTEWOHL, Otto. Born 11 March 1894 in Braunschweig. Member of Young Socialist Workers (SAJ) and SPD 1910. Member of Braunschweig *Landtag* 1920–5. Minister of Interior, Education and Justice of *Land* Braunschweig 1921–3. Member of Reichstag, Chairman of *Land* Braunschweig branch of the SPD 1925–33. Commercial traveller in Berlin 1933–. Imprisoned for seven months in 1938–9. Chairman of CC, SPD 1945–6. Member of CC, SED 1946–64. Member of Central Secretariat/Politburo 1946–64. Member of VK 1949–64. Chairman of Council of Ministers 1949–64. Died 21 September 1964.

GRÜNEBERG, Gerhard. Born 29 August 1921 in Lehnin, *Kreis* Brandenburg. Soldier and prisoner-of-war 1941–5. Member of KPD 1945. First SED Secretary of *Kreis* Guben 1947–8. Secretary and member of SED *Land* Brandenburg executive 1949–52. First Secretary of *Bezirk*

Frankfurt/Oder 1952–8. Secretary of CC 1958–. Candidate member February–July 1958. Member of CC 1958–. Member of VK 1958–. Candidate member December 1959–September 1966. Member of Politburo September 1966–. Secretary for agriculture of CC 1960–. Minister and member of Presidium of Council of Ministers July 1962–February 1963.

HAGER, Kurt (also known as Felix Albin). Born 24 July 1912 in Bietigheim, Enz. Member of KPD 1930, 1945. Fought in Spanish Civil War 1937–9. Émigré in France and England. Head of party education section, KPD 1945. Head of propaganda 1949. Head of science and universities 1952, in CC, SED. Professor of Philosophy, Humboldt University 1949–. Candidate member 1950–4. Member of CC 1954–. Secretary for science and culture of CC 1955–. Candidate member 1958–63. Member of Politburo 1963–. Member of VK 1958–.

HALBRITTER, Walter. Born 17 November 1927 in Hoym, *Kreis* Aschersleben. Member of SED 1946. Section Head, Ministry of Finance 1951–4. Section Head in planning and finance section of CC 1954–61. Deputy Minister of Finance 1961–3. Deputy Chairman of State Planning Commission and Chairman of the committee on labour and wages 1963–5. Head of the Bureau of Prices of the Council of Ministers December 1965–. Member of CC April 1967–. Candidate member of Politburo April 1967–October 1973. Member of the Presidium of the Council of Ministers and members of the VK 1967–.

HERRMANN, Joachim. Born 29 October 1928 in Berlin. Member of SED 1946. Deputy editor 1949–52, chief editor FDJ organ *Junge Welt* 1952–60. Member of Central Council of FDJ 1952–9. Secretary of Central Council of FDJ 1958–9. Chief editor *Berliner Zeitung* 1962–5. Member of SED *Bezirk* Berlin executive 1962–7. State Secretary for All-German/West German affairs December 1965–June 1971. Candidate member 1967–71. Member of CC 1971–. Chief editor *Neues Deutschland* June 1971–76. Secretary of CC 1976–. Candidate member of Politburo 1976–.

HERRNSTADT, Rudolf. Born 17 March 1903 in Gleiwitz. Member of KPD 1924. Emigrated to USSR 1933. Soviet citizen. Co-founder of NKFD 1943. Chief editor *Berliner Zeitung* 1945. Chief editor *Neues Deutschland* 1949–53. Member of CC and Candidate member of Politburo 1950–3. Removed from CC and Politburo on 26 July 1953 for 'factionalism'. Expelled from SED on 23 January 1954. Employed in German Central Archives, Merseburg 1954–66. Died on 28 August 1966.

HERTWIG, Hans-Joachim. Born 16 July 1928 in Schmiedeberg. Member of SPD 1945. Secretary and Deputy Chairman of Ernst Thälmann Pioneer movement 1960–6. Member of CC, SED 1954–. SED Secretary for science, education and culture October 1966–September 1968. Second Secretary September 1968–May 1971, First Secretary of *Bezirk* Frankfurt/Oder May 1971–. Member of VK 1971–.

HOFFMANN, Karl-Heinz. Born 28 November 1910 in Mannheim. Member of KPD 1930. Emigrated to the USSR 1935. Fought in Spanish Civil War 1936–9. Returned to the USSR 1939, to Germany 1945. Worked in SED *Land* Berlin executive, then Head of Political culture section of chief administration of People's Police. Inspector General and Head of chief administration for training 1950. Candidate member 1950–2. Member of CC 1952–. Member of VK 1950–. Lt-General of KVP and Deputy Minister of the Interior and Head of the KVP 1952–5. First Deputy Minister for National Defence 1956–60. Lt-General of NVA October 1959. Minister of National Defence July 1960–. General of the Army March 1961. Member of Politburo October 1973–. Member of National Defence Council.

HONECKER, Erich. Born 25 August 1912 in Neunkirchen, Saar. Member of KPD 1929. Secretary of Communist Youth Association (KJV) in Saar 1931. Arrested 1935 and sentenced to ten years' imprisonment in 1937. Youth Secretary of CC, KPD 1945. First Secretary of FDJ 1946–55. Member of CC, SED 1946–. Member of VK 1949–. Candidate member 1950–8. Member of Politburo 1958–. Secretary of CC 1958–71. Secretary 1960–71; Chairman of National Defence Council 1971–. First Secretary of CC 3 May 1971. Secretary-General of CC 1976–. Member of Council of State 1971–.

HONECKER, Margot (née Feist). Born 17 April 1927 in Halle/Saale. Member of KPD 1945. FDJ Head of culture and education section 1947–8. Secretary for culture and education in *Land* Saxony-Anhalt 1948–9. Head of Young Pioneers section, then Secretary for Young Pioneers in Central Council of FDJ 1949–53. Member of Central Council of FDJ 1946. Member of VK 1949–54, 1967–. Candidate member 1950–63. Member of CC 1963–. Married Erich Honecker

236 *Marxism-Leninism in the German Democratic Republic*

1953. Section Head, Ministry of Education 1958. Deputy Minister August 1958–November 1963. Minister of Education November 1963–.

JAROWINSKY, Werner. Born 25 April 1927 in Leningrad. Member of KPD 1945. Student of economics at Humboldt University and University of Halle/Saale 1948–51. Doctorate 1956. Sectional Head, Ministry of Trade and Supply, 1956–9. Deputy Minister 1959–. State Secretary and first Deputy Minister of Trade and Supply 1961–3. Member of CC 1963–. Candidate member of Politburo 1963–. Member of VK 1963–. Secretary for trade and supply of CC November 1963–.

JENDRETZKY, Hans. Born 20 July 1897 in Berlin. Member of KPD 1920. KPD Secretary in Frankfurt/Oder 1928. Imprisoned 1934–7, 1944–5; in concentration camp 1937–8. *Stadtrat* for labour in Berlin 1945. Chairman of FDGB 1946–8. SED First Secretary of *Bezirk* Berlin 1948–53. Member of VK 1949–53, 1958–. Member of CC 1946–54, 1957–. Candidate member of Politburo 1950–3. Removed from Politburo July 1953 as supporter of Zaisser-Herrnstadt 'faction'. Rehabilitated 29 July 1956. Deputy Minister of the Interior 1957–60. State Secretary and Head of secretariat of Council of Ministers 1960–1. Chief of Central Commission for State Control 1961–3.

KARSTEN, August. Born 20 December 1888 in Peine. Member of USPD 1917–22. Member of SPD 1922. Member of control commission 1920–4. Member of Reichstag 1920–33. Imprisoned for short spells 1933–45. Member of SPD 1945. Member of CC, SPD 1945. Member of Central Secretariat, SED 1946–9, then relieved of all party posts.

KERN, Käthe. Born 22 July 1900 in Darmstadt. Member of SPD 1920. Member of SPD *Bezirk* Berlin committee 1928–33, 1945–6. Imprisoned for short spells 1933–45. Head of women's secretariat and member of CC, SPD 1945–6. Member of CC, SED 1946–. Head of women's secretariat of CC, SED 1946–9. Member of VK 1949–. Head of section, Ministry of Health 1949–70.

KLEIBER, Günther. Born 16 September 1931 in Eula, *Kreis* Borna. Member of SED 1949. Engineering student at Universities of Rostock and Dresden 1953–8. Lecturer, University of Dresden, 1958–62. Head of section on electronics and data processing SED *Bezirk* Dresden 1964–6. State Secretary for co-ordination and management of introduction and use of electronic data processing of Council of Ministers

December 1966–June 1971. Member of CC 1967–. Candidate member of Politburo 1967–. Member of VK 1967–. Deputy Chairman of the Council of Ministers June 1971–. Minister for General Machine Building 1973–.

KOHL, Michael. Born 28 September 1929 in Sondershausen. Member of SED. Lecturer in international law, University of Jena 1956–. Head of law section, Ministry of Foreign Affairs, 1961–3. Head of fundamental questions section 1964–5. State Secretary, Council of Ministers May 1965–. Head of GDR Permanent Mission in West Germany June 1974–. Candidate member CC 1976–.

KROLIKOWSKI, Herbert. Born 15 March 1924 in Oels, Silesia. Labour service 1942, then soldier, prisoner-of-war in the USSR until 1949. Member of SED 1952. Diplomat at GDR embassy to USSR 1955–8. Head of Scandinavian section, Ministry of Foreign Affairs 1958–60. Head of first European section (USSR), Ministry of Foreign Affairs 1962–3. Deputy Minister of Foreign Affairs 1963–9. GDR Ambassador to Czechoslovakia August 1969–October 1973. First Deputy Minister of Foreign Affairs January 1975–. Candidate member of CC June 1971.

KROLIKOWSKI, Werner. Born 12 March 1928 in Oels, Silesia. Member of SED 1946. Head of agitation SED *Land* Mecklenburg 1950–2, then First Secretary of *Kreis* Ribnitz-Damgarten until December 1952 when he was dismissed for infraction of the party statute. First secretary of *Kreis* Greifswald 1954–8. Secretary for agitation and propaganda *Bezirk* Rostock 1958–60. First Secretary of *Bezirk* Dresden May 1960–October 1972. Member of CC 1963–. Member of VK 1963–. Member of Politburo June 1971–. Secretary for economy of CC October 1973–October 1976. First Deputy Chairman of Council of Ministers October 1976–.

KURELLA, Alfred. Born 2 May 1905 in Brieg. Member of KPD 1918. Worked in Comintern 1927–32. In USSR 1934–54. Member of SED 1954. Director of Institute of Literature, Leipzig 1954–7. Member of presiding council of DKB 1957–75. Head of commission for cultural questions of Politburo 1957–63. Candidate member 1958–63. Member of CC 1963–75. Member of VK 1958–75. Vice-President of Academy of Arts 1965–75. Died 12 June 1975.

LAMBERZ, Werner. Born 14 April 1929 in Mayen, Rhineland. Member of SED 1947. FDJ secretary of *Land* Brandenburg 1951–2. Student at Komsomol University, Moscow, 1952–3. Member and Secretary of Central Council of FDJ 1953–63. Candidate member 1963–7. Member of CC 1967–78. Secretary for agitation of CC 1967–78. Head of foreign information section 1963–6. Head of section of agitation of CC 1966–71. Member of VK 1967–78. Candidate member December 1970–June 1971. Member of Politburo June 1971–8. Killed in air accident 6 March 1978.

LANGE, Ingeborg. Born 24 July 1927 in Leipzig. Member of KPD 1945. Secretary of Central Council of FDJ 1952–61. Member of VK 1952–4, 1963–. Employed in CC 1961– (Head of section on women and Chairman of commission on women of Politburo). Candidate member 1963–4. Member of CC 1964–. Candidate member of Politburo October 1973–. Secretary for women of CC October 1973–.

LEHMANN, Helmut. Born 1 December 1882 in Berlin. Member of SPD 1905. Full-time union official 1907–. Deputy chairman of German *Krankenkassenverband* 1914–23. Chairman 1923–33. Arrested several times after 1933, condemned for attempted high treason 1944. Member of CC, SPD 1945. Member of CC, SED 1946–59. Member of Central Secretariat/Politburo 1946–50. Member of VK 1950–9. Died 9 February 1959.

LEUSCHNER, Bruno. Born 12 August 1910. Member of KPD 1931, 1945. Imprisoned in concentration camps 1936–45. Head of economics section of CC, KPD 1945–6. Head of economics section CC, SED 1946–. Head of planning section in DWK 1947. State secretary in Ministry of Planning 1949. Member of VK 1949–64. Deputy Chairman 1950–2. Chairman of State Planning Commission 1952–61. Member of CC, SED 1950–65. Candidate member 1953–8. Member of Politburo 1958–65. Deputy Chairman of Council of Ministers 1955–65. Member of Council of State 1960–3. GDR representative in Comecon 1961–5. Died 10 February 1965.

MATERN, Hermann. Born 17 June 1893 in Burg bei Magdeburg. Member of SPD 1911. Member of USPD 1918. Member of KPD 1919. KPD Secretary of *Bezirk* Magdeburg-Anhalt 1928. Secretary in East Prussia mid-1932–April 1933. Secretary in Pomerania (Stettin) April 1933–July 1933. Arrested 14 July 1933; escaped from Altdamm prison 19

September 1934. Émigré from 1934 in Czechoslovakia, Switzerland, Austria, France, the Netherlands, Denmark, Norway and Sweden. Moved to Moscow May 1941. Co-founder of NKFD 1943. Headed group to Dresden May 1945. Chairman of KPD in *Land* Saxony 1945. Chairman of SED *Land* Berlin executive April 1946–. Member of CC, SED 1946–71. Member of Central Secretariat/Politburo 1946–71. Chairman of Central Party Control Commission January 1949–71. Member of VK 1949–71. Died 24 January 1971.

MEIER, Otto. Born 3 January 1889 in Magdeburg. Member of SPD 1911–7, 1922–46. Member of USPD 1917–22. Member of Prussian *Landtag* 1921–33. Illegal party work 1933–. Arrested 1944. Member of CC, SPD 1945. Member of CC and Central Secretariat Politburo, SED 1946–50. Afterwards politically unimportant. Died 10 April 1962.

MERKER, Paul. Born 1 February 1894 in Oberlossnitz bei Dresden. Member of USPD 1917–8. Member of KPD 1919. KPD functionary responsible for trade union matters. Member of *Land* Berlin executive of illegal KPD 1933. Émigré in France and Mexico. Founder of *Freies Deutschland* movement in Mexico and editor of newspaper of same name. Returned to Germany July 1946. Member of SED 1946. Member of CC 1946–50. Member of Central Secretariat/Politburo 1946–50. State Secretary in Ministry of Agriculture and Forestry 1949–50. Expelled from SED because of contacts with Noel H. Field 24 April 1950. Arrested 20 December 1952 as 'hostile agent'. Released 1956. Not rehabilitated. Reader for *Volk und Wissen* Publishing Co. 1957. Chairman of *Kreis* Königs Wusterhausen committee of Society for German-Soviet Friendship 1961–9. Died 13 May 1969.

MEWIS, Karl. Born 22 November 1907 in Hann.-Münden. Member of KPD 1924, 1945. KPD functionary until 1933. Fought in Spanish Civil War 1936–9. Émigré in Sweden as KPD functionary under pseudonym of Fritz Arndt. Imprisoned in Sweden 1942–3. KPD functionary in *Land* Mecklenburg 1945. SED Secretary of *Land* Berlin 1946–9. Member of VK 1949–63. Second Secretary 1949–51, First Secretary 1951–2 of *Land* Mecklenburg. Candidate member 1950–2. Member of CC 1952–. First secretary of *Bezirk* Rostock 1952–61. Candidate member of Politburo 1958–63. Member of Council of State 1960–3. Minister and Chairman of State Planning Commission July 1961– January 1963. GDR Ambassador to Poland April 1963–November 68.

MIELKE, Erich. Born 28 December 1907 in Berlin. Member of KPD 1925. Involved in murder of Police Captains Anlauf and Lenk in Berlin April 1931. Fled country. Fought in Spanish Civil War 1936–9. Émigré in the USSR. Returned to Germany 1945. Vice-President of Central Administration of the Interior in Berlin-Wilhelmsruh 1946. Built up political police with Wilhelm Zaisser. State Secretary in Ministry of State Security 1950–3, 1955–7. Member of CC 1950–. Deputy State Secretary for state security in Ministry of the Interior 1953–5. Minister of State Security 1957–. Member of VK 1958–. Colonel-General October 1959. Candidate member 1971–6. Member of Politburo 1976–. Member of National Defence Council.

MITTAG, Günter. Born 8 October 1926 in Stettin. Member of SED 1946. Employed in CC 1951. Head of transport and communications section of CC 1953–8. Secretary of economic commission of Politburo 1958–61. Candidate member 1958–62. Member of CC 1962–. Deputy Chairman and Secretary of Council of National Economy 1961–2. Secretary for economy of CC June 1962–October 1973, October 1976–. Candidate member January 1963–September 1966. Member of Politburo September 1966–. Member of VK 1963–. Member of Council of State 1963–71. First Deputy Chairman of Council of Ministers October 1973–October 1976.

MÜCKENBERGER, Erich. Born 8 June 1910 in Chemnitz. Member of SPD 1927, 1945. SED *Kreis* secretary and city deputy Chemnitz (Karl-Marx-Stadt) 1946–8. Second Secretary of *Land* Saxony 1948–9. First Secretary of *Land* Thuringia 1949–52. Member of VK 1949–. Member of CC 1950–. Candidate member 1950–8. Member of Politburo 1958–. First Secretary of *Bezirk* Erfurt 1952–3. Secretary for agriculture of CC 1953–60. First Secretary of *Bezirk* Frankfurt/Oder 1961–71. Chairman of Central Party Control Commission 1971–.

MÜLLER, Margarete. Born 18 February 1931 in Neustadt, Upper Silesia. Member of SED 1951. Student at University of Leningrad 1953–8. Chairman of *Pionier* collective farm in Kotelow. *Kreis* Neubrandenburg February 1960–. Candidate member 1960–2. Member of SED *Bezirk* Neubrandenburg bureau 1962–3. Member of CC January 1963. Candidate member of Politburo 1963–. Member of VK 1963–. Member of Council of State 1971–.

NAUMANN, Konrad. Born 25 November 1928 in Leipzig. Member of

KPD 1945. Chairman of FDJ in Leipzig 1947–8. FDJ Secretary for labour *Land* Mecklenburg 1949–51. FDJ First Secretary of *Bezirk* Frankfurt/Oder 1952–7. Member of Central Council of FDJ 1952–67. Secretary of Central Council of FDJ 1957–64. Candidate member 1963–6. Member of CC 1966–. Member of VK 1967–. SED Secretary for party organs 1964–7. Second Secretary 1967–71, First Secretary *Bezirk* Berlin May 1971–. Candidate member October 1973–June 1976. Member of Politburo June 1976–.

NEUMANN, Alfred. Born 15 December 1909 in Berlin. Member of KPD 1929, 1945. Émigré in the USSR 1934. Fought in the Spanish Civil War 1938–9. Interned in France 1939–40. Returned to Germany 1941; arrested and sentenced to eight years' imprisonment in 1942. SED Secretary of *Kreis* Berlin-Neukölln 1946. Deputy Oberbürgermeister of East Berlin 1951–3. First Secretary of *Bezirk* Berlin 1953–7. Member of CC 1954–. Member of VK 1954–. Candidate member 1954–8. Member of Politburo 1958–. Secretary of CC 1957–61. Minister and Chairman of Council of National Economy 1961–5. Member of Presidium of Council of Ministers 1962–. Deputy Chairman 1965–8. First Deputy Chairman of Council of Ministers 1968–. Minister for Materials 1965–8.

NORDEN, Albert. Born 4 December 1904 in Myslowitz, East Upper Silesia. Member of KPD 1920. Chief editor *Ruhr-Echo*, Essen 1930, then deputy chief editor *Rote Fahne* until 1933. Émigré in France, Czechoslovakia and USA. Publisher of *Germany Today* in USA. Returned to Germany 1946. Chief press officer of DWK. Chief editor *Deutschland Stimme* 1948–9. Head of press section in GDR bureau of information 1949. Government speaker at press conferences, Secretary of committee for German unity 1954. Member of CC 1955–. Secretary of CC 1955–. Member of Politburo 1958–. Member of VK 1958–. Secretary and Head of commission on agitation of Politburo February 1963–.

OELSSNER, Fred. Born 27 February 1903 in Leipzig. Member of KPD 1920, 1945. Student in Moscow 1926–32. Employed in CC, KPD 1932–3. Émigré in Czechoslovakia and France 1933, then to the USSR 1935. Head of German department of Radio Moscow during Second World War. Head of agitation department of CC, KPD 1945–6. Head of party education in CC, SED 1946–50. Member of CC 1947–58. Member of VK 1949–58. Member of small secretariat of Politburo 1949–50. Member of Politburo 1950–8. Secretary for propaganda of CC 1950–5 and chief editor of *Einheit* until 1956. Deputy Chairman of Council of Ministers 1955–8. Removed from Politburo and relieved of all his state functions on 6 February 1958 because of criticism of Ulbricht's economic policy. Director of Institute of Social Sciences of Academy of Sciences of GDR 1958–69.

OTT, Harry. Born 15 October 1933. Student at State Institute for International Relations, Moscow 1953, then in Ministry of Foreign Affairs, then in international relations section of CC. Deputy Head of section 1966–74. GDR Ambassador to the USSR March 1974–. Member of CC 1976–.

PIECK, Wilhelm. Born 3 January 1876 in Guben. Member of SPD 1895–1918. Deserted from German army in 1918. Member of KPD 1918. Member of CC, KPD 1918. Member of Prussian *Landtag* 1921–8, 1932–3. Member of Reichstag 1928–33. Member of Comintern *apparat* 1928. Émigré in France 1933. Chairman of CC, KPD 1935. Later moved to the USSR. Chairman of the KPD in SBZ 1945–6. Co-chairman (with Otto Grotewohl) of SED 1946–54. President of German People's Council 1948. President of the GDR 1949–60. Member of VK 1949–60. Member of CC 1946–60. Member of Central Secretariat/Politburo 1946–60. Died 7 September 1960.

PISNIK, Alois. Born 8 September 1911 in Leoben, Styria, Austria. Member of Socialist Party of Austria (SPÖ) 1928. Member of Communist Party of Austria (KPÖ) 1933. Imprisoned 1935–6 in Austria. Sentenced to ten years' imprisonment in 1940 (in prison in Halle/Saale). Member of KPD 1945. SED Organisational Secretary in *Land* Saxony-Anhalt 1946–9. Member of Saxon *Landtag* 1948–52. SED Second Secretary of *Land* Saxony 1949–52. Member of CC 1950–. First Secretary of *Bezirk* Magdeburg 1952–. Candidate member of Politburo 1958–63. Member of VK 1958–.

RAU, Heinrich. Born 2 April 1899 in Feuerbach bei Stuttgart. Co-founder of KPD 1918. Section head in CC, KPD 1920. In the USSR 1936–7. Fought in the Spanish Civil War 1937–8. Interned in France 1939; transferred to Germany 1942, in Mauthausen until 1945. Minister of the Economy in *Land* Brandenburg 1946. Chairman of DWK 1946–9. Member of CC 1949–58. Member of Politburo 1949–58. Member of VK 1949–58. Minister for Economic Planning 1949. Deputy Chairman of the Council of Ministers and Chairman of the State Planning

Commission 1950–3. Minister for Machine Building 1953–5. Minister for Foreign Trade and Intra-German Trade 1955–8. Deputy chairman of the Council of Ministers 1955–8. Died 1958.

SCHIRDEWAN, Karl. Born 14 May 1907 in Königsberg, East Prussia. Member of KPD 1925, 1945. Arrested 1935, imprisoned 1935–8, then in concentration camps. Member of CC, SED, responsible for researching into activities of party members during National Socialist era 1946. Head of Western commission of CC 1947. First Secretary of *Land* Saxony March 1952. First Secretary of *Bezirk* Leipzig October 1952. Secretary for development and control of leading party organs and mass organisations section of CC December 1952. Member of CC 1952–8. Member of Secretariat 1952–8. Member of Politburo 1953–February 1958. Member of VK 1952–8. Together with Wollweber relieved of all party offices for 'factionalism' on 6 February 1958. Head of GDR State Archival Administration, Potsdam 1958–65. Engaged in self-criticism on 15 April 1959.

SCHMIDT, Elli. Born 9 August 1908 in Berlin. Member of KPD 1927. Head of women's secretariat in *Bezirk* Berlin-Brandenburg executive 1927. Illegal activity for KPD in Germany 1933–7. Émigré in Czechoslovakia, France. Moved to the USSR in 1940. Head of women's secretariat in CC, KPD and CC, SED 1945–9. Chairman of Democratic Women's Association of Germany (DFD) 1949–September 1953. Member of VK 1949–50. Member of Central Secretariat Politburo of SED 1946–50. Member of CC 1950–July 1953. Candidate member of Politburo 1950–July 1953. Relieved of all party functions as a result of her support of Zaisser-Herrnstadt 'faction'. Rehabilitated 29 July 1956. Head of German Fashion Institute December 1953–67.

SCHÖN, Otto. Born 9 August 1905 in Königsberg, East Prussia. Member of KPD 1925, 1945. KPD Secretary in Berlin, Saxony 1928. Imprisoned 1933–7. Member of SED *Land* Saxony executive 1947–50. Second Secretary of *Land* Saxony 1949–50. Member of CC 1950–68. Member of secretariat of CC 1950–3. Member of VK 1958–68. Head of bureau of Politburo of CC 1953–68. Died 15 September 1968.

SCHUMANN, Horst. Born 6 February 1924 in Berlin. Member of KPD 1945. FDJ First Secretary of *Land* Saxony 1950–2. FDJ First Secretary of *Bezirk* Leipzig 1952–3. Member of Central Council of FDJ 1952–67. Head of youth and sport section in CC, SED 1954–9. Candidate member July 1958–May 1959. Member of CC, SED May 1959–. First Secretary of Central Council of FDJ May 1959–May 1967. Member of Council of State 1960–71. Member of VK 1963–. SED Second Secretary June 1969–November 1970, First Secretary of *Bezirk* Leipzig November 1970–.

SCHÜRER, Gerhard. Born 14 April 1921 in Zwickau. Member of SED 1948. Employed in CC, SED 1953–62 (Head of planning and finance section 1960–2). Member of economic commission of Politburo 1960–2. Deputy Chairman 1962–3. First Deputy Chairman 1963–5. Chairman of State Planning Commission and member of Presidium of Council of Ministers December 1965–. Member of CC February 1963–. Deputy Chairman of Council of Ministers July 1967–. Member of VK 1967–. Candidate member of Politburo October 1973–. Member of National Defence Council.

SELBMANN, Fritz. Born 29 September 1899 in Lauterbach, Hesse. Member of KPD 1922. KPD *Bezirk* Head in Upper Silesia 1930, in Saxony 1931–3. Member of Reichstag 1932–3. Imprisoned in concentration camps 1933–45. Minister for the Economy and Economic Planning of *Land* Saxony 1946. Deputy Chairman of DWK 1948–9. Minister for Industry, Minister for Heavy Industry and Minister for Mining 1949–55. Member of VK 1954–63. Member of CC 1954–8. Deputy Chairman of Council of Ministers 1956–8. Deputy Chairman of State Planning Commission 1958–61. Deputy Chairman of Council of National Economy 1961. Chairman of commission on scientific technical services of State Planning Commission 1964. Died 26 January 1975.

SINDERMANN, Horst. Born 5 September 1915 in Dresden. Imprisoned 1934–45. Member of KPD 1945. Chief editor *Sächsische Volkszeitung*, Dresden 1945–6. Chief editor *Volksstimme*, Chemnitz 1946–7. SED First Secretary of *Kreis* Chemnitz and Leipzig 1947–9. Chief editor *Freiheit*, Halle/Saale 1950–3. Employed in CC, SED 1953–63. Candidate member 1958–63. Member of CC 1963–. Candidate member 1963–7. Member of Politburo 1967–. Member of VK 1963–. First Secretary of *Bezirk* Halle 1963–71. First Deputy Chairman of the Council of Ministers May 1971–October 1973. Chairman of Council of Ministers October 1973–October 1976. President of VK October 1976–.

STOPH, Willi. Born 9 July 1914 in Berlin. Member of KPD 1931, 1945. National service (military) 1935–7. Soldier in Second World War. Head of building materials and construction industry section of CC, KPD 1945–6 and of CC, SED 1946–7. Head of economic policy section of CC 1948–50. Member of VK 1950–. Member of secretariat of CC 1950–3. Minister of the Interior 1952–5. Member of Politburo 1953–. Deputy Chairman of Council of Ministers 1954–64. Minister of National Defence 1956–60. Colonel-General 1956. General of the Army 1 October 1959. Involved in co-ordination and control of implementation of decrees of CC and Council of Ministers 1960. First Deputy Chairman 1962–4; then Chairman of Council of Ministers 1964– October 1973, October 1976–. Member 1963–4. Deputy Chairman 1964–October 1973. Chairman of Council of State October 1973– October 1976.

TISCH, Harry. Born 28 March 1927 in Heinrichswalde, *Kreis* Ueckermünde. Member of KPD 1945. Trade union official, then Chairman of I. G. Metall *Land* Mecklenburg 1948–53. SED Secretary for the economy in *Bezirk* Rostock 1955–9. First Secretary of *Bezirk* Rostock 1961–75. Member of CC 1963–. Member of VK 1963–. Candidate member June 1971–5. Member of Politburo 1975–. Chairman of FDGB 1975–. Member of National Defence Council.

ULBRICHT, Walter. Born 30 June 1893 in Leipzig. Member of SPD 1912– 9. Soldier 1915–8. Member of *Spartakusbund* 1918. Member of KPD 1919. Member of CC, KPD 1923–. Secretary of CC, KPD 1923–. Member of Reichstag 1928–33. Head of KPD *Bezirk* Berlin-Brandenburg Grenzmark executive 1929–. Sentenced to two years in a fortress for high treason 1930. Émigré in France October 1933–8, in the USSR 1938–45. Secretary of Politburo of KPD in exile 1934–. Cofounder of NKFD 1943. Returned to Berlin as leader of Group April 1945. Key figure with Wilhelm Pieck in KPD. Deputy Chairman of SED 1946–50. Member of CC, SED 1946–73. Member of Central Secretariat/Politburo 1946–73. Secretary of CC 1946–71. Member of VK 1949–73. First Deputy Chairman of Council of Ministers 1949–60. Secretary-General of SED 1950–3. First Secretary of the CC July 1953– May 1971. Chairman of SED May 1971–August 1973. Chairman of National Defence Council February 1960–May 1971. Chairman of the Council of State September 1960–August 1973. Died 1 August 1973.

VERNER, Paul. Born 26 April 1911 in Chemnitz. Member of KPD 1929. Fought in Spanish Civil War 1936–9. Imprisoned in Sweden 1939–43. Industrial worker in Sweden 1943–5. Returned to Germany 1945. Co-founder of FDJ 1946. Member of secretariat of the Central Council of the FDJ 1946–9. Member of CC, SED 1950–. Member of the secretariat of CC, SED 1950–3, then Head of all-German affairs section of CC. Member of secretariat of CC 1958–. Candidate member 1958–63. Member of Politburo 1963–. Member of VK 1958–. First Secretary of *Bezirk* Berlin 1959–71. Secretary for security of CC 1971–. Member of Council of State 1971–. Member of National Defence Council.

VIEWEG, Kurt. Born 29 October 1911 in Göttingen. Member of KPD 1932, 1945. Émigré in Denmark and Sweden after 1933. Secretary-General of Mutual Peasant Aid (VdgB) 1949–53. Secretary for agriculture of CC 1950–3. Member of CC 1950–4, Professor and Director of the Institute of Agricultural Economics of the Academy of Agricultural Sciences of the GDR until 1957. Relieved of his functions because of 'revisionism' in 1957. Fled to West Germany. Returned to GDR in 1958 and sentenced to twelve years' imprisonment. Released in mid-1960s.

WANDEL, Paul. Born 16 February 1905 in Mannheim. Member of KPD 1923, 1945. Émigré in the USSR 1933. Member of CPSU. Worked for Comintern. Chief editor of *Deutsche Volkszeitung*, organ of KPD 1945. President of Central Administration for Education 1945–9. Minister of Education 1949–52. Member of CC, SED 1946–58. Member of VK 1949–58. Secretary for culture and education of CC 1953–7. Dismissed in October 1957, for lack of 'ruthlessness in carrying out cultural policy'. GDR Ambassador to the People's Republic of China 1958–61. Deputy Minister of Foreign Affairs 1961–4. President of League for Friendship among Peoples 1964–.

WARNKE, Herbert. Born 24 February 1902 in Hamburg. Member of KPD 1923, 1945. Involved in trade union affairs in Hamburg until 1933. Member of Reichstag 1932–3. Illegal work for KPD in Germany 1933–6. Émigré in Denmark 1936, Sweden 1938 and imprisoned there 1939–43. Returned to Germany 1945. Chairman of *Land* Mecklenburg committee of FDGB 1946, then Head of Works' council section in FDGB executive. Chairman of FDGB executive 1948–75. Member of VK 1949–75. Member of CC 1950–75. Member of secretariat of CC 1950–

3. Candidate member 1953–8. Member of Politburo 1958–75. Died 26 March 1975.

WINZER, Otto. Born 3 April 1902 in Berlin. Member of KPD 1919, 1945. Émigré in France, the Netherlands and the USSR 1935–45. Returned with the Ulbricht Group April 1945. Member of CC, KPD 1945–6. Counsellor for education in Gross-Berlin city council 1945–6. Member of Berlin city parliament 1946–8. Member of CC, SED 1947–75. State secretary and Head of private chancery of State President 1949–56. Member of VK 1950–75. Ambassador and Deputy Minister of Foreign Affairs 1956–8. First Deputy Minister and State Secretary in Ministry of Foreign Affairs 1958–65. Minister of Foreign Affairs June 1965–75. Died 3 March 1975.

WOLLWEBER, Ernst. Born 28 October 1898 in Hann.-Münden. Member of KPD 1919, 1945. Member of Prussian *Landtag* 1928–32. Member of Reichstag 1932. Illegal party work for KPD in Germany after 1933, then emigrated to Scandinavia. Comintern official there. Arrested in Sweden in 1940 and sentenced to three years' imprisonment. Transferred to USSR at request of Soviet government. Deputy Head 1946, Head of Directorate of Shipping 1947. State Secretary in Ministry of Transport 1949–53. State Secretary for Shipping May 1953. State Secretary for state security and Deputy Minister of the Interior July 1953–November 1955. Minister of State Security 1955–7. Member of CC, SED 1954–8. Member of VK 1954–8. Together with Karl Schirdewan, removed from CC on 6 February 1958, for 'factionalism'. Died 3 March 1967.

ZAISSER, Wilhelm. Born 19 January 1893 in Rotthausen-Gelsenkirchen. Member of KPD 1920. Leader of Red Army in Ruhr 1920. Moved to the USSR 1923. Participated in Canton uprising; later involved politically in Mukden. Returned to Germany 1930. Fought in Spanish Civil War under name of General Gomes. Returned to the USSR. Chief of Police in *Land* Saxony-Anhalt 1945. Minister of the Interior of *Land* Saxony 1948. Built up political police with Erich Mielke. Minister of State Security 1950-July 1953. Member of CC 1950–3. Member of Politburo 1950–3. Together with Rudolf Herrnstadt relieved of all his functions for 'factionalism'. Expelled from SED 1954. Died 3 March 1958.

ZILLER, Gerhart. Born 19 April 1912 in Dresden. Member of KPD 1930, 1945. *Stadtrat* for economic affairs in Meissen May 1945. Head of industry section in *Land* administration, later of *Land* government in

Saxony August 1945. Minister for Industry and Transport in *Land* Saxony April 1949. GDR Minister for Machine Construction October 1950. Minister for Heavy Industry December 1952–January 1954. Member of CC 1953–7. Secretary for economy of CC 1953–7. Member of VK 1953–7. Belonged to Schirdewan-Wollweber 'faction'. Committed suicide 14 December 1957.

Select Bibliography

NEWSPAPERS AND PERIODICALS

Beiträge zur Geschichte der Arbeiterbewegung
DDR-Report
Deutschland Archiv 1968–
Einheit
Forum
Neuer Weg
Neues Deutschland
SBZ Archiv 1950–68
Tribüne
Wirtschaftswissenschaft
Zeitschrift für Geschichtswissenschaft
Zeitschrift für Philosophie

BOOKS AND ARTICLES

General
A bis Z Ein Taschen- und Nachschlagebuch über den anderen Teil Deutschlands (Bonn, 1969).
Bichler, Hans, and Clemens Szamatolski, *Landwirtschaft in der DDR* (Berlin, 1973).
Brandt, Heinz *Ein Traum der nicht entführbar ist Mein Weg zwischen Ost und West*, 2nd ed. (Munich, 1978).
Bröll, Werner, *Die Wirtschaft der DDR Lage und Aussichten*, 2nd ed. (Munich, 1973).
Buch, Günther, *Namen und Daten Biographien wichtiger Personen der DDR* (Bonn, Berlin and Bad Godesberg, 1973).
Buhr, Manfred, and Alfred Kosing, *Kleines Wörterbuch der marxistisch-leninistischen Philosophie* (Berlin, DDR, 1975).
Childs, David, *East Germany* (London, 1969).
DDR-Handbuch (Cologne, 1975).

Deuerlein, Ernst, *DDR 1945–1970: Geschichte und Bestandsaufnahme*, 5th ed. (Munich, 1974).

Die DDR: Entwicklung, Probleme, Perspektiven (Frankfurt-am-Main, 1972).

Diepenthal, Wolfgang, *Drei Volksdemokratien* (Cologne, 1974).

Dokumente der Sozialistischen Einheitspartei Deutschlands, 13 vols (Berlin, DDR, 1948–74).

Duhnke, Horst, *Die KPD von 1933 bis 1945* (Cologne, 1972).

Duhnke, Horst, *Stalinismus in Deutschland Die Geschichte der sowjetischen Besatzungszone* (Cologne and Berlin, 1955).

Ehlert, Willi (ed.), *Wörterbuch der Ökonomie Sozialismus* (Berlin, DDR, 1973).

End, Heinrich, *Zweimal deutsche Aussenpolitik: Internationale Dimensionen des innerdeutschen Konflikts 1949–1972* (Cologne, 1973).

Erfolgreiche internationale Wirtschaftspolitik der SED (Berlin, DDR, 1971).

Förtsch, Eckart, *Die SED* (Stuttgart, 1969).

Forster, Thomas H., *Die NVA Kernstück der Landesverteidigung der DDR*, 4th ed. (Cologne, 1972).

Frank, Henning, *20 Jahre Zone* (Munich, 1965).

Gast, Gabriele, *Die politische Rolle der Frau in der DDR* (Düsseldorf, 1973).

Glaessner, Gert-Joachim, *Herrschaft durch Kader Leitung der Gesellschaft und Kaderpolitik in der DDR* (Opladen, 1977).

Gregory, Paul, and Gert Leptin, 'Similar Societies under Differing Economic Systems: The Case of the Two Germanys', *Soviet Studies*, vol. xxix, no. 4 (October 1977) pp. 519–42.

Hanhardt, Arthur M. Jr., *The German Democratic Republic* (Baltimore, 1968).

Hearnden, Arthur, *Education in the Two Germanies* (Oxford, 1974).

Helwig, Gisela, *Zwischen Familie und Beruf Die Stellung der Frau in beiden deutschen Staaten* (Cologne, 1974).

Heyen, Rolf, *Jugend in der DDR* (Bad Honnef and Darmstadt, 1972).

Hoffmann, U., *Die Veränderungen in der Sozialstruktur des Ministerrates der DDR 1949 bis 1969* (Düsseldorf, 1971).

Horn, Werner, *Der Kampf der SED um die Festigung der DDR und den Ubergang zur zweiten Etappe der Revolution (1949–1952)* (Berlin, DDR, 1960).

Horn, Werner, et al., *20 Jahre Sozialistische Einheitspartei Deutschlands Beiträge* (Berlin, DDR, 1966).

Hümmler, Heinz, *Die Partei* (Berlin, DDR, 1967).

Immler, Hans *Agrarpolitik in der DDR* (Cologne, 1971).

Introducing the GDR (Verlag Zeit im Bild Dresden, 1971).

Kaden, Albrecht, *Einheit oder Freiheit* (Hanover, 1964).

Kleines politisches Wörterbuch (Dietz Verlag Berlin, DDR, 1973).

Krieg, Harald, *LDP und NDP in der 'DDR' 1949–1958* (Cologne and Opladen, 1965).

Lapp, Peter Joachim, *Der Staatsrat im politischen System der DDR (1960–1971)* (Opladen, 1972).

Leonhard, Wolfgang, *Sowjetideologie Heute II: Die Politischen Lehren* (Frankfurt-am-Main, 1972).

Leptin, Gert, *Die deutsche Wirtschaft nach 1945: Ein Ost-West Vergleich* (Opladen, 1971).

Leptin, Gert (ed.), *Die Rolle der DDR in Osteuropa* (Berlin, 1974).

Lippmann, Heinz, *Honecker: Porträt eines Nachfolgers* (Cologne, 1971).

Lades, Hans (ed.), *20 Jahre Deutsche Demokratische Republik* (Munich, 1969).

Ludz, Peter C., *Die DDR zwischen Ost und West: Politische Analysen 1961 bis 1976)* (Munich, 1977).

Ludz, Peter C. (ed.), *Soziologie und Marxismus in der Deutschen Demokratischen Republik*, 2 vols (Neuwied and Berlin, 1972).

Ludz, Peter C. (ed.), *Studien und Materialien zur Soziologie in der DDR*, 2nd ed. (Cologne and Opladen, 1970).

Ludz, Peter C., *The Changing Party Elite in East Germany* (Cambridge, Massachusetts, 1972).

McCauley, Martin, 'East Germany', in Martin McCauley, *Communist Power in Europe 1944–1949* (London and New York, 1977).

Mahncke, Dieter, *Berlin im geteilten Deutschland* (Munich, 1973).

Mampel, Siegfried, *Die Entwicklung der Verfassungsordnung in der sowjetisch besetzten Zone Deutschlands von 1945 bis 1963* (Tübingen, 1964).

Materialien zum Bericht zur Lage der Nation 1974 (Bonn, 1974).

Mitzscherling, Peter, *et al., DDR-Wirtschaft Eine Bestandsaufnahme* (Frankfurt-am-Main, 1974).

Protokoll der 1. Parteikonferenz der Sozialistischen Einheitspartei Deutschlands, 25. bis 28. Januar 1949 im Hause der Deutschen Wirtschaftskommission zu Berlin, 2nd ed. (Berlin, DDR, 1950).

Protokoll der Verhandlungen der 2. Parteikonferenz der Sozialistischen Einheitspartei Deutschlands, 9. bis 12. Juli 1952 in der Werner-Seelenbinder-Halle zu Berlin (Berlin, DDR, 1952).

Protokoll der Verhandlungen der 3. Parteikonferenz der Sozialistischen Einheitspartei Deutschlands, 24. März bis 30. März 1956 in der Werner-Seelenbinder-Halle zu Berlin (Berlin, DDR, 1956).

Protokoll des Vereinigungsparteitages der Sozialdemokratischen Partei Deutschlands (SPD) und der Kommunistischen Partei Deutschlands (KPD) am 21. und 22. April 1946 in der Staatsoper 'Admiralspalast' in Berlin (Berlin, DDR, 1946).

Protokoll der Verhandlungen des II. Parteitages des Sozialistischen Einheitspartei Deutschlands, 20. bis 24. September 1947 in der Deutschen Staatsoper zu Berlin (Berlin, DDR, 1947).

Protokoll der Verhandlungen des III. Parteitages der Sozialistischen Einheitspartei Deutschlands, 20. bis 24. Juli 1950 in der Werner-Seelenbinder-Halle zu Berlin, 2 vols (Berlin, DDR, 1951).

Protokoll der Verhandlungen des IV. Parteitages der Sozialistischen Einheitspartei Deutschlands, 30. März bis 6. April 1954 in der Werner-Seelenbinder-Halle zu Berlin, 2 vols (Berlin, DDR, 1954).

Protokoll der Verhandlungen des V. Parteitages der Sozialistischen Einheitspartei Deutschlands, 10. bis 16 Juli 1958 in der Werner-Seelenbinder-Halle zu Berlin, 2 vols (Berlin, DDR, 1959).

Protokoll der Verhandlungen des VI. Parteitages der Sozialistischen Einheitspartei Deutschlands, 15. bis 21. Januar 1963 in der Werner-Seelenbinder-Halle zu Berlin, 4 vols (Berlin, DDR, 1963).

Protokoll der Verhandlungen des VII. parteitages der Sozialistischen Einheitspartei Deutschlands, 17. bis 22 April 1967 in der Werner-Seelenbinder-Halle zu Berlin, 4 vols (Berlin, DDR, 1967).

Protokoll der Verhandlungen des VIII. Parteitages der Sozialistischen Einheitspartei Deutschlands, 15. bis 19. Juni 1971 in der Werner-Seelenbinder-Halle zu Berlin, 2 vols (Berlin, DDR, 1971).

Protokoll der Verhandlungen des IX. Parteitages der Sozialistischen Einheitspartei Deutschlands, 18. bis 22. Mai 1976 im Palast der Republik in Berlin, 2 vols (Berlin, DDR, 1976).

Richert, Ernst, *Agitation und Propaganda: Das System der publizistischen Massenführung in der Sowjetzone* (Berlin, 1958).

Richert, Ernst, *Das zweite Deutschland: Ein Staat, der nicht sein darf* (Gütersloh, 1964).

Richert, Ernst, *Macht ohne Mandat*, 2nd ed. (Cologne and Opladen, 1963).

SBZ Biographie: Ein biographisches Nachschlagebuch über die Sowjetische Besatzungszone Deutschlands (Bonn and Berlin, 1965).

SBZ von 1945 bis 1954 (Bonn and Berlin, 1964).

Schlenk, Hans, *Der Binnenhandel der DDR* (Cologne, 1970).

Schwarze, Hannes Werner, *The GDR Today: Life in the 'Other' Germany* (London, 1973).

Schwarzenbach, Rudolf, *Die Kaderpolitik der SED in der Staatsverwaltung* (Cologne, 1976).

Schweizer, Carl Christoph, *Die deutsche Nation Aussagen von Bismarck bis Honecker Dokumentation* (Cologne, 1976).

Sikora, Franz, *Sozialistische Solidarität und nationale Interessen: Polen, Tschechoslowakei, DDR* (Cologne, 1977).

Slusser, Robert (ed.), *Soviet Economic Policy in Postwar Germany A Collection of Papers by former Soviet Officials* (New York, 1953).

Sontheimer, Kurt, and Wilhelm Bleek, *Die DDR: Politik, Gesellschaft, Wirtschaft* (Hamburg, 1973).

Statistisches Jahrbuch der DDR various years.

Stern, Carola, 'East Germany', in William E. Griffith (ed.), *Communism in Europe*, vol. 2 (Cambridge, Massachusetts, and London, 1966).

Stern, Carola, *Porträt einer bolschewistischen Partei* (Cologne, 1957).

Stern, Carola, *Ulbricht: Eine politische Biographie* (Cologne and Berlin, 1963).

Thomas, Rüdiger, *Modell DDR: Die kalkulierte Emanzipation*, 4th ed. (Munich, 1974).

Ulbricht, Walter, *Zur Geschichte der deutschen Arbeiterbewegung*, 10 vols (Berlin, DDR, 1953–71).

US Congress Senate Committee on Foreign Relations; *Documents on Germany 1944–1961* (Washington, DC, 1961).

von Münch, Ingo, *Quellentexte zur Rechtslage des Deutschen Reiches, der BRD und der DDR*, 2 vols (Stuttgart, 1974–6).

Weber, Hermann, *DDR: Grundriss der Geschichte 1945–1976* (Hanover, 1976).

Weber, Hermann, *Der deutsche Kommunismus: Dokumente* (Cologne and Berlin, 1963).

Weber, Hermann, *Die Sozialistische Einheitspartei Deutschlands 1946–1971* (Hanover, 1971).

Weber, Hermann, *Die Wandlung des deutschen Kommunismus Die Stalinisierung der KPD in der Weimarer Republik*, 2 vols (Frankfurt-am-Main, 1969).

Weber, Hermann, *Von der SBZ zur DDR 1945–1968* (Hanover, 1968).

Weber, Hermann, and Fred Oldenburg, *25 Jahre SED Chronik einer Partei* (Cologne, 1971).

Weber, Werner, and Werner Jahn *Synopse zur Deutschlandpolitik 1941 bis 1973* (Göttingen, 1973).

Wettig, Gerhard, *Die Sowjetunion, die DDR und die Deutschland-Frage*

1965–1976: Einvernehmen und Konflikt im sozialistischen Lager (Stuttgart, 1976).

Windsor, Philip, *Germany and the Management of Détente* (New York, 1971).

Wörterbuch zum sozialistischen Staat (Berlin, DDR, 1974).

Wörterbuch zur sozialistischen Jugendpolitik (Berlin, DDR, 1975).

Zauberman, Alfred, *Industrial Progress in Poland, Czechoslovakia and East Germany 1937–1962* (London 1964)

20 Jahre Sozialistische Einheitspartei Deutschlands Beiträge (Berlin, DDR, 1966).

20 Jahre SED – 20 Jahre schöpferischer Marxismus (Berlin, DDR, 1967).

Chapter 1

Adler, Hans, *Berlin in jenen Tagen Berichte aus der Zeit von 1945–1948* (Berlin, DDR, 1959).

Agsten, Rudolf, and Manfred Bogisch, *Bürgertum am Wendepunkt: Die Herausbildung der antifaschistisch-demokratischen und antiimperialistischen Grundhaltung bei den Mitgliedern der LDPD 1945–1946* (Berlin, DDR, 1970).

Agsten, Rudolf, and Manfred Bogisch, *LDPD auf dem Weg in die DDR Zur Geschichte der LDPD in den Jahren 1946–1949* (Berlin, DDR, 1974).

Benser, Günther, *Vereint sind wir unbesiegbar: Wie die SED entstand* (Berlin, DDR, 1961).

Berendt, Armin, *Wilhelm Külz* (Berlin, DDR, 1968).

Doernberg, Stefan, *Die Geburt eines neuen Deutschlands 1945–1949* (Berlin, DDR, 1959).

Fischer, Alexander, *Sowjetische Deutschlandpolitik im Zweiten Weltkrieg 1941–1945* (Stuttgart, 1975).

Gniffke, Erich W., *Jahre mit Ulbricht* (Cologne, 1966).

Goroschkowa G. N., *Die deutsche Volkskongressbewegung für Einheit und gerechten Frieden 1947–49* (Berlin, DDR, 1963).

Gruenewald, Wilhard, *Die Münchener Ministerpräsidentenkonferenz 1947: Anlass und Scheitern eines gesamtdeutschen Unternehmens* (Meisenheim/Glau, 1971).

Krippendorff, Ekkehart, *Die Liberal-Demokratische Partei Deutschlands in den sowjetischen Besatzungszone 1945–1948* (Düsseldorf, n. d.).

Krisch, Harry, *German Politics under Soviet Occupation* (New York and London, 1974).

Kulbach, Roderich, and Helmut Weber, *Parteien im Blocksystem der DDR* (Cologne, 1969).

Laschitza, Horst, *Kämpferische Demokratie gegen Faschismus* (Berlin, DDR, 1969).

Leonhard, Wolfgang, *Die Revolution entlässt ihre Kinder* (Frankfurt-am-Main, 1972).

McCauley, Martin, 'Liberal Democrats in the Soviet Zone of Germany 1945–47', *Journal of Contemporary History*, vol. 12, no. 4 (October 1977) pp. 779–89.

Mattedi, Norbert, *Gründung und Entwicklung der Parteien in der Sowjetischen Besatzungszone Deutschlands 1945–1949* (Bonn, 1966).

Moraw, Frank, *Die Parole der 'Einheit' und die Sozialdemokratie* (Bonn and Bad Godesberg, 1973).

Neef, Helmut, *Der Freiheit Morgenrot: Das deutsche Volk im Kampf um Einheit und Frieden 1945 bis 1947* (Berlin, DDR, 1960).

Nettl, J. P., *The Eastern Zone and Soviet Policy in Germany 1945–50* (London, 1951).

Niethammer, Lutz, *et al.*, *Arbeiterinitiative 1945* (Wuppertal, 1976).

'Oberbürgermeister in Jena 1945/46: Aus den Erinnerungen von Dr Heinrich Troeger', *Vierteljahrshefte für Zeitgeschichte*, 4, (October 1977) pp. 889–930.

Schaffer, Gordon, *Russian Zone* (London, 1947).

Scheurig, Bodo, *Free Germany*. (Middletown Connecticut 1969).

Schiller, Klaus J., *Die Sorben in der antifascistisch-demokratischen Umwälzung 1945–1949* (Bautzen, 1976).

Schoenhals, K., 'The "Free Germany" Movement and its Impact upon the German Democratic Republic', *East Central Europe*, 1, 2 (1974) pp. 115–31.

Staritz, Dietrich, *Sozialismus in einem halben Land: Zur Programmatik und Politik der KPD/SED in der Phase der antifaschistisch-demokratischen Umwälzung in der DDR* (Berlin, 1976).

Thomas, Siegfried, *Entscheidung in Berlin: Zur Entstehungsgeschichte der SED in der deutschen Hauptstadt 1945–46* (Berlin, DDR, 1964).

Wolff, Willy, *An der Seite der Roten Armee: Zum Wirken des National-komitees 'Freies Deutschland' an der sowjetisch-deutschen Front* 2nd ed. (Berlin, DDR, 1975).

Chapter 2

Baring, Arnulf, *Uprising in East Germany June 17, 1953* (London, 1972).

Goldman, Marshall I., *Soviet Foreign Aid* (New York, 1967).

Grotewohl, Otto, *Dreissig Jahre später*, 4th ed. (Berlin, DDR, 1952).

Köhler, Heinz, *Economic Integration in the Soviet Bloc: With an East German Case Study* (New York, 1965).
Schenk, Fritz, *Im Vorzimmer der Diktatur* (Cologne, 1962).

Chapter 3

Berlin and the Problem of German Unification (London, HMSO, 1969).
Croan, Melvin, 'Reality and Illusion in Soviet-German Relations', *Survey*, nos 44–5 (October 1962) pp. 12–28.
Jänicke, Martin, *Der dritte Weg: Die antistalinistische Opposition gegen Ulbricht seit 1953* (Cologne, 1964).
Mallinckrodt, Anita Dasbach, *Propaganda hinter der Mauer* (Stuttgart, 1971).
Otnosheniya SSSR s GDR 1945–1955gg: Dokumenty i Materialy (Moscow, 1974).
Schultz, Joachim *Der Funktionär in der Einheitspartei: Kaderpolitik und Bürokratisierung in der SED* (Stuttgart and Düsseldorf, 1956).

Chapter 4

Auf dem Wege der sozialistischen Menschengemeinschaft: Eine Sammlung von Dokumenten zur Bündnispolitik und Kirchenpolitik 1967–1970 (Berlin, DDR, 1971).
Baylis, Thomas A., *The Technical Intelligentsia and the East German Elite* (Berkeley, Los Angeles, and London, 1974).
Croan, Melvin, 'Czechoslovakia, Ulbricht and the German Problem', *Problems of Communism*, vol. XVIII, no. 1 (January/February 1969) pp. 1–7.
Dem VI. Parteitag entgegen (Berlin, DDR, 1962).
Fünfter Tätigkeitsbericht 1965–1969 (Bonn and Berlin, 1969).
Hoffmann, Ernst, 'Zwei aktuelle Probleme der geschichtlichen Entwicklungsfolge fortschreitender Gesellschaftsformationen', *Zeitschrift für Geschichtswissenschaft*, no. 10 (1968) pp. 1265–88.
Keren, Michael, 'The New Economic System in the GDR: An Obituary', *Soviet Studies*, vol. XXIV (April 1973) pp. 554–87.
McInnes, Neil, 'Havemann and the Dialectic', *Survey*, no. 62 (January 1967) pp. 25–37.
Melzer, Manfred, 'Der Entscheidungsspielraum des VEB in der DDR', *Vierteljahrshefte zur Wirtschaftsforschung*, Jg (1970) Zweites Heft.
Melzer, Manfred, 'Das Anlagevermögen der mitteldeutschen Industrie', *ibid.*, Jg (1968) Erstes Heft, pp. 105–32.
Melzer, Manfred, 'Preispolitik und Preisbildungspolitik in der DDR', *ibid.*, Jg. (1969) Drittes Heft, pp. 313–53.

Miller, Dorothy, and Harry Trend, 'Economic Reforms in East Germany', *Problems of Communism*, vol. xv, no. 2 (March/April 1966) pp. 29–36.

Mittag, Günter, *Die Bedeutung des Buches 'Politische Ökonomie des Sozialismus und ihre Anwendung in der DDR' für die weitere Gestaltung des ökonomischen Systems des Sozialismus in der DDR und die Entwicklung des ökonomischen Denkens der Werktätigen* (Berlin, DDR, 1970).

Politische Ökonomie des Sozialismus und ihre Anwendung in der DDR (Berlin, DDR, 1969).

Pritzel, Konstantin, *Die wirtschaftliche Integration der sowjetischen Besatzungszone Deutschlands in den Ostblock und ihre politischen Aspekte* (Bonn and Berlin, 1962).

Rush, Myron, *How Communist States Change their Rulers* (Ithaca and London, 1974).

Spittmann, Ilse 'East Germany The Swinging Pendulum', *Problems of Communism*, vol xvi, no. 4 (July/August 1967) pp. 14–20.

Ulbricht, Walter, *Die Bedeutung des Werkes 'Das Kapital' von Karl Marx für die Schaffung des entwickelten gesellschaftlichen Systems des Sozialismus in der DDR und den Kampf gegen das staatsmonopolistische Herrschaftssystem in Westdeutschland* (Berlin, DDR, 1967).

Ulbricht, Walter, *Die nationale Mission der DDR und das geistige Schaffen in unserem Staat* (Berlin, DDR, 1966).

Ulbricht, Walter, *Probleme des Perspektivplans bis 1970* (Berlin, DDR, 1966).

Ulbricht, Walter, *Whither Germany?: Speeches and Essays on the National Question* (Dresden, 1966).

Ulbricht, Walter, *Zum neuen Ökonomischen System der Planung und Leitung* (Berlin, DDR, 1966).

Weidig, Rudi, *Sozialistische Gemeinschaftsarbeit* (Berlin, DDR, 1969).

Chapter 5

Bahro, Rudolf, *Die Alternative: Zur Kritik des real existierenden Sozialismus* (Cologne, 1977).

Bahro, Rudolf, *Eine Dokumentation* (Cologne, 1977).

Bildungs- und Erziehungsplan für den Kindergarten (Berlin, DDR, 1967).

Biskup, Reinhold, *Deutschlands offene Handelsgrenze: Die DDR als Nutzniesser des EWG-Protokolls über den innerdeutschen Handel* (Berlin, 1976).

Cramer, Dettmar, *Deutschland nach dem Grundvertrag* (Stuttgart, 1973).

Croan, Melvin, *East Germany: The Soviet Connection* (Beverly Hills and London, 1976).

'Deutschland Politik Öffentliche Anhörungen des Ausschusses für innerdeutsche Beziehungen des deutschen Bundestages 1977', *Zur Sache* (Bonn) no. 4 (1977).

Die Entwicklung der Beziehungen zwischen der Bundesrepublik Deutschland und der Deutschen Demokratischen Republik 1969–1976 (Bonn, 1977).

Dokumentation zur Entspannungspolitik der Bundesregierung (Bonn, 1977).

Fricke, Karl Wilhelm, *Programm und Statut der SED vom 22. Mai 1976* (Cologne, 1976).

Jahresbericht der Bundesregierung 1976 (Bonn, 1977).

Keren, Michael, *The Rise and Fall of the New Economic System in the GDR* (Jerusalem, 1974).

Lamm, Hans Siegfried, and Siegfried Kupper, *DDR und Dritte Welt* (Munich, 1976).

Lindemann, Hans, and Kurt Müller, *Auswärtige Kulturpolitik der DDR* (Bonn and Bad Godesberg, 1974).

Müller-Römer, Dietrich, *Die neue Verfassung der DDR* (Cologne, 1974).

Münzner, Willi, *et al.*, *Dokumente und Materialien der Zusammenarbeit zwischen der SED und der Kommunistischen Partei der Sowjetunion 1971 bis 1974* (Berlin, DDR, 1975).

Radde, Jürgen, *Der diplomatische Dienst der DDR: Namen und Daten* (Cologne, 1977).

Radde, Jürgen, *Die aussenpolitische Führungselite der DDR* (Cologne, 1976).

Rahmenprogramm für Arbeitsgemeinschaften der Klassen 9 und 10 – Wehrausbildung (Berlin, DDR, 1973).

Rodejohann-Recke, H., 'Sozialistische Wehrerziehung in der DDR', in Studiengruppe Militärpolitik, *Die Nationale Volksarmee: Ein Anti-Weissbuch zum Militär in der DDR* (Hamburg, 1976).

Schwarz, Hans-Peter, *Zwischenbilanz der KSZE* (Stuttgart, 1977).

Sowjetunion 1975/76: Innenpolitik, Wirtschaft, Aussenpolitik Analyse und Bilanz (Munich, 1976).

Weber, Hermann, *Die SED nach Ulbricht* (Hanover, 1974).

Weber, Hermann, *SED: Chronik einer Partei 1971–1976* (Cologne, 1976).

Index

Abgrenzung, 109, 195, 204–8
Abramisov, Pyotr, 174–5, 200
Abusch, Alexander, 67
Ackermann, Anton, xiv, 26, 29–30, 41–3, 55–6, 79, 89, 229; activities of group, 4; German road to socialism, 15, 22, 52; heads group, 1
Adenauer, Konrad, 41
Administrations of Nationalised Enterprises (VVB), 95, 105
Africa, 185, 209
African National Congress, 209
Agriculture, 21, 28, 32, 91–3, 104, 106, 136, 190; collectivisation, 74, 89, 91–2, 105–7, 111, 118, 190, 215; land reform, 5, 18, 21, 38; LPG, 104, 115
Albania, 98, 219–20
Albrecht, Rudolf, 58
Allied Control Commission (ACC), 2–3, 49, 69; set up, 2
Andropov, Yuri, 188
Angola, 209
Apel, Erich, 105, 133–4, 151, 229
Arzumanyan, A. A., 159
Associations of Nationalised Enterprises (VVB), 73, 105, 126, 128–9, 135–6, 147
Austria, 12, 47
Axen, Hermann, 144, 147, 151–2, 188, 223–4, 229

Bahr, Egon, 161, 201–2
Bahro, Rudolf, 225, 228
Bartsch, Karl-Heinz, 151, 230
Basic Treaty with the FRG, 184, 191, 194, 202, 206, 216
Bauer, Leo, 66–7
Baumann, Edith, 230

Bautzen, 60
Bavaria, 37, 40
Becher, Johannes R., 5, 99–100, 230
Behrens, Fritz, 98, 102–3, 116
Belgrade, 221–2
Beling, Walter, 26, 66, 230
Benary, Arne, 102–3, 116
Benjamin, Hilde, 60, 231
Bentzien, Hans, 133
Beria, L. P., 41, 46, 50, 78
Berlin, xi, 1–6, 13, 15–17, 34, 36, 42, 44–5, 52, 73, 75–6, 78, 82, 86, 90, 96, 102, 109, 114, 119, 156–9, 161–5, 172, 184, 186–8, 191, 193, 210; administration set up, 4; airlift, 49
Berlin Agreement, 164–5, 173, 191, 200, 203, 207
Berlinguer, E., 220
Berzarin, Colonel-General N. E., 4
Bidault, G., 3
Biermann, Wolf, 133, 223, 225
Bierut, B., 87
Biskup, Reinhold, 207
Bismarck, Otto von, 33
Bloc of antifascist democratic parties, 6
Bloch, Ernst, 98–100
Bolz, Lothar, 58
Bonn, 87, 108, 161–2, 167, 169
Brandenburg, 17, 31, 35, 42
Brandt, Helmut, 60
Brandt, Willy, 161–2, 192, 203
Bredel, Willi, 42, 96
Bremen, xi
Brest-Litovsk, Treaty of, 69
Brezhnev, Leonid Ilich, 133, 158, 163–5, 171, 199–200, 210, 214, 220–1
Brezhnev Doctrine, 221

Brill, Hermann, 13, 15, 44
Brundert, Willi, 60
Brus, Wlodzimierz, 103
Bucharest, 158
Buchenwald, 44, 60
Budapest, 71, 163, 219
Bulganin, Marshal, 88
Bulgaria, 66, 158, 169
Bundesrat, 165
Bundestag, 157, 164–5
Bundesversammlung, 157
Busse, Ernst, 44, 56

Calau, 41
Carl Zeiss Jena, 48
Carrillo, S., 220, 224
Carsten, Francis, x
Casablanca, 1
Ceausescu, N., 220
Central German Administrations (DZV), 28, 40, 59; set up, 3
Chemnitz, xii
China, People's Republic of, 100, 133
Christian Democratic Union of Germany (CDU), 6, 18, 22, 31–2, 34, 38, 46, 58–60, 65, 73, 115, 120
Christian Democratic Union/Christian Social Union (CDU/CSU), 38, 160–1
Churchill, Winston, S., 49; at Casablanca, 1
Clay, General Lucius, 37
CMEA *see* Comecon
Comecon, 71, 94–5, 174–5, 179, 185, 194–201, 213
Comintern *see* Communist International
Commissions of Workers' and Peasants' Inspectorate (ABI), 122
Committee for State Security (KGB) (USSR), 188
Communist Information Bureau (Cominform), 46, 49, 51, 218
Communist International (Comintern), xi, 49
Communist party of Albania, 46
Communist Party of Austria, 223
Communist Party of Czechoslovakia, 98, 224

Communist Party of Denmark, 223
Communist Party of Germany (KPD), 3–4, 7–8, 11–13, 18, 20–2, 25, 36–8, 41, 43–4, 47, 53–4, 61, 64, 66–7, 85, 87, 90, 101, 104, 110, 113, 116, 143, 160, 180, 188; and religion, 32; and Roman Catholic Church, 32; backs down, xii; Berne conference, xiii; calls social democrats social fascists, xii; commissions set up, xiii; conference of sixty, 12–14; electoral success, xii; first congress, xi; formation of, xi; leadership flees, xiii; manifesto, 7–9; membership, ix, xii, 16–17, 63; Muscovite leadership, 9; policy in SBZ, 3; programme, xiii; refounded, 5–6; sets up work groups, xiii
Communist Party of Greece, 223
Communist Party of Norway, 223
Communist Party of the Soviet Union (CPSU), 22–3, 50, 55, 57, 61, 88, 90, 93, 95, 99–100, 138, 149, 156, 166–8, 170, 172, 174, 182, 184, 194, 199–200, 210, 218–20, 223–5
Communist Party of Spain (PCE), 219, 222–5
Communist Party of Yugoslavia, 51–2
Communist Youth Movement (KJV), 180
Constitution, 204–5, 226–7
Corghi, Benito, 224
Cottbus, 120, 155, 214
CPSU *see* Communist Party of the Soviet Union
Cunhal, A., 223
Cybernetics, 136–7, 166–7, 183, 216
Czechoslovakia, 66–8, 71, 86, 94, 114, 121, 123, 135, 137, 140, 158, 167–70, 172, 217, 219, 222, 224

Dahlem, Franz, 26, 28–9, 37, 55–6, 67, 78, 89, 231
Dahrendorf, Gustav, 7, 10, 13, 15
Democratic Peasants' Party of Germany (DBD), 58, 120
Democratic Women's Association of Germany (DFD), 31, 155

Dessau, 45, 60
Deutsche Demokratische Partei, 5
DKP *see* German Communist Party
Dohlus, Horst, 149, 186–7, 214, 231
Dortmund, 159–60
Dreger, Egon, 42
Dresden, 5, 119, 151, 186–7
Dubček, Alexander, 168–9
DWK *see* German Economic Commission

East Prussia, 35
Ebert, Friedrich, 28, 55, 151, 152, 163, 231
Economic Planning, 21, 59, 72–4, 80, 88–95, 121–31, 134–40, 177, 184–5, 190–1, 194–201, 207, 216, 221–2, 226–7
Egypt, 208, 227
Ehard, Hans, 38
Eisenach, 16
Eisenhower, President Dwight D., 112
Ende, Lex, 66
Engels, Friedrich, 22, 96
Erfurt, 162
Erpenbeck, Fritz, 41
Eurocommunists, 221–5
European Advisory Commission, 1
European Defence Community (EDC), 83–4
Ewald, Georg, 151, 154, 232

Fascism, xiv, 22
FDGB *see* Free German Trades Union Association
FDJ *see* Free German Youth Movement
Fechner, Max, 26, 28–9, 35, 56–7, 76, 79, 232
Fedyuninsky, Colonel-General, 1
Felfe, Werner, 186, 214, 232
Fiedler, Artur, 42
Field, Noel H., 66–7
Finland, 208
First International, 159
Fischer, Kurt, 5, 42, 56
Fischer, Oskar, 200, 211, 213, 232
Florin, Peter, 42, 213, 233
FNLA, 209
France, 2–3, 38, 48, 68, 85, 109, 114,

180, 201, 222; and Ruhr, 35; and Saar, 35; forces in Berlin, 4; uses veto, 3; zone of occupation, 40, 43, 82
Frankfurt-an-der-Oder, 41, 186
Free Democratic Party (FDP), 38
Free German Trades Union Association (FDGB), 12, 18, 31, 73, 90–1, 102, 114, 123, 138, 155, 188; founded, 18
Free German Youth Movement (FDJ), 31, 90, 123, 180, 182, 186–8, 192, 212, 214–15; founded, 19
French Communist Party (PCF), 219, 222–5
FRELIMO, 209
FRG *see* West Germany
Fröhlich, Paul, 99, 120, 133, 151, 233
Frölich, August, 44
Fuhrmann, Bruno, 66
Fulton, Missouri, 49

Gast, Gabriele, 156
de Gaulle, General Charles, 3
Geneva, 86, 112
Gera, 102
German Communist Party (DKP), 206, 219
German Economic Commission (DWK), 59, 72–3, 94; set up, 40
German People's Congress for Unity and a Just Peace, 58–9
German People's Council, 58–9
Germany, 4, 9, 47, 49, 64, 82, 101, 180; attacks USSR, xiii; central German government, 2; division of, 1–2
Germer, Karl, 13
Gestapo, xiii
Gniffke, Erich, 7, 10, 26, 28–9, 31, 37, 40, 44, 56, 64, 233
Goldenbaum, Ernst, 58
Goldhammer, Bruno, 66
Gomulka, W., 87
Gotha, 16
Graf, Engelbert, 7
Great Britain, 2–3, 47, 85, 109, 114, 201; forces in Berlin, 4; zone of occupation, 38, 43, 82

262 *Index*

Greif, Heinrich, 5, 42
Greiner, Ferdinand, 42
Gromyko, Andrei A., 112, 161–3, 200
Grotewohl, Otto, 7, 11–15, 26, 28–9, 53, 55–7. 59, 63–4, 71–2, 75–6, 87, 151, 171, 174, 202, 233; and Oder Neisse Line, 36; influenced by Tyulpanov, 15; speech censored, 10–11
Grünberg, Gottfried, 42–3
Grüneberg, Gerhard, 147, 151–2, 233
Gruppe Internationale (Spartacus League), xi
GST *see* Society for Sport and technology
Gundelach, Gustav, 41
Gypner, Richard, 28, 41

Hagen, Eva-Maria, 225
Hagen, Nina, 225
Hager, Kurt, 98–100, 104, 147, 151, 152, 183, 216, 223, 234
Halbritter, Walter, 151, 154, 186–7, 234
Halle, 16, 63, 72, 90, 101, 120, 186, 214
Hamburg, xii, 13
Hanover, 11
Harich, Wolfgang, 98–9
Haufe, Arno, 79
Havemann, Robert, 131–2, 223, 225
Hegel, G., 98
Heilmann, Professor, 58
Helsinki Conference, 165, 174
Helsinki Final Act, 185, 199, 205, 214, 219–20
Hentschke, Herbert, 42
Herrmann, Joachim, 160, 186–8, 214, 234
Herrnstadt, Rudolf, 42, 78–9, 89, 101, 234
Hertwig, Hans-Joachim, 186, 235
Herwegen Leo, 60
Hesse, 37–8, 66
Heym, Stefan, 133
Hitler, Adolf, xiv, 55, 96, 101
Hoffmann, Heinrich, 13
Hoffmann, Heinz, 186, 188, 211, 235
Hofmann, Artur, 42
Honecker, Erich, 65, 97, 124, 133, 142, 147, 149, 151–2, 164–5, 170, 172, 174–5, 235; heads FDJ, 19; heads SED, 180–225
Honecker, Margot, 155, 192, 211, 235
Hörnle, Edwin, 5–6; and land reform, 18
Hungary, 66–7, 96–7, 101, 158, 169, 198; elections in, 12; and NEM, 123–4

Iceland, 219–20
Independent Social Democratic Party of Germany (USPD), xi
Italian Communist Party (PCI), 132, 219, 222–5
Italy, 48, 222

Japan, 134
Jarowinsky, Werner, 147, 149, 151, 154, 236
Jena, 43
Jendretzky, Hans, 79, 89, 237
Jews, 67
Jodl, A., 2
Jogiches, Leo, xi
Jugendweihe, 92, 99
Junkers, ix, 18

Kafka, Franz, 168
Kahmann, Fritz, 42
Kaiser, Jacob, 19, 31–2, 46, 58
Kaliningrad, 199
Karlovy Vary, 158, 169, 219–20
Karsten, August, 26, 236
Kassel, 162
Kennedy, John F., 112–13
Kern, Käthe, 28, 236
KGB *see* Committee for State Security (USSR)
Khrushchev, Nikita Sergeevich, 65, 86, 88–9, 92–3, 95–7, 99, 105, 110–13, 122, 124, 167, 172, 181, 218; on Ulbricht, 100
Kirsch, Sarah, 225
Kissinger, Henry, 163
Klaus, Georg, 166, 183–4
Kleiber, Günther, 151, 154, 188, 236
Knutsen, Martin Gunnar, 223
Kohl, Michael, 201, 237
Köhler, Bruno, 30

Köhler, Heinz, 70
Kohlmey, Günther, 103
Kolesnichenko, General, 44
Kommandatura, 2, 82
Konev, Marshal, 1
Königsberg, 199
Köppe, Walter, 41
Kostov, Traitscho, 66–7
Kosygin, Alexei, 158, 162, 181
KPD *see* Communist Party of Germany
Kreikemeyer, Willi, 66
Krenz, Egon, 214
Krisch, Henry, 10
Krolikowski, Herbert, 213, 237
Krolikowski, Werner, 120, 151–2, 185–7, 214, 237
Krug, Manfred, 225
Kuckhoff, Greta, 103
Kuczynski, Jürgen, 99–100, 116, 182
Kühn, Lotte, 29–30
Kulturbund, 31
Külz, Wilhelm, 14
Kunze, Reiner, 225
Kurella, Alfred, 133, 237
KVP *see* People's Police in Barracks

Labour Party (Great Britain), 11
Lamberz, Werner, 147, 149, 151, 153, 185–6, 188, 209, 238
Land Reform *see* Agriculture
Lange, Fritz, 56
Lange, Ingeborg, 186–7, 238
Lange, Oskar, 103
Langhoff, Wolfgang, 66
Larsen, Reider, 223
League of Communists of Yugoslavia, 221–2
League of Democratic Socialists, 44
Lehmann, Helmut, 26, 29, 55, 238
Lehmann, Richard, 9
Leipzig, 9, 16, 99, 114, 186
Lemmer, Ernst, 19, 31, 58
Lenin, Vladimir Ilich, 14, 50, 91–3, 96, 143, 165, 173–4; on Comintern, xi
Leonhard, Wolfgang, 1, 41
Leuschner, Bruno, 59, 95, 104, 106–7, 151, 238
Liberal Democratic Party of Germany (LDPD), 14, 18, 22, 31–2, 34, 38, 58–60, 65, 72–3, 120; founded, 6
Liberman, Evsei, 122–3
Liblice Conference, 168
Liebknecht, Karl, xi, 113
Lippmann, Heinz, 90
Local elections, 33–4
Loest, Erich, 99
London, 1, 49, 58
Ludz, Peter, 205
Lukács, György, 98
Lusaka, 209
Luxemburg, Rosa, xi

Machel, President, 227
Madrid, 224
Magdeburg, 107
Magnitogorsk, 174
Mahle, Hans, 41
Makarov, Lieutenant-General V. E., 49
Malchow, 42
Malenkov, G. M., 50, 78, 88–9, 92
Maputo, 209
Marchais, G., 220
Maron, Karl, 41
Marshall Plan, 49
Marx, Karl, 22, 96, 98, 165, 168
Mass Organisations, xiv, 31, 34, 145–7, 213
Matern, Hermann, 5, 28, 42, 151, 238
Mecklenburg, 1, 16–17, 33–4, 43, 191
Meier, Otto, 26, 29, 239
Merker, Paul, 26, 29–30, 55, 65, 67–8, 239
Mewis, Karl, 106, 239
Mexico, 67
Meyer, Henry, 6
Middle East, 185
Mielke, Erich, 67, 151, 154, 185–8, 214, 240
Mies, Herbert, 219
Mikoyan, A., 5, 69
Ministry of Agriculture and Forestry, 65
Ministry of State Security (SSD), 60
Mittag, Günter, 105, 131, 135, 147, 151, 153, 165, 181, 186–7, 214, 240

Modrow, Hans, 187
Molotov, V. M., 85, 97, 100
Moscow, xii–xiv, 1, 4, 20, 32, 43, 49,
    52, 76, 86, 95, 97, 101, 108, 159, 161,
    163–4, 174, 210, 219
Moscow Treaty, 162, 165, 174
Mozambique, 209
Mückenberger, Erich, 55, 98, 151,
    153, 240
Müller, Margarete, 151, 154, 240
Müller, Vicenz, 97
Munich, 38, 40

Nasser, President, 227
National Committee for a Free Ger-
    many (NKFD), 9, 25, 45
National Democratic Party of Ger-
    many (NDPD), 58, 120
National Front, 58
National People's Army (NVA), 25,
    55, 85, 193, 209–10, 213
National Socialist German Workers'
    Party (NSDAP), 4–6, 32–3, 54, 59;
    seizure of power, xii
Naumann, Konrad, 186, 214, 240
Neubecker, Fritz, 13
Neumann, Alfred, 98, 107, 133, 151,
    153, 187, 241
Nimeiri, President, 209
Nixon, Richard, 163
NKFD see National Committee for a
    Free Germany
NKVD see People's Commissariat for
    Internal Affairs (USSR)
Norden, Albert, 98, 101, 133, 147, 151,
    153, 241
North Atlantic Treaty Organisation
    (NATO), 85–6, 97, 203
North Rhine Westphalia, 38
Nothnagel, Alfred, 9
NSDAP see National Socialist Ger-
    man Workers' Party
Nuschke, Otto, 60, 76, 78
NVA see National People's Army

Oder-Neisse Line, xiv, 2, 35–6
Oelssner, Fred, 5, 42, 53, 92, 95, 97, 99,
    101–2, 104, 116–17, 241
Opportunism, 51–2

Orenburg-Uzhgorod Pipeline, 195
Ott, Harry, 213, 242

Paris, xiii, 49, 112, 164
Party Control Commission, 26
Party of Labour (Netherlands), 46
PCE see Communist Party of Spain
PCF see French Communist Party
PCI see Italian Communist Party
PCP see Portuguese Communist Party
Peking, 163
People's Commissariat of Internal Af-
    fairs (NKVD) (USSR), 46, 56, 60
People's Police in Barracks (KVP), 25,
    55, 85
Pieck, Arthur, 7
Pieck, Wilhelm, xiv, 5, 7, 10, 12–13,
    26, 28, 36, 43, 55–7, 59, 71, 108, 171,
    174, 242
Pisnik, Alois, 242
Podgorny, Nikolai, 158, 181
Poland, 35–6, 71, 86–7, 89, 96–7, 167,
    169, 195
Politburo see Socialist Unity Party
    (SED)
Pomerania, 35, 42
Population, 74, 111–13, 118, 120, 215
Portuguese Communist Party (PCP),
    223
Potsdam, 102
Potsdam Agreement, xiii, 2–3, 18, 21,
    70
Potsdam Conference, 35, 46, 80
Prague, xiii, 70, 201
Protestant Churches, x, 32, 92, 99
Pskov, 69
Pushkin, Ambassador, 97

Raab, Karl, 42
Rajk, Laszlo, 66–7
Rau, Heinrich, 59, 94–5, 242
Red Army see Soviet Army
Refugees, 16, 28, 35, 111, 118
Reichstag, xii
Reims, 2
Reinhold, Otto, 92, 170
Reparations see Soviet Union
Revisionism, 52
Rhodesia, 209

Ribnitz-Damgarten, 187
Roberto, Holden, 209
Roman Catholic Church, x, 32, 92, 99
Romania, 158, 195, 219–20
Roosevelt, Franklin D., 1
Rostock, 151, 185
Rudolfstein-Hirschberg, 224
Ruhr, xi, 3
Rumpf, Willy, 95
Russian Communist Party (Bolsheviks) (RKP), xi–xii
Russian Social Democratic Labour Party (RSDRP), 50

Saar, 35, 65, 180
Sachsenhausen, 60
Sagan, 42
Sägebrecht, Willy, 42
Saxony, xii, 1, 5, 16–17, 30–1, 34, 45, 56, 79, 180
Schäffer, Fritz, 97
Scharf, Hans, 209
Scheel, Walter, 162
Schirdewan, Karl, 56, 95–102, 243
Schmidt, Elli, 28, 37, 79, 89, 243
Schmidt, Waldemar, 78
Schneider, Maria, 156
Scholz, Paul, 95
Schön, Otto, 108, 243
Schramm, Bruno, 42
Schreiber, Fritz, 28, 63
Schumacher, Kurt, 11, 13–14, 41, 44, 64
Schumann, Horst, 133, 186, 243
Schürer, Gerhard, 186, 188, 244
Schwarz, Georg, 9
Schwerin, 43, 102
Scientific-Technical Revolution, 136–40, 166, 177, 183
SED *see* Socialist Unity Party
Šejna, Karel, 113
Selbmann, Fritz, 56, 59, 75, 95, 101, 104, 116–17, 244
Semenov, Vladimir, 41, 78
SEW, 206
Sindermann, Horst, 151, 153, 181, 186–7, 214, 244
Silesia, 35, 42
Slansky, Rudolf, 66, 98

SMAD *see* Soviet Military Administration in Germany
Sobottka, Gustav, 43; heads group, 1, 42
Social Democratic Party of Germany (SPD), xii, 3, 7, 12–14, 18, 20–2, 24, 34, 36, 43–4, 53–5, 63–4, 85, 87, 91, 143, 159–61; called social fascists, xii; CC, 13–15; complaints against KPD, 10; conference of sixty, 12–14; founding of West German SPD party, 11; fusion with KPD, ix, 19, 41; manifesto, 8–9; membership, 16–17, 63; opposes fusion with KPD, 13, 15; refounded, 5–6
Socialism, 7, Christian, 31; German, ix; German road to, ix, 1–46; Soviet, ix; with a German face, x, 118–79
Socialist Unity Party of Germany (SED), 35, 47, 59, 119; and Berlin Conference, 218–21; and economy under Honecker, 184, 189–91, 194–201, 207, 211–12, 216; and German road to socialism, 22, 52–3; and Germany, 38, 40, 58, 83–4, 87, 97, 108–13, 159–61, 201–2, 204–8; and national socialists, 32; and NES/ESS, 121–31, 134–41, 167, 181, 183, 186–7, 189; and Oder-Neisse Line, 35–6; and religion, 32; and the German nation, 38, 201–4, 226; apparatus, 25; Central Committee (CC), 24, 26, 28, 36–7, 51–2, 55–6, 67–8, 75–6, 79, 89, 93, 96, 98, 100–5, 129, 135, 144–7, 158, 160, 166, 171, 174, 186–7, 212–13, 216–18; Central Secretariat, 26, 28–31, 37, 54, 56–7, 65; *Chistka*, 23, 50, 57, 61–9; Conference I, 50, 54, 63–4; II, 61, 74, 76; III, 96; Congress II, 23, 26, 37, 46, 51, 54, 63, 79; III, 50, 55, 73; IV, 90–1; V, 101; VI, 124, 134, 138, 141, 150, 155; VII, 134, 138, 141, 146–7, 151, 155, 175; VIII, 141–2, 146, 151, 155, 175, 183, 185, 188, 203, 205, 211, 216; IX, 187–8, 210–8; elec-

(contd.)
tions, 33–4; *Kreis* organisation, 24; land reform, 32; membership, 17, 68–9, 90, 115, 140–56, 214–15; opposition in, 23; party of a new type, 14, 47–81; Politburo, x, 54–5, 68, 75–6, 78–9, 88–91, 98–9, 101–2, 119, 149–54, 167, 171, 185–8, 191, 213–14, 218; programme, 20–1, 170, 216–17; recruitment, 22–3; Secretariat, 24, 56, 68, 98–102, 105, 147–50, 175, 186, 188, 218; social composition of, 23, 140–2; statute, 217–18; tactics used against social democrats, 24; women, 155–6, 215; youth under Honecker, 191–4
Socialist Workers' Party (Hungary), 163
Society for Sport and Technology (GST), 193
Sofia, 224
Sokolovsky, General/Marshal, 3, 29–30
Sölle, Horst, 213
Sorbs, 147, 156, 226
Soviet Army, 1, 3, 5, 9, 20, 42, 45
Soviet companies (SAG), 70
Soviet Military Administration in Germany (SMAD), 10–16, 18–19, 29–30, 32, 34, 36, 41, 44, 57–8, 72–3, 87; and FDGB, 19; and FDJ, 19; censors Grotewohl, 11; established, 2; Order no. 2, 6, 19; Order no. 103, 31; Order no. 124, 30; Order no. 167, 70; policy, 3
Soviet Union (USSR), xii, 3, 5, 11, 35–6, 38, 48–9, 52–3, 55, 60, 64, 69–70, 72, 78, 80–3, 89, 91, 93, 100, 105–6, 108, 112, 122, 133, 137, 156, 163, 167, 171–3, 194–201, 222; allied intervention, 47; antifascist schools in, 25; credits for GDR, 114; German attack, xiii; German policy, 82–8, 108–14; prisoners-of-war in, 16, 25, 32, 80; reparations, 18, 31, 48, 55, 69–74, 80–1; sequestrations, 31, 48
Spartacus League *see* *Gruppe Internationale*

SPD *see* Social Democratic Party of Germany
Staatspartei, x
Stalin Iosif Vissarionovich, xii, 1, 5, 30, 46, 48–50, 53, 67, 69–70, 76, 88, 96, 98, 133, 218
Stargard, 42
State Planning Commission (SPK), 94–5, 105–7, 127, 129, 131, 135
Steinhoff, Karl, 55
Stempel, Günter, 60
Stephan, Oskar, 42
Stern, Carola, 12, 68
Stoph, Willi, 86, 151, 153, 161–2, 179, 181, 186–7, 214, 245
Sudan, 209
Sudetenland, 25
Suhl, 102
Switalla, Anton, 42
Syria, 208
Szklarska Poręba, 46, 218

Tehran Conference, 1
Teubner, Hans, 66
Thalbach, Katharina, 225
Thälmann, Ernst, xii
Thuringia, 12–13, 17, 44–5, 56
Timmermann, Heinz, 223
Tisch, Harry, 151, 154, 185, 188, 212, 245
Tito, Josif Broz, 46, 50, 53, 66, 220–5
Titoism, 52, 59
Trade Unions, (*see also* FDGB), 6, 19, 30, 40
Treaty of Friendship, Co-operation and Mutual Aid with the USSR, 199, 216
Trotsky, Lev Davidovich, 53
Trotskyism, 52
Truman Doctrine, 49
Tyulpanov, Colonel S. I., 15, 30, 41, 57

Ulbricht, Walter, xiii, 4, 7, 9, 17, 20, 26, 28–30, 36–7, 41–3, 46, 50–1, 55–7, 59–60, 63, 65, 67, 73–6, 78–9, 86–90, 92, 95–102, 147, 150–1, 153, 158–9, 180, 182, 184, 186, 188, 191, 217, 221, 245; and Berlin, 108–13,

156–9, 161–5; and foreign policy, 108; and Germany, 108–9, 173, 203; and KPD leadership, 20; and Munich conference, 40–1; and socialism in Germany, 46, 98, 111, 165–71; and Stalin, 96–7; and the economy, 102–7, 115, 118, 121–31, 133–40; and wives, 29; dismissed, 163, 167, 171–6; heads commission in Moscow, xiv; heads group, 1; launches socialism with a German face, x, 165–71; rejects united party of the left, 7

United Nations, x, 83, 184, 194, 201–2, 205, 208, 213

United States of America, 2–3, 11, 47, 49, 65, 85, 106, 109, 114, 157, 201; forces in Berlin, 4; zone of occupation, 40, 43, 46, 82

Uschkamp, Irma, 155

USPD *see* Independent Social Democratic Party of Germany

USSR *see* Soviet Union

Varga, Eugene, 48

Verner, Paul, 108, 147, 151, 153, 188, 217, 245

Vienna, 112

Vieweg, Kurt, 30, 98, 104, 107, 116, 246

Volkskammer, 59, 61, 100, 118, 120, 159, 181, 194, 214, 226

Wachtel, Ingo, 56

Walde, Werner, 214

'Waldheim Trials', 60

Wandel, Paul, 5–6, 98–100, 104, 246

Waren, 44

Warnke, Hans, 56

Warnke, Herbert, 151, 246

Warsaw, 71, 219

Warsaw Pact, 86, 113, 158, 163, 200–1

Washington, 108, 112

Watt, James, 136

Wehrmacht, xiii, 5; capitulates, 2

Weimar Republic, xii–xiv, 11

Weinert, Erich, xiv

Weiss, Gerhard, 213

Weisswater, 216

Weiterer, Maria, 66

West Berlin, 55, 67, 106, 110–13, 118, 133, 156–9, 173, 184, 191, 199–202, 206

West European Union (WEU), 85

West Germany (FRG), 18, 38, 40, 46, 55, 68, 71, 73, 78, 81–5, 87, 90, 93, 97, 105–7, 109–10, 114, 119, 121, 133, 156–65, 167, 169, 175, 191, 198–9, 201–2, 204–8, 211; set up, 49

Wiener, Norbert, 136

Winzer, Otto, 41, 158, 178, 188, 246

Wismut, 70, 102

Wittkowski, Margarete, 155

Wolf, Georg, 42

Wollweber, Ernst, 95, 97–101, 247

Works' Councils, 21, 73; conference of, xii; elections, 11

Württemberg, 37

Yalta Conference, 2

Yom Kippur War, 189, 197

Yugoslavia, 51, 64, 98, 218–25, 227

Zaisser, Wilhelm, 78–9, 89, 101, 247

Zentrumspartei, 5

Zhdanov, A. A., 41

Zhukov, Marshal G., 1, 29

Ziller, Gerhart, 95, 98, 100, 104, 247

Zilliacus, Konni, 37

Zimbabwe, 209

Zimmermann, Hartmut, x, 19

Zionists, 65–7

Zipperer, William, 9

Zwerenz, Gerhard, 99